The Book of the Axe

George Philip R. Pulman

THE

BOOK OF THE AXE:

CONTAINING

A PISCATORIAL DESCRIPTION OF THAT STREAM,

AND A

HISTORY OF ALL THE PARISHES

AND REMARKABLE SPOTS UPON ITS BANKS;

WITH SEVERAL ILLUSTRATIONS, AND A MAP.

BY GEORGE P. R. PULMAN,

AUTHOR OF 'RUSTIC SKETCHES,' 'THE VADE MECUM OF FLY-FISHING
FOR TROUT,' ETC. ETC.

LONDON:
LONGMAN, BROWN, GREEN, AND LONGMANS.
1854.

CREWKERNE:
Printed by G. P. R. Pulman,
Market-place.

PREFACE.

———•———

WHAT may be called an *outline* of this work was published about ten years since, when two editions were rapidly sold off; and the work has for at least eight years been out of print.

As the demand for copies continued, and as a large amount of new materials had been collected, the author was induced to reconstruct the work; and he now presents it in a form so altered that the title alone is almost the only original feature.

It has been his object to trace the Axe from rise to mouth, and to describe both the piscatorial attractions of that far-famed stream, and the most striking scenery in the lovely valley through which it flows;— to wander, in fact, with rod in hand, along its ' mazy margin ;'—to discourse, as pleasantly as may be, upon its famous spots;—to keep time, in merriness, with the music of its rippling ' stickles,' and to moralise,

in a graver fashion, with its solemn depths, as each
might successively create the emotion;—to step aside
at every interesting place and learn its history;—
to plunge into the depths of antiquity, among the
musty records of the Past, calling up the scenes and
beings which have long since disappeared;—and anon
to ramble on again in what is hoped may prove the
profitable enjoyment of the Present.

Angling forms a perfectly natural association with
the description of a river; but care has been taken,
in spite of almost irresistible temptation, to make it
not so prominent a feature of the work as to be
otherwise than a vehicle for the historical and topographical information—a relief, in short, to the
'dryness,' as it is sometimes called, of antiquarian
subjects.   The author, indeed, has been anxious to
prove the correctness of Walton's idea, that

> 'Of recreation there is none
> So free as fishing is alone;
> All other pastimes do no less
> Than mind and body both possess:
> My *hand* alone my work can do,
> So I *can fish and study too.*'

And he has not been unmindful of the opinion
of Lord Bacon, that 'It is good in discourse and

speech of conversation to vary and intermingle speech of the present occasion with arguments, tales with reasons, asking of questions with telling of opinions, and jest with earnest; for it is a dull thing to tire, and, as we say now, to jade a thing too far.'

The following are the principal places of which a sketch of their history and present condition will be found in these pages:—in DORSETSHIRE—Chedding-ton, Beaminster, Mosterton, Broadwinsor, Thorn-combe (including Ford Abbey), Hawkchurch, and Chardstock; in SOMERSETSHIRE—Crewkerne, Way-ford, Seaborough, Winsham, Chard, and Cricket Saint Thomas; and in DEVONSHIRE—Axminster (including Newenham Abbey), Kilmington, Mus-bury (including Ashe House), Shute and Whitford, Colyton (including Colyford), Seaton and Beer, and Axmouth.

It would be affectation to deny that the treatment of so extensive a subject has proved, in some degree, laborious. The labor, however, has been one of love; for the author has felt, while the work was growing beneath his hand, that he was, in one sense, engaged in the payment of a grateful tribute to the lovely river which has been the scene of so many of his happiest hours, and 'the lisp of whose waters' has lost none of its fascinations.

His warmest thanks are offered to those for whose friendly assistance, in the contribution of information on many subjects, he is so much indebted;—to those, also, who have supplied the illustrations;—and lastly, but not in the least degree, to those whose names compose a subscription-list of which he may justly be proud, and whose encouragement and support have stimulated him to exertion. 'And so,' in the words of a famous old author, 'he craves a favorable acceptation of this tedious travail, with a toleration of all such faults as haply therein lie hidden, and which, by diligent reading, may soon be espied.'

Crewkerne, Lady-day, 1854.

LIST OF THE ILLUSTRATIONS, ETC.

———◆———

THE BOOK OF THE AXE.

ETC. ETC.

INTRODUCTORY CHAPTER.

THE Axe is one of the most beautiful and interesting of the numerous sparkling trout streams which contribute so much to the character of Devonshire as the Arcadia of England.

Notwithstanding that the river rises in Dorsetshire and flows for some distance along the edge of Somersetshire, its claims to be regarded as a Devonshire stream must remain unaffected, when it is remembered that not only is the most beautiful part of its course within the last named county, which

supplies its principal tributaries, but also that it possesses the prevailing characteristics of those delightful
streams and their associations for which that charming
county is peculiarly celebrated. [1]

We propose to describe the Axe as an angling
stream—tracing it minutely from rise to mouth, with
fly-rod in hand, and with an imaginary angler by our
side; and also to treat of it with reference to the
various objects of interest—antiquarian, scenic, and
otherwise,—which occur so frequently in the valley
through which it winds.

As an angling stream the merits of the Axe are
indisputable. Its pellucid waters flow along their
gravelly bed in an uninterrupted alternation of stickle
and range.[2] Its banks are remarkably free from en-
cumbering bushes, and at convenient intervals they
are broken into sandy beaches shelving to the water's
edge. These are satisfactory recommendations, and
as we proceed we shall have to enumerate others
which are equally so, especially when we come, presently, to speak of the piscatory productions of
which the stream is so prolific.

[1] There is a river of the same name, but of a very different character,
in the heart of Somersetshire. It rises among the Mendip Hills—one
branch at Wookey Hole, near Wells, and another at the far-famed Cheddar
Cliffs. The united stream flows by Axbridge, Wear, and Bleadon, and
falls into the Bristol Channel near Brean Down.

[2] In the West of England, the rough and shallow parts of rivers,
called elsewhere 'scours' and 'runs,' are characteristically denominated
'*stickles*,' in contradistinction to the deep and smoother parts, which bear
the name of 'ranges.'

And not less to the tourist than to the angler does the Axe commend itself. It flows through one of those luxuriant and delightful valleys to be found in Devonshire alone—a valley so full of fertility that it seems incapable of being contained within the undulating hills by which it is enclosed—so diversified and beautiful that the eye never tires of beholding it. The elm-crowned hedge rows trace it everywhere, like lines upon a map. Narrow winding lanes, half buried between their flower covered banks, conduct to its picturesque recesses, where, away from the busy haunts of men, the honeysuckled cottage excites the wanderer's admiration, embosomed as it is in poetry and peace, and where the primitive farm house holds out to him its old fashioned openhearted hospitality. Anon some crumbling ruin, or some majestic ancient pile, arrests his eager footsteps, and with a silence more eloquent than words, may preach to him a solemn lesson. Directing his gaze along the glorious landscape, he detects the tiny river, like a vein of virgin silver, threading its early course among the distant meadows which the wild flowers are 'painting with delight.' Further down he beholds it approaching some pleasant little village, half hidden by orchards, where the blacksmith rings out joyful music, and where the school children are gamboling upon the green. Again it stretches away and glistens in the sunshine among the quiet velvet meadows yonder, in which the famous 'great red cows of Devon'

are quietly pasturing. And now, still flowing onwards, and gradually augmenting, it winds about a
pleasant country town, which rises picturesquely from
its banks along the hill side, and forms a pleasing
object in the distant landscape. A little further
down, where man and his habitations for a while
are left again, a sparkling tributary renders up to it
the liquid treasures of a charming little valley, into
the umbrageous recesses of which the gazer's eye
can linger with delight. And returning to the stream
which he has traced so far, he beholds it widening as
it flows along, and sobering like the life of an aged
man which is passing solemnly away. He remarks
that towards the bottom of the valley the hills recede
to form a more expanded plain for the stately river
to roll itself along, and also that the craggy cliffs
with which those hills are abruptly terminated in the
sea beyond, form not unfitting portals for the glorious exit. And then arises the spontaneous reflection, that like as the stream is received into the ocean
which is rolling yonder like the breathings of a
troubled bosom, even so is the river of the Present
perpetually swallowed up by the ocean of the Future
—even so are the fleeting things of Time borne away
for ever into the mysterious unfathomableness of the
Eternity beyond!

But before setting out upon our imaginary wanderings through the valley into which we have thus
taken a kind of bird's eye glance, in anticipation of

the beauties which we shall have to explore, it will be
necessary to clear the way by the disposal of sundry
miscellaneous topics which cannot be more appropriately discussed than in an introductory chapter :—

And in order to 'begin at the beginning,' it will
be desirable to take a rapid survey of the geological
formation of the valley. Sir Henry De La Beche,
in his invaluable 'Geological Report of Cornwall,
Devon, and West Somerset,' describes the process by
which, in common with other geologists, he supposes
the valleys in this particular part of the district were
originally formed. Grounding the theory upon the
remarkable fact that nearly all the ranges of green
sand hills which extend for a great distance along the
verge of Devon, Somerset, and Dorset, are of about
a uniform height, and that in most cases the strata
of the hills on one side of a valley are found to cor-
respond in arrangement and direction with the strata
of the hills on the opposite side, it is concluded that
there was a time when those hills were united, or
rather, when what are now valleys were parts of
one and the same level range of table land, in which
the action of running water upon the soft and yielding
soil, operating for countless centuries, scooped out by
degrees the numerous valleys which now diversify
and adorn the landscape. This may seem a startling
tale to those who are not familiar with the wonders
which geology is continually revealing; but any one
who thoughtfully brings his mind to bear upon the

facts on which the theory is founded, and remembers the peculiarities of form and direction of our own particular valley, for example,—winding as it does towards the sea, and increasing in width as it advances downwards, precisely as the volume of water must have increased—will find it easy to receive as a scientific truth, conclusions which are really by no means speculative, but have been arrived at by a process of the strictest philosophical induction. It must be remembered, however, that the formation of *all* valleys is not pretended to be attributed to aqueous agency, and that the theory to which we have referred is only, in this instance, of local, though of course not of exclusive, application. The materials of the hills out of which the valley of the Axe is formed, are green-sand, as already hinted, resting upon beds of lias and new red sandstone—the whole surmounted, on some of the hills in the upper part of the valley, by a thin stratum of chalk. The inferior oolite also appears in that part of the valley, and near Hawkchurch and Ford Abbey. The lias shows itself near Axminster; and the new red sandstone, in the form of marl, one of the component parts of that bed, becomes conspicuous from that town downwards,— particularly on the western side of the valley. The presence of marl is a sure indication of fertility, and the lias contains inexhaustible treasures in the fossil remains of the plants and animals of the pre-Adamite earth.

From geology to agriculture is a natural transition. The farms in the valley of the Axe, in common with those throughout the county of Devon, are generally small; but they are rich in dairy produce, and while it must be confessed that the ridges of a few of the hills have a shallow flinty soil, hardly capable of supporting sheep, yet the hill-sides generally are put to excellent tillage, and the plains are very rich as grazing ground. On the marl of the lower parts are extensive and luxuriant orchards, from which large quantities of the far-famed Devonshire cider are annually produced.

The name of the river is of obvious etymology. In common with the names of many other natural objects, it has descended to us from a time when a language was spoken in this country of which such names are almost the only relics—a language which has for centuries been superseded as completely as the aboriginal race itself with which it was vernacular. The root of the word is ancient British, and signifies *water*. Of the same origin, also, are the names of Usk, Exe, and those of many other rivers, similarly modernised. In Ptolemy's 'Description of the British Island Albion,' the Axe, according to Horsley, is called Alænus—the name by which it was known to the Romans. The natives, however, at the same time, undoubtedly retained the original name, which, with a slight alteration, as already stated, has been transmitted to us through the eventful changes of succeeding centuries.

Among the relics of the past which every district more or less contains, those which refer to the Roman occupation of the country, and to a more remote period, must always present indisputable claims to the attention of the modern investigator. In the remains of old mural fortifications, we can easily read the condition of the country at the period to which they point, when rude and hostile tribes were incessantly engaged in the defence of their own territories and in making aggressions upon the territories of their neighbours; and the ancient roads and trackways suggest a more pleasing train of contemplation, in the requirements of the increasing civilization which they bespeak. Perhaps few localities of like extent contain more interesting remains of both those kinds than the valley which we have undertaken to describe. Of its numerous hill fortresses we shall speak in future pages, but it may be worth while, in this place, to take a hasty glance at the ancient roads which intersected it in every direction, for their few existing remains are rapidly disappearing before the unsparing utilitarianism of modern times. That those ancient roads should have been numerous in this part of the country, will not excite surprise, when it is remembered that the West of England was precisely the place where they were earliest required for the natives to carry on that commercial intercourse with the Greeks and Phœnicians which commenced at a period far beyond authentic record. The ancient British, however, in all probability, never carried the art of road-making to very great perfection. Their roads, which wound along the hills, from fortress to fortress, and from the mining districts to the coast, were little better than mere beaten trackways, over which their merchandise was carried upon pack horses. [1] It is to the Romans, therefore, who adopted those trackways, and straightened and improved them in their own peculiar and wonderful manner, that we are mainly indebted for the interesting fragments which remain, as we undoubtedly are for the principal modern roads, which have been formed upon the ancient foundations. [2] It is said, though on what authority we are not informed, that the original trackways were made by a British king named Molmutius, about the year A. M. 3527, and that Agricola gave them a more regular form and character. [3] But the greatest improvements were made by Trajan, who thoroughly repaired and levelled them, and built bridges over the principal rivers. The remains of some of those bridges exist to this day, especially in the form of *foundations* upon which subsequent bridges have been erected. 'The Romans,' says Tacitus, 'compelled the Britons to wear out and consume their bodies and hands in repairing the roads, clearing

[1] Wright's ' *The Celt, the Roman, and the Saxon.*'
[2] Ibid.
[3] Phelps's ' *History of Somerset.*' Vol. I, p. 130.

woods, and paving fens, for the passage of the troops, the conveyance of provisions, and other civil and military purposes.'

Four principal roads were thus constructed by the Romans, upon the ancient British trackways. Two of these roads passed through a considerable portion of the valley of the Axe, and innumerable branches from the main roads crossed the country in different directions. Although but little of their actual remains exist, as may be expected after the lapse of so many centuries, yet the means have not been wanting by which to trace them with minuteness and certainty.[1] The names of the two roads alluded to, are 'the Ikeneld Street,'[2] or the 'Via Icenia,' which commenced on the coast of Norfolk, the country of the Iceni, and led to the Land's End,—and 'the Fosseway,' which, in the words of an old chronicler, went 'fram the south-west to north-est into Englonde's end.' The Ikeneld went from Dorchester to Eggardun fort and Bridport, and entered the valley of the Axe near Hunter's Lodge, where it crossed the Lyme Regis and Crewkerne turnpike road, and passed down Gore lane to Axminster. Thence it pro-

[1] Among the most successful of those who have given their attention to this interesting and difficult subject, must be mentioned Mr. Davidson, of Secktor House, whose work on ' The British and Roman Remains in the Vicinity of Axminster' displays great research, and is an invaluable record of facts and observations of local and general interest.

[2] The word street, or strete, is derived from the Latin Stratum, and frequently occurs in the names of places on the line of the ancient roads.

ceeded over Kilmington common to Cockroad, Mor-
cock's Hill, Hembury Fort, and Exeter. A branch
of the same road left Morcombelake and passed
through Charmouth and Lyme Regis over the hills
to Colyford, Sidbury and Woodbury Castles, and
Exeter—throwing off a branch at Colyford to Hembury Fort through Colyton, where its course is
indicated by the name of *Ridgeway*.

A branch of the Ikeneld also proceeded from Dorchester, which in those remote ages was a place of
great importance, as its numerous remains attest,[1]
and passing very nearly along the present road to
Crewkerne, through Maiden Newton and the Hore
Stones (themselves a relic of the ancient road, in
which they served as a boundary mark), it led over
Beaminster Down and Horn Hill, through Broadwinsor, to the forts on Pillesdon Pen and Lambart's
Castle,—thence over Hawkchurch Common, through
what are now for the most part enclosures, to Stan-
bury, or, as it is vulgarly called, Stammery Hill, and
Secktor, to Lane Orchard, where it joined the main
line. At this place, also, it threw out a short branch
across the fields, where its traces still exist, to Evil

---

[1] Maiden Castle, near Dorchester, the site of the original town, is a
very extensive and interesting ancient British Fort, which was subsequently adopted by the Romans; and the amphitheatre, near the station
of the Southampton and Dorchester Railway, is one of the most perfect
of its kind in the kingdom. Barrows and forts, indeed, in this interesting
locality, arrest the eye in every direction. See Savage's '*History of
Dorchester.*'

Lane, and met the Fosseway at its entrance to Axminster, whence a branch went on to Musbury and
Hochsdun Castles, and the mouth of the Axe.
What appears to be a portion of this ancient branch
was distinctly visible during the last summer on the
present turnpike road, near the gateway to Stedcombe
House. The fact of such a road leading direct to
Axmouth is sufficient proof of the importance of the
place at that early period—an importance, indeed,
which the voice of tradition very confidently affirms.

The Fosseway, which was the great ancient road
from Bath and Ilchester to Exeter and the West, has
given considerable trouble to the antiquaries who
have attempted to trace it beyond Petherton Bridge,
to which point its course is sufficiently clear. Mr.
Davidson, however, appears to have set the matter at
rest in a manner which admits of no dispute, and the
reader who wishes to pursue the subject—since we
profess to give only a rapid sketch of the course of
the main lines, and of a few of their principal
branches—will do well to consult his work, and to
compare it with the account of those ancient roads
in Lysons's 'Magna Britannia.'

From the ancient ford over the Parrott at Petherton Bridge, the Fosse appears to have proceeded, in
one of its branches, to Watergore [1] and Dinnington,

---

[1] The name gore, which is applied to so many of our old muddy lanes,
appears to be derived from the Anglo-Saxon gor, dirt. The propriety of
its modern application is indisputable.

whence it passed the higher lodge of Hinton Park, and proceeded to Chillington Down and along the hill by Windwhistle to White Down. It then passed over Chard Common, and through the hamlets of Street and Perry Street, to Titherleigh and Streteford, now Weycroft Bridge. Here it crossed the river and passed by Millbrook into the town of Axminster, throwing a trajectus up Stony Lane to join the Ikeneld, which it also joined in the centre of the town, at the ancient fort which is supposed to have occupied the site of the present market-place, and proceeded with the Ikeneld in the different directions already indicated.[1] A Roman vicinal way, originally of British construction, appears also to have led from Neroche Castle over Buckland Hill, through Whitestanton, to Baaley Down, where it divided—one branch leading to Membury Castle and Axminster, and the other over Smallridge Hill, where, as well as on Baaley Down, it may be traced along the turf to Weycroft Bridge, or Streteford, where it joined the Fosse. Weycroft also appears to have been the point of junction with a vicinal way which branched from the Fosse at Whitedown, and passing Ford Abbey, Highridge, Parkway or Portway, Sylvanus's Wood, Olditch, and Cansey wood (a corruption of *Causeway* wood),[2] led directly to Lambart's Castle—

[1] '*British and Roman Remains in the Vicinity of Axminster.*' p. 34.
[2] All those names are remarkably significant, and leave no doubt as to the course of this ancient road.

a branch being thrown off to Weycroft along the
ridge of the hill.

The Ikeneld and Fosse were connected by vicinal
ways in several parts of their course. Such a con-
necting branch diverged from the main road at
Wynniard's gap, where there are the remains of an
ancient entrenchment, [1] and it appears to have passed
through the parishes of North Perrott, Haselbury,
West Chinnock, and Chiselborough, reaching the
fort on Ham Hill and joining the Fosse near Stoke.
Another, not mentioned by any previous writer, very
probably passed from the road near Lambart's Castle
to a junction with the Fosse near Windwhistle. Its
course would seem to be distinctly indicated by certain names which are often found along the ancient
roads, such as Cold Harbor, Stony Knapps, and
Wayford. Cold Harbor is always a safe indication.
It is derived partly from the British and partly from
the Gallic. *Col,* in the former language, signifies an
eminence, and *arbhar,* in the latter, an army. Hence
the united words mean, undoubtedly, a *statio mili-
taris,* or resting place. [2] The term *stony* is simply a
corruption of the ancient name of the road itself—
the *stone*-way, from the materials with which it was

[1] This in some works is called, without due consideration, a Roman
fort. It is, undoubtedly, in common with nearly all the other remains of
a similar character in the locality, of ancient British formation, although
subsequently used by the Romans in their subjugation of the country.

[2] See Sir Richard Colt Hoare's '*Ancient Wiltshire.*'

constructed. [1] Wayford requires no explanation.

Among the other vicinal ways, we shall mention only that which diverged from the Ikeneld at the foot of Barrowshot Hill, between Hunter's Lodge and Axminster. It passed down Woodbury and Fairy (or Farway [2]) lanes, near Wick, [3] to join the road which led to Axmouth and Seaton.

[1] Vitruvius has given exact directions for making a road. They began, it appears, by making two parallel furrows, of the intended width of the road, and then removed all the loose earth between them till they came to the hard solid ground, and they filled up this excavation with fine earth hard beaten in. This first layer was called the *pavimentum*. Upon it was laid the first bed of the road, consisting of small squared stones, nicely ranged on the ground, which was sometimes left dry, but often a large quantity of fresh mortar was poured into it. This layer was termed *statumen*. The next was called *rudus* or *ruderatio*, and consisted of a mass of small stones, broken to pieces and mixed with lime, in the proportion of one part of broken stones to two parts of lime. The third layer, or bed, which was termed *nucleus*, was formed of a mixture of lime, chalk, pounded or broken tiles, or earth, beaten together, or of gravel, or sand and lime mixed with clay. Upon this was laid the surface or pavement of the road, which was called technically *summum dorsum*, or *summa crusta*. It was composed sometimes of stones set like the paving stones in our streets, and sometimes of flag-stones cut square or polygonally, and also, probably oftener, of a firm bed of gravel and lime. The roads were thus raised higher than the surrounding grounds, and on this account the mass was termed *agger*. The result of the above process would be a Roman road of the most perfect description; but we must not suppose that in any part of the empire these directions were always strictly adhered to. On the contrary, there are few Roman roads existing which do not in some way or other vary from them; some are entirely without the *nucleus*, in others there was no *statumen*. Nevertheless, there is always found a sufficiently close resemblance between the structure of the old Roman roads as they exist, and the directions given above.—'*The Celt, the Roman, and the Saxon.*'

[2] From the Anglo-Saxon, 'far-an,' to go, and 'wœg,' a way.—*Mr. Davidson.*

[3] From *Vicus,*—an evidence of the Roman road.—*Ibid.*

In concluding this subject, we shall merely add that the Roman roads were adopted and held in great estimation by the Anglo-Saxons, who called them ' *the military ways,*' while the term '*country roads*' was applied to the older British trackways. The highways of the Anglo-Saxons were distinguished by the designation '*anes wænes gang,*' or one waggon's way, four feet broad, and ' *twegna wæna ganweg,*' or two waggons' way, probably eight feet, or more,— a distinction which shows the origin of our narrow village roads.[1]

We have already alluded, in general terms, to the excellence of the Axe as an angling stream. It is now time to give some particular consideration to the object of the angler's skill, in doing which we shall have to draw a comparison between the past and the present condition of the river, and to furnish an instance, in a humble way, of the foolish tendency, in small matters as in great, to commit the short-sighted sacrifice of future benefits for the sake of present gratification and selfishness—to act, in a word, the well known fable of the goose with the golden eggs.

The Axe produces the following species of fish :— salmon, sea trout, bull trout, common trout, parr, roach, dace, lamprey, flounder, and three varieties of the common eel; besides the usual small species which form the angler's baits rather than the object

---

[1] Fosbroke's '*Encyclopædia of Antiquities.*'   page 580.

of his skill, such as the minnow, the stone-loach, and the stickleback. It is stated by Polwhele, that of all the Devonshire rivers the perch is found only in the Axe and the Clist. The Axe is certainly not a perch-producing stream, and although we are aware that some years since a few perch were captured near Ford Abbey, we had reason to believe that they had escaped from some artificial ponds in the neighbourhood, and therefore had not been bred in the river. In the same manner was the presence of a large carp accounted for in a stickle near Weycroft Bridge, where it was captured by the unusual means of an artificial fly. These accidental occurrences cannot, of course, be admitted to establish the position of such species as indigenous to the stream, and therefore we have no hesitation in saying that Polwhele's statement, as far as regards the Axe, must be erroneous.

The classing of the Axe as a trout stream is not affected by the presence of the *coarse* fish, roach and dace—the *vilains* of the water—for though abundant in some places in the lower parts of the stream, yet they bear no proportion to the aristocratic class *salmonidæ*, in its representative the common trout, and formerly in that of *salmo salar* himself. The trout of the Axe are very vigorous and of a brilliant appearance, and although they seldom cut red, their culinary qualities are excellent. They do not reach a large size, on account, probably (to say nothing

D

about the agency of the poachers), of the comparative
scarcity of large flies on a stream so free from over-
hanging bushes, [1] Perhaps six ounces may be considered as the average weight, it being rare to capture
a trout above a pound.   A fish of the former weight,
however, from the strength and activity of Axe-bred
fish, will call forth as much skill on the part of the
angler as one of treble the size in many other rivers.

It is not improbable that the grayling would
flourish in the Axe, if judiciously introduced.   The
character of the stream, as a succession of pools and
stickles, appears to be exactly suitable for it, and the
experiment of introduction could be tried at a small
expense.   Many people, anglers, even, confound the
grayling *(salmo thymallus)* with the young of the
salmon under its local name of *gravelling*.   We need
hardly say that the species are entirely distinct.   The
grayling is supposed by some to have been originally

---

[1] The May flies, which contribute so much to the growth and culinary
recommendation of trout, are not found on the Axe, except in very small
numbers in the upper part of the river.   During the last ten years there
has evidently been a considerable falling off in the flies which are common
to the stream—such as the duns, for instance, which used at times to
appear in myriads.   It may be worth while to inquire whether this fact
may not be explained by the unprecedented mildness of the winters of
recent years, owing to which the larvæ were precociously matured, and
the flies thus produced were exposed to the occasional frosts, and so were
killed before depositing their eggs.   The reader is referred to the account
of an interesting experiment on the nutritive qualities of different kinds
of food, in Stoddart's *'Scottish Angler.'*   It is quoted also in Yarrell's
'History of British Fishes,' and in the *'Vade Mecum of Fly-fishing
for Trout.'*

imported into this country from the continent. [1] It is plentiful in Hampshire, Wiltshire, and some of the Midland Counties, and being in perfection in the Autumn, it affords the means, on the rivers in which it is bred, of an agreeable prolongation of the angling season.

As we write in the hope of attracting the attention of influential parties, and of the local anglers as a body, to the condition of a stream which, instead of being the source of considerable employment and trade, is allowed to become the common property of all who choose to join in the disgraceful process of exterminating its once magnificent breed of fish, we shall perhaps be pardoned for devoting a short space to a consideration of the more prominent habits of the migratory *salmonidæ*, which appear to be not generally understood. The three migratory species in the Axe, are the Salmon, the Sea-trout, and the Bull-trout. [2] It will suffice to confine our remarks to the

---

[1] See '*Salmonia*,' by Sir Humphrey Davy.

[2] The sea trout (*salmo trutta*, probably identical with *salmo hucho*) is easily distinguished from the salmon by the larger size of its spots, which somewhat resemble the letter X, by the generally darker color of its body, and by its lighter fins. It differs, also, in the shape of its gill covers and in the number of its fin-rays. It seems to prefer the Yarty to the Axe, and would increase with great rapidity if properly protected. It is of delicious quality for the table—superior, perhaps, even to the salmon itself. The bull trout (*salmo eriox*) is comparatively rare in our waters. It is a much *coarser* fish than either the salmon or the sea trout, and infinitely inferior as an article of food, its flesh being yellow and dry. The general color of the exterior of the body is darker, and its scales are smaller than those of the salmon; while its caudal fin, or tail,

salmon, the most numerous and valuable of the three. The habits of all, indeed, are so nearly identical that the description of more than one, in this place, would be unnecessary :—

Fishes in general multiply their species by eggs, which are brought into contact with the milt *after* their ejection from the female, [1] and which require the contact of water saturated with air to render them productive. These circumstances show the necessity for that wonderful instinct of the salmon, which, previously to the spawning season in autumn and the early part of winter, quits the sea and makes its way through the roughest streams and over apparently insurmountable weirs, to the upper parts of rivers, and into their tributaries, where the ova may be deposited in pure and aërated water. In this migration a beautiful instance is furnished of the protecting instinct which is so wisely implanted in the humblest creatures ; for instead of rushing at once

---

unlike that of its congeners, becomes *rounded*, instead of forked or square, after the fish has attained its first year. Very few specimens have been taken in the Axe, to our knowledge. The largest we ever saw weighed eleven pounds. It was taken at Whitford, in 1842, by the fishermen of the late Sir W. Pole, Bart.

[1] See The '*Angler's Companion to the Rivers and Lakes of Scotland,*' in which this position is attempted to be controverted upon grounds which, if proved to be tenable, would completely overturn the old and, till lately, the universally received opinions as to the procreation of fishes. A condensed account of Mr. Stoddart's theory will be found in the '*Vade Mecum of Fly-fishing for Trout.*' See, also, the '*North British Review*' for May, 1848, in which the theory is criticised with great severity and acumen.

from the salt water into the fresh, which, before its organs of breathing had become fitted for the change in the constitution of its element, would be immediately fatal to the fish, it remains in the brackish water, within the influence of the tide, until the necessary change shall have been effected, when it slowly proceeds along its course. A wonderful instance, this, of the powers of modification which are exercised not only in man but in the inferior objects of creation!

Arrived at the spot to which instinct prompts as adapted to its purpose, the process of spawning commences, and soon after it is effected both the male and female fish set about returning to the sea, by the same slow stages as those by which they arrived— leaving the ova buried in the sand, to be hatched, in due time, by the influence of the water and the air. The number of eggs deposited by a single fish depends upon the size of the individual. From experiments made a few years since, we found that the average was a thousand to each pound weight of the fish, and that the rule applied to both salmon and trout. Thus a trout of eight ounces, for example, contained the exact number of five hundred eggs, and a salmon of twelve pounds that of eleven thousand six hundred. We are of course unable to say that this is the natural law, although we venture to throw out the hint. It is during the time of spawning, when the fish, as an article of food, are almost in a poisonous condition, [1] and when the loss of one fish to a river involves the loss of embryo thousands which should go to form the next year's stock, that the short-sighted poachers put their detestable arts into operation. From the moment the poor fish ventures into the river till it returns again to the sea, it is, in the Axe, in defiance of fence-days or close time, [2] an object of unceasing persecution. Hundreds become victims to the poachers ere they reach their spawning ground, and those that by chance ascend so far, instead of the protection which under such circumstances the humblest animal should in right receive, no means are left untried to discover the defenceless fish, which of course become an easy prey. Thus salmon, which, if properly protected, would in due time produce invaluable progeny, are slaughtered when positively valueless, and in a state unfit for human food. Sir Humphrey Davy expressed surprise

[1] A few years since a whole family was poisoned at Carlisle by dining heartily on a salmon which was taken in the act of spawning. Trout, in the same condition, are equally noxious.

[2] These are certain periods set apart by the legislature for cessation from the capture of salmon. What is called the close time is the whole of *every* Sunday, when no flood-hatch is allowed to be down nor any other obstruction to the passage of fish permitted. The fence-days are variously fixed to suit the peculiarity of different rivers. On the Axe they commence (nominally, alas!) on the 20th of November (at least a month too late) and expire on the 18th of April. Within this period no one can *legally* be in possession of 'a fish of the salmon kind,' and the purchaser of such a fish is punishable, on information to a magistrate, equally with the seller, or with the poacher himself. The purchaser, in fact, is by far the most culpable, for he *encourages* an offence for which, unlike the poor poacher, he cannot have the shadow of an excuse.

that the rivers of Devonshire were comparatively unproductive of salmon.[1] He could not have been aware of the shameful practices which for years have been in operation to account for a circumstance by no means *natural*. While we are now writing, thousands of embryo salmon, we have reason to fear, are in the act of being destroyed in the river of which we are treating, by the vagabonds who are allowed to ply their nefarious arts with barefaced impunity, and in defiance of a law for the especial protection of the valuable fish which they so wantonly destroy.

But to return to the spawn deposited in the sand by the parent fish, and left, we will imagine, in comparative security. It becomes vivified, according to the temperature, in the course of from ninety to one hundred and twenty days. Many of the little fish, as may be expected, fall an easy prey to other fishes, the voracious trout in particular, and as soon as those which escape acquire sufficient strength to frequent the stickles, many of them are sure to be taken with the fly, and basketed as trophies by the 'pretender to the angle,' who calls them *parr*, and says that they would grow no larger if permitted to remain in the water. He is wrong, of course—as he might know if he condescended to reflect. The little fish, if left alone, would remain in the river for a year,

---

[1] ' *Salmonia*,' page 123, first edit.

when their coating of scales, which up to that time appears as if impressed on the sides with finger marks, would become moulted off and reveal them in the *gravelling* dress, in which they would descend to the sea with the floods of spring. [1] In the course of a very few months, they would return again to the river as *salmon-peal*, to be slaughtered on every hand after the manner of the few which *do*, in some mysterious manner, contrive every summer to enrich, for a little while, the thankless waters of the Axe and its tributaries. The following year would find them veritable salmon of six or eight pounds weight, and of a quality fit to grace the table of a prince, as all Axe salmon are. [2]

What is wanted to restore the Axe to its pristine position among the salmon rivers of the West, is simply to put in force the laws which relate to the subject—to maintain a liberal and an encouraging policy towards *all* anglers, whatever their station in life,—to adopt rules for the regulation of the angling season, and for the weight and character of the fish to be caught—and, lastly, to discountenance poaching in every possible form. Apply this system, and we will answer for it that the river would very

[1] The finger marks referred to are the distinguishing characteristics of the whole of the genus *salmo* in their infant state. The angler should always bear this fact in mind, and return to the water *all* small fish marked in this unmistakable manner.

[2] See Mr. Shaw's pamphlet on ' *The growth of Salmon in Fresh Water.*' Also, the ' *Book of the Salmon,*' by 'Ephemera' and Andrew Young.

soon become full of the choicest fish, an object of
attraction far and near, and the source of profit and
delight, in a variety of ways, to the dwellers upon
its lovely banks. Let it be remembered, that salmon
have been taken in the stream weighing thirty and
forty pounds each, [1]—that the capture, with the fly,
of three or four large fish a day was of frequent occurrence,—that within the memory of persons still
living the salmon of the Axe, in the choicest season,
were so abundant as to be often sold at three-pence
and four-pence per pound,—and that it was then
usual to insert a clause in indentures by which masters were restricted from dining their apprentices
upon that piscine delicacy oftener than three times a
week! Need we add another syllable upon the
subject?

We shall conclude this 'chapter of miscellanies'
with a few paragraphs relating to the Axe, extracted
from the scarce and curious works of some old topographical writers. And first for a passage from the
'*Itinerary*' of William de Worcester :—

'Ab Excestre usque Seynt Mary Otteray X miliaria, et ab Otteray usque Axmyster X miliaria, et ab
Axmyster usque Taunton XII miliaria. Axmyster

---

[1] The late Rev. William Wills, of Axminster, once caught a salmon of
32lbs., and the late Mr. James Woolley one of 42lbs., with nine others on the
same day of from 12 to 20lbs. each. This was near Whitford. Mr.
Wills records that he was present at the taking, from *three pools* only,
below Yarty bridge, and in less than two hours, of as many large salmon
as completely filled a post chaise!

villa distat ab Excestre XX miliaria. Axwater currit per villam Axmyster, *ubi est pons magnus*, et incipit ejus fons per IV miliaria, in boriali et orientali ultra villam Axmyster per VIII miliaria, et cadit in mari apud portum vocatum Seton havyn, per distantiam V miliarium ab Axmyster ex parte meridionali.'

Holingshed says that ' The Ax rises out of an hill called Axnol, belonging to Sir Giles Strangeways, near Cheddington, thence runs to Mosterdon, whence it goes to Seborough, Clapton, Wayford bridge, Winsham, and Ford, and, crossing an angle of this county, passes to Axminster, thence to Musbury, Culliford, and Axmouth. At Ford the Ax receives a rill from the east by Hawkchurch, and soon after another from the north-west, from Wambroke by Chardstock. Above Culliford it meets with a water that rises above Cotleigh, and goes from thence by Widworthy and Culliton, and there receiving a rill, proceeds to the confluence below Culliford bridge into Ax, and thence with it to the sea. Below Axminster it crosses the Yare, which comes from Buckland by Whitestanton, Yarcombe, Longbridge, Stockland, and Kilmington bridge, at which last it receives a brook which comes from the south by Dalwood.'

The following is from Leland's ' *Itinerary*,' vol. III, pp. 72 and 73 :—

' *The Descent and Course of the River of Ax from the Hed.*—Ax riseth a mile est from Bemistre, a market toun in Dorsetshir, at a place caullid Axnoll, a ground longging to Sir Giles Strangewaies, in a more on the hangging of an hille; and thens rennith south west a four miles to Forde Abbey, standing in Devonshir, on the farther ripe of it. And here about it is a limes to Devonshir and Somersetshir. Ax then rennith to Axmistre, a pratie quick market toun, a three miles lower ripa citeriori. This toun is in Devonshir. Ax then rennith through Axmistre bridge of stone, about a quarter of a mile lower than Axmistre toun. Somewhat lower than this bridge enterith Artey ryver, being sometyme a raging water, into Ax ryver. Artey riseth by north west, and enterith into Ax by est. There is a stone bridge on Artey, about half a mile from the place wher it enterith into Ax. This bridge of some is caullid Kilmington bridge, a village not very far from it. Ax rennith a mile dim. lower through Ax bridge of two arches of stone. This bridge *serveth not to passe over at high tydes, otherwise it doth.* Then Ax rennith half a mile lower to Axmouth toun, and a quarter of a mile lower it goith undre White Clif into the ocean se, there caullid Ax bay.'

In Coker's ' *Survey of Dorset* ' we find this passage:—' Not far from hence is Ax, where out of an hill called Axeknoll issue three springs, which taking their courses as manie several wayes growe rivers of good bignesse; the principal of them, taking name from the place, passeth ere long into Devonshir, and after crossing an angle of this countie, taketh his course to Axminster, a well known towne unto which it imparteth the name.'

Last of all we copy a few verses from the curious old work entitled ' *Polyolbion, or a Poetical Description of England,*' by the celebrated Michael Drayton —'my honest old friend,' as father Izaac styles him. In these verses the poet confers a little more classical renown upon our neighbourhood than other writers seem inclined to do :—

' where

Great Brute first disembarq'd his wand'ring Trojans, there
His offspring (after long expulst the inner land,
When they the Saxon power no longer could withstand)
Found refuge in their flight; where *Ax* and *Otrey* first
Gave these poor soules to drink, opprest with grievous thirst.'

THE FIRST SONG.

The whole story to which these lines refer is, of course, fabulous. Brute, or Brutus, say the ancient chroniclers, was the first king of this island, and the founder of the British nation.[1] He was the son of Sylvius, and the grandson of Ascanius the son of Æneas. A quarrel arising amongst his family, he left Italy and paid an unwelcome visit to this country. Some traditions say that he landed alone, and others that he was accompanied by many warriors and their families. After many struggles he destroyed the giants who then inhabited Albion, and called the island by his own name. At his death the island was

---

[1] Robert of Gloucester, Geoffrey of Monmouth, Huntington, &c.

divided between his three sons—Socrine had England, Camber had Wales, and Albanack had Scotland.

Totnes is said by some writers to be the scene of 'Great Brute's' debarkation. Prince, the celebrated author of the '*Worthies of Devon*,' writing in 1701, informs us that 'there is yet remaining towards the lower end of the town of Totnes, a certain rock called Brute's stone, which tradition here, *more pleasantly than positively*, says is that which Brute first set his foot upon when he came ashore.[1] Of which adventure Havillan, an ancient Cornish poet, following the authority of the British History, thus sang long since, as he is quoted by an author of the highest reputation among us in these affairs,' although with no great faith as to what he says,—

> " Inde dato cursu, Brutus comitatus Achate,
> Gallorum spoliis cumulatis navibus æquor
> Exarat, et superis aurag; faventibus usus
> Littora fœlices intrat Totonesia portus ! "

thus translated into English :—

> " From hence great Brute with his Achates steer'd,
> Full frought with Gallic spoils their ships appeard ;
> The Gods did guide his sails and course,
> The winds were at command,
> And *Totnes* was the happy shore
> Where first he came to land." '

[1] 'Brute's Stone' is still in existence at Totnes, where Prince was vicar, and the tradition which attaches to it is as familiar to the inhabitants at the present moment as it was 150 years ago, when ' *The Worthies of Devon* ' was written.

[2] Camden ' *Brit. in Dev.*' ult edit. p. 27.

Other writers imagine that Bridport is the place which was honored by the landing of Brute, and that the original name of that town was *Bruteport* [1]—a specimen of the imaginative tendencies of some antiquaries who would seek to establish a favorite theory by the assistance, indiscriminately, of fable and of fact.

[1] Hutchings's 'History of Dorset.'

CHAPTER II.

AND here we are at the rise of the river, after a delightful walk over the hills, in winding lanes, across sundry daisied fields, and at last through a perfect *chevaux-de-frize* of 'brake and briar' into Cheddington Copse, where the infant stream is gurgling itself into existence![1] It will be a three miles' ramble

---

[1] 'Various opinions have been held by ancient as well as modern philosophers respecting the origin of springs and rivers; but the true cause is now pretty well ascertained. It is well known that the heat of the sun draws up vast quantities of vapour from the sea, which being carried by the wind to all parts of the globe, and converted by the cold into rain and dew, falls down upon the earth. Part of it runs down into the lower places, forming rivulets; part serves for the purposes of vegetation; and the rest descends into hollow caverns within the earth, and breaking out by the sides of the hills forms little springs. Many of these springs running into the valleys increase the brooks or rivulets, and several of these meeting together make a river. Dr. Halley says, "the vapours that are raised copiously from the sea, and carried by the winds to the ridges of mountains, are conveyed to their tops by the current of air; where the water being presently precipitated, enters the crannies of the mountains, down which it glides into the caverns, till it meets with a stratum of earth or stone of a nature sufficiently solid to sustain it. When this reservoir is filled, the superfluous water, following the direction of the stratum,

for us down the meads, Piscator, ere we shall arrive
at fishing ground; so that now we must content ourselves with chatting, historically and topographically,
about this unfishable upper part (as we have decided upon tracing the *entire* stream), and by-and-by
we will commence our sport in earnest—*cum grano
salis*, as a thing of course. We shall have enough to
do, good friend, when we arrive among the speckled
beauties lower down.

The stream is generally believed to rise exclusively
at Axeknoller, but in reality it has two principal
sources, the more important of which is in the copse
already mentioned. This copse is situated on a
hanger on the northern side of the semi-funnel like
extremity of the valley. It is about two stone-throws
from the branch on the farm of Axeknoller, which is
in the parish of Beaminster. There is nothing striking or romantic about either source. That at Ched-

runs over at the lowest place, and in its passage meets perhaps with other
little streams, which have a similar origin. These gradually descend till
they meet with an aperture at the side or foot of the mountain, through
which they escape, and form a spring or the source of a brook or rivulet.
Several brooks or rivulets uniting their streams, form small rivers, and
these again being joined by other small rivers, and united in one common
channel form such streams as the Rhine, Rhone, Danube, &c." Several
springs yield always the same quantity of water equally when the least
rain or vapour is afforded, and when rain falls in the greatest quantities;
and as the fall of rain, snow, &c., is inconstant or variable, we have here
a constant effect produced from an inconstant cause, which is an unphilo-
sophical conclusion. Some naturalists, therefore, have recourse to the sea,
and derive the origin of several springs immediately from thence by sup-
posing a subterraneous circulation of percolated waters from the fountains
of the deep.'—*Keith on the Globes.*

dington Copse, as our artists have illustrated, trickles
out of the side of a bank, in a very humble and
unobtrusive manner; and the copse itself is small and
common place, filled with brushwood growing rankly
in the spongy soil among the fir and other trees.

The village of Cheddington is situated at the distance of about a mile north of the source of the
river. It occupies a very commanding position upon
the range of hills which encloses on the east the great
valley in which the town of Crewkerne is situated.
The prospect from the ancient earthwork at the back
of the Wynniard's Gap Inn,[1] is very magnificent,
and it ranges in three directions. To the west and
north it embraces a wide extent of country into
the heart of Somerset to the Langport hills, sweeping over the town of Crewkerne, which lies very
snugly at the distance of about four miles—and
over villages and homesteads in every direction, the
unequalled Somersetshire churches presenting themselves more or less distinctly, and pointing out,
appropriately, the collected abodes of men. Among
the most striking objects in the distance, are Blagdon
Hill, near Taunton, and the monument at Burton
Pynsent, near Langport; towards the north-east
Glastonbury Tor and the Mendip Hills; and nearer
home, the hills in the neighbourhood of Yeovil, and
the noble entrenchment upon Hamdon Hill, which

[1] See page 14.

F

looks a comparative mole-heap among its more tower-ing neighbours. [1]   All these eminences, more or less defined according to their relative distances, form beautiful undulations against the horizon; and the intermediate valleys are clothed in the richest verdure, and amply adorned with trees.   Towards the east are

[1] Ham, or Hamdon, Hill is situated about five miles north of Crew-kerne, and in the parishes of Norton, Montacute, and Stoke. It formed one of a chain of forts about which more will be said in a future page. In common with the other forts with which it was connected, it is supposed to be of Ancient British origin, although subsequently occupied and adapted by the Romans. A miniature amphitheatre, familiarly called 'the frying-pan,' exists at the northern angle, and also a series of low perfo-rated stones, regularly disposed, and apparently used originally either for securing tents or for the Roman cavalry. At all events they are exceed-ingly curious, and of undoubted antiquity. The earthworks were origi-nally of great strength, and they enclose an area of not less than 210 acres, of which the circumference is three miles. The hill commands a magnificent prospect over 300 miles of country, in different directions, and it is said that in clear weather no less than eighty churches are visi-ble. The far-famed Ham stone quarries, from which the materials for most of the churches and other public buildings within a wide circuit have been supplied, are of the most remote antiquity. They are exceed-ingly interesting, and constantly worked, the principal proprietors being Mr. Charles Trask and Mr. John Trask, of Norton, and Mr. Staple, of Stoke. 'The quarries,' says Mr. Charles Trask, in an intelligent re-ply to our inquiries, 'are of great depth, and a section presents, next to the soil, several layers of ochre, then a few beds of stone of an impure description, after which from sixty to seventy feet of good stone, in layers of from six inches to three feet in thickness, of which the lowest are con-sidered the best. The stone is a magnesian limestone, of a creamy yellow color, and contains 50 per cent. of carbonate of lime, 30 per cent. of phosphate of magnesia, and an intermixture of iron. The quarries ex-hibit several vertical fissures, called 'gullies,' which branch out into innumerable smaller fissures, some of which are so narrow as to be hardly visible. They all present the evidence of fire, and are undoubtedly the effect of volcanic action.' The name of the hill is derived from the Anglo-Saxon, *ham,* an inhabited place, and the British, *dun,* a hill.

the dreary Dorset hills and downs, presenting a striking diversity in the prospect; while on the south,
where the view is very confined, are the bold eminences of Lewisdon and Pillesdon Pen, near Broadwinsor, and a few of the other hills which occur in
the direction of the coast between Bridport and
Lyme Regis.

Altogether, friend Piscator, we have beheld a
scene by which we are amply repaid for the fatigue of
scaling the rather formidable hill, and for the no little
probability, in our attempts to descend, of an undig-
nified roll into the village street below, if not, indeed,
plump through one of the roofs, to be ushered, *nolens
volens*, into the 'domestic mysteries' of the inhabitants! But not so. We have heroically preserved
our perpendicular, and here we are in the midst of
the ten or a dozen houses which constitute this pretty
little rural retreat, the history of which we must now
explore.

There does not appear, however, to be a great deal
said about the little place in early times. No mention is made of it in Domesday Book, [1] probably

---

[1] Domesday Book is the most ancient and valuable record in England.
It was compiled by order of William the Conqueror, and contains a
general survey of the Kingdom, with the exception of four of the north-
ernmost Counties. Every manor and 'vill' is mentioned and described—
the value and extent of each, with the number of tenants, 'villains,' 'cottarii,'
'servi,' cattle, &c., together with the name of the owner and the nature
of his tenure. The value is shown at the time the document was compiled, and also as it stood in the time of Edward the Confessor. The
work is in two volumes, on vellum, written in a legible hand, in nearly a

because it was then included in some adjoining parish; but at a very ancient period the place belonged to a family who either gave it their own name or else derived their name from it—namely, the *Cheddingtons*. Of this family little more is known than that it became extinct before the reign of Henry the VI, [1] when, by the daughter of Nicholas Cheddington, the property came to John Buller, of Somerset. Afterwards John Hornesbowe and Thomas Boller held one fee, late Cheddington's, of the Bishop of Sarum in chief, as did subsequently the heirs of John Spreveshew and John Bowler. In the 28th year of Henry VI, John Crokehorn, whose family was one of great local influence, and had a seat at Childhay, held lands at Cheddington 'of John Bolour,

pure Roman character, with a mixture of Saxon. The first volume consists of 382 leaves, appropriated to 31 counties, in double columns and on both sides, and the second volume contains the three counties of Essex, Suffolk, and Norfolk, on 450 leaves, in single columns, and in a large character. Domesday was compiled in the space of a single year (1085-6,) by commissioners appointed by the king, and it has ever since been regarded as the great legal document by which most of the landed property in England is held, appeals being always made to it in the decision of law cases. It is deposited in the chapter house at Westminster. The name, which sounds so ominously, is said by Stow to be a corruption of *Domus Dei*, the name of the apartment in the king's treasury in which the volumes were formerly kept. Other authors have given different explanations. What is called the Exeter Domesday appears to have been compiled at the same time with the Exchequer Domesday, and probably for local use. It originally contained surveys of the five Western Counties, in two volumes, but is now little more than a fragment. It is in the custody of the Dean and Chapter of Exeter.

[1] Its arms were Az. on a chevron A. between three plates, three crosslets Sa.

Esq, as of his manor here.' About the year 1500 the Bampfields, of Poltimore, presented to the rectory, which shows that that family had then some concern in the property of the parish, which appears afterwards to have passed to unknown owners, for in the 38th year of Elizabeth, Giles Penny, Esq., at his death, held lands of William Ouseley and Christopher Mintern, 'as of their manor of Cheddington, value £4.'

The parish of Cheddington is in the hundred and union of Beaminster, which is also its polling place, and in the deanery and magisterial division of Bridport. It contains a population of only 189 souls, out of which there are five registered voters for the county of Dorset. The amount of poor rate levied in 1851 was £150 9s. 3d. The living is a rectory, and the present incumbent is the Rev. Rowland Huyshe, of East Coker, the officiating minister being the Rev. Thomas Babb. It is valued in the King's Books at £8 8s. 10d., and the tithes are commuted at £138 10s. The village contains some respectable houses, one of the most interesting being the old farm-house inhabited by Mr. John Symes. The principal landed proprietor is William Trevelyan Cox, Esq., who occupies a magnificent residence at the entrance to the village from Wynniard's Gap. It is in the Tudor style of domestic architecture, and was erected in 1840. The gardens and grounds are spacious, and very tastefully laid out. They are especially interesting to us, Piscator, from their containing the source of the river Parrot. Moreover, they possess an air of peculiar solemnity, for among the shrubs and flowers are the remains of the old church-yard, in which

'The rude forefathers of the hamlet sleep,'—

the ivy and the honeysuckle festooning gracefully, yet mournfully, about the tombs. It is a solemn lesson which those grounds should preach—the living and the dead so immediately in contact, and the beauties and delights of nature so entwined, as it were, with the end of all things! Nevertheless, it is a pleasant resting-place from the toils of life, and let us hope, Piscator, that we may neither of us find a less appropriate or hallowed one!

It is not a little remarkable that so many as four rivers should rise in Cheddington and the adjoining parishes, and at a comparatively trifling distance from each other. At Corscombe, within a mile of the source of the Parrot, and not much more than a mile from the source of the Axe, rises the river Yeo, which flows to Yeovil and falls into the Parrot near Langport. The Brit rises on Beaminster Down, at about the same distance from Axeknoller, and flows to Beaminster and Bridport. The direction of the Parrot is north-west. That river gives its name to the villages of South and North Perrot, and flows within a mile of Crewkerne to South Petherton, whence it goes to Langport, and falls into the sea near Bridgwater. The Axe flows south-westward, in a course of about five and twenty miles.

Cheddington church is a modern building, erected after the removal of the older structure, in 1840, and at the distance of a few yards from the original site, in the grounds of Mr. Cox. It is a plain, genuine nineteenth-century building, in imitation of the perpendicular style of the fifteenth century,—the style which prevailed immediately before our ecclesiastical architecture had begun to undergo the rapid course of degeneracy which has distinguished it in modern times. The church consists of a nave and chancel, [1] 68 feet long, with a porch at the west end which is entered by two doorways and lighted by an end window. A vestry projects from the south wall of the nave, and the western gable is surmounted by a bell turret. The building is lighted by four windows in the north wall and three in the south, placed between buttresses. These windows are of two lights,

---

[1] Churches, formerly, were almost always built in the form of a cross, which also symbolised the position of our Saviour's body at the crucifixion. The chancel represented his head and the upper part of the cross; the transept his extended arms; and the nave his body and legs. The chancel contained the altar, and was the place in which the service was performed. It was regarded as the most sacred part of the edifice, and was divided from the nave by *rails*, in Latin called *cancelli*—a circumstance from which it derives its name. The nave was the largest part of the church, and it is said to have been so called from the French *nef*. Some authors, however, have resort to the Latin, and say that the root of the word is *navis*, a *ship*, and that the nave is thus symbolical of the church of Christ being tossed about by the waves of this troublesome world.

with feathered headings, surmounted by a quatrefoil, [1]
and they are furnished with weather mouldings
resting upon corbels of foliage and other ornaments.
The eastern window, which was preserved from the
former building, consists of three lights, with foliated
heads, surmounted by quatrefoils, that in the apex
containing the letters I. H. S. in stained glass. The
communion table is of Caen stone, placed between
pinnacled tablets of the same material, upon which
the commandments are cut. The pulpit and reading
desk are placed against the south pier of the chancel
arch. A neat marble tablet, the only one in the
church, is placed against the wall near the opposite
pier, to the memory of William Hody, Esq., who
died June 19th, 1739, aged 74 years; and to that of
his son William, who died February 22nd, 1780, aged
70 years. [2] Arms, A. a fess barry, indented V and Sa.
between two cotizes counterchanged, in a border engrailed Sa.

Axeknoller is said by Hutchings, who wrote in
1774, to be 'a village consisting of about twelve
houses, two miles north-est from Beaminster, belonging to several owners. The hundred of est Ax-
naller was held, 39 Eliz., by James Hannan, of the

---

[1] The quatrefoil was an imitation of the primrose, which, being one of
the first flowers of the spring, was considered as the harbinger of revived
nature, and was adopted by our church architects to signify, emblemati-
cally, that the gospel, the harbinger of peace and immortality, was there
preached. The trefoil was the emblem of the Trinity.

[2] These were probably members of the Pillesdon family of that name.

hundred of Beminster, value £3.' There are now no traces of a village, and the only buildings are those in connection with the farms of higher and lower Axeknoller, which are about a quarter of a mile apart. What was formerly known, for miles about the neighbourhood, as Axeknoller church, was really nothing but a venerable oak, under the branches of which the rustic patriarchs were wont to seat themselves in the summer evenings, to enjoy their pipes and jugs, while their children amused themselves in play. This agreeable manner of spending the evening, was, more facetiously than reverently, called 'going to church;' and hence we should not be surprised to find some matter of fact scribe, one of these odd days, putting a literal construction upon the phrase, and gravely informing the public that Axeknoller 'was once a flourishing village, with an ancient and a well-attended church.'

Away over the hills, at the distance of about two miles to the south of Axeknoller, is the town of Beaminster, very comfortably nestled among the beautifully undulating eminences by which it is surrounded. Its situation is indeed delightful. Sheltered from the piercing winds of the north and east, and watered by the sparkling Brit,[1] it presents a

---

[1] This stream, of which mention has been made at page 38, is called by Coker the *Birt*, and by Hollingshed the *Bride*. Drayton thus refers to it under the name of *Bert* :—

'Whereas the little Lim along doth easelie creep,
And Car that coming downe unto the troubled deep

desirable spot in which the lover of nature and of
seclusion may find a fitting resting place, and is an
object upon which the eye can linger, from a distance,
with satisfaction and delight.   But as a place of bustle
and of business it has no pretensions.   In common
with all the other towns in this part of the country,
it suffers greatly from the want of the accommodation of railways which contributes so essentially to
those desirable characteristics. [1]   Beaminster formerly
possessed extensive manufactories of sailcloth, which
afforded employment to a considerable portion of the
population; and when those declined, the introduction of a woollen manufacture proved a scarcely less
fruitful source of occupation.   Inability to compete

Brings on the neighbouring *Bert*, whose bat'ning mellowed banke
From all the British soyles for hempe most largely ranke,
Doth bear away the best to Bertport, which hath gain'd
That praise from every place,' &c.—POLYOLBION. *The Second Song.*

[1] Several attempts have been made, from time to time, to open up this
important part of the country to the advantages of railway communication,
but hitherto without success.   The valley of the Axe, in particular, has
for many years been the frequent scene of the 'mappings' and the 'measur-
ings' which were supposed to be precursory to *bona fide* engineering
operations.   Ever since the year 1824-5, when it was proposed to construct
the celebrated ship-canal from Seaton to Watchett, for which, indeed, an
act of Parliament was obtained, there has been no intermission to the
alternate expectations and disappointments by which the temper of the
too confiding inhabitants of the locality has been tried.   After years of
fierce contention between the promoters of 'the central line,' and the promoters of 'the coast' and other lines, the ground seems at last to be left
in the quiet possession of the Great Western Company, to carry out, if they
please, their 'Devon and Dorset railway' from Stoke Canon, near Exeter,
to a junction with the Wilts, Somerset, and Weymouth line, near Maiden
Newton.   We shall see.

with the steam machinery of the North, and comparative isolation from the great seats of commerce, have resulted in the almost total extinction of both those branches of trade, and Beaminster has thus lost all claim to the distinction of a manufacturing town. Recently, however, an establishment for the preparation of flax, on a new chemical principle, has been introduced with every prospect of success. But the town carries on a trade in agricultural productions, and has a weekly market on Thursdays, and an annual fair on September 19th. The grants for these were obtained in the 12th year of Edward the First (1284) by William Ewel, prebendary of Sarum.

Beaminster was, until lately, in the parish of Netherbury, to which its church was only a chapel of ease.[1] But it is now a separate parish, and in 1849 was made a perpetual curacy. The living is valued in the King's Books, among the possessions of the Abbey of Sherborne, at £20 6s. 6d. for Beaminster Prima, and £22 5s. 7½d. for Beaminster Secunda; and the tithes for the two are commuted at £270 for the rectorial, belonging to a layman, and £300 for the vicarial. The Rev. A. C. Richings is the present incumbent. Beaminster gives its name to a prebendal stall in the cathedral of Salisbury. The parish consists of the two

[1] During the Commonwealth, Beaminster appears to have been made a distinct parish. Its minister was Joseph Crabbe, who enjoyed, at the same time, the living of Netherbury. He was ejected at the Restoration, when he conformed, and afterwards became vicar of Axminster; and Beaminster was again united to Netherbury.

manors just mentioned, namely, Beaminster Prima and Beaminster Secunda, which are held under the prebendary, on the tenure of 'customary copyhold,' for a term of twenty-one years. The present lessee of Beaminster Prima is Baruch Fox, Esq., and that of Beaminster Secunda, Samuel Cox, Esq. The town is also the centre of a union composed of the following parishes :— Beaminster, Bettiscombe, Broadwinsor, Burstock, Cheddington, East and West Chelborough, Corscombe, Evershot, Halstock, Hook, Mapperton, Marshwood, Melbury Osmond, Melbury Sampford, Mosterton, Netherbury, South Perrot, Pillesdon, Poorstock, North Poorton, Rampisham, Stoke Abbot, Wraxhall, Misterton, and Seaborough. The last two parishes are in Somerset. Beaminster is also one of the polling places for Dorsetshire, and is the capital of a hundred to which it gives its name.

In Domesday Book, 'Beminstre' is surveyed amongst the lands of the bishop of Sarum, but it was one of those manors which were 'de victu monachorum Scireburnens.' The bishop's demesnes were sixteen hides,[1] value £16. The lands of four of the bishop's men were ten hides and a half, value £7. In the 4th year of William Rufus (1091) Osmond, bishop of Salisbury, gave Begeminster, and the knight's fee

[1] The hide was a quantity of land which appears to have differed in different counties. Some writers fix the amount, generally, at sixty-four acres, others at ninety-six, others at one hundred, and others at one hundred and twenty acres. In Jacob's Law Dictionary it is said to have been, in the time of Edward III (1320), one hundred acres.

there, to the church of Sarum. Leland, who wrote in the time of Henry VIII, describes it as 'a praty market toune, and usith much husbandry, and lyith in one street from north to south, and in another from west to est. There is a fair chapelle of ease in this toune. Netherby is the paroch chirch to it; and Bemistre is a prebend to the chirch at Saresbyri.' Quarter sessions were held in the town during the first seven years of the reign of Charles the First (1625 to 1632), after which they were removed to Bridport; and in 1638 there was an order of sessions for erecting a house of correction at the expense of the division. [1]

The principal street, called Hay's Hill street, is pleasantly situated, and contains some respectable buildings and some handsome shops. The market-place, over which is the town hall, stands in an open space towards its southern extremity. The other principal streets are North-street and East or Flax-street. The town contains two churches,—a new church having been erected in 1850. It also contains two chapels, one of which belongs to the Wesleyans, erected in 1838, and the other to the Independents, erected in 1749. The population, according to the census of 1851, is 2842; the number of registered voters for the county, 119; and the amount of poor's rate for 1852, £392. In common with many other towns in a locality in which the use of thatch was

[1] Hutchings.

formerly universal, Beaminster has at different times experienced some calamitous fires. These have been the means of materially improving the appearance of the town, by removing many old and ugly buildings by which the narrow streets were inconveniently crowded. During the civil war the town was made a considerable station for the troops of the King, and in 1645, during a quarrel among the men under Prince Maurice, it was wilfully set on fire at five different places at once, and almost entirely consumed. It also suffered from an accidental fire in 1686-7, 'when a handsome Market-house, built on pillars, was destroyed;' [1] and in 1781, upwards of eighty houses fell a prey to 'the devouring element.' The principal streets are now paved, and the town is lighted with gas.

The most celebrated man whom Beaminster appears to have produced was Dr. Sprat, bishop of Worcester, who was born in 1636 and died in 1713. He was the son of a clergyman, and was celebrated as a historian and a poet. Among his writings in verse, are a poem on the Death of Cromwell, and an Ode on the Plague of Athens. He also wrote a Life of Cowley, and the History of the Royal Society, of which he was one of the earliest members. Mr. Macaulay pronounces this history to be 'an eloquent production.' [2] The History of the Rye House Plot,

[1] Hutchings.
[2] See Macaulay's *History of England*, vol. 1, page 406.

and a volume of Sermons, are among his other works. Some authors make Tallaton, in Devonshire, his birthplace; but his epitaph satisfactorily decides the question in favor of Beaminster.

Among the charities for which Beaminster, in common with most other places, is indebted to the consideration and liberality of our 'benighted' forefathers, as it is the fashion to consider them, are an almshouse, which was founded about the year 1627, by Sir John Strode, for six poor men and women, not confined to the inhabitants of Beaminster only. This was endowed with two-third parts of a farm called Bilshay, in the parish of Loders, but subject to disbursements and to a charge of £6 a year to the poor of Symondsbury. It was endowed, also, with a house in Beaminster 'formerly belonging to a chantry, now the almshouse,' and with other property. The buildings are on the north-west side of the church yard. Beaminster also possesses a charity school, at which thirty poor boys are educated. This was founded by Frances Tucker, spinster, who by will dated December 8th, 1682, bequeathed for that purpose a farm called South Mapperton, in Mapperton and Beaminster, and £30 a year for ever for the binding out, as 'apprentices to some honest calling, of three or four of the said boys yearly, as far as the money would reach—one whereof, at least, if not two, to be sent to sea, if fitted for it; such boys to be successively chosen by her executors.' This school had also other endowments from the same source. It was originally intended for *twenty* poor scholars, but a few years since it was thought advisable to alter the design of the founder so far as to increase the number of scholars to thirty, by the appropriation of the money intended for the binding of apprentices, which is thus discontinued. Gilbert Adams, in 1626, gave to the poor of the parish, by will dated February 20th, £200 in money, with part of which the old workhouse was erected. The poor are also indebted to Thomas Keat, William Hillary, and Francis Champion for donations in money and in bread ' for ever.'[1]

The parish church is situated on the south-western side of the town, and is an object of considerable interest, although of no great architectural beauty. The tower is by far the best part of the building, and it forms a highly ornamental feature in the surrounding landscape. It is square and embattled, with buttresses and gargoyles, and has a staircase turret towards the eastern angle of the north side. The gargoyles are very curious, as is generally the case,—the ancient architects appearing to delight in allowing their fancies to revel in the productions of those

'Gorgons, and hydras, and chimeras dire,'

the imputed object of which must not be passed over in silence, although at the expense of a slight interruption in our description of this Church:—Lions'

[1] See Boswell's ' *Charities, &c., for Dorset.*'

heads, of stone or baked earth, were used by the Romans to convey water from their roofs, and this idea appears to have been seized upon by the builders of our early churches. Accordingly, the grotesque looking objects attached to church towers were designed, as antiquaries inform us, to represent evil spirits embodied and frightened beyond measure at the sound of the bells, for bells, in early days, were supposed to have wonderful powers imparted to them by the holy water with which, on their being placed in towers, they were always ceremoniously besprinkled by a priest. [1]

But to return. The tower of Beaminster church consists of three storeys, marked by stringcourses, and it has windows in the belfry pierced for light and sound. Its buttresses are furnished at some of the set-offs with pinnacles, and at others with grotesque figures of animals. In the centre of the western face of the tower, there is, among other carvings in stone, a group representing the crucifixion; and in one of the canopied niches, of which there are several, is a crowned figure, intended, probably, for King Henry

[1] 'The grinning figures for spouts,' says Fosbroke, 'are said to have been invented by Marchion of Arezzo, architect to Pope Innocent III, who died in 1262.' Other authorities, as stated in the text, assign a much earlier date to the 'invention.' The word gargoyle is sometimes used in a different sense, signifying a *corbel* rather than a water spout, as in the 'Vulgaria,' by Hormanus, printed by Richard Pynson, in 1525:—'I wyll have *gargyllis* vnder the beamys heedis.' And again:—'make me a trusse standynge out upon *gargellys*, that I may se about.'—*Glossary of Architecture.*

H

VII. The tower contains a clock and chimes, and eight very musical bells.

The church, which we had almost forgotten to state is dedicated to the Virgin Mary, consists of a nave, under a plain coved roof, a chancel, north and south aisles [1] to the nave, a north aisle to the chancel, forming a chantry chapel, erected in 1505, [2] and a porch on the north side. The church anciently contained also a chantry chapel at the eastern end of the south aisle. It was founded in the year 1407, by Robert Grey, an inhabitant of the town, who endowed it with two messuages and sixty-two acres of land. At the suppression of chantries, in 1547, the rector of this chantry was John Mintern, who received a pension of £6 per annum. The building and endowing of chantry chapels by private individuals was a very common practice in the Roman Catholic times. The object, of course, was the spiritual benefit supposed to result to the founders of those chapels from the prayers of the church which were thus insured. Bequests of money for the building and repair of

[1] The aisles of a church are situated at the sides of the nave, from which they are separated by arches; and there are sometimes aisles to the chancel. The name appears to be derived from the French word *aile*, a wing.

[2] This we learn from an inscription on a board over a depressed perpendicular window in the north wall of the chancel aisle, or chapel:—'This aisle was built by Mr. John Hillary, of Meerhay, in the 20th year of the reign of King Henry VII, in the year of our Lord 1505, and beautified by Mrs. Mary Mills, of Meerhay, in the year 1767; repaired and newly covered with lead by William Clarke, of Beaminster, Esquire.

churches were also frequently made. The erection
of chantries may no doubt be accounted for in the
circumstance of private masses not having been permitted at the high altar.

The aisles are divided from the nave by five pointed
arches on each side, springing from capitals, some of
which are rudely sculptured with vine leaves and
grapes. The chancel is entered under a paneled arch,
and in the walls of the ground floor of the tower—the
western entrance to the church—there are other
paneled arches, now filled up. The nave and aisles
are lighted by five windows on the south, and four
on the north side, and by dormer windows in the
roof. Each of the side windows is formed within
a pointed arch, and is divided by mullions into
three lights, with cusped headings [1] surmounted by
two series of plain sexagonal compartments, which no
doubt were originally filled in with the ornamental
tracery peculiar to the style of which the windows
are now mutilations. The east window is of similar
design, but composed of five lights; and the chancel
is also lighted by small side windows which must be

---

[1] Mullions are the upright bars of stone by which a window is divided
into *lights*, as the intermediate spaces are called. The upper part of the
mullion—the part immediately underneath the commencement of the
tracery in the head of the window—is usually ornamented with small
projecting arcs or *foils*, called *featherings*, or *cusps*, the last word, very
probably, having been originally applied in the same sense as that in
which Chaucer speaks of 'yé cuspys of yé moone.' According to the
number of these cusps, or foils, in connection, they are called trefoils,
quatrefoils, cinquefoils, &c.

excepted from the remark just made, inasmuch as they exhibit some of the characteristic beauties of the perpendicular style. One of them, on the south side, is filled with painted glass representing the resurrection, and other scripture scenes, with a palm tree in the upper part, and the initials 'P. C.' The subjects were designed by Pugin and executed by Hardiman. This window was erected, as set forth in an inscription, 'to the memory of Peter, only son of Peter and Anne Cox, who died at Bekfeya, on Mount Lebanon, September 6th, 1850, aged 23 years.'

In the chancel wall, on the south side of the altar, will be found that interesting object the piscina, within a plain pointed niche, in which is also a stone shelf; [1] but there are no traces of sedilia, [2] as may be expected from the alterations which this part of the building has evidently undergone. Remains of the

[1] In the Roman Catholic service, the piscina was the place where the chalice was rinsed, and where the priest poured away the water in which he had washed his hands before the communion. The water was conveyed away by a drain underneath. The shelf over the piscina was constructed sometimes of stone and sometimes of wood. It is supposed by some to have been used as a credence—that is, the place where the elements were deposited previously to their oblation. Others think that it was used for placing the cruets which contained the holy oil.

[2] Sedilia were stone seats within recesses, in the south wall of the chancel, for the use of the officiating priests. The puritans, when in power, were so anxious to remove every vestige of the Roman Catholic worship, and to wreck their vengeance even upon the walls, that very few churches escaped their mutilations—the good and the bad, the ugly and the interesting being indiscriminately sacrificed,—somewhat after the fashion of our modern church 'restorers,' but from a widely different motive.

piscina are also to be seen in each of the chantry chapels before mentioned. As usual, the church is deformed with galleries—one in each aisle, and one across the nave, at the west end. The last contains a small organ. These galleries contribute to the heaviness of the building, which, without them, would not be remarkable for the opposite characteristic. The vestry is at the west end of the south aisle, and the font stands under the tower, in its proper position near the western entrance of the church. It is of blue lias, square and shallow. On one of its sides are carved some circular arches, as if of Norman date, to which they are not improbably a truthful index; while the vilest of rude chiseling ('enlightened-age'-work, of course,) has effectually erased from the other sides, and from the top, every trace of ornament and of antiquity. Some ancient open benches, of carved oak, still remain at the west end of the nave, but the greater portion of the church is filled with the cumbrous pews with which churches in general are deformed. [1] The pulpit and reading desk stand

[1] Prior to the year 1430, the only seats with which our churches appear to have been furnished were the stone benches which ran around the walls of the building, the men occupying the south side and the women the north. The larger portion of the congregation, when not kneeling, were of course compelled to stand. About the period just mentioned, small open wood benches were introduced. They were afterwards increased in size and adorned with the choicest productions of the carver's art. About the commencement of the seventeenth century, these were gradually superseded by what are now more strictly understood by the word *pews*, as used in the text. See the '*History and Statisticks of Pues*,' published by the Ecclesiological, late Cambridge Cambden, Society.

against the piers of the chancel arch, having recently been removed from the nave. The pulpit is certainly not improved in form by the change to a position on the ground which it was never intended to occupy. Originally it was placed above the reading desk, to which it formed a kind of second storey, standing on its smaller end. Its present position upon the floor, therefore, where it looks like a gigantic whip-top, is preposterously out of place. It is of black oak, carved in a similar style to the pulpit in Axminster church, which it appears to have formerly resembled in other respects. The style of carving probably points to the middle of the seventeenth century as the date of the execution of the work. The church, we must not omit to state, is lighted with gas.

To sum up this imperfect account, we may observe that the prevailing style of the building is that of the perpendicular, with evident provincialisms of a character indicative of the decline of the art,—very inferior, as a whole, to the churches in the same style which are so great an ornament to the neighbouring county of Somerset. The date of the erection of the greater part of the building, therefore, may be presumed to be about the close of the fifteenth century. [1] The tower, undoubtedly, dates

---

[1] The perpendicular style, or, as it is variously denominated, the Tudor, the Florid, and the third or late pointed Gothic, is the last of the four styles of *pointed* architecture (reckoning the Semi-Norman style as one) which, at the death of King Stephen (1154), succeeded each other after the abandonment of the Norman style, with its *circular* arch and

a few years later, for it is on record that in 1503 a legacy was given towards the expenses of its erection.

Among the monuments in Beaminster Church, of which some are very curious and others very imposing, is a magnificent one, of marble, in the south

its peculiar mouldings. The period of the perpendicular style extends from about the year 1380 (Richard II) to the time of Henry VIII. After the Reformation, the true principles of ecclesiastical architecture were lost, and a debased, incongruous manner of church-building prevailed, which has only lately begun to exhibit the slightest indication of improvement—that improvement, at the very best, consisting merely in a more faithful imitation than formerly of mediæval art, without the most remote approach to originality of design. The chief characteristics of the perpendicular style, and those also which can be most easily recognised, are:—

FIRST.—The carrying of the mullions *perpendicularly* through the tracery in the head of the window, dividing it into panel-like compartments—the centre mullion often branching off to form the head into sub-arches. The prevailing idea represented in the tracery, in short, is *perpendicularity*.

SECOND.—The division of lofty windows into stages by means of horizontal bars of stone, called *transoms*, of which the three western windows of Crewkerne church, as well as some of the windows on the north side of that magnificent building, are admirable examples.

THIRD.—The employment of the depressed four-centred or Tudor arch, for windows and otherwise,—the arches which support the roof, &c, being frequently *paneled*, as are sometimes, also, the buttresses.

FOURTH.—The door-ways having generally a square head or moulding over the arch, the *spandrils* (as the triangular spaces between the arch and the head are called) being filled with trefoils or quatrefoils, or with a device or foliage.

Specimens of this style may be found, more or less, in almost every ancient church, either in the form of modern work in imitation of the ancient, or in that of the original work itself—a general reparation of the older churches, and an extensive erection of new ones, having taken place during the fifteenth century, and modern repairs, regardless of the original style of particular buildings, being usually made in imitation of the perpendicular.

aisle, with an inscription in Latin, to the memory of some members of the ancient family of Strode, of Parnham. This family derived its name from the manor of Strode, about two miles from Beaminster, —now the residence and property of George Gollop, Esq., to whose family it has belonged for many generations, having passed into it by the marriage of an ancestor with a daughter of the Strodes. Parnham came into the hands of the Strode family ' by matching,' says Coker, 'with the heirs of Parnham, or Parram, and here have they flourished, in knight's degree, even before the date of ancient evidences.' The family became extinct in 1764, by the death of Thomas Strode, Esq., the last of the name, and the property at Parnham passed into the hands of Sir John Oglander, Bart., of Nunwell, in the Isle of Wight (where the family has been seated from the Conquest), in right of Elizabeth, daughter of Sir John Strode, by his second wife, Ann Paulett, who married Sir William Oglander. [1] Parnham house and park are situated in a delightful spot near Netherbury, on the banks of the Brit, and at the distance of a mile from Beaminster. The present owner and occupier is Sir Henry Oglander, bart., who succeeded

[1] Sir John Strode, of Chantmarle, knt., who was born in 1624, paid £1470 for assisting the king's forces, February 10, 1644, being then a prisoner at Taunton. He was ordered up in safe custody, but, March 3rd, was left to be disposed of by the committee of the county, and in the following year his farm at Parnham, value £200 per annum, was sequestered.—*Hutchings.*

his father, the late Sir William Oglander, at his death, in January, 1852. The arms of the Strodes, of Par-nam, were:—ermine, on a quarter sable, a crescent surmounted by a mullet, argent. Those of Og-lander (anciently Okelander, or De Orglandris) are:—azure, a stork between three croslets fitché or; and their crest is a boar's head couped, or. The arms of Gollop are:—gules, on a bend, or, a lion passant guardant, sable. Crest:—a demi-lion barry, or and sable, holding in his dexter paw a broken arrow.

In the chancel are marble tablets erected to the memory of some members of the Cox and Russell families; and inscribed upon a brass plate, affixed to a marble monument, in the south aisle, is the follow-ing, in old English characters, to the memory, it is said, of a priest, who died when on a journey:—

'Pray for the soul of Sr. John Gone,
Whose body lies buried under this tomb,
On whose soul Jesu have mercy. Pat. nost. ave.'

There are also many old brasses in different parts of the church; and upon the floor are numerous records of the mouldering remains, in the vaults be-neath, of those who once played their parts upon the stage of life and then disappeared from it for ever.

In the unusual situation of the top of a hill, at a retired spot called Knowle, about a mile and a quarter from Beaminster, in the direction of Stoke, is a burying-place of a different character from that around the old church. It is totally distinct from any

religious establishment, and had its origin in a somewhat romantic incident, which we shall briefly relate :—Mr. James Daniel, a lawyer of Beaminster, and
great-great-grandfather to the present family of that
name, was induced by the persecutions inflicted upon
the non-conformists—the body to which he belonged
—to join the standard of Monmouth, when that unfortunate personage landed at Lyme, in 1685, and to
be present at the decisive battle of Sedgemoor. Mr.
Daniel was among the number of those who escaped
from the field, and who took refuge from their pursuers in flight.   Many of his comrades were captured
on the road, but he succeeded in reaching Beaminster,
and in placing himself once more beneath the shelter
of his beloved home. Not long, however, was he
permitted to remain there undisturbed; for being a
man of influence and of property, a reward was soon
offered for his apprehension,—a reward which too
many, in those distressing times, were eager enough
to earn.   The monster Jeffreys was presiding at Dorchester, and scores of lives had already been sacrificed
to his miscalled 'justice.' Every day brought in
fresh victims, and the arrival of Mr. Daniel, as a
prisoner, was eagerly expected. But as yet the fugitive, by concealing himself in a chamber, had
eluded all pursuit. He soon, however, found it un-
wise to remain in Beaminster, and accordingly prepared for departure, first offering up a fervent prayer,
in answer to which he imagined that a voice from

heaven had whispered to him 'flee to the west.' He religiously obeyed the mandate, and shortly afterwards found himself at Knowle. A barn then occupied the spot which has since been appropriated to a more sacred purpose, and thither he directed his steps, concealing himself, on his arrival, beneath some straw with which the floor of the barn was covered— agitated enough, no doubt, but still maintaining an unshaken faith in the protection of the Providence in whom he trusted. Scarcely had he effected his concealment ere the voices of his pursuers were wafted to his agonised ear. The soldiers of James, and the emissaries of Jeffreys, were but too ready to do the bidding and to imitate the character of their abominable masters. The premises at Beaminster had been unsuccessfully searched, and information had been furnished of the probable retreat of the fugitive. Accordingly, the pursuers, like bloodhounds pouncing upon their prey, rushed madly into the barn, not doubting of a successful issue. But, strange to say, their minutest search was fruitless. In vain were their bayonets thrust eagerly into the straw, which was as eagerly trampled by their impatient feet. In vain their practised eyes peered anxiously into every nook and corner likely to afford concealment. Again and again was the search renewed, but invariably with the same result. At length it was given over, and the barn was left to the undisturbed possession of the fugitive, whose feelings may be imagined but cannot be described. Preserved, as he believed, by the immediate agency of Providence, he determined, in the first outpourings of his gratitude, upon the sacred appropriation of the spot to the final depository of his mortal remains, after the trials of the earth should have passed away. In after years, when the heat of persecution had subsided, and when the men of the west could talk in safety about the memory of their beloved Monmouth, and with righteous indignation about the horrors of 'the bloody assize,' and the judge whose atrocities were so familiar in their locality, the barn at Knowle was removed, and the bones of the old man, over whose furrowed brow a hundred years had passed, and whose wonderful escape had formed the theme of many a fireside conversation, were borne to their last resting place upon the spot which he so long had selected for the purpose, and which, to the present moment, has been adopted as the only burying-ground of his descendants. [1]

A few words about the new church, and we must take our leave of Beaminster. But first we may be pardoned for observing, once for all, that as ecclesiastical architecture is confessedly almost a 'lost art'— the *animus* by which it was anciently fostered not being a characteristic of an 'enlightened' age,—we shall, in the course of our ramble, be unlikely to fall

[1] The writer is indebted to James Daniel, of Beaminster, Esquire, for the particulars of this remarkable escape of his ancestor.

in with any modern building requiring more than a few passing remarks. Our space is limited even for the accounts which we are anxious to give of the glorious structures of the 'benighted' past, the inimitable beauties of which, in spite of the effects of time, of fanaticism, and of modern 'restorations,' are still so apparent and deserve so much our appreciation and regard. Those venerable buildings, upon which we shall so often stumble, in village and in town, will always lure us, friend Piscator, from our angling fascinations to their sacred shades, for our own gratification, and, let us hope, for thine good reader, also! A powerful claim, in truth, old churches have upon our consideration. Of all that man has made they best—most fittingly—adorn the landscape. As monuments they stand to the piety and to the scientific and mechanical attainments of our forefathers, centuries ago. Hallowed to us they must ever be by their solemn associations with the past, and by the reflections which they must inspire about the future!

The new church is situated at the end of Flax-street, in Watley Mead. It is dedicated to the Holy Trinity, and was consecrated June 17, 1851. The endowment is £50 a year. It is a neat stone structure, consisting of a nave, with side aisles built against the body of the building, a chancel, and a porch on the south side. A bell is contained in a turret placed between the nave and chancel. There is also a clerestory, with trefoil and quatrefoil lights.

The aisles and body of the church are lighted on each side with double trefoil-headed *lancet* windows, as we suppose we must call them. The west window is of four lights, with three circles in the head containing quatrefoils; and the east window may be said to consist of three trefoil-headed lancets within a pointed arch. The interior of the building is appropriately fitted up, and great liberality on the part of the inhabitants appears to have been displayed in the providing of the necessary funds.

But we have lingered long enough at Beaminster, seeing that that town cannot by any possibility be regarded as a fishing station for the Axe. The considerable space which we have given to it must be accounted for in the circumstance of the river's partly rising in the parish—a circumstance which could not but possess the fullest claims upon our attention. Let us now, however, friend Piscator, bend our steps forthwith to Mosterton, which lies upon the turnpike road half way to Crewkerne—a good three miles or so. There we shall meet again with the charming little stream along the banks of which we hope to rove so pleasantly. [1]   *   *   *   *   *

[1] About a mile and a half from Beaminster, on the Crewkerne road, is a tunnel through Horn Hill, the construction of which materially improved the former line of road. On a board over each entrance to the tunnel is the following information :—' The public are principally indebted for the erection of this tunnel to the zealous exertions of Giles Russell, of Beaminster, Gent. Begun, August, 1831; finished, June, 1832. M. Lane, Civil Engineer.'

Mosterton, or Mosterne, is a large hamlet and tithing in Dorsetshire, on the border of Somerset. It is in the hundred of Beaminster-Forum-and-Red-Hove, [1] the diocese of Salisbury, the deanery of Bridport, and the union of Beaminster. The parish contains an area of 850 acres, and a population of 346 souls. The registered voters are 18, and the amount

[1] The division of England into counties is very ancient, but it is believed to have been reduced to its present form by Alfred the Great, who also subdivided the counties into hundreds, and the hundreds, again, into tithings. The object of this parcelling out of the country was the due administration of justice, which was thereby most admirably accomplished. Parishes were a purely ecclesiastical division. They existed, as well as mother-churches, as early as the time of Edgar, about the year 970; for the consecration of tithes, before that time, being *arbitrary*, it was ordained, by a law of that king, that all tithes should be paid '*ecclesiæ ad quam parochia pertinet.*' As the name imports, a hundred families composed a Hundred. The courts at which the business of the Hundred was transacted, were, in ancient times, invariably held in conspicuous fortified places; and in a modernised form they have been continued to be held in the same places till a comparatively recent period. Every ten of these hundred families formed, in the Saxon times, a tithing, or fribourg, over which an officer presided. Every man in the kingdom was expected to belong to some tithing, and men who did not were imprisoned until they could prevail upon others to take them in, or to become pledges for their good behaviour. In these tithings, every man was a security for the rest. Hence the term 'frankpledge' applied to such a community. So stringent was the law at that period, that if any one took a stranger in, and suffered him to remain under his roof for three nights, and if the stranger afterwards committed any crime, the person so harboring him was considered as having made himself a pledge for him, as if for one of his own family, and was, upon the absconding of the offender, required to make amends to the injured person. A system like this must have contributed most effectively to the prevention of crime, as well as to the detection of offenders. It inculcated, besides, a feeling of mutual interest altogether inexperienced in the society of modern times.—See Reeves's '*History of the English Law.*'

of poor rate last year was £140. In Domesday book, 'Mortestorne' was held by Richard de Redvers. Afterwards it came to the Blunt family, in which it remained until about the close of the fourteenth century. In 1424 (Henry VI.) Richard More, de Piket, and Elizabeth his wife, held at their deaths the 'manor of Mortestorne and the capital messuage there called Blunt's Court,' with other property. The Earls of March, also, had an interest in the parish. The manor continued in the More family until the beginning of the sixteenth century, after which it passed to several unknown owners—the tenements were sold in fee, and all the tenants became freeholders and the manor extinct. The principal landowners in the parish are now Sir Henry Oglander, Bart., Thomas Hussey, Esq., and Captain Steele.

Mosterton church, a chapel of ease to South Perrott, stood formerly at Chapel Court, about half a mile from Mosterton, in the direction of Crewkerne, where the churchyard still remains. The graves and tombs, away in the fields and apart from any building in connection with them, are calculated to produce a solemn effect upon the thoughtful wayfarer along the adjacent turnpike road. A faculty for burying in this churchyard was procured in 1750. Among the tombs is one which stood originally in the old church, to the memory of Elizabeth Hood, who died August 2, 1745, aged 43 years. The noble family of Hood belonged, originally, to Mosterton, as we shall have to relate in our account of Cricket Saint Thomas. A small brass, taken from the old church, in which it had been placed to the memory of some members of a family called Clarke, was shown to us, on a recent visit, by the occupier of a house at Mosterton which was formerly the residence of the Hood family. We mention this brass for the sake of the quaintly expressed motto which follows the inscription:—

> 'It's true Fair Tombs doe's do yé deed no Good,
>   Yet shews yé Donars Love and Gratitude.'

The old church, or rather chapel, was pulled down in 1831-2, and a new one erected in the centre of the hamlet. The new church, which was consecrated in 1833, is built in imitation (as we suppose it must be called), of the Early English style. [1] It consists of

---

[1] The builder was a whimsical individual of whom it would be uncharitable to speak severely, especially after reading the inscription upon his tomb in South Perrott churchyard, from which it appears that he was a self-taught artist without school-instruction. Some years before his death, he caused his grave to be dug, as well as that of his wife (who was also living), the two graves being separated from each other by a wall of single bricks, in which was an aperture for the convenience of the buried couple's *shaking hands,* when in some imaginary state of existence which the old man's superstitious fancies had suggested. The inscription is as follows, the dates and ages having been filled in on the death of the parties :—' To the memory of Elias Dawe, who died June 23, 1847, aged 72 years; and also of Elizabeth his wife, who died March 23, 1848, aged 83 years. The above Elias Dawe was a carpenter of this parish and Cheddington 47 years and never served an apprenticeship, or ever went to school one day in his life. He built two churches in his time. He was *old in years, in honors, in wisdom, and in virtue.* His afflictions were sanctified, and laying hold of that hope which brings a man peace at the last, he closed a life of usefulness by a death of tranquillity.'

K

a nave and chancel, lighted by *lancet* windows, which are furnished with weather mouldings resting upon corbels of *unique* design. There is a tower at the west end, containing one bell, and a porch on the north side. A gallery crosses the western end of the nave, and the pulpit and reading desk are placed one on each side of the chancel arch. The pews are neatly arranged, and admit of 359 sittings. The present rector is the Rev. John Wills, and the tithes are commuted at £170. [1]

[1] The Early English, or First Pointed Gothic, was the style of ecclesiastical architecture which prevailed during the thirteenth century. Like the Perpendicular (page 54) it is peculiar to this country. It succeeded the Semi-Norman style, to which it is in many respects a perfect contrast. It is light, chaste, and exceedingly graceful, and can always be easily recognised by the acutely-pointed arch, the slender detached shaft, the steeply pitched roof, and the graceful spire by which the tower is generally terminated. The ornaments and mouldings are also characteristic, particularly that which is called the tooth-ornament, which is peculiar to this style. But the lancet window is the most striking feature. It is long, narrow, of one light, acutely pointed, and deeply splayed—resembling in shape the instrument after which it is named. In large churches, and for the end windows of small ones, three, and sometimes four, of these lancet windows are placed side by side, the highest in the centre, and a hood moulding is carried in a graceful manner over the whole. Salisbury cathedral, and the nave and transepts of Wells cathedral, are magnificent specimens of the Early English style. The best specimen in our immediate neighbourhood is the parish church of Ottery Saint Mary. The style can be traced in certain parts of some of the churches in the valley of the Axe, intermixed, in every case, with other styles. The little church at Wayford, though by no means an elegant one, is yet the most complete specimen; and there are lancet windows, and other Early English work, in the churches of Winsham, Thorncombe, Axminster, and other places. Some parts of Ford Abbey, also, present some exquisite work in this interesting style.

Mosterton possesses a factory for the spinning of flax, which was formerly on a more extensive scale than at present, although it still affords employment to several hands. The river at the back of the factory is ponded, for the purpose of driving the machinery,—forming a considerable stretch of water, which contains some trout and eels. As there happens to be a breeze, Piscator, this pleasant April morning, you may as well, as a relief, indulge in a few initiatory casts, by way of getting your hand in for the ground below, at which we must commence in earnest. The village inn, too, will afford, perchance, a glass of home-brewed and a crust, which may not be unwelcome. [1] There! You have hooked a capital fish already—a lively though not a *spotless* beauty! But you handle him nervously. The first fish for the season is apt to discompose one for a moment. The first plunge—the strike—and the rush which follows—send the blood through one's veins like quicksilver, and make the heart beat audibly; while a kind of electric shock affects the system when the struggler yields at last, and when the angler flings his speckled prize upon the green sward. But, after all, this puts new life into a man! It excites his hopes—it exhilarates his spirits—it communicates, in a word, the mysterious influence

[1] In the course of our narrative, we shall not forget to point out the various respectable hostelries near the stream, a knowledge of which is important both to the tourist and to the angler.

peculiar to sporting—the influence which puzzles
the philosopher, and which is altogether beyond the
comprehension of the 'fashionable gent,' who affects
to ridicule the angler and to take pity upon his possession of 'patience.'   But——what a fish was
that which came up under the alder opposite ! There !
—thanks to your nervousness, or to something else,
you have caught the bush instead of the fish, and
your line is fast enough.

But hold, Piscator,—prithee, hold ! You hate,
you say, a brawling brook when fringed with bushes,
and have not yet your nerves in tune. Nevertheless,
old friend, that flinging down of your rod so petu-
lantly—that stamping like a maniac—are unseemly
in so good a craftsman and so good a man ! It is, to
say the least, unangler-like.   Imagine Father Izaac
indulging in such pranks—the good old man who
sang with milkmaids, and who spake such words of
wisdom ! Why verily you get from bad to worse !
That impatient tug has smashed your top, and left
your collar dangling in the bush. We blush for you,
old friend, and shall forthwith retire to the alehouse,
leaving you alone with your reflections, to repair the
damage to your tackle, to regain your lost serenity,
and to gratify the curiosity of that bull in the
meadow where your flies are dangling, for he has for
some minutes, we observe, been lavishing his attention upon us in a way which makes one feel uncom-
fortable.   You will find time, while we are engaged

with the crust and home-brewed, about which you express yourself to be indifferent,—to wander up the stream—to try a few casts near Picket mill,[1]—in the event of your finding sufficient water there, which is somewhat problematical,—and to insinuate your flies into the few little open places which you will discover in the interval between the mill and the factory pond, on the margin of which we are now about to separate for a little while.   *   *   *

All hail, Piscator! We have timed our luncheon to the minute, and we are by the factory pond again to find you just arrived, and well disposed to listen to our further chattings. You have, we rejoice to find, regained your equanimity—at no time very long disturbed—and you have admirably repaired your broken tackle. You have, as you inform us, adopted our advice—have wandered up the stream and caught a trout near Picket mill—have found below some tiny stickles, much too small for fishing—have extracted from the factory pond a couple more of speckled juveniles—have been attacked, as we expected, by the aforesaid bull, when peacefully engaged in disentangling your collar on the other side—and have been sent galloping across the river, which has sufficed to cool you down to amiability. More-

[1] This mill, called also Buckham Mill, is the first below the source of the river. The stream in this part, except in the factory pond, can be hardly considered adapted for fly-fishing, strictly speaking, on account of its smallness, although it might, at certain seasons, be fished successfully with the worm.

over, you have carefully stowed your tackle, without
the slightest hope of employing it again until we shall
arrive, by-and-by, at Seaborough Bridge, about two
miles further down the stream,—the intervening
ground being quite unfishable!

CHAPTER III.

MOSTERTON BRIDGE, which has two arches, is the first stone bridge on the stream. The river thence to Seaborough, a distance of about two miles, is very small, and is much diverted from its channel for the purpose of irrigation. A considerable part of the interval, on the banks of the river, is occupied by 'Mosterton Meadow,' which from time immemorial was common to those of the parishioners who occupied certain other lands. An act for its enclosure, which was obtained in 1851, is now in the course of being carried into effect. The Dorsetshire parish of Broadwinsor abuts upon the river, on the left bank, at Mosterton Bridge, as it also does at the distance of a quarter of a mile above. At a short distance below the bridge, the stream divides the parishes of Mosterton and Broadwinsor for about three hundred yards, after which it flows exclusively within the Mosterton boundary as far as Little Winsor on the left, and West Farm on the right bank, whence it again divides the parishes as far as Seaborough.

The village of Broadwinsor is about three miles south from Mosterton Bridge. It is situated upon the high road from Beaminster to Axminster and Lyme Regis, and on one of the two direct roads from Bridport to Crewkerne. It is about three miles north-west from Beaminster. Broadwinsor is a liberty and manor, the lord of which is William Pinney, of Somerton, Esq. It was a hundred up to the time of Henry II (1154), when it was granted the franchise.[1] It is in the diocese of Salisbury,

---

[1] Franchise and Liberty are used as synonymous terms, and their definition is, a royal privilege, or branch of the King's prerogative, subsisting in the hands of a subject. Being therefore derived from the crown, they must arise from the King's grant; or, in some cases, may be held by prescription, which pre-supposes a grant. The kinds of them are various, and almost infinite. They may be vested in either natural persons or bodies politic—in one man or in many; but the same identical franchise that has before been granted to one, cannot be bestowed on another, for that would prejudice the former grant. To be a County Palatine is a franchise, vested in a number of persons. It is likewise a franchise for a number of persons to be incorporated, and subsist as a body politic, with a power to maintain perpetual succession, and do other corporate acts; and each individual member of such corporation is also said to have a franchise or freedom. Other franchises are, to hold a court leet; to have a manor or lordship; or, at least, to have a lordship paramount; to have waifs, estrays, wrecks, treasure-trove, royal fish, forfeitures and deodands; to have a court of one's own, or liberty of holding pleas, and trying causes; to have the cognizance of pleas, which is a still greater liberty, being an exclusive right, so that no other court shall try causes arising within that jurisdiction; to have a bailiwick, or liberty, exempt from the sheriff of the County, wherein the grantee only, and his officers, are to execute all process; to have a fair or market, with the right of taking toll, either there or at any other public places, as at bridges, wharfs, or the like, which tolls

and the deanery of Bridport. The parish comprises about 5780 acres, and is divided into five tithings, namely, Broadwinsor, Childhay, Drimpton, Little-winsor, and Dibberford.[1] Of these tithings it may be as well to state at once that Childhay was anciently the property of a family of the same name, from which it passed, by marriage, in the reign of Edward III (1327-1377), into the hands of John De Cruckerne, to whose family allusion has been already made.[2] An heiress brought the manor, by marriage, at the close of the sixteenth century, to Arthur Champernon, of Devonshire, and by a second marriage to Henry Drake, after which it became the property of the Bragges, from whom it was sequestered in 1645. It has since belonged to the Tucker family of Weymouth, and is now, or was lately, the property of John Lillingstone, Esq. The mansion-house, at which the owners of the manor, in ancient times, resided, was held for the Parliament by Lady

must have a reasonable cause of commencement (as in consideration of repairs, or the like,) else the franchise is illegal and void; or, lastly, to have a forest, chase, park, warren, or fishery, endowed with privileges of royalty. &c., &c. *Blackstone's Commentaries.*

[1] Although it is stated in the note from Reeves's '*History of the English Law,*' page 63, that every ten families formed a tithing, in the Anglo-Saxon division of the country, it must not be understood that every tithing was necessarily *limited* to ten families, but rather that ten was the smallest number of which a tithing could be composed.

[2] Page 36. The arms of this ancient and long extinct family were:—gules, on a chevron, between three bugle horns argent, stringed or, as many cross crosslets fitché of the second.

Drake, during the civil war in the reign of Charles I, and in an attack by a body of the King's troops it was partly destroyed by fire. The portion of the mansion which still remains is built in the Tudor style of domestic architecture.

Drimpton is situated on the Crewkerne road, about half-way between Broadwinsor and Clapton. It is a large hamlet, and many of the inhabitants are employed in Mr. Haydon's factory, at Greenham, which is in the parish of Crewkerne. The machinery of this factory is driven by a small tributary to the Axe which rises under Pillesdon Pen, and falls into the Axe below Clapton Bridge.

Littlewinsor was among the possessions of Ford Abbey, and at the dissolution it was granted to Robert Chidley, from whom it passed to several successive owners. Among these was Amias Pawlet, who in 1574 obtained 100 acres from John Pollard. A few years afterwards the name of William Rowsewell appears as the owner, and in 1646 that of Mr. Bondfield, whose 'high rents, value £6 13s. 4d. were sequestered.' [1]

The parish of Broadwinsor contains a population of 1516, of which 53 are registered voters. In 1841 the number of inhabitants was greater by 144. Hutchings thinks that the name Broadwinsor was originally suggested by 'the winding border that separates the

---

[1] Hutchings.

parish from the county of Somerset.' In Domesday
Book, Broadwinsor is surveyed in three parcels,
namely, first, 'Windesore,' which consisted of 'three
virgates,'[1] and was 'held by Hanger, son of Odin,
one of the king's servants;' second, 'Windesorte,'
perhaps erroneously spelled by the Norman scribe;
and third, 'Windresore' (probably Littlewinsor),
which consisted of 'four hides, and was held by
William de Moin.'

The manor was given by Henry II (1154-1189)
to Gervais de Windsor, who held it by grand ser-
geantry.[2] 'From this Gervais,' says Coker, 'flourished
knights of great repute,' who lived at Broadwinsor
and were lords of the hundred. The representative
of the family in 1332, was a female named Alice, who
was twice married. She 'joined with her second
husband, John Everard,' continues Coker, 'to pass
away this manor to Sir Hugh Courtney the elder.'
It remained in the possession of this powerful family
(afterwards Earls of Devon) and their kindred, for
many generations. In 1691, the manor and hundred

---

[1] A virgate was a measure of land which appears to have differed in
extent in different parts of the country, and about which there is a disa-
greement among several authors. The extremes at which the measure
has been estimated are fifteen and sixty acres. Du Cange, it will be sufficient to state, quotes an ancient MS. in which a virgate is made to corres-
pond, uniformly, to one-fourth of a hide, or twenty-four acres; and there
appears to be a preponderance of authorities in favor of this estimate.

[2] 'Per servitium moram faciendi ad scaccarium D. regis, ad denar' dicit'
regis, ibid. ponderandum et quolibet die pro servitio illo accipiet XII d.
de burso D. regis.' Coker's *Survey of Dorset.*

were granted to William Pole and William Courtney. How long it continued in this ownership is not recorded; but sometime afterwards, the manor appears, from the great number of freeholders, to have been sold by parcels in fee. In 1774, the liberty and manor belonged to Sir John Pole, Bart., of Shute.

The village is large and well sheltered by the lofty hills among which it is situated.[1] Many of the inhabitants are employed in weaving—some at their own homes and others at the extensive manufactory of sailcloth which belongs to Mr. Studley. A fair is held on Trinity Monday, and a market, hardly more than *nominal*, on Fridays. A chapel for the Independents was erected in the village in 1821, and a chapel of ease at Blackdown in 1839-40. The latter, which is dedicated to the Holy Trinity, is not endowed.

During the 'troublous times' of the civil war, Broadwinsor, although a place of trifling importance,

[1] Lewesdon and Pillesdon are among the highest eminences in this part of the country. Lewesdon is 960 feet, and Pillesdon 934 feet above the level of the sea. They command magnificent prospects, and serve as landmarks to the sailors on the coast, who call them the Cow and the Calf. A lodge is said by Coker to have formerly stood on the top of Pillesdon Pen, where the remains of Ancient British earthworks are still conspicuous. The word 'Pen,' which is applied to several elevated places in this locality, signifies, in the British language, a point or headland. Conig Castle, a rampart-crowned eminence situated nearer to Lambert's Castle, is said by Mr. Davidson to derive its name from the Anglo-Saxon 'cyng,' or 'cyning,' a king, and to be so called from its having been, 'in all probability, the camp of Egbert, when he encountered the Danes at Charmouth, in the year 833.' See '*The British and Roman Remains*,' Hutchings's '*Dorset*,' Coker's '*Survey*', &c.

was not exempt from the excitement and confusion
which prevailed so universally at that unhappy period
of our country's history. Besides being the scene of
active operations, in the attack upon Childhay House,
it will always be memorable from the circumstance of
a visit which it received from the fugitive Charles II,
who was afforded timely shelter and protection at the
village inn. We shall briefly relate the story of this
visit, which ranks among the numerous romantic adventures of the King in his attempts to escape to the
continent :—

After the decisive battle of Worcester, which was
fought on the sixth of September, 1651, the King
fled to Trent, near Yeovil and Sherborne, and took
refuge in the house of Colonel Wyndham, in which
he remained for some time, waiting an opportunity
to leave the country. Through the instrumentality
of Captain Ellesden, of Lyme, who was a friend of
Colonel Wyndham's, a vessel, belonging to a trust-
worthy man named Stephen Limbry, of Lyme, was
at length engaged for the hazardous service, and a
particular part of Charmouth beach was selected as
the place of embarkation. Accordingly, in the morning of September 22, the King, in disguise, set out
for Charmouth on horseback. Behind him, with a
view to disarm suspicion, was seated Mrs. Julian
Conigsbury, a member of the Wyndham family.
The rest of the party were Lord Wilmot, Colonel
Wyndham, and a serving man. They arrived, in the

evening, at Charmouth, where a room at the inn had been previously engaged. [1] Soon afterwards Limbry made his appearance and reported that his arrangements were complete, and that he should be ready with his vessel at the place and time appointed. He then returned to Lyme to take leave of his wife, whom he had previously made acquainted with his engagement. The proclamation for apprehending the King, and for prohibiting the going on shipboard for a certain time of any person without a license, had just been published at Lyme, and the anxious spouse was so alarmed at the risk which her husband was about to incur, although in ignorance of the quality of his employer, that she locked him into a room and turned a deaf ear to his urgent entreaties for liberation. [2] At midnight the royal fugitive and his party repaired to the place of embarkation, only to be doomed, of course, to disappointment. After waiting a considerable time, and there appearing to be no hope of the arrival of the vessel, it was decided to return to Trent without delay—the unaccountable conduct of Limbry very naturally engendering the

[1] The room at Charmouth in which Charles was waiting to embark is still to be seen.

[2] 'All the persuasions he used for his own liberty were in vain, for the more he entreated the more her violent passion increased,—breaking forth into such clamours and lamentations that he feared, if he should any longer contend, both himself and the gentleman he promised to transport would be *cast away in the storm without ever going to sea.'* *Boscobel Tracts.*

suspicion of treachery. Early in the morning, therefore, the party set forth upon their return, intending to pass through Bridport and Broadwinsor. Both of those places were occupied by the forces of the Parliament, but as it was deemed advisable to vary the route of the preceding day, the risk was determined to be run. It happened that Lord Wilmot was obliged to remain behind at Charmouth, after the rest of the party had set out, in order to have his horse shod. The smith whom he employed suspected, from the peculiar manner in which the shoes had been previously fitted, that the party had come from the north, and that it contained some influential royalists, if not the King himself. As soon as Lord Wilmot had departed, these suspicions were communicated to the minister of the place, Bartholomew Wesley, who hastened to the nearest justice of the peace for a warrant. Failing in his object, for some reason not clearly explained,[1] he at once proceeded to raise a pursuing party on his own account. He was assisted by a Captain Massey, 'as errant a Hotspur as himself,' who directed the subsequent operations. Arrangements were soon completed, and 'the hot-mettled company' started on the London road, expecting to

---

[1] The *Boscobel Tract* says:—' He (Wesley) ran to Mr. Butler, of Commer, the justice of the peace, to have dispatched abroad his warrants to raise the country for the apprehending the King and those persons the last night with him at Charmouth. But he *spends his mouth in vain,*— a deaf ear is turned upon him—no warrant would be issued forth.' &c.

come up with the fugitives at Dorchester.   The decision of the. King to return to Trent was thus most
fortunate ; for his pursuers, in their eagerness,. had
overshot their mark by proceeding to Dorchester,
while the King and his devoted little party were
safely sheltered at Broadwinsor.[1]

The church occupies an elevated situation on the
north side of the village.   It has lately been extensively repaired.   A considerable part of the building,
including the tower and the aisles, are in the style of
the fifteenth century ;[2] but there are unmistakable
evidences of a much older foundation, in the massive
circular piers and pointed arches of the nave.   These
are four in number on each side, and are undoubtedly
semi-Norman.[3]   There is also a small circular-headed
doorway, in the chancel, ornamented with the characteristic zig-zag moulding.   The date of these
Norman erections may thus be safely fixed at the
latter part of the twelfth century—soon after the
commencement of one of the great eras in the history
of church building.[4]   The chancel, perhaps, is of more

[1]   There are slightly different versions of this romantic incident, but
we have given the essential and most reliable points of it on the authority
of Lord Clarendon, and on that of the *Boscobel Tracts*, which were the
production of a female member of the Wyndham family.   A more detailed account than ours will be found in Mr. Roberts's '*History of
Lyme Regis.*'
[2]   The perpendicular style.   See page 54.
[3]   A note in explanation of this style will be found in our description
of Thorncombe church.
[4]   'They (the Normans) revived, by their arrival (1066), the obser-
vances of religion, which were everywhere grown lifeless in England. You

recent date by about a century and a half. The
capitals of the piers on the north side of the nave
are circular, and those on the opposite side are square,
with the peculiar ornamentation of this early style.
The east end of the north or Childhay aisle was
originally a chantry chapel, as appears from the
piscina which still remains there, within an ogee
niche of several mouldings, enclosing a trefoiled arch.
Over the north aisle was formerly a school-room.
From what we have already said, it will be understood that the church consists of a chancel, nave, and
two side aisles. It has, also, a clerestory [1] which is
embattled on the south side, as is also the aisle on the
same side—a tower at the west end, and a porch on
the south side. The chancel, which is of extraordinary length, is lighted by six side windows and the
east window. The latter consists of three rude lancet
shaped lights, with trefoil headings, under a pointed

might see churches rise in every village, and monasteries in the towns and
cities, *built after a style unknown before;* you might behold the country
flourishing with renovated rites; so that each wealthy man accounted
that day lost to him, which he had neglected to signalize by some magnificent action.' *William of Malmesbury.*

[1] The clerestory, or, in modern orthography, the clearstory, is the upper
storey or row of windows over the nave, which is thus more effectually
lighted than it could be from the aisle windows alone, although at the
sacrifice of the steep and graceful roof. In the absence of the clerestory
the same object is frequently attained by means of dormer or attic
windows set upon the sloping sides of the roof. These are generally a
deformity to the building. Clerestories may be almost said to form a
distinguishing feature in Third Pointed or Perpendicular churches, for
they are comparatively rare in those of an older date, except in the shape
of additions to the original building.

M

arch with a hood moulding within. The side windows are of two lights, with feathered headings, and with rude hood mouldings also. The windows of the nave are chiefly flat-headed. The one or two exceptions are admirable specimens of the Perpendicular style. The eight windows of the clerestory are also flat-headed, and of two lights. Six of them are placed on the south side, the opposite wall being chiefly occupied, in the interior, by monuments. A large gallery spans the western end of the nave, and over it is a smaller gallery appropriated to the choir. The front of the lower gallery exhibits some old oak carving of similar design to that on the front of the gallery at Winsham, and on the pulpits at Beaminster, Axminster, and many other places—the work, probably, of the seventeenth century.

The font, which stands in the north aisle, is perhaps coeval with the oldest parts of the church, and deserves the particular attention of the visitor. It is a large square bason of stone resting upon a single shaft, or rather a cluster of shafts, composed of a large central cylinder, with four circular columns of smaller size set against it at equal distances from each other. Fonts are generally very interesting objects. They are frequently ancient, even in cases in which the churches are comparatively modern; for in the olden time they were regarded with a degree of reverence which made them objects of especial preservation. Hence the reason why Norman fonts are very numerous.[1] The position of the font opposite the western entrance to a church, is symbolical of entrance into the Church of Christ. Some other positions are also allowed to be appropriate, but they are always near to a doorway, and if, in modern times, the font is found elsewhere, the conclusion may be arrived at that it has been moved from its original place, or else that an ancient doorway near it has been blocked. At Broadwinsor the font has been moved more than once, having occupied its present position but a few years only. A piscina of similar design to that of the one already mentioned, occupies the usual situation in the south wall of the chancel, near its eastern end. The pulpit and reading desk are placed in the nave, against the south pier of the chancel arch. They bear evidence of some antiquity, and are curiously ornamented with carving. There is no vestry.

The tower, which rises to the height of about fifty-six feet, is square and embattled. It is ornamented with gargoyles and pinnacles, and has a turret on the north side, which is also embattled and surmounted by a low vane.[2] The tower contains a

---

[1] By an ancient ecclesiastical constitution (A. D. 1236), a font of stone, sufficiently capacious for total immersion, was required to be placed in every church in which it might happen, from whatever cause, to be then absent.

[2] The use of vanes on towers is of remote antiquity. That vanes were used by the Anglo-Saxon church architects is evident from a curious engraving in the '*Archæologia*,' vol 25, and from other authorities. The

clock [1] and five bells, and is lighted by four windows
in the middle storey, and, on the west side, by a
larger window below, of three rude lancet lights,
corresponding with those of the eastern window.
Beneath this window is a doorway which forms the
western entrance to the church. The tower is
strengthened by buttresses, one of which bears sufficient evidence of its modern erection in the multi-
tude of meaningless set-offs which contrast it so
unfavorably with those of the other buttresses.
The walls of the aisles are also furnished with buttresses, as well as with gargoyles.

During the recent restoration of this ancient
church, it was observed that many of the stones in

form of the cock, so generally adopted, was intended, according to Du
Cange and others, to remind the rector of vigilance; and it is supposed,
also, to refer to the fall of St. Peter. So universally did this form prevail
originally, that vanes of the most dissimilar pattern came in time to
receive the general name of weather-*cocks.* See Britton's '*Architectural
Antiquities.*'

[1] The period when clocks were invented is involved in the obscurity
of what are called 'the dark ages.' They are mentioned about the year
840, when Rabanus Maurus is said to have sent a clock and a bell to a
friend. But they were probably very imperfect for several centuries afterwards, and arrived to greater perfection by degrees. The custom of having
faces or dial plates to clocks is of much later origin, and did not come
into use until a comparatively recent period, as we have numerous
sun-dials erected even in the seventeenth century, and they were then
much more commonly used than clocks. Most of the large round faces,
with glaring gilt numerals, which now disfigure so many beautiful bell-
towers, were erected during the last century. There are a few ancient
examples in which the figures are ingeniously introduced in the tracery
of a Catherine wheel window, the effect of which is very elegant, and forms
a singular contrast to the shining circles of modern days. See '*The Glossary of Architecture.*'

the oldest walls bore unmistakable evidence of the action of fire, and of their having been placed in positions very different from those which they originally occupied. This fact, in conjunction with the different styles in which the principal parts of the edifice are erected, may serve to throw some light upon the history of the building, and to explain the manner in which its present characteristics have been successively assumed. As we have already said, there remains enough to prove that the date of the oldest parts may be fixed at the latter end of the twelfth century, and that the chancel was subsequently erected. The evidences of fire, of which mention has just been made, would seem to show that at some time during the fifteenth century, the body of the church and the tower were burnt—that the chancel escaped—and that the edifice was rebuilt, with the addition of aisles and a clerestory, in the Perpendicular style which then prevailed;—the original Semi-Norman arches of the 'nave, which resisted the influence of 'the devouring element,' being retained and adopted for the new structure. Such may be regarded as, at least, a plausible explanation; but in the absence of documentary evidence, it must, of course, be taken only at its worth.

In the belfry are some remains of the ancient rood screen and rood loft, which were removed from their place between the nave and chancel in the year 1818, when the building underwent repair.

On entering the church the eye is immediately
arrested by a large marble monument over the north
arches of the nave, against the clerestory wall. It is
erected to the memory of Edmund Hallson, who died
October 12, 1839, aged 79 years; of his daughter
Mary, wife of John Gorman, who died June 2, 1826,
aged 26 years; and of Edmund Hallson Gorman, son
of the last named John and Mary Gorman, who died
March 22, 1834, at the age of 21.

A board near this monument records that Edmund
Hallson, late of Bridport, a native of Broadwinsor,
bequeathed by will dated February 23, 1839, the sum
of £1080, to be invested in the funds, £30 of the
yearly interest thereof to be applied to the support
of a schoolmaster 'professing the religion of the
Church of England,' for the education of male children of the parish; the remainder of the interest to
be annually divided among the poor 'who profess
and follow the doctrines of the Established Church.'[1]
Against the same wall of the clerestory are monuments to the memory of Buncombe Eveleigh and
some other members of his family. In the chancel is
a small mural monument to the memory of Benjamin
Studley, who died January 1, 1775, aged 43 years,
and of John his son, who died April 5, 1809, aged
41 years. Over the altar is a small tablet with the

---

[1] Robert Smith, M.D., founded, in 1725, a school at Blackdown, for the
education of thirteen boys of Broadwinsor and Burstock. He endowed it
with lands in the tithing of Childay. See Boswell's *Charities of Dorset.*

following inscription :—' Neare to this lye the body of Edith the wife of Hugh Gundrey and daughter of Benjamin Studley, of Broadwinsor, who died the 15th day of January Ano. dom. 1695-6.' On the east side of the porch, in the south aisle, is a large mural monument, consisting of two ovals placed one above the other, with angels and other decorations. Upon the upper and larger oval are some laudatory verses, and upon the under one is the following :—' Near this place lyes the body of Ann, wife of Edward Forward, of Axminster, gent., daughter of the Revd. and learned Thomas Watton, late vicar of this place, and of Lydia his wife. She was maryed the 20th December, 1727, and departed this life the 20th of March following, ætat. suæ 20.'

From a board in the church it appears that the poor of the parish receive annually in bread the interest of £50, bequeathed to them, in 1795, by John Stanton. There is also a piece of land in the parish yielding about £17 per annum, appropriated to ' the beautifying of the church.'

The living is a vicarage, valued in the king's books at £15 8s. 9d., and the tithes are commuted at £750. The rectorial tithes belong to the vicars choral of Salisbury Cathedral, and are by them let to lay impropriators.[1] The church is dedicated to St. John the Baptist.

[1] A parsonage, or a rectory, is a parish church endowed with a house, glebe, and tithes, &c, and such originally were all parish churches. Glebe

The celebrated Thomas Fuller, author of the
'*Worthies of England*,' and other learned works, was
vicar of this parish in 1635.   He was a zealous loyalist, and became chaplain to King Charles I, whom he
attended at the sieges of Basing House and Exeter.
The '*Worthies of England*' is an invaluable contribution to biographical literature, and displays a great
amount of learning and research.   Many anecdotes
are related of Dr. Fuller's powers of memory, which
are said to have been extraordinary, and also of his
punning, to which he was much addicted.   As with
all punsters, however, it happened, very justly, that
the laugh was not always on his own side.   Attempt-
ing, on one occasion, to enjoy a joke at the expense
of a gentleman named Sparrowhawk, he met with
the following retort :—' What is the difference,' said
the Doctor, who was very corpulent, ' between an
owl and a sparrowhawk ? ' ' An owl,' replied the per-

is the church lands exclusive of the tithes. A *parson* is a rector of a
church parochial, and is called *persona ecclesiæ* because he taketh upon
him tho person of the church, and is seized in right of his church; that in
his person the church might sue for and defend her right, and also be sued
by any that hath an elder right.   The word Ecclesia is always applied to
a parsonage, as Vicaria is to a vicarage. A *Vicar (Vicarius, quasi vice
fungens rectoris)* is the priest of that parish where the predial tithes
[corn and crops generally] are appropriated. The parson or rector has
the predial tithes to himself. At first the vicar was a mere curate to the
impropriator, temporary and removable at pleasure; but by degrees he got
a settled maintenance of glebe and some kind of tithes, and now claims his
dues, either by endowment of the impropriator, or by *prescription*, because
the ordinary hath power to increase his allowance. See 15 Richard II,
c. 6.—4 Henry IV, c. 12. Wood's '*Institute of the Laws of England.*'

son addressed, ' is *fuller* in the head, *fuller* in the body, and *fuller* all over.' Dr. Fuller was born, in 1608, at Aldwinkle, Northamptonshire,—the birth-place of Dryden,—and died at Cranfield, August 15, 1661.

But we must now take our leave of Broadwinsor, and transport ourselves, *per saltum*, to Seaborough, which stands on the right bank of the river, at the distance of about two miles below Mosterton Bridge. Seaborough is a scattered little village, in a retired situation on the side of a hill,—out of the way of all the great thoroughfares, and amid the beauties of the fields and the associations of rural life. The rippling of the little stream, and the other melodies of nature, with the sounds of agricultural industry, are all that break its solitude and interfere with its repose. The village lies south from Crewkerne, at the distance of two miles and a half. It is in the county of Somerset, the parish being divided by the Axe from that of Broadwinsor, in Dorset, as before stated. It is in the hundred of Crewkerne and the union of Beaminster, to which it sends one guardian. The little parish consists of about 560 acres, and its population is 104 only, of which but four are registered voters for the western division of the county.[1] Ilminster is its polling-place, as it is, also,

[1] The word County *(comitatus)* is derived from *Comes*, the Count of the Franks—that is, the Earl, or Alderman, as the Saxons called him, of the Shire, to whom its government was entrusted. This government he usually exercised by his Deputy, still called in Latin *Vice-comes*, and in English *the Sheriff, Shrieve*, or *Shire-reeve*, signifying the officer of the

the polling-place of all the other parishes in Somerset which we shall have to describe.

The account of Seaborough in Domesday Book is as follows:—' The bishop [of Sarum] holds *Seveberge*. Alward held it in the time of King Edward, and gelded for a hide and a half. [1] The arable is one carucate and a half, [2]—yet there are two ploughs, and two villains, and four cottagers, and two servants. [3]

Shire, upon whom, in process of time, the civil administration of it is now totally devolved. See Blackstone's ' *Commentaries on the Laws of England.*'

[1] That is, the tax called Danegeldt was paid for that quantity of land. This tax was first levied in the reign of Ethelred, and it was continued (with a slight intermission during the reign of Edward the Confessor) till the end of Henry II (about 1189). 'In this year' (991), says the Anglo-Saxon Chronicle, ' it was decreed that tribute, for the first time, should be given to the Danish-men, on account of the great terror which they caused by the sea coast.' Other authorities say that the amount so raised was applied to the hiring of Danish and other ships with which to protect the nation from piratical attacks. After the Conquest, this tax, although retaining its original name, was applied to very different purposes to suit the exigences of the state or the caprice of the monarch. The rate of taxation varied from two shillings for every hide of arable land—the amount first fixed,—to six shillings per hide,—the amount which was paid in the time of the Conqueror.

[2] The carucate was a measure of land which, at the time of Domesday Book, was less than a hide (see page 44). More anciently, the terms hide and carucate were synonymous. Carucate, in Domesday Book, means as much land as a man could manage with one plough in a year.

[3] At the time of Domesday Book, a *free* laborer was unknown in England. The feudal lord was the owner not only of the soil but of its inhabitants also, over whom he had absolute control. A great part of the manual labor was performed by two classes of the people, called in Domesday ' Villani' and ' Servi.' The *villains* were the resident tenants annexed to the manor, and although allowed to hold small portions of land, in order to support themselves, they could be disposed of at the will of the lord and transferred by deed to a different owner. In after

There is half a mill, rendering ten-pence, and nine acres of meadow, and ten acres of wood. Pasture half a mile long and half a furlong broad. To this manor is added another *Seveberge*. Aluer held it in the time of King Edward, and gelded for a hide and a half. There are two ploughs, with one villain, and five cottagers, [1] and half a mill, rendering ten-pence, and nine acres of meadow, and ten acres of wood. Pasture half a mile long and half a furlong broad. These two lands are not of the bishopric of Sarisberie. Bishop Osmund held them for one manor, and Walter of him. They were and are worth sixty shillings. In the time of King Edward they belonged to Crewkerne, the King's manor, and they who held them could not be separated from it, and paid to Crewkerne a customary rent of twelve sheep with their lambs, and one pig of iron from every freeman.'

As a reward for the services rendered by the principal personages who assisted in the conquest of England by the Normans, the grateful monarch bestowed upon them the estates of the Saxon landholders, whom he unceremoniously dispossessed. But the estates so granted were made liable, among other conditions, to certain military service, proportioned

---

ages they became *copyholders*. The *servi* were employed in the most servile and laborious works, and were slaves in the fullest sense of the word. Villainage was not extinct before the time of Queen Elizabeth.

[1] 'Cottagers' paid a rent to the lord, or rendered some service to him in the shape of a certain amount of manual labour, in return for small parcels of land, such as gardens.

to their value and population. [1]   Le Sieur de Vaus,
or Vallibus, was the fortunate individual who, shortly
after the compilation of Domesday Book, obtained,
among other lands, the manor of Seaborough.   The
feudal service attached to this possession was that of
one soldier.   In the time of Henry III (1216-1272),
the manor was enjoyed by Ralph de Vallibus, the
descendant of the first Norman possessor.   Henry
had engaged in a crusade, and Ralph de Vallibus
was called upon for his ' military service.'   The ' one
soldier' whom he selected from Seaborough, was
John Gole, or Golde, who accordingly departed for
the Holy Land.   He was present at the siege of
Damietta, and so greatly distinguished himself, that,
after his return, De Vallibus presented him with an
estate at Seaborough.   This was about the year 1229,
and the deed by which the estate was conveyed
has been preserved, we believe, to the present day.   At
all events it was perfect in the time of Collinson,
who wrote in 1791. [2]

The heir of Ralph de Vallibus was an only
daughter, named Grecia, who, in 1245, transferred
the property, with the advowson of the church, by

[1] Every tenant of the crown was bound to furnish an armed
soldier for each knight's fee, and to maintain him in the field for forty
days, every time that the King went to war.   This was afterwards commuted by Henry II into a money payment of twenty shillings for each
knight's fee, which was called an *escuage*, or tax for furnishing a *bow-
man.*—Eccleston's '*Introduction to English Antiquities.*'

[2] See the '*History of Somerset*,' vol. 2, page 172.

marriage, to a family named Rochford, in which they remained until 1321, when Ralph De Rochford sold them to John Golde, of Seaborough,—a descendant of the valiant crusader just spoken of. In this family the property continued for nearly 300 years. Some of the Goldes lie buried in Crewkerne church, and have some curious old brasses erected to their memory. [1] With the extinction of the family is associated a tragical occurrence which we proceed to relate :—

About the middle of the sixteenth century, its only surviving male member was John Golde, who resided on his estate at Seaborough. An unfriendly feeling had long subsisted between himself and Mr. Weeks, who was then the owner and occupier of Henley Farm. One morning, in harvest time, Mr. Weeks was busily engaged in superintending his workmen in one of his fields. At that period hawking was the favorite amusement of country gentlemen, and a party who were engaged in its pursuit in the plain below, attracted the attention of Mr. Weeks and his reapers. Mr. Golde, who was passionately attached to the amusement, had often been cautioned against trespassing upon the lands of his unfriendly neighbour. He was one of the party on the morning in question. The sport was most exciting, and the horsemen were galloping in different directions as

[1] See our account of Crewkerne Church.

the movements of the contending birds required
different positions from which to command a view.
Mr. Golde, in the eagerness of the sport, had become
separated from his friends, and in order to rejoin
them had ridden into Mr Weeks's field. No sooner
had he done so than the owner, who had long been
waiting an opportunity for a personal encounter,
rushed down, with his men, upon his foe. A furious
quarrel immediately commenced, and Weeks, in the
height of his passion, directed his men to fell Mr.
Golde from his horse. They instantly proceeded to
do so, and one of them struck him a blow with a rake
which brought him to the earth a corpse. Weeks
and two of his men were a few days afterwards taken
into custody, and at an assize which was held on the
occasion at Crewkerne, they were found guilty and
sentenced to be hanged. The market-place at Crewkerne is said, by the voice of tradition, to be the scene
of their execution.

The murdered Mr. Golde having no issue, the
manor of Seaborough, on the death of his widow,
descended to his four sisters. Margaret, the eldest of
them, married Richard Martin, Esq., who was the
second son of Sir William Martin, of Athelhamstone,
Dorset, knight, by Christina his second wife,
daughter of Sir Amias Powlet, of Hinton St. George,
knight. The second daughter, Catherine, who married Mr. Henry Hoskins, died childless, and the
share of the third daughter, Alice, who had married

Mr. Strechley, of Devonshire, was sold, after the death of her husband, to Mr. Bale, the husband of the youngest daughter, Anne. Mr. Martin and Mr. Bale thus became the sole owners of the property, and they both resided at the mansion-house. 'But they were too near neighbours,' says Collinson, 'to continue long good friends, and the ways to each other's grounds became also matter of contention. Wherefore, Mr. Hugh Martin, grandson of Mr. Richard Martin, who married the eldest sister of the Goldes, pulled down his third part of the mansion, and carrying off the materials built the house in Seaborough, in 1591, in which some of the Martins have dwelt ever since. [1] The two-third parts continued in the family of Bale till about the year 1682, when Mr. James Bale sold them to Sir John Strode, of Parnham, knight.' The rest of the manor was sold in fee to the respective tenants, and subsequently a portion of it was repurchased by the Martins. The principal landowners are now Sir Henry Oglander, Bart, who inherits the property of the Strode family there, [2] and John Studley, Esq., of Broadwinsor.

The tranquillity of Seaborough, in former ages, was frequently interrupted by causes which gallantry induces us to assert cannot possibly be in operation now. At all events they are not recognised by law, and therefore———— But to return:—The village

[1] A view of Seaborough House is contained in the initial letter, page 1.
[2] See page 56.

appears to have been pestered by '*scolding women*,' who were obviously injurious to the comfort of its more amiable denizens, and to the poetry and peace of the locality. But the machinery of the manorial law was very properly put into operation, and the most rigorous measures were adopted, from time to time, in the hope of removing so great a scandal— a scandal peculiar, of course, to ancient times. The law, in days of yore, regarded a common scold as a 'public nuisance'—an offender liable to indict- ment, and punishable in a manner so unique and so characteristic as to deserve description [1] here :— 'A post was fixed in a pond. Upon the former was placed a transverse beam, turning on a swivel, with a chair at one end of it. In this the scolding woman was placed, and the end turned to the pond and let down into the water.' [2] It is recorded of Seaborough, that in the third year of Richard III (1486), two fair denizens of that sweet retreat—Isabella Pery and Alianora Slade by name,—were presented at the ma- norial court as 'common scolds,' and fined in a penny each. But as a kind of *quid pro quo*, an order was

---

[1] 'A common scold, *communis rixatrix* (for our law-Latin *confines it to the feminine gender*) is a public *nuisance* to her neighbourhood. For which offence she may be indicted, and if convicted shall be sentenced to be placed in a certain engine of correction called the trebucket, castiga- tory, or cucking-stool, which, in the Saxon language, is said to signify the scolding stool, though now it is frequently corrupted into *ducking-stool*, because the residue of the judgment is, that when she is so placed therein she shall be plunged in the water for her punishment.'—*Blackstone.*

[2] Fosbroke's '*Encyclopædia of Antiquities.*'

made at the same court that the tenants of the manor *should not scold their wives,* under pain of forfeiting their tenements and cottages. What a picture of domestic felicity the village ought to have presented, after those rigorous but salutary proceedings—a perfect paradise of connubial delights! But, alas! for human imperfections,—we find that in the twenty-third year of Henry VIII (not fifty years afterwards) an order was made that ' tenants' wives should not scold, under the penalty of *a six and eight-penny fine*—half to go to the repairs of the chapel, and the other half to the lord of the manor.' [1]

Bethink thee, after this, Piscator, of the many unhappily-tempered dames of Seaborough whose angelic forms, in days of yore, have been received into the limpid waters of our beloved Axe—therein to be purified of those grievous infirmities which generate rebellion against a husband's rightful rule, and thus obscure the genial sunshine of the matrimonial sky!

The church is a small plain building, the date of which, although sufficiently indicated by the character of its architecture, is more exactly ascertainable than that of most other churches, the records of which are so seldom to be found. It is recorded, that in the third year of King Henry V (1415), John Golde, who then possessed the manor and advowson of Seaborough, gave, by license from the King, to John

[1] See ' *Collinson's History of Somerset,*' vol. 2, page 173.

o

Threddar, parson of the church of Seaborough, a
certain parcel of land in the village, one hundred feet
in length and sixty feet in breadth, for the building
of a new church there. 'This church,' says Collinson, 'being in the latter end of the sixteenth century
found too small for the inhabitants, an additional
building was made to it on the north side; but A.D.
1728,[1] the old part of the church being damaged in
the roof and walls, and this additional building being
found defective and inconvenient, a faculty was obtained for pulling down that part thereof and for
erecting in its place an aisle twelve feet square, which
was accordingly done, and the church was new roofed,
new seated, and handsomely adorned.'[2] The building
now consists of a nave and chancel, with a transept
(or an aisle, as Collinson calls it,) on the north side,
and a porch on the opposite side. Two of the side
windows of the nave, and the window at the west
end, are pretty little specimens of the Perpendicular
style, which prevailed when the church was first built.
The other windows, with one exception, are flat
headed, with foliated lights. The exception referred
to is the window in the transept or aisle, which, if
not a nondescript, is at best a very imperfect imitation of the Middle Pointed, or Decorated character[3]—

[1] This must be a mistake, as the date carved upon a stone over the
'aisle' window is 1722.

[2] 'History of Somerset.'

[3] See our account of Axminster Church.

a faithful manifestation of the modern architectural incongruities which succeeded the true ecclesiastical styles.

The pulpit and reading-desk are placed against the piers of the chancel arch, and the font stands underneath the gallery at the west end of the nave. It is composed of Ham stone, and is octagonal in shape, on a stem of corresponding design. It was undoubtedly constructed at the time when the church was built,—namely, the beginning of the fifteenth century. A small organ has lately been placed, by the present rector, in the gallery just spoken of. A turret of peculiar, and certainly not very elegant form, surmounts the western end of the building, and contains two small bells. In the chancel are two mural monuments, upon one of which is the following inscription :—' M. S. Adami Martin, armig. qui, tanquam semper moriturus, vivens; tanquam semper victurus, mortuus est. Die 15 Jan. 1738, ætat. 66.' A bust of the subject of this inscription surmounts the monument. It is of the size of life, and is very beautifully executed in white marble. The other monument is in memory of Sarah Cayley, relict of William Cayley, Esq., M.P. for Dover, who died June 11, 1791.

The following is a list of some of the incumbents of Seaborough :—Stephen,[1] in 1244; Thomas Bruce,

---

[1] Sometime in the reign of Henry III (1244) one Stephen was rector of Seaborough, and held a tenement in the manor of Sampitt, from Endo,

14 Edward II (1321); [1] Jocelinus Pim, presented by
John Golde, 15 Edward III (1342); William Le
King, towards the end of Edward III (1361); John
Threddar, 1415; John Blackden, about 1490; Tho-
mas Crokehorn, September 25, 1573; Robert Gibbs,
January 9, 1595; Richard Brain, July 7, 1610; John
Sharpe, March 30, 1671; John Tidball, 1709; Faith-
ful Aishe, 1711; Thomas Edgar, 1717; John Adams,
1756; John Wills, 1779; William Butler, 1806; [2]

of *Sandpat*, now called Stephen's Lea, which from him undoubtedly had
its name—although it is likely that some other rector of Seaborough had
the same lands before him, from these words in the deed:—quas predicte
domini (Rectores) de Seveberg aliquando de me——————. When the
rectors of Seaborough parted with this tenement (perhaps in exchange for
glebe at Seaborough) they reserved to themselves and successors the tithe
thereof, for which it is supposed they afterwards compounded at eightpence a year.—*From a MS. in the possession of the Rev. C. J. Shawe.*

[1] During the reign of Edward I (1272-1307) the use of *surnames*
began to be extended among the bulk of the people, having previously
been *partially* adopted by the landowners from about the time of the
Norman Conquest. In Domesday Book the surnames are almost invariably preceded by *De*, which implies possession of a place, or residence
there,—Le Sieur *de* Vaus, for example. Personal qualities, trades, and
offices, became in time the source of numberless names which descended
from father to son, until at length, about the time of Edward VI (1546-
1533), hardly any one was without a surname. The origin of the word
surname may be traced to the custom which anciently prevailed of writing
it, in charters and other public documents, not in a line with the original
name but above it, between the lines. The name so placed was designated,
from the circumstance, *suprænomen.* See *Du Cange, Camden, &c. &c.*

[2] The late Rev. William Wills, of Axminster, who is remembered
with great respect by the old anglers of the Axe, was for many
years the officiating minister at Seaborough when the living was held by
the Rev. W. Butler. In Mr. Wills we personally possessed a valued
friend and preceptor, whose kind instructions, both in the closet and the
field, we have reason to remember with gratitude. We cannot but feel,

Charles James Shawe (the present rector), instituted in 1837. [1]

The living is a rectory, in the deanery of Crewkerne. It is valued in the King's Books at £16 15*s.* The tithes are commuted at £137.

The Rectory house stands on the west side of the church. The following inscription, upon the south front, sufficiently explains its history:—Johannes Wills, S.T.P. hujus parochiæ rector, necnon collegii Wadhami apud Oxon. Guardianus, hanc domum sua impensa ædificandam curavit, A.D. 1784.' The building overlooks the little river, which is murmuring so delightfully this afternoon, and tempting us, Piscator, from the musty records of the past, among which we have so long been lingering, to rove along its daisied banks, and to allure the spangled trout from his sub-aqueous home!

Let us then forthwith betake ourselves to the little bridge below the rectory, and, commencing at the stickle there, fish down a mile or so to Clapton. We cannot call the ground first-rate, Piscator. The stream is yet but small, and it is greatly bush-encumbered. There are, however, a few delightful *open* stickles, over which a well-thrown fly, at a favorable time, can be seldom passed in vain, if the 'hand'

therefore, that it would be unpardonable not to embrace an opportunity of mentioning his name in a work upon the river which he loved so well, and with which that name will long be most agreeably associated.

[1] Mrs. Shawe is a lineal descendant from the Martin family.

that throws it be but 'cannie.' For, of a verity, there is no lack of fish; and sheltered as they are beneath the bushes and among the roots, they often reach a goodly size, and put the angler well upon his mettle. Let us reckon, friend, upon two hours' work to fish to Clapton Bridge, whence a three miles' walk along the turnpike road will bring us into Crewkerne. In that fair town we mean to rest for the night, intending, at an early hour in the morning, to be at Clapton Bridge again—to resume our angling earnestly—to trace each winding of the sparkling stream, and explore each shady nook—to sharpen every sense in the admiration of the beauties and the wonders spread so lavishly around us—to rest, awhile, upon the flower-bespangled bank and chat as pleasantly as may be—and anon to resume our ramble downwards, in the keenest appreciation of the delights and charms of our delightful and contemplative pastime !

CHAPTER IV.

RIGHT welcome, in the beauty of evening, as we trudge along the turnpike road from Clapton,— turning our backs till morning upon the valley of the Axe—are the indications, which manifest themselves at every step, of our approach to our resting-place for the night! No trifling labor has been ours to-day, Piscator. When 'morning ope'd its cold grey eye' and found the world still slumbering, *we* were awake, old friend, and journeying. The 'clarion' of Chanticleer, borne blithely on the early breeze, was music to us as we 'brushed, with hasty steps, the dews away.' The 'gates of day' were opened gloriously. 'The frolic wind that breathes the spring,' in all its early freshness, gave vigor to our steps and sent us onward joyfully. We breathed an atmosphere of beauty, and each breath was grateful as the fumes of incense. The lowland mist soon shrank before the increasing sunbeams, and rolled itself along the hill-sides, like a mighty filmy curtain, in a thousand graceful forms. How enraptured were we at the glorious landscapes thus successively revealed—how beguiled along our way, unconscious of fatigue, insensible of distance! How well pleased, at last, to reach our destination, and, as we traced the infant stream, to fancy Naiades breathing music in each shady nook, and disporting in each rippling eddy! All the live long day a-foot, Piscator,—diverging right and left, and 'taking notes' of things noteworthy in the different parishes into which the limpid waters wander! And yet we are not foot-sore, even now, old friend, but somewhat leg-lorn. For what, in truth, are *miles* to us—to us who look contemptuously upon all means of locomotion saving those which God has given to us? To-day's exploring, friend, is but the key-note to the lengthened tune we have to play—the step initiatory ere we wander forth in earnest. Right welcome, notwithstanding, are the prospects of a supper and an early bed, for the strongest man is verily but weak. The home-bound laborers whom we meet at every turn, enjoying heartily their evening 'weed,' will not, we trow, discuss their meal more heartily than we, nor press their pillows heavier. The birds which even now are chanting vespers in the twilight—filling 'the wide expanse' with melody, and calling Echo from each grove and hill,—will not, we hope, be earlier astir than we, Piscator, in the morning.

There lies the good old town below us, nestled

snugly between its sheltering hills—a very picture,
friend, of comfort and repose. Old Bincombe, which
in winter rears its friendly head against the northern
blast, is now all beauteous in its spring-tide clothing.
St. Reigne and the Warren hills, with the keeper's
cottage, in which a candle twinkles among the sombre
firs, like a beacon in the olden time, confine the picture on the opposite side; while the eye passes over
the town between those guardian eminences, into a
splendid Somersetshire valley which is fairly mantled
by the evening shades. But there is light enough to
discern the fine old church—unmatched for many a
mile—looming indistinctly out among its guardian
trees, and towering above the abodes of men, which
are clustering, as if admiringly, about it. How the
picture would be heightened if a sparkling trout-
stream, like the Axe, were rippling musically beneath
its sacred walls! How improved would be the landscape if men more reverently regarded nature's works
—if they condescended to believe that even *trees*, for
instance, were not 'made in vain,' but 'for admirable
ends.' You mark, Piscator, in the neighbourhood of
the town, the paucity of those delightful hedge-row
ornaments which in Devonshire have been described
as 'the beauty of its landscapes and the disgrace
of its agriculture.' [1] Our rambles soon will bring
us into some of the scenes in which this 'beauty' and

[1] Report, in the *Times* Newspaper, of the proceedings at Exeter in
July, 1850, of the Royal Agricultural Society of England.

this 'disgrace' are said to be associated; and there, we suppose, we shall have to learn the lesson (intolerable dunces as we are!) that the 'wisdom' of one generation is really the 'foolishness' of another—that, in the case of agriculture, 'improvement' is antagonistic to 'beauty'—and that we are very silly folks for expressing the hope that the day is distant when that 'beauty' and that 'disgrace' shall be removed from England's 'garden.'

But we have passed the Hermitage Brewery and are fairly into the town. A walk through Sheepmarket-street, and a few yards beyond, will bring us to our quarters, and then for supper and a chat about the history of Crewkerne.

Right welcome, friend,—right welcome!

*   *   *   *   *   *

Crewkerne, as we have said before, is three miles distant, in a northerly direction, from its hamlet Clapton.[1] It is on the verge of Western Somerset, the river Axe dividing the parish from Dorsetshire at the north-western extremity of the latter county; and the river Parrott, which rises in Dorset, about four miles from Crewkerne,[2] flows at the distance from the town of a mile and a quarter, where it is crossed by a bridge on the road to Yeovil. The parish comprises an area of about 6200 acres, including an iso-

[1] The other hamlets in the parish are Hewish, Woolminstone, Furland (where there was anciently a chapel), Roundham, and Laymore.

[2] See page 38.

CREWKERNE.

W Spreat Lith Exeter.

lated portion beyond Clapton, which is surrounded by the parishes of Thorncombe, Wayford, and Broadwinsor. Crewkerne is the capital of a hundred, to which it gives its name; and the parish contains six tithings and a half.[1] It is a deanery, in the diocese of Bath and Wells. It is included in the Union of Chard, to which it sends three guardians, and in the Western Division of the County, its polling place being Ilminster. The population in 1851 was 4498, of which number 126 were registered voters. A County Court is held at Crewkerne, J. M. Carrow, Esq., being the present judge, and its jurisdiction extends to twenty-five surrounding parishes.[2] The town, however, cannot boast of Petty Sessions, and strange to

[1] These tithings are as follow:—Crewkerne, or the town tithing (formerly five tithings); Easthams, one-fourth of a tithing; Furland, one-eighth of a tithing; part of Coombe tithing, the other part being in Wayford parish, and comprising Ashcombe Farm, the whole being one-eighth of a tithing; Woolminstone, one-fourth of a tithing; Hewish, one-fourth of a tithing; Clapton, one-fourth of a tithing; part of Oathill tithing, the other part being in Wayford parish, and comprising Berechapel Farm, the whole being one-fourth of a tithing;—making together the six tithings and a half. The other tithings in the hundred of Crewkerne are—Misterton, one full tithing; Merriott, one full tithing; Hinton St. George, one full tithing; Seaborough, one-fourth of a tithing; Wayford, one-fourth of a tithing; amounting to three and a half tithings, which, with the above six and a half tithings, make a total of ten tithings, and constitute the hundred of Crewkerne. See page 63.

[2] Namely:—Chillington, Cudworth, Chiselborough, Cheddington, Dinnington, Hinton St. George, Haselbury, Kingstone, Lopen, Merriott, Middle Chinnock, Misterton, Mosterton, North Perrott, Seavington St. Michael, Seavington St. Mary, South Petherton, Shepton Beauchamp, Stocklinch Ottersey, Stocklinch St. Magdalen, Seaborough, South Perrott, Wayford, West Chinnock, and West Dowlish.

say it has now no resident magistrate. The magisterial business—very greatly to the inconvenience of the inhabitants, and not unfrequently to the detriment of justice—is transacted at Ilminster and Chard, both eight miles distant!

The town is pleasantly situated in a valley, as already stated.[1] It wears a very clean and respectable appearance, and is well laid out, the streets being wide and open, and the buildings generally good. There is nothing, however, particularly attractive in any of its approaches, as regards the buildings, and a stranger entering the town for the first time, and forming an opinion of the place from its outskirts, would probably be agreeably surprised on walking through the principal streets. These streets are six in number, namely, North, South, East, and West-streets, Sheep-market-street, and Church-street, with the usual accompaniments of lanes and alleys. In the centre of the town is a large open space, in the middle of which is the market-house, containing the shambles, town hall, and reading rooms. This building was erected about the year 1730, and was considerably repaired and altered on the removal of the old shambles in 1836. The buildings around the market-house are mostly good, and they include some handsome shops and private residences, together with the principal hotel. The town is 132 miles from London, and about mid-distance between the railway stations at

---

[1] See page 33.

Dorchester on the South Western, and Taunton on the Great Western lines—namely, twenty miles.

Crewkerne is an ancient place, having been well known in the time of the Saxons, from which its name has been transmitted. The full signification of the word is *the place of retirement, or hermitage, at the cross,*—a designation which conveys an idea of the place at a time when hermitages and cells were more numerous than churches. [1] Beyond this period the authentic history of the locality can hardly be expected to reach. There is no doubt, however, that for a long period after the arrival of the Saxons, the river Parrott was the boundary between the ' West Angles' and the ' Welch' [i.e. the British] who were driven westward by degrees; for it is recorded in the Anglo Saxon Chronicle, that in the year 658 ' Kenwalk fought against the Welsh at Peonna [whither they had arrived in the invasion of the Saxon territory]; and he drove them as far as Pedrida. This was fought after he came from East Anglia. He was there three years in exile. Thither had Penda driven him, and deprived him of his kingdom, because he had forsaken his sister.' The place called Pen by the old Saxon Chronicler is supposed, with great show of probability, to have been *Pendomer,* about five miles east from Crewkerne; and *Pedrida* is well known as the ancient name of the river Parrott. There would seem to be some reason for witholding the pursuit at

[1] Collinson's *Somerset.*

'Pedrida,' and nothing is more likely than that the
Britons should then have arrived within their recog-
nized territories, and therefore that the object of the
Saxons in driving them out of the territory which
they had invaded, was so far accomplished.[1] The
neighbourhood of Crewkerne, then, from its border
situation, was the frequent scene of strife and
slaughter in those early times. No records tell the
fearful tales, however. A mere rough outline has
come down to us of all that appertains to this eventful period. Let Caffreland and India, of the present
day, help those whose fancy needs assistance in the
picturing to themselves of those savage scenes in ages
past, for history only echoes and repeats itself. The
Britons—poor, oppressed, betrayed, and beaten,—
were driven into corners of the land, whence at times
undying patriotism and love of liberty, would send
them forth in fierce but futile strugglings with the
triumphant invaders of their island and the fell
destroyers of their race. The Pedride was, however,
but a temporary boundary; for the advancing Saxons
could not be withstood, and in time their rule extended to the Exe. At Exeter 'the Welch and
Saxons dwelt harmoniously together;' but feuds and
jealousies at last sprang up, and the Saxons, in the

---

[1] There are other reasons which render this opinion almost a matter of
certainty. See Barnes's '*Poems in the Dorset Dialect,*' page 8. Sir
Richard Colt Hoare, however, selects a locality in Wiltshire for the scene
of the Battle of Peonna, or Penn; but he does not seem to be borne out
by evidence.—See '*Ancient Wiltshire.*'

tenth century, drove out their British neighbours, and fixed the Tamar as their western boundary. [1]

There are probably no existing indications of Crewkerne having been the site of a Roman station. It is not situated upon either of the great Roman roads which traversed the West of England, [2] although it is likely that a vicinal way, to connect the Ikeneld and Fosse, passed very near it. [3] The dis-

[1] This event is described as follows by William of Malmesbury, who at the same time gives an interesting account of the 'Metropolis of the West' in ancient times, and draws an unflattering picture of the agricultural condition of a locality which is now unmatched for rural beauty and fertility:—'Departing thence, he [King Athelstan] turned towards the Western Britons, who are called the Cornwallish, because, situated in the west of Britain, they are opposite to the extremity of Gaul. Fiercely attacking, he obliged them to retreat from Exeter, which, till that time, they had inhabited with equal privileges with the Angles, fixing the boundary of their province on the other side of the river Tamar, as he had appointed the river Wye to the North Britons. This city, then, which he had cleansed *by purging it of its contaminated race*, he fortified with towers and surrounded with a wall of squared stone. And, though the barren and unfruitful soil can scarcely produce indifferent oats, and frequently only the empty husk without the grain, yet, owing to the magnificence of the city, the opulence of its inhabitants, and the constant resort of strangers, every kind of merchandise is there so abundant that nothing is wanting which can conduce to human comfort. Many noble traces of him are to be seen in that city, as well as in the neighbouring district, which will be better described by the conversation of the natives than by my narrative.'

[2] See our Introductory Chapter.

[3] A spot near the first mile stone from Crewkerne, on the road to Chard, still bears the name of 'Hore Stones,' which seems to indicate an ancient road (see page 11); but the almost total absence of the records of any local archæological investigation has now rendered researches of this nature extremely difficult—the face of the country, in the immediate vicinity of Crewkerne, having, within a few years, become completely altered by cultivation. The important station at Ilchester, and the great

covery, within the boundaries of the town, of no Roman coins, nor of any other vestiges, amounts almost to a proof that the spot was not inhabited by the wonderful people who invariably left behind them some unmistakeable evidences of their former presence. [1]

We must be satisfied, therefore, with a Saxon origin for the town of Crewkerne; and there cannot be a doubt that it was originally a place of considerable importance. This fact, indeed, is proved in the circumstance of its having been selected as one of the towns of Somersetshire at which a mint for the coinage of the royal money was established. [2] Of the productions of the Crewkerne mint, there are still remaining specimens (not more than four or five in the whole) of the coinage of Ethelred II (978-1016), Canute (1016-1035), and Harold I (1035-1040). We are enabled to present our readers with an engraving

encampment upon Hamdon Hill, were undoubtedly approached in various directions by vicinal ways of which no traces now remain.

[1] Several Anglo-Saxon sceattas have been found at different times in the town and its immediate vicinity. Sceattas were very small coins invariably made of silver. 'The word in the singular,' says Mr. Wright, 'is *sceat* or *scæt;* and to pay your *sceat* was, literally, to pay your reckoning. This has been by course of time corrupted into the modern alehouse phrase of *paying your shot.*'—Wright's ' *The Celt, the Roman, and the Saxon.*'

[2] In ancient times the coinage was not confined to a single central mint, as at present, but was effected at numerous places throughout the country, at which the King's 'moneyers' were stationed. The places selected for this purpose in Somerset, were, Bath, Ilchester, Taunton, Watchet, Crewkerne, Langport, Bruton, and '*Mile,*'—probably Milborne Port.

of one of these curious and ancient coins, of which the original is in the museum of Stockholm. This museum, which is one of the richest in the world, has been very ably described by M. Hildebrand. It contains an immense number of the ancient coins of this country,—the remains, no doubt, of the tribute which the northern nations exacted from our Saxon ancestors in the shape of Danegeldt. [1]

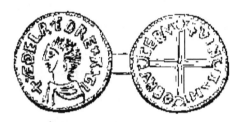

This coin, it will be seen, is of the reign of Ethelred. Its inscription, in addition to the name of the town and that of the monarch, with his title, includes, as was customary at the time, the name of the 'moneyer' (M'O) 'VINAS.' The latest Crewkerne coin known is one of the reign of Harold I, soon after which the mint was probably closed. There is no record of the circumstance, but as no coins of the more important town of Bath are known later than the time of Henry II, there appears to be room for very little doubt. The mint at Ilchester was closed about the middle of the thirteenth century, after which time the local money was supplied by the mints at Exeter and Bristol; until at length, in the

[1] See page 90.

Q

reign of Queen Mary, the privilege of coining in the provincial towns was taken away. [1] The custom, however, was revived a few years afterwards, although without the royal authority. Elizabeth would never consent to the issuing of a *copper* coinage, and the want of small change becoming inconvenient, the magistrates, in many of the large towns, took upon themselves to issue *tokens*, made of lead or brass, as the representatives of current coins to be paid by the issuers on demand. Their example was quickly followed, in the smaller places, by the tradesmen and manufacturers, and during the unsettled times of the civil war, when the government of the country was obviously in a very unsettled state, the practice was carried on to a great extent. A few of the large towns contrived to obtain formal licenses for the coinage of tokens; but in the great majority of cases the issue was made without the shadow of authority, and several places were afterwards punished for the offence by fine and otherwise. But generally speaking the coinage of tokens was regarded as a public privilege, as it really was for a long period. The people of Crewkerne, among the rest, not having the immediate fear of government before their eyes, were very active in the issuing of this spurious but convenient currency. Many of their tokens are in the cabinets of the curious to this day. We subjoin a

---

[1] See a paper on the Somersetshire Coins in the '*First Report of the Somerset Archæological and Natural History Society.*'

figure of a brass halfpenny or farthing token,[1] which was found, a few months since, in the neighbourhood of Axminster. At least three similar tokens, bearing

precisely the same inscription, have fallen under our notice—a proof, perhaps, of the prolificacy of John Shire's mint, and of his extensive vending of the pills and potions of which his device of a mortar is emblematical.

But to return to our notice of Crewkerne in the chronological order from which these remarks on the coinage have caused us to digress:—The manor, in ancient times, was held by the king himself, and endowed with many privileges, one of which, at least, would at the present day be deemed invaluable. We allude to the exemption from all taxations which the

---

[1] The usual weight of the farthing token was from thirteen to fifteen grains. The specimen referred to in the text weighs *nineteen* grains, and is in almost perfect preservation. It may not be amiss, perhaps, to remark, first, that the initials J. S. A. are those of the coiner and his wife, which in the token coinage were always placed in this manner—and, secondly, that the issuing of tokens has not been completely discontinued beyond a very few years. So recently as 1811-12, when change was very scarce, nearly all the large towns issued silver shilling tokens; and Savage states that in the latter year the Messrs. Cox, of Taunton, issued penny copper tokens. See Savage's '*History of Taunton,*' Pinkerton on *Metals,* Akerman's '*London Tokens,*' &c. &c.

town enjoyed in the time of Henry II. What an enviable community these ancient Crewkernites must have formed—making, as they did, their own money, and keeping it for their own use! *Ex pede Herculem!*

. The account in Domesday is as follows:—The king holds *Cruche.* Eddiva held it in the time of King Edward, but paid no geld, nor is it known how many hides are there. The arable is forty carucates. [1] In demesne [2] are five carucates, and twelve servants, and twenty-six coliberts, [3] and forty-two villains, and forty-five cottagers, with twenty ploughs. There are four mills of forty shillings rent, and a *market* rendering four pounds. [4] There are sixty acres of meadow. Pasture half a mile long and four fur-

---

[1] See page 90.

[2] Demesne has divers significations, but the more common one is to signify the lord's chief seat or mansion, with the lands belonging to it, which the lord kept and reserved for his own use, in opposition to such lands as were held of him by services.—Willis's '*History of Buckingham.*'

[3] The coliberti occupied a middle rank between the servile and the free tenants. They were tenants in free socage, holding their freedom of tenure on condition of certain services, among which were the care of rivers and watercourses, and the providing of fish for the lord's table.— See Du Cange.—Spelman's '*Glossary,*' &c. &c.

[4] Crewkerne market thus was evidently subsisting before the Norman Conquest, having no doubt been granted by one of the Saxon monarchs who held the manor. It is to be regretted that determined efforts are not made to place in a more flourishing condition than at present a weekly market which was formerly of considerable importance. The excellence of the six 'sheep markets' in spring, and their increasing attractions, only show what *might* be done in the establishing of a weekly, or at least a fortnightly, market, which should be worthy of the town it would so greatly benefit.

longs broad. A wood four furlongs long and two furlongs broad. It yields forty-six pounds of white money. From this manor is severed Estham. In the time of King Edward it was of the farm of the manor, and could not be separated from it. Turstin holds it of Earl Morton. It is worth fifty shillings.'[1]

In the time of Henry II (1154-1189) Baldwin de Redvers, baron of Oakhampton, Devonshire, became possessed, by his marriage with the heiress of Ralph de Dol in Berry,[2] of the manor of Crewkerne, which, in the reign of King John (1199-1216), passed, by the marriage of a daughter of the Redvers, into the family of Courtenay, Earls of Devon. In this rich and powerful family it continued until the middle of the fifteenth century, when their estates were forfeited to the crown by the attainder of some members of the family who were executed for treason, which caused the extinction of the first male line.

[1] Collinson gives the following as a note:—'The manor of Eastham (so called to distinguish it from Roundham) in another part of the Record [Domesday] is thus further surveyed: "Turstin holds of the Earl [Morton above mentioned]. Goduin, the King's bailiff, held, in the time of King Edward, with *Cruche*, a manor belonging to the King, and could not be severed from the farm, and gelded for two hides. The arable is two carucates, which are in demesne, with ten cottagers, and one servant. There is a mill of twelve shillings rent, and twelve acres of meadow, and twenty acres of wood. It was and is worth fifty shillings." It afterwards went with the manor of Crewkerne. The benefice was rectorial, now a sinecure, the church being destroyed, and the village, formerly considerable, depopulated.' The foundations of the church are still discernible in a field called Chapel Close, on Easthams farm.

[2] Dugdale.

In the year 1478 (18 Edward IV), the manor was granted to George, Duke of Clarence; but it was afterwards restored to the Courtenays.   In 1581 (23 Elizabeth), John Arundel had the fourth part of the manor of Crewkerne Magna and Parva, and had license to alienate the same, with 140 messuages there and elsewhere, to Sir Amias Poulett, who died seized of the same September 26, 1588. The manor has ever since belonged to the Poulett family, its present owner being John Earl Poulett, of Hinton St. George.

Leland, whose description of the country in the middle of the sixteenth century is so highly valued as a topographical contribution, thus quaintly and briefly expresses himself:—' Crokehorn is sette under the rootes of an hille.   Ther I saw nothing very notable.   Yet ther ys a praty crosse environed with smaul pillers, and a praty toune house yn the market place.' [1]   The ' praty crosse' has long since been removed, but what are said to be some of its ' pillers' are still to be found in sundry porches in the town.

An idea of Crewkerne, and of the social condition of the people, in the days of Queen Elizabeth, may

---

[1]   *Itinerary*, vol. ii. p. 94. Leland was appointed 'Antiquary' to King Henry VIII, who empowered him to examine all the libraries of the cathedrals, abbeys, and colleges in the kingdom. He undertook to write a work on the Antiquities of England, and spent six years in travelling for the purpose of collecting materials, but died insane before its completion. Most of his collections have since been published by different editors.

be formed from a few extracts from 'A Surveye and Rentall of the sayde Mannor, renewed and made April 26, 1599:' [1]—'The lordshyppe of Crokerne is a stately lordshyppe, and a greate markett towne, and standeth in the high way between London and Ex-ceccer. The style of this lordshyppe, with his members, very good, and fruitefulle for corne, pasture, and meadowe; and the towne well furnished with wood, water, and all other comodyties. The lands very fynable and much desyred, because of the resorte of people to the markett, and alsoe of strangers traveylinge from London into all the west partes. The sayde lordshyppe is devyed into seven several tythings, or villages, that is to say, Crokerne Magna, Crokerne Parva, Mysterton, Wollmyston, Combe, Clapton, and Hewishe, which are all within the lordshyppe and parish of Crokerne; and all the tennants within them, and of every of them, holde theire lands of the lords, either by free deede or else by copy; and every of the sayde tythings or villages have theire severall grounds inclosed, and alsoe common fields, wherein the tennants of the sayde tythings have their lands lyinge, devyed as in all other common fields. The common of pasture of the same fields after harvest, in stray time, doth belonge onely to the tennants of the sayde tything; and none of the tythings or villages doe intercommon with other, but every

[1] We are indebted to W. Sparks, Esq. for the loan of a copy of this interesting document, no part of which has ever before been published.

tythinge hath the comudythe of his owne fields seve-
ally to themselves, as if the same were severall mannors
(excepte Crokerne Magna and Crokerne Parva, which
doe intercommon together), and have but three common fields together. The demeanes of his lordshyppe
are large and greate, and granted out by copy amongst
the tennants so longe and many years past that there
remaineth noe memory of them amongst the tennants, eyther of theire own knowledge or by the
reporte of theire auncesters. Whether the lord's
auncesters had any habitation there, or not, it doth
not appeare; but by supposall there is a close adjoininge to the church, towards the southe, called Courte
Burton, and one other, adjoininge to the same, called
Courte Orcharde, *wherein standeth an olde house of
stone, which some time, as it should seeme, was a chapple;* [1] and it appeareth that there hath byn muche
more buyldinge, but to what use and purpose no man
knoweth.'

The tenures and services of the 'free' and 'customary' tenants are next described, and then follows
an account of the Hundred Courts, the Court Baron,[2]

[1] No vestige of this 'olde house' remains, but there is a tradition that
the principal part of the town was once below the church, on the south
and west.

[2] The Court Baron (called also the Hall-mote, from the place in which
it was held) was a court 'incident,' says Blackstone, 'to every manor in
the kingdom, to be holden by the steward. It is of two natures. The one
is a customary court appertaining entirely to the copyholders, in which
their estates are transferred by surrender, &c., &c. The other is a court
of common law, and it is the court of the Barons, by which name the

and the nomination, by the lords, of the Hundred Bailiff:—'The tything man of each tything is bound to be at the lord's *three weeks' courts*,' and to 'bringe with him fower of his neighbours, which they call "fower posts," and there, at every courte, to present all matters as of right they ought to present.'

The fair and markets (still held on the same days) are referred to thus:—'Within the town of Crokerne is a markett every Satterday, well served and furnished with all kindes of wares and victuals oute of all partes of the countrye, and muche accesse thether by reason of the saide markett; and on Bartholomew day, yearly, a greate fayre. The tolle, [1]

freeholders were sometimes anciently called; for that it is held before the freeholders who owe suit and service to the manor, the steward being rather the registrar than the judge. The freeholders' court was composed of the lord's tenants, who were the *peers* of each other, and were bound by their feudal tenure to assist their lord in the dispensation of domestic justice'—such as deciding all controversies relating to the right of lands, personal actions of debt, trespass, &c., below forty shillings damages. It was formerly held every three weeks. 'If,' says Mr. Watkins, 'the party was dissatisfied with the judgment of his peers, he might have appealed to them; that is, he might have *fought them*—he might have *dared them to the combat and appealed to the decision of heaven.* If he did not appeal till judgment was pronounced, he was *obliged to fight the whole bench.* And it is observable, that their sense of honor, and of their own importance and independency, was such, that the lord could not (and cannot even now, in this nation, unless warranted by custom,) compel the free suitors, as between suitor and suitor, to be sworn. This would have been to call their honor in question. Hence, perhaps, the suitors in a Court Baron are called the *homage,* or *homagers,* or *benchers,* and not *the jury,* to this day.' These courts are now merely nominal.—See Watkins's '*Treatise on Copyholds.*'

[1] Toll (or tolne) was first invented that contracts might be made openly and before witnesses.—Wood's '*Institute.*'

R

stallage, and proffytes, as well of the fayre as of the markett, appertayneth to the lords, and is worth fourty pounds yearly. [1] The lords, in times past, have byn accustomed to elect and choose one man, at their pleasure, and name hym *a Portreve*, whose office was always to collecte and gather yerely the proffytes of the markett and fayre, and to yelde accompte thereof at the auditt. But now the sayde office is granted by coppy for terme of lyves, accordinge to the custome, payinge yerely to the lord fower pounds thyrteene shillinges and fower pence.' [2]

The election of Reeve, and the payment of heriots, are next treated of. A single case will serve as a specimen —' If the husbande joyne any of his wyves in the coppy with hym, if the same wyfe dye, and he marry another and dye, his seconde wyfe shall have her widowe's estate in all his landes whereof she ought to be endowed by the custome of thys lordshyppe; for in thys mannor the nameynge one wyfe or more in the coppy doth not extinguishe the righte of

[1] In Saxon times, when fairs and markets were first established, Sunday was the usual market day, but, by the efforts of the church, Saturday was at length generally substituted. Fairs were also commonly held near some cathedral, church, or monastery, on the anniversary of its dedication (wake)—a custom which prevails to this day in many places. The old Roman roads still presented considerable facilities of communication, and were aided, it is supposed, in some places, by artificial canals.— Eccleston's *Introduction to English Antiquities.*

[2] The 'proffytes of the marketts and faire,' are now the property of a private individual, having passed from the Poulett family either by sale or in exchange for lands.

wydowe's estate of his other wyves, as in other mannors it dothe.'

The document concludes with an account of the
'severall commons,' and of the various privileges
attached to them. Roundham common, which was
enclosed about thirty-five years since, is thus
described :—'Within the lordshyppe of Crokerne
Magna is a common of waste grounde of the lord's,
called Rownam, conteyninge fower score acres, wherein the cottagers inhabitynge within the towne of
Crokerne have common of pasture for theire beastes
from the first Holly Roode Daye untylle the naty-
vytye of our Lord God,' &c., &c.

Of Cory Meadow the 'Surveye' states that 'No
tennant shall have or use any common in the sayde
meadowe, *but only the cottagers*, every of them with
theire beasts, as before in Rownam;'' and of Crewkerne Magna and Crewkerne Parva, that 'Every
tennant holdinge one tenemente, eyther buylded or
decayed, shall keepe in the common fieldes fower
score and tenne sheepe ; and if he have twoe tenementes he shall keepe nyne score sheepe; and if he
have three, fower, or more tenementes, he shall
keepe but nyne score sheepe, albeit he have twenty
tenementes.'

Cosmo III, Grand Duke of Tuscany, who visited
this country in 1669, accompanied by a secretary to
describe his travels, and by an artist to illustrate
them, speaks of Crewkerne as 'a village' through

which he passed on his way from Hinton House to
Dorchester.   This term must have been used indefi-
nitely, or, perhaps, without a knowledge of its true
meaning, since Honiton, Frampton, and 'Southprad'
[South Perrott], among many other places, are all
alike denominated *villages*, while both Crewkerne and
Honiton must at the same time have really been
flourishing *towns*.   Perhaps his Highness supposed
that Crewkerne contained nothing worthy of his
notice, and therefore hastened on to a more attractive
locality. [1]

The part which was played by Crewkerne in the
civil war between the king and the parliament, in the
seventeenth century, was not a conspicuous one; and
the town appears not to have been the scene of such
stirring events as those by which so many other places
in the neighbourhood are distinguished.   It was,

---

[1]   Cosmo's travels were translated and published in 1821, with illustrations from the original sketches—forming a very curious and interesting
picture of the state of the country as it was presented to an intelligent
foreigner nearly two hundred years ago.   The duke's account of Hinton
House, 'the villa of my Lord Paulet,' with its gardens, terraces, and
parterres,—'very different from the common style,'—of its park, containing six hundred deer 'of two sorts,' and of its 'wood for pheasants'—
is sufficiently quaint; but, perhaps, not more so than his description of
fly-fishing, which the party had an opportunity of observing at Dorchester.
Peculiar to the Anglo-Saxon race as this elegant amusement has been
from the earliest period, it is easy to imagine the surprise of the Italians
on seeing it practised for the first time:—'Their mode of angling here,'
he says, 'is very different from the common one; for where our fishermen
hold the hook still for a long time in the same place, these keep it in con-
tinual motion, *darting the line into the water like the lash of a whip;
then, drawing it along a few paces, they throw it in afresh, repeating this
operation till the fish is caught.*'

however, frequently occupied by the troops of the contending parties, in their marches to and from the localities in which their more active services were required. Very easy, therefore, is it to imagine the excitement and social disorganization which Crewkerne experienced in common with even the most insignificant places.

The outrages of a lawless soldiery, in truth, are in themselves a sufficient infliction, and to these outrages the town, from its situation, must have been peculiarly exposed. Taunton, at the distance of twenty miles, held a prominent position on behalf of the parliament, and Lyme Regis, at a shorter distance in another direction, was early enlisted on the same side and soon became the 'Key of the West of England;' [1] while Hinton St. George, in the immediate vicinity of Crewkerne, was the quarters of Lord Poulett, who greatly distinguished himself for the king, and held an important command in the royal army. [2]

[1] See Roberts's 'History of Lyme Regis,' which contains a very interesting and detailed account of the important proceedings at Lyme and the West of England generally. See, also, Savage's 'History of Taunton.'

[2] 'His Highness, upon his arrival at Bristol, found the West in this condition: all Dorsetshire entirely possessed by the rebels, save only what Sir Lewis Dives could protect by his small garrison at Sherborne, and the island of Portland, which could not provide for its own subsistence; the garrison of Taunton, with that party of horse and dragoons which relieved it, commanding a very large circuit, and disturbing other parts in Somersetshire; Devonshire intent upon the blocking up of Plymouth, at one end, and open to incursions from Lyme, and prejudiced by Taunton, at the other end; the king's garrisons, in all three counties, being stronger in

Monmouth's expedition, a few years afterwards, found the West of England again the scene of unnatural contention and of bloodshed. Almost idolized as was the Duke by the generality of the people, who groaned under the tyranny of James, his 'progresses' were a series of splendid triumphs, which shadowed most unfaithfully his after downfall. Barrington Court, the seat of William Strode,—Whitelackington, the mansion of the Spekes, [1]—Ford Abbey, the magnificent home of Edmund Prideaux,—and Hinton St. George, where Monmouth's visit was celebrated in the park by a feast of junket, [2]—are a few of the places in this locality at which the favorite was hospitably entertained and fondly welcomed. However altered might have become the feeling towards him of many of the local gentry, it is certain

fortifications (which yet were not finished in any place, and but begun in some) than in men, or any provisions to endure an enemy; whilst the Lord Goring's forces equally infested the borders of Dorset, Somerset, and Devon, by unheard of rapine, without applying themselves to any enterprize upon the rebels.' Clarendon's '*History of the Rebellion.*'

[1] At Whitelackington still stands the enormous chestnut tree, under which the Duke and his party took refreshment.

[2] 'While in Hinton Park, Elizabeth Percy, who had heard of the festive party, made a rush at the Duke of Monmouth and touched his hand. She was a martyr to the king's evil, and had received no benefit from the advice of surgeons, nor even from a *seventh son*, to whom she had travelled ten miles. After touching the Duke, all her wounds were healed in two days. A hand-bill was circulated in folio, setting forth this marvellous cure; and a document, signed by Henry Clark, minister of Crewkerne, two captains, a clergyman, and four others, lay at the Amsterdam Coffee-house, Bartholomew-lane, London.'—Roberts's '*Life of the Duke of Monmouth.*'

that the majority of the people who assembled at those places from far and near to greet him, were not less enthusiastic when he afterwards repeated his visit in a different character, and when, upon the plains of Sedgemoor, they battled for his cause and reaped the bitter fruits of his defeat. [1] The writer of the Axminster '*Church Book*' of the Independent Chapel[2] thus describes the immediate effect of King James's triumph :—' Now did the rage of the adversary increase, and, like a flood, swell to a great height, insomuch that many poor creatures, yea, many of the Lord's own professing people, were constrained to hide themselves in woods and corners where they could find places for shelter from the fury of the adversary, divers being taken captive, some shut up in prison-houses, others hanged up immediately by the hands of the enemy. Ah! how did the Lord, by this amazing providence, correct the vain confidence, creature-dependence, and trusting in an arm of flesh, which was the great sin of the nation in this day!'

[1] The Battle of Sedgemoor was fought on Monday July 6, 1685.

[2] The full title of this manuscript is '*Ecclesiastica, or a Book of Remembrance.*' Similar records were very commonly kept by the dissenting congregations. They served to show the progress of 'the cause,' and to chronicle the cruel persecutions of its early professors. The Axminster manuscript, along with a great deal of interesting local matter, presents a vivid picture of the state of the country generally at the period at which it was written. As a literary composition it is exceedingly creditable to the author, whose phraseology and style are amusingly characteristic. We shall, in future pages, make further extracts from this interesting document.

The 'reign of terror' had indeed begun. King James, incapable of mercy, immediately commenced a signal vengeance upon the misguided people who had favored, directly or indirectly, the pretensions of the unfortunate object of their preference. A fitting instrument to carry out his plans was found in Jeffreys, who forthwith set out upon his horrid mission. The result, while history lasts, will never be forgotten. A writer at the time describes thus forcibly the awful scenes presented in a portion of the kingdom which nature would seem to have selected as the appropriate abiding place of beauty and of peace :—' He [Jeffreys] made all the West an Aceldema. Some places quite depopulated, and nothing to be seen in 'em but forsaken walls, unlucky gibbets, and ghostly carkases. The trees were loaden almost as thick with *quarters* as with leaves. The houses and steeples covered as close with heads as at other times, in that country, with crows or ravens. Nothing could be liker hell than all those parts; nothing so like the devil as he. Caldrons hissing, carkases boyling, pitch and tar sparkling and glowing, blood and limbs boyling, and tearing, and mangling, and he the great director of all; and, in a word, discharging his place who sent him, the best deserving to be the late king's chief justice there, and chancellor after, of any man that breath'd since Cain or Judas.'

[1] From '*A New Martyrology; or, the Bloody Assizes.*'

No pen has ever chronicled a tithe of the misery, the cruelty, and the moral degradation of those unhappy times of regal tyranny and of its offspring revolution. A nation fighting for its dearest rights —the rights of conscience and the rights of liberty— is in the abstract (if *compelled* to fight) a really noble object of contemplation. It will always enlist the sympathies of the true hearted among its contemporary communities, and the respect and love of succeeding generations. But let us draw aside the veil from even the most righteous and most successful of civil wars,—let us look with an impartial eye upon the imposing picture which will be thus revealed,—and we shall be horrified at the enormous *moral* expense at which the triumphant result has been obtained. A thousand instances of the purest heroism and of the most patriotic zeal, will surely present themselves to our admiration. A thousand instances of the worst of human passions, displayed for the worst of individual purposes, will as surely appal and sicken us;—will operate upon our moral sense like the poisonous simoom upon an eastern prospect which is *apparently* so healthful and so fair ! But we must not pursue this theme. We have been led almost unconsciously into these remarks—forgetting for a moment that it is neither our object nor our province to trace the history and to moralize upon the effects of the social disturbances and the political changes which characterize an eventful century,—greatly instrumental as they have been in securing the peace, the prosperity, and the happiness which as a nation we now enjoy! This is the work of a far more able pen, and we, in all humility, must confine ourselves to a few of the leading particulars of those intestine wars, in connection with the various places in the locality upon which we have undertaken to treat. [1]

Crewkerne is the scene of the execution of ten out of the three hundred and thirty-one unhappy beings who suffered capital punishment on the sentence of Jeffreys. [2] Their names were John Spore, Roger Burnell, William Pether, James Every, Robert Hill, Nicholas Adams, Richard Stephens, Robert Halswell, John Bussell, and William Lashley. '*The New Martyrology*' contains an account of the sufferings of a person who was first a loyalist and afterwards a partizan of Monmouth. An extract may perhaps be interesting:—'Captain Madders, at the time of the Duke's landing, was a constable at Crewkerne, in the county of Somerset, and so diligent and active for the king in his office, that when two gentlemen of Lyme came there, and brought the news of the

[1] Abundant information may be obtained from Clarendon's '*History of the Rebellion;*' Macaulay's '*History of England;*' Roberts's '*Life of the Duke of Monmouth,*' &c. &c.

[2] This is a very small proportion of the total loss of life in Monmouth's ill-fated rebellion. About 2500 fell in battle,—hundreds died of their wounds,—and nearly a thousand were transported, of whom great numbers died in slavery.

Duke's landing, and desired horses to ride post to acquaint his Majesty therewith, he immediately secured horses for them, the town being generally *otherwise bent* [that is, on the side of Monmouth], and assisted them so far as any loyal in those times could do; which was represented to the Lord Chief Justice [at the trial], in expectation thereby to save his life. But an enquiry being made about his religion, and returned by a very worthy gentleman of those parts that he was a good protestant, an honest man, and had a very good character amongst his neighbours: "O then," says he, [Jeffreys] "I'le hold a wager with you he is a presbyterian; I can smell them forty miles." * * * Being brought to the place of execution [at Dorchester], he was the last man, except one, executed; and he behaved himself, whilst the rest [ten] were executing, with great zeal.' * * * After making a public prayer 'he came once down the ladder and prayed again privately; then mounted the ladder again, the sheriff saying, "Mr. Madders, if you please, you may have more liberty." He answered, "No, I thank you, Mr. Sheriff, now I am ready." * * * So blessing and praising God, he was translated from earth to heaven.'

Of the many local traditions of these afflicting times, transmitted orally from generation to generation, we select one now almost forgotten, which relates to a circumstance deserving to be ranked

among the *minor* 'popular delusions' of Dr. Mac-
kay:—Two industrious aged men, of great respectability, it is said, carried on an extensive business
as tallow chandlers in a house still standing in East-
street.   An idea, the ludicrousness of which is
equalled only by its absurdity, got possession of the
minds of the populace, that these thrifty, but, as it
appears, very amiable old gentlemen, were in the habit
of purchasing the dead bodies of the victims of the
rebellion, at Sedgemoor and elsewhere, for the purpose of *boiling them down for the sake of their tallow.*
In a short time, the idea acquired so much force, that
a mob was actually formed, the object of which was
to wreak signal vengeance upon the parties suspected
of the unnatural practice.   The chandlers' house was
accordingly surrounded, and after a time a few of the
mob effected an entrance, determined upon the execution of Lynch law.   The parties attacked, becoming
alarmed at a proceeding which at its commencement
they had regarded as too absurd to be treated seriously,
proceeded to secrete themselves among the rafters of
the roof.   But it unfortunately happened, that one
of the brothers, in dragging himself through the
aperture of the ceiling which led to the intended
hiding-place, was discovered by the ringleader of the
mob and immediately seized.   The promise of a considerable reward, however,—which was actually paid
in the shape of an annuity—not only silenced the
discoverer, but secured his assistance in the effectual

concealment of the chandlers,—a concealment of six months' duration,—and also in the ultimate diversion of his followers from a pursuit which they reluctantly abandoned.

The living of Crewkerne is a perpetual Curacy [1] in the gift of the Dean and Chapter of Winchester, and the present incumbent, instituted during the present year (1853), is the Rev. Alexander Ramsay. The tithes, which belong to Thomas Hussey, Esq., the lay impropriator, are commuted at £1300, subject to the annual payment of £80 to the curate, for his stipend, and to the cost of keeping in repair the chancel of the parish church. [2]

Crewkerne possessed, in ancient times, an ecclesias-

---

[1] '*Perpetual Curacies.* Previous to the dissolution of monasteries and religious houses, the churches and chapels belonging to their manors and possessions were served by monks and curates sent out from the abbey or priory for the purpose. This privilege was confined to benefices given *ad mensam monachorum* (to the support of the table of the monks), and not appropriated in the common form, but given by way of union *de jure*. The like liberty of not appointing a perpetual curate or *vicar*, was sometimes granted by dispensation in benefices not annexed to their tables, in consideration of the poverty of their house, or the contiguity of the church or chapel. But when such appropriation, together with the charge of providing for the cure (after the dissolution of religious houses), were transferred from *spiritual* to *lay*, and single persons, who were not capable of serving them, and who by consequence were obliged to nominate some particular person to the ordinary for his license to serve the cure, the curates became by these means so far *perpetual* as not to be wholly at the pleasure of the appropriator, nor removable but by due revocation of the license of the ordinary.'—Gibson's '*Codex.*'

[2] The living has been augmented since 1812, from the Royal Bounty and by Parliamentary Grant, to the total amount of £1000, which has been applied to the erection of a dwelling-house for the incumbent.

tical establishment of an extensive character. Its
church, to which large possessions were attached, was
given by William the Conqueror to the famous abbey
at Caen, in Normandy, which he founded and muni-
ficently endowed. [1]   This property is thus described
in Domesday :—'The church of St. Stephen (Caen)
holds of the King the Church of Cruche.   There
are ten hides.   The arable is thirteen carucates.
Thereof in demesne are two hides, and there is one
carucate, with one servant, and eleven villains, and
two coliberts, [2] and seventeen cottagers, with six
ploughs.   There are ten acres of meadow, and half a
mile of pasture in length and breadth.   Of these ten
hides. a knight holds of the abbot three hides, and
has there two carucates, with one servant, and six
villains, and two cottagers, with four ploughs.   There
is a mill of five shillings rent, and ten acres of
meadow, and half a mile of pasture in length and
breadth.   It is worth to the abbot seven pounds, and
to the knight four pounds.' [3]

[1] 'Besides the immense bounties which he [William] in his life time
conferred thereon, he, on his death, was fain to give it all his favorite trin-
kets, the crown which he used to wear at high festivals, his sceptre and
rod, his cup set with precious stones, his golden candlesticks, and all his
other regalia; nay, even the bugle horn, which he used to carry at his
back, went to pot!   It seems it was some difficulty to recover these matters from the abbey; for it is evident that King William II gave the
manor of Coker, in this County, and a large parcel of exemptions, to
redeem what had been so foolishly squandered.'—Collinson's 'Somerset.'

[2] See page 116.

[3] The Abbey of Glastonbury also possessed property in this parish, for
we find that Kentwin, king of the West Saxons (676-685), presented it
with three hides of land in Crewkerne.

The impropriate tithes were granted to Winchester cathedral in the year 1547 (2 Edward VI), and they passed into the possession of their present owner about fifty years ago. 'The church,' says Collinson, 'was anciently divided into three portions, the first of which was in 1292 valued at fifty marks (in 1554 at £56 12s. 11d.), the second at sixteen, and the third at ten. [1] 1 Edward II [1308] it was found not to the king's detriment to grant to Agnes de Monceaux a license settling the sum of £4 4s. 3d. rent in Crewkerne on a certain chaplain in this church to celebrate mass daily in perpetuum. [2] The last incumbent of this service was John Godge, who [at the suppression of chantries in 1547] received the sum of £4 3s. 4d., by way of pension.' [3]

Three rectors and two chantry chaplains were formerly attached to this church; and it is probable that they lived together, in a monastic manner, in a building on the north-west side of the church, the ruins of which were removed in 1846. [4] This building is popularly believed to have been *an abbey*, and the name of Abbey-street has been given to the street in

[1] *Taxad. Spiritual.*

[2] Inq. ad quod damnum, 1 Edward II.

[3] The Courtenays were probably also the founders of a chantry chapel in this church.—*From a private communication from the Rev. Dr. Oliver, of Exeter.*

[4] We have been favored with a private communication on this subject by the Rev. W. Phelps, author of a History of Somerset which is now in the course of publication.

which it stood. We are almost sorry to disturb this popular belief, but we can assure our Crewkerne friends that it has been formed without the slightest historical authority—that, in fact, the proud fanes of an abbey never graced their town—and, therefore, that the building in question must be regarded as one of a far less dignified character. The character which we have assigned to it—namely, that of a residence of the officiating priests—is in all probability the correct one.

The great ornament of Crewkerne is its magnificent church, which occupies an elevated position on the north-western side of the town. It is dedicated to St. Bartholomew, and the fair, or wake, as already stated, is still held on the anniversary of that Saint (September 4).[1] It affords us considerable pleasure to state that we have been favored by Edward Freeman, Esq., of Trinity College, Oxford, with an original account of the architecture of this church. Mr. Freeman, who is justly celebrated as a writer on architectural and ecclesiological subjects, has long paid great attention to the ecclesiastical buildings of Somersetshire. His account of this interesting church, therefore, will not fail to be regarded as a valuable contribution to our pages. The annotations, we should mention, are our own:—

'Crewkerne Church is unquestionably one of the finest among the magnificent specimens of the latest

[1] See pages 121 and 122.

or Perpendicular era of Gothic Architecture with which the county of Somerset abounds; and while, on the whole, it may be considered as belonging to the local style of the district, it is by no means wanting in peculiarities of its own. [1] It is a large cruciform building, with a central tower. There are aisles to the nave, but the choir has no regular aisles. There is, however, a remarkable arrangement of chapels between the choir and the north transept.

[WEST FRONT OF CREWKERNE CHURCH.]

'The west front is one of the finest belonging to any parish church in England. In many respects it

---

[1] The Church was erected, on the site of a more ancient structure, during the latter half of the fifteenth century. 'Henry VII, on coming to the throne,' says Dr. Toulmin, 'rebuilt many of the Somersetshire churches in the style of the Florid Gothic, [Perpendicular] in reward for the attachment of that county to the Lancastrian party in the civil wars between the houses of York and Lancaster.' Somersetshire is celebrated for its Perpendicular churches, which possess peculiarities of a very decided and beautiful character. The buildings which preceded them are supposed to have been, 'for the most part, of no very great pretensions.'

T

resembles that of Yatton, in the northern part of the county; but it bears a still closer similarity to that of Bath Abbey, and there can be little hesitation, in this case, in setting the parochial before the cathedral example. The end of the nave is flanked by octagonal turrets, between which is a magnificent Perpendicular window of seven lights. A highly enriched doorway below somewhat recalls that of King's College Chapel, at Cambridge. The height and general proportion of the whole front are admirable.

'The nave is short and lofty, consisting only of three wide bays, but rising considerably above the rest of the church. [1] The aisles are lighted by large windows of six lights. [2] In the clerestory there are two small windows in each bay, but the effect of this part of the building is somewhat lost, owing to its being partially concealed by the large battlement of the aisles,—the form usual in the southern part of Somersetshire, instead of the elegant pierced parapets of the north.

'The north transept is very large, and, both from its size and the especial care evidently bestowed on its

[1] The length of the nave is 56 feet, which is the same as its width inclusive of the aisles. The total length of the church is 122 feet, and the width of the transepts 102 feet.

[2] All the windows are furnished with weather mouldings, most of which rest upon beautifully finished corbels of human heads. The gargoyles with which the building is ornamented are also very exquisitely carved. See page 49.

workmanship, forms one of the most conspicuous portions of the building. The part of the transept which projects beyond the aisle is considerably higher than any part of the church except the nave clerestory; and we must forestal our description of the interior to mention that it is parted off at the same point by an arch, so as to make it in every respect a distinct chapel.[1] The transept has three large windows with very flat heads, that to the north of six lights, those to the east and west of five.[2] The north doorway cuts into the north window in a remarkable manner. The northern chapels might be described as an aisle to the choir, occupying two of its three bays, with an additional chapel against the western bay of the aisle. The outline they produce from the north-east is one singularly varied for the style and date of the building.

'The choir is considerably lower than the nave. Its walls are not higher than those of the aisles and chapels, but it rises above them by reason of its high-

[1] The south transept was also a chapel, as is evident by the piscina which still remains in its south wall. Against the mullions of the south-easternmost window of this transept is a mutilated figure of what appears to be St. Michael and the Dragon. See 'Handbook of English Ecclesiology,' Fosbroke's 'Encyclopædia of Antiquities,' Bloxam's 'Gothic Architecture.' &c., &c.

[2] On the west side of this transept there is, besides, a small window of four lights placed over a doorway now walled up. The north transept is commonly called the Woolminstone Chapel. The remains of several members of the Merefield family, who formerly resided at Woolminstone House, lie buried there. The larger west window of this transept is shown in the engraving, page 137.

pitched roof. The same may be said of the south transept also, which is very inferior in magnificence to its fellow. Under the east window was formerly a vestry, placed behind the high altar, according to what seems to be a Somersetshire localism, occurring at Ilminster and North Petherton; also at Hawkhurst, in Kent. The vestry is now destroyed, but the doors at the east end are sure evidence of its existence.[1] In the centre of the nave, on the south side, is a large and handsome porch, with a parvise,[2] rising the full height of the aisle.[3]

[1] 'On each side of the communion table,' says Collinson, 'is a door leading into a small room, which was formerly a confessional, or place where, in days of popery, a reverend confessor sat in form to hear the declarations of his penitents and to dispense absolutions. The virtues and advantages of confession are not improperly expressed by some figures over the doors which lead into this apartment. That by which the penitents entered has two swine carved over it, to signify their pollution; over that by which they returned are two angels, to represent their purity and innocence.'—See '*Fosbroke's Encyclopædia of Antiquities*,' page 124. 'Some persons,' say the writers of '*A Handbook of English Ecclesiology*,' page 197, 'have denied that there are such things as ancient confessionals at all, but, it seems to us, without sufficient reason.' Tradition speaks very positively in favor of the confessional at Crewkerne, and of the symbolization of the figures carved over the doorways which led into it. There is room, however, for considerable doubt on the latter point. The hog formed part of the arms of Richard III, and the figures over both doorways are supporting shields.

[2] The parvise is a room over the porch of a church, which is sometimes used as a school, or record room. In ancient times it was frequently the residence of a chantry priest (see page 50). It was approached by a winding staircase either from within or without the building. The floor of the parvise at Crewkerne was removed in 1822 [see the following note], but the *external* features of a parvise remain unaltered.

[3] The doorway of this porch has been blocked since the year 1822, and the porch itself is appropriated to pews. Its ceiling is ornamented with

'The tower, rising from the intersection, is the least satisfactory part of the church, and is especially inferior to its magnificent neighbour at Ilminster. It is very plain, with a battlement, small double angle pinnacles, and a polygonal turret at the south-east corner. There is a single very long belfry window in each face, of a kind very different from that which is generally found in Somerset. [1] The difference in height between the several parts of the church prevents any claim for the tower to justness of proportion from any point.

'Within, much magnificence of general effect is derived from the great height of the nave; [2] but the

the beautiful fan-tracery so frequently employed in buildings of the Perpendicular style. Over the doorway, on the outside, is a canopied niche for a small statue. This is the proper situation for a figure of the patron saint, and such a figure, no doubt, once occupied the niche referred to. A door on the opposite side of the church, opening into the north aisle, was also closed in 1822, and in lieu of these appropriate entrances, the *transepts* were made to serve the purpose of porches, and a doorway was opened into each of them—very greatly to the injury of the beautiful windows into which they are so clumsily cut, and hence to the deformity of the building.

[1] The tower rises to the height of about eighty feet. It contains a clock and chimes and six bells, upon one of which is the date 1698. Prior to 1820, the number of bells was five only. They occupied the second storey of the tower,—that now occupied by the clock and chimes—and were rung from the floor of the church. In that year they were raised to their present position in the upper part of the tower, and a sixth bell was added. Upon the great bell is the following inscription:—'*Me resonare jubent pietas, mors, atque voluptas.* Cast by Thomas Bayley, Bridgwater, 1767. John Wills, Churchwarden.' The interior of the tower bears evidence of fire, and it is said that about 150 years ago the wood work was accidentally burned.

[2] About 44 feet.

details are plain compared with those of many other churches in the county, and the great width of the pier-arches must be allowed to be a considerable drawback. A fine coved roof—the local form—rises from small shafts resting on the clerestory string, and furnished with angel capitals. The lantern arches are of the same character as those in the nave, but, as is so often the case, they are far too low.

' The choir and chapels are precluded by their smaller dimensions from rivaling the general majesty of the nave, but their architectural details are of a more delicate character. All the arches in this part of the church are four-centred.[1] The sections of the piers and mouldings of the arches are very elaborate. The clustered pillar in the north transept, from which four arches spring in different directions, is worthy of especial admiration. Both within and without we may remark the much greater attention displayed in the workmanship on the north side, the chapels formed there being doubtless the private additions of individual benefactors, although harmonized into one general design.'[2]

In the south wall of the chancel is a niche within an acutely pointed foliated arch containing a piscina,

[1] That is, the arches are struck from four centres within—a form almost peculiar to the Perpendicular style. 'The four-centred arch,' says the author of ' *The Glossary of Architecture,*' ' was introduced soon after the middle of the 15th century, and was generally prevalent from that time till the expiration of Gothic architecture.'

[2] See page 135.

with a stone shelf. [1]—evidently of much older date than the church. [2] Near the piscina is a curious old brass on which is the figure of a knight in full armour, kneeling, and beneath it the following inscription, in old English characters:—'*Pray for the soule of* Thomas Golde, Esquire, which deceased the XIV day of September, the yeare of our Lord MDXXV, on whose soule *Jesu have mercy.*'[3] Against the same wall is a handsome tablet to the memory of the late John Hussey, Esq., owner of the rectory impropriate, who died at Bath, November 6, 1848, aged 59. There are also inscriptions to the memory of two of his daughters. There is a marble monument to some members of the Hawksley family, and a small tablet to the memory of Samuel Wills, Esq., and his wife.

In the chapel, or north aisle to the chancel, are two curious old brasses inscribed to some members of the Sweet family, once goldsmiths at Crewkerne. The

---

[1] See page 52.

[2] The chancel of a church [see page 39] was always regarded with particular veneration, and when the rest of an old church was taken down, it was frequently preserved, and employed for its original purpose in the new building. Even in cases in which the chancel was removed, along with the rest of the church, some *parts* of it were generally retained as relics. The presence of a piscina of older date than the church at Crewkerne, may thus be very reasonably accounted for. The same remark applies to the font, which is undoubtedly by far the most ancient object in connection with this church and its furniture. See page 82.

[3] The words in italics have been almost erased with a chisel—the work, no doubt, of some puritan fanatic in the time of Cromwell. On an old brass in the south transept are the arms of the Martins, of Seaborough. See page 93.

oldest date is 1683.   There is also a tablet to the
memory of 'Elizabeth Wyke, wife of John Wyke
of Henly, esquier . . . . born 1565, died 1615.'
The inscription includes an acrostic, which is copied
by Collinson.[1]

In the north-west corner of the chancel aisle, or
chapel, is a large and handsome marble monument to
the memory of Thomas Way, 1723.   Opposite this
monument is a tablet to the memory of 'Isaac Sparks,
Esq., solicitor, who died April 26, 1841;' and beneath this a small brass inscribed to Mrs. Joan
Burnard, 'who dy'd September 2, 1754.'   Other members of the Sparks and Burnard families have monuments in different parts of the church.

In the north transept are several other monuments
besides those to the Merefields, already mentioned.
Among them is a neat tablet of Caen stone to the
memory of the Rev. George Swaine Swansborough,
A.M., second master of Crewkerne Grammar School,
and assistant curate of Misterton.   He died at Weymouth, September 28, 1848, and this tablet was
erected by a few of his friends and pupils, by whom
he was held in great respect.

In the south transept are several monuments, including one to some members of the family of Cox,
of Cheddington,[2] and there are also a few curious
old brasses.

[1] In this aisle or chapel is the church chest, which is small and made
of oak.   It bears the date 1672.
[2] See page 37.

The pulpit and reading desk, which were presented by the late Countess Poulett, in 1808, stand at the eastern end of the nave, and the font is placed at the opposite end. [1] A small gallery occupies the eastern end of each of the nave-aisles, extending into the transepts, and a large gallery spans the entire width of the nave and aisles at the western end. In the last is an organ, [2] which was presented in 1823 by

[1] The font bears evidence of great antiquity. It is of granite, and ornamented with arches very similar to those on the font in Beaminster church, as described at page 53. It rests upon a square pedestal with circular pillars at the angles.

[2] 'Organs,' says Dr. Burney, in his '*History of Music,*' 'were introduced into some of the churches in France about A.D. 775. The first that was seen in France was sent as a present to King Pepin. St. Dunstan appears to have been the constructor of one of the finest organs in England in the tenth century.' Puritanical fanaticism, in the time of Cromwell, discovered a heinous sin in the sublime tones of the organ, and accordingly an ordinance for the removal of organs from all churches was issued in 1644. They were replaced at the Restoration, as rapidly as persons could be found to erect and play them—for during the Protectorate, both organ builders and performers had become extremely scarce. At the present time it is impossible to say what the modern love of 'congregational *singing*' (?) will produce; for really if the 'enlightened age' comes seriously to the conclusion that mere noise is *music*, and that the extemporaneous performance of a whole congregation, with every species of individual disqualification, is preferable to a really *musical* performance by a few trained voices alone, singing as harmony can only be sung, from music scientifically arranged;—if this, we say, is seriously to be the decision, it becomes a question whether the builders of organs for religious purposes will not, like Othello, find their 'occupation gone,' and whether musicians also may not as well abandon the study of the 'art divine,' and spare themselves the trouble of arranging their sacred compositions in accordance with the laws of harmony. But we are notoriously a people of *manias,* and the congregational singing mania, like that of Hullah's *music* teaching, may, perhaps, ere long experience a reaction. The time may come with music, as with ecclesiastical architecture, when men will

the Rev. Dr. Ashe, at that time the incumbent of the parish. The church is kept in admirable order, and lighted with gas. [1]

But our limits forbid the further extension of our remarks upon this very interesting building, and we must take our leave of the subject by stating that in consequence of the insufficiency of the present accommodation, subscriptions have been raised for the building of a Chapel of Ease, in South-street, the foundation stone of which was laid August 31, 1852.

The residence of the incumbent, to which allusion has been already made at page 133, is at the distance of about three hundred yards to the west of the church, beyond Pople's Well [2] on the Hinton road. The incumbent formerly resided in a house on the

imitaté once more their pious forefathers in bestowing all the *best* they can to their Creator's service, and when, in their songs of thankfulness and praise, they will manifest their gratitude by the exercise of the *highest* faculties with which He has endowed them.

[1] The gas works by which the town and church are lighted were erected in 1837.

[2] A great degree of sanctity was in ancient times associated with wells; and in connection with almost every church there was a well from which the water used for baptism, and other sacred purposes, was obtained. The church well was itself an object of attraction to the afflicted, who sought for cures in the supposed miraculous properties of its waters. Various superstitions were also attached to certain springs, and many of them cannot even now be correctly spoken of in the past tense alone. 'Beauty Spring,' for example, at the outskirts of Crewkerne, on the Merriott road, is believed to possess invaluable properties as a cosmetic at sunrise on the first of March; and many a simple lass resorts to it on this day in the hope of experiencing its virtues.

eastern side of the church, and within a few yards of it. This was probably allotted to him at the Reformation, when the building familiarly known as the Abbey[1] was dismantled. It is thus referred to in a Survey of the Rectory, &c., of ' Crookehorne,'[2] made in April 1650, 'by virtue of a commission to us granted, grounded upon an Act of Parliament for the abolishing of Deans, Chapters, Canons, Prebends, and other offices, and tythes of and belonging' to Cathedrals, Churches, Chapels, &c., namely:—' One parsonage house, with a garden, orcharde, and other necessary outhousing, containing by estimation one acre and a half, situate on the east side of the church-yard, we value worth ffour pounds per annum.'

The schools in connection with the established church are well conducted and numerously attended. The handsome building in which they are held, at the western entrance to the town, was erected in 1847.

The dissenting places of worship in the town are:— the Unitarian Chapel, in Hermitage-street, erected in 1733; the Baptist Chapel, in North-street, erected in 1820; and the Wesleyan Chapel, in South-street,

[1] See page 135.

[2] In the possession of J. Hussey, Esq., to whom the writer is indebted for its inspection. The same gentleman has also a copy of a Survey of the Rectory made in 1799 by Mr. Webb, of Salisbury, in which the roads in the neighbourhood of the town are described as being 'narrow and bad.' The reverse is now the case. The Crewkerne roads have been greatly improved within a few years, and are now among the best in the county, the business of the turnpike trust being most efficiently conducted in all its departments.

erected in 1832. Sunday schools are attached to each of these establishments. The schools of the Unitarian Chapel are among the oldest in the West of England. They were founded, in 1788, by the celebrated Raikes. Some members of the Blake family—a collateral branch of the family of the famous Admiral Blake, and formerly influential inhabitants of the town,—are buried in this chapel.

We annex a table of the Crewkerne Charities, referring the reader for more minute particulars than our limits enable us to supply, to the Government Commissioners' *Report of the Charities of Somersetshire.*

As the table shows, there are in Crewkerne two valuable charities in the shape of almshouses. They are situated in West-street. The new almshouse is handsomely built, on an elevated site, with an excellent garden in the rear. A garden is also attached to the old almshouse.[1]

But by far the most valuable institution in Crewkerne is its Free Grammar School, to which extensive buildings and playgrounds are appropriated in Carter-street, on the north side of the church.[2] These have

[1] The following inscription is cut on a stone in the front of the building:—'To the honor of God and for the reliefe of 8 poore people of the towne of Cr., this hovse was bvilt by Mathew Chvbb, of Dorchester, in the C. of D. Gent, & Margaret his wife, In Ano Domini 1604. "Blessed is he that considereth the poore and needie, the Lorde will deliver him in the tyme of trovble."' *Psalme* 41. 1.

[2] 'By a deed of feoffment dated August 25, 1675, a dwelling-house with the appurtenances, situate in Carter Street, in Crewkerne, was con-

Crewkerne Charities and Benefactions.

Donors and Date of Grant.	Donations.	Application.	Objects.	Time of Distribution.	By Whom.
John de Combe,	Free Grammar School, lingstone's.	Classical Education.	The children of pa...		Trustees of the
Wm. Budd, 1730.	Twenty pounds.	Four years, without Interest.	Two industrious tradesmen, with bondsmen.	Every four years	Minister & Churchwardens.
Eliz. Cookson, 1762.	The use of £50.	Teaching to read.	Poor children.		Minister & Churchwardens.
Wm. Sharlock, May 1, 1786.	£100, 3 per cent. consols.	1s. each.	Poor persons.	St. Thomas's-day.	Minister, Churchwardens, & Overseers.
Mary Ann Taylor, 3rd Nov. 1837.	£140, 3 per cent. consols.	£2 a year each.	Church Sunday School & Infant School of Crewkerne.	Annually at Christmas.	Rev. Dr. Penny, Wm. Sparks, & John Sparks.
Jane Hawksley, 9th Sep. 1837.	£352 11s. 4d, 3 per cent. consols.	Dividends towards the support of	Poor persons in Chubb's almshouse.	Annually on Christmas Eve.	Wm. Sparks, Isaac Sparks, & John Sparks.
James Hawksley, 25th May, 1845.	£48 19s. 9d., 3 per cent. consols.	The like.	Poor persons of Crewkerne above 70 years of age.	Annually on 6th January.	Isaac Jennings Sparks & John Sparks.

been greatly enlarged and improved within the last ten years. The school is one of the most ancient in the kingdom, there being not more than ten of an older foundation than 1499. Its founder, John Combe, was a native of Crewkerne, and for many years precentor of Exeter Cathedral. [1] The school was endowed by its founder, and by subsequent benefactors, with lands and houses at Crewkerne, Merriott, Haselbury, Sturminster Marshall, Maiden Newton, Pillesdon, and other places, producing an annual income of about £300. The original grant appears to have consisted of 'the lands and inheritance of one John Combe, clerk, situated at Crewkerne, Combe St. Reigne, and Merriott. At Combe St. Reigne' [2] (we quote from a speech of the Rev. Dr. Penny, at the School Meeting in 1851)—'there was a religious house, probably connected with the Abbey of Ford, and after John Combe had been elevated to the office

veyed to the trustees.'—['*Commissioners' Report*.'] The inscription over a doorway on the south side of the school-house, is as follows:—'Memoriæ sacrum Mri. Johannis Combe, quondam Præcentoris Eccles. Cathedral Exon. qui Scholam hanc Grammaticæ fundavit anno 1499, et Mri. Gul. Oualii, olim Rectoris Eccles. Shepton Bechamiæ beneficentissimi Scholæ hujus Patroni posuit R. Cossins, 1701. "Venite, filii, obedite mihi, timorem Domini ego vos docebo." '

[1] The Rev. Dr. Oliver, of Exeter, in a polite reply to our inquiries, says:—'There is no doubt that John Combe died early in 1499. His initials are still to be seen on the beautiful chimney piece which he erected in the hall of the precentor's house, in the Close at Exeter. But I cannot trace his pedigree.'

[2] 'Westward of Crewkerne, and between that town and Chard, is a hill called Rana Hill, on which was a chapel dedicated to St. Reyn, which contained her bones.'—*Collinson*.

of precentor, he conceived that the best way in which
he could benefit his native town and promote the
glory of God among its inhabitants, would be by
founding a free Grammar School there, to be taught
by " one honest and discreet learned person, to be
appointed by the feoffees."   The name of Combe
appears from time to time among the feoffees, and at
an annual meeting held on the 20th of January,
1719, it is recorded that a Mr. John Combe, of
Combe (a descendant from the founder of the said
school), was appointed master.'

Attached to the school are four exhibitions founded
by the Rev. W. Ouseley, of Shepton Beauchamp, in
1625, of five pounds per annum, confined to free
boys; and three exhibitions of twenty-five pounds a
year, tenable for four years, founded in 1847 by
T. Hoskins, Esq. (the warden), the late Lord Wynford, [1] and the feoffees of the school. Two of these
are confined to boys proceeding to the Universities,
and one is further extended to the learned pro-
fessions.

The school is now in a very flourishing state, having a large number of boarders in addition to the
free-scholars. It is under the very efficient management of the Rev. C. Penny, D.D., Rector of Chaff-
combe and Domestic Chaplain to Earl Poulett. He
is assisted by three other masters, one of whom is also

[1] Mr. Justice Best (afterwards Lord Wynford) was educated at the
Crewkerne Grammar School under the late Dr. Ashe.

in Holy Orders. Upon the exclusively *classical* basis which was once the sole standard of literary attainments, the Rev. Dr., aware of the far different requirements of an altered age, has engrafted a complete system of modern education, including the mathematics and the modern languages,—the latter being taught by a foreign resident professor.

A few years since, a seal, of which we give an engraving, was found appended to a very old document

relating to the school. Some curiosity about this seal was excited at the time of its discovery, and it was at first supposed to have been the ancient arms of the town. The design, however, is clearly not an armorial ensign but simply a device, which, together with the legend, appears to have been adopted at an early period. Instances of this nature frequently occur in seals belonging to corporations to which arms have never been assigned, in their corporate capacity, for the institutions entrusted to their care. [1]

----

[1] We are indebted for a very courteous letter from the authorities at the Herald's College, to whom we have submitted the seal in question.

Our account of this school has been intentionally minute in order to convey some idea of the great advantages enjoyed by the town in the possession of such an establishment—an establishment at which that greatest of all earthly blessings, a first-rate education may be obtained, and at the same time a field may be presented, through the exhibitions, in which a diligent and clever youth may find a path to the highest social distinction.

We have devoted considerable attention to Crewkerne, because we regard it as an angling station for the upper part of the Axe, which washes, as we have said before, the southernmost extremity of the parish, about three miles from the town. A little miscellaneous information will conclude this account:—Few persons, perhaps, are aware that the father of the well-known Thomas Paine (author of ' *The Rights of Man*,' &c.), was born in Crewkerne, and buried, April 16, 1749, at Cheddington, of which place his wife, the mother of the individual referred to, is presumed to have been a native. The elder Paine was a staymaker, and lived for many years at Thetford, in Norfolk, where his son was born. [1]

Crewkerne, we should have stated before, possesses some extensive manufactories of sailcloth, twines, girth web, and horse-hair seating, the different pro-

[1] From memoranda by J. Bellamy, Esq., of Guernsey, kindly presented to the writer, along with other interesting documents relating to the locality.

prietors of which are Mr. Matthews, Mr. Bird, and Mr. Rowe. The first three articles are also extensively manufactured in some of the neighbouring villages, particularly at Chinnock and Merriott, by the Messrs. Hayward, whose establishment is very extensive; at North Perrott, by Mr. Smith;[1] and at Haselbury, by Mr. Pitt and others. These manufactories afford employment to a very considerable part of the laboring population of the locality.

[1] At North Perrott, also, there has lately been introduced by Mr. Smith a new manufacture of fancy twine of a peculiar and beautiful description—gold and silver wire being interwoven with the threads.

CHAPTER V.

WE are up, Piscator, before the sun, this 'fine, fresh, May morning,' and really there is no trifling satisfaction in turning one's back upon 'the din of towns'— in leaving man and his habitations for a time, with all the cares, and strivings, and trumpery conventionalities of what is called '*civilization*,' for the freedom of the verdant meads, by 'babbling brooks,' amid the poetry and balm of nature!

Notwithstanding that the supper, last night, was unexceptionable—that the punch was like the nectar of the gods—that the cigars were veritable wafters away of care—that our cozy evening's gossip was not perhaps uninteresting—and that the bed was an irresistible inviter of repose, 'the sheets smelling of lavender,' and so forth, as father Izaac hath it;— notwithstanding all these fascinations, we boldly repeat that there is a satisfaction in being up with the lark and in leaving them behind us, while we seek

the delightful little stream away in the meadows,
where man intrudeth seldom, and where the only
sounds are the sounds of nature,—the music of the
birds, the sighing of the breeze, the rippling of the
stream, and the bleating of the sheep, borne down,
like the voice of Æolus, from the hills. What a
relief from the cares and anxieties of a life which is
made by many such a life as that of the fabled Ixion
at his eternal wheel, or Sisyphus with his ever-rolling
stone;—the life, old friend, which thousands are
content to follow, without a thought or wish beyond
it;—forgetting that

> 'To study God, God's student, man, was made
> To read him as in nature's text conveyed;
> Not as in heaven, but as he did descend
> To earth, his easier book, where, to suspend
> And save his miracles, each little flower,
> And lesser fly, shows his familiar power.' [1]

Everything around us, as we quit the slumbering
town and stride into the fields which lead by Hewish
to the Axe, inspires us with joy and admiration.
How light and springy are our steps! They are as
the steps of earliest youth. How exhilarated are we
by the breath of morning! This elasticity of step
and buoyancy of soul could be produced by such an
influence alone. Around and within us, friend, is the
secret of our inspiration. And how, indeed, should
it be otherwise, when the pulse of nature beats so

[1] Sir William Davenant.

audibly, in the fullness of perennial youth, and at a time of beauty and of joy ?   'For lo! the winter is past, the rain is over and gone, the flowers appear on the earth, the time of the singing of birds is come, and the voice of the turtle is heard in the land.'

High up 'in ether' is a speck, almost invisible in the grey of morning.   But it poureth down a flood of melody which seems to fill the whole expanse of atmosphere.   That tiny throat is warbling nature's music most delightfully.   Aroused by the first flush of dawn, while 'morning trembled o'er the sky,' the little avial chorister went up 'at heaven's gate' to pay its glorious tribute.   The thrush in yonder elm was awakened by the melody, and at once poured forth its flute-like lay.   The cuckoo, 'harbinger of spring,' proclaimed, in yonder copse, his welcome presence.   A hundred feathered throats soon formed a matchless chorus, and the early sun-beams, twinkling in the dew-drops, now awake a countless host of animated things, which also tune, in various notes, their Almighty Maker's praise.

What human heart can be insensible to sounds like these?   Who can but feel as Walton felt, when he exclaimed :—'Lord, what music hast thou not provided for thy saints in heaven, when thou affordest bad men such music upon earth !'   Who can but bring to mind the poet's charming lines, trilled forth so musically thus :—

'Beautiful creatures of freedom and light,
  Oh! where is the eye that groweth not bright
  As it watches you trimming your soft, glossy coats,
  Swelling your bosoms and ruffling your throats?
  Oh! I would not ask, as the old ditties sing,
  To be "happy as sand-boy," or "happy as king;"
  For the joy is more blissful that bids me declare,
  "I'm as happy as all the wild birds in the air."
  I will tell them to find me a grave, when I die,
  Where no marble will shut out the glorious sky;
  Let them give me a tomb where the daisy will bloom,
  Where the moon will shine down, and the leveret pass by;
  But be sure there's a tree stretching out, high and wide,
  Where the linnet, the thrush, and the woodlark may hide;
  For the truest and purest of requiems heard,
  Is the eloquent hymn of the beautiful Bird.' [1]

And the influences which we have enumerated are but a few of those in operation on a lovely morning such as this. No one can help finding who will only condescend to seek for them. No one who believes that man was formed not wholly for the grovellings of to-day, can fail to take them home and profit by them. How many thousands know as well as we, old friend, that a day passed rationally among the charms of nature will greatly rub the rust of life away, and fit us better for our daily duties! How many thousands, 'city pent,' may justly envy our delightful ramble;—poor pining souls!

Why you have leaped that style amazingly, old friend! The influences of Morning are in active operation, doubtlessly. The anticipation of our future wanderings, 'by mazy burn in flow'ry brae,' is

[1] Eliza Cook.

evidently of a most inspiring nature.　Else why that
rivaling of the avial choir—that hearty and not un-
melodious outburst?—

> 'I in these flowery meads would be;—
> These crystal streams should solace me;
> To whose harmonious bubbling noise
> I with my angle would rejoice.'

And as heartily, old friend, do we adopt the sentiment and *encore* the strain.　But let us have a little
sober chat, for we are passing objects which deserve
it:—That hamlet at our right, among the fields,
which is sending up its early smoke and beginning so
determinedly the business of the day, as you witness
in the dairy operations there, is Hewish, friend.　The
trickling streamlet which meanders through these
'flowery meads,' about which you sang just now, is
fitly named therefrom. [1]　Upon the hills at our left is
Henley Farm, the place where Mr. Weeks was murdered. [2]　We can hardly see the house from this
position, for we now are getting rapidly *behind* the

---

[1]　The Hewish Brook rises on Coombe Farm, and falls into the Axe at
Clapton Bridge.　It is, speaking generally, too small for the fly, but in one
or two of the meadows near its mouth a few trout may sometimes be
caught, and it is invaluable as a breeding stream.

[2]　See page 93.　The name *Henley* is derived from the British *Hen*,
old, and Saxon *Leag*, a field or pasture.　Henley was formerly so considerable as to give its name to an eminent family of large possessions in
Somerset, Dorset, and Devon.　Robert Henley was sheriff of Somersetshire in 1612, and his grandson, Robert, was created a baronet June 30,
1660.　The title is now extinct.　Anthony Henley, Esq., 'that friend and
ornament to music, poetry, and jovial society in the reign of Queen Anne,'
was a member of this family.　See *Collinson*.

hill on which it stands; but from most points in the neighbourhood of Crewkerne it is a conspicuous and pleasing object. Its steep old gables, and its towering chimneys, stand picturesquely up against the sky; and the few large trees surrounding it enhance materially its fine effect. [1] The turnpike road to Lyme, along which we trudged last evening, on our way from Clapton, lies between us and the farm. [2] The fields through which we now are passing will soon enable us to regain this road at the turnpike which we near so rapidly. This turnpike is within a mile of Clapton. [3] * * * * *

[1] At *Coniger Hill*, on Henley farm, [see Note at page 79 for the definition of a word of apparently similar origin] are the remains of a small earthwork, of probably Roman construction. Innumerable musket bullets are found in a sandpit on its south side, and are also frequently turned up by the plough in the adjoining fields. They are of iron, in an almost totally oxydised state. Human bones have also at different times been dug up in the same places. It may be permitted, therefore, to hazard the conjecture, that a skirmish might have taken place there—perhaps during the civil war in the reign of Charles I.—and that one of the contending parties availed themselves of the ancient fort. But this is pure conjecture, and we leave the reader to account for the *facts* in any other way he pleases.

[2] The four cross way about a mile from Crewkerne, on this road, is distinguished by the name of 'Maiden Beech Tree,' from a magnificent old tree which formerly stood in the north-west corner of a field abutting on the main road. This tree, a perfect ornament to the neighbourhood, was blown down during the night of December 8, 1827. The late Miss Taylor, of Crewkerne, who was owner of the field, with extreme good taste, caused its place to be supplied by a small plantation of beeches on the spot which the old tree had occupied. Her object was to perpetuate a name which had been known for ages, and to provide for future generations a similar ornament to that which their forefathers had admired so greatly. *From a Communication by Mr. Moss, of Crewkerne.*

[3] There is a little inn at Clapton which affords a tolerable glass of ale or cider, as well as accommodation for a horse.

But we have already passed through the hamlet,
and have arrived at the ' lower mill,' with the bridge a
few yards beyond us.　A leap over the hedge opposite, and we find ourselves again in the lovely
meadows through which the Axe meanders.　And
while we hastily arrange our tackle, let us also arrange our programme of the day's proceedings :—
A good two hours' fishing, friend, will bring us
breakfast time.　Our wallet will supply the ' needful.'
Two hours more—for we must fish rapidly over this
part of the stream, so much remains to be explored
below,—will find us at Winsham, a village three
miles down from Clapton, about which we must
discourse awhile.　Knap Inn, a mile still lower down,
will tempt us to a homely dinner ; and while we are
discussing that, we must find time for antiquarian
lore, with which, indeed, we must beguile our *saunterings*, as we cannot stop to linger over every stickle,
or over every fish that we may land.　We must leave
abundance for the reader's imagination to supply.
The outline which we shall attempt to draw of that
which relates to our actual piscatorial tracings and
exploits, must, to a great extent, be filled in by himself.　A tithe alone of the delights and triumphs of
an angler's day, on such a stream, could hardly be
contained within a goodly tome ; and we have many
days, and many things besides, to talk about.　A
pleasant saunter down the meads from Knap, will
bring us, in ' the shades of evening,' to Axminster,

CLAPTON BRIDGE.—LOOKING UP THE STREAM.

our sleeping place, by far the most important angling station on the stream. A lengthened ramble, truly, friend, the distance by the stream, from Clapton, being more than twenty miles. We will do our best, however, to beguile the way. At Axminster we have some time to linger, for abundant are its notabilities and a very Eden is its lovely neighbourhood.

As yet, however, we are not off from Clapton Bridge. Your tackle, friend, is quickly ready, for you have not been inactive while we sketched our day's proceedings. But, man, you are beside yourself! The stream, you say, exceedeth all your expectations;—its crystal waters ripple on their pebbly bed in a series of delightful pools and stickles [1] to the sea. It is, in truth, a perfect trout-stream. These meadows, also, seem to you an angler's paradise! The dew drops sparkle on the velvet turf like ten thousand diamonds in an emerald field. The balmy breeze, which curls the ranges, is redolent of spring, and augurs sport by and by, when the clouds arise, and when a gentle shower patters on the new born leaves. And so you rapturously launch forth—too incoherently, though, to be melodious:—

> 'Again the merry month of May
> Has made our hills and valleys gay;
> The birds rejoice in leafy bowers,
> The bees hum round the breathing flowers;
> Blythe Morning lifts his rosy eye,
> And Evening's tears are tears of joy.'—*Burns.*

[1] See page 2.

Y

Hush! There is a goodly trout under the opposite bank of this stickle below the bridge! He is just turned out for breakfast, and the grannams which the morning's sun is bringing into life,[1] begin to flit about the alders temptingly. There! he rose—slowly and with dignity, like a sultan at his sherbet. Just wet your line above, and show him your red palmer. Now steady, we beseech thee, friend! He moved;— but try again. Well done! you struck to admiration, and the hook is fast enough, for he keeps deeply in the water, 'indignant of the guile'—a certain indication of his goodly size. He leaves to smaller fry ignoble flouncings at the surface. Be careful, now, while giving him the spring of your rod. A good manœuvre, of a verity! He rushes madly, and your line is whizzing from the reel. Wind up,—wind up! But look! Give *to* him, as he leaps above the surface. Like a foe who finds that he has fought his fight, and found resistance further to be vain, he turns upon his side and yields. What a splendid object as he rests upon the greensward, with which his golden, olive, pink, and silver tints so exquisitely harmonize! But basket him, old friend, and try again. He is at least a pound.[2] There is hardly a stickle hence to

[1] For a list of flies, not only for the Axe but for every other stream in the three kingdoms, see the '*Vade Mecum of Fly-fishing for Trout,*' published by Messrs. Longman and Co.

[2] It is not often that a trout of this weight is taken in the Axe. The average weight is about six ounces, but even *small* fish are extremely vigorous, and afford exciting 'play.' In the upper parts of the stream

Winsham (and the limit might be greatly extended) in which you will not move a fish. As you will soon find, however, a considerable part of the stream above and below Bere Chapel is unfishable, on account of the overhanging alders. But your fly has suffered in the struggle. Select another, friend,—a neat blue dun— and while you do so let us say a word or two about Bere Chapel. It is a farm house, picturesquely situated, as you will perceive when we reach it, upon the left bank of the river, and at about mid-distance between Clapton and Winsham. It is surrounded by lovely woods, some of which slope to the water's edge and add materially to the beauty and variety of the river scenery. Bere Chapel was doubtless originally appropriated to a religious purpose, as some of its old walls, as well as its name, attest; but we have been unsuccessful in our researches for its history. It was very probably connected with the neighbouring Abbey of Ford, as the farm or rather manor is now tithe free,[1] and its name

the trout are generally rather larger than those below Axminster, where, however, the frequent capture of salmon peal, and occasionally that of salmon, much more than makes amends for the somewhat smaller trout and shorter supply of them.

[1] 'Spiritual persons or corporations,' says Blackstone, 'as Monasteries, Abbots, Bishops, and the like, were always capable of having their lands totally discharged of tithes by various ways; as, first, by real composition; second, by the Pope's Bull of exemption; third, by unity of possession,— as when the rectory of a parish and lands in the same parish both belonged to a religious house, those lands were discharged of tithes by this unity of possession; fourth, by prescription,—having never been liable to tithes, by being always in spiritual hands; fifth, by virtue of their order,—

might have been derived from that of the family of
De La Beere, which had a mansion at Beerhall, an
isolated part of the Parish of Axminster, and within
a short distance of Bere Chapel. It is now the property of Lord Portman, of Bryanstone House, Dorset.

But you are ready to resume. Ah! a small one,
friend, and quite unbasketable. He is under six
inches in length, and no true sportsman could think
of retaining such a 'worthless prize.' [1] We shall
meet with six or eight good 'keepable' fish by the
time we reach our halting-place, for the beauty of the
stream is here almost equalled by its prolificacy.

as the Knights Templars, Cistercians, and others, whose lands were
privileged by the Pope with a discharge of tithes. Though, upon the
dissolution of Abbeys by Henry VIII, most of these exemptions from
tithes would have fallen with them, and the lands become titheable again,
had they not been supported and upheld by the Statute 31, Henry VIII,
c. 13., which enacts that all persons who should come to the possession of
the lands of any Abbey then dissolved, should hold them free and discharged of tithes in as large and ample a manner as the Abbeys themselves
formerly held them.' To this one of the editors of Blackstone has
annoted:—'This possession is peculiar to that statute, and therefore all
the lands belonging to the lesser Monasteries, dissolved by the 27 Henry
VIII, cap 28, are now liable to pay tithes.' 'From this original,' continues Blackstone, 'have sprung all the lands which, being in lay hands,
do at present claim to be tithe free; for if a man can shew his lands to
have been such Abbey lands, and also immemorially discharged of tithes
by any of the means above mentioned, this is now a good prescription
de non decimando. But he must shew both these requisites; for Abbey
lands, without a special ground of discharge, are not discharged, of course;
neither will any prescription *de non decimando* avail in total discharge of
tithes, unless it relates to such Abbey lands.'

[1] It is a pity that so many of those who fancy themselves anglers do
not observe more rigidly the practice of returning small fish to the water.
'All's the fish that come to the hook' is too often the maxim of those
who ought to know better.

But our 'discoursing' must not be forgotten :—
Wayford, friend, is the name of the village at our
right, upon the hill-side, so pleasantly situated among
the gardens and the orchards. [1] The parish of Wayford comprises about 1150 acres, and its population
is 238. It is in the hundred of Crewkerne, [2] the
union of Chard, and the western division of the county
of Somerset. The history of the little place is quickly
told. In Domesday Book it is not mentioned, for at
the time of the compilation of that volume it was
included in the parish of Crewkerne ; [3] and we are
not aware of its association with any historical event
sufficiently important to give it a conspicuous place
in subsequent writings.

The living is a rectory, valued in the King's Books
at £5 1s. 5½d. The tithes are commuted at £235,
out of which £100 a year is paid to the lay impropriator, T. Hussey, Esq., who owns the great tithes. [4]
The Rev. Henry Caddell is the present incumbent.

The Church is a plain old building in the form of
a parallelogram, 69 feet long by 16 feet wide. It

[1] See pages 14 and 15.

[2] See page 107.

[3] ' I surmise that both Wayford and Seaborough were once Chapelries
of Crewkerne; for, till within a few years back, it was the custom, on Easter
Sunday, to place the keys of both churches upon the communion table of
Crewkerne church, and at the same time to pay sixpence for each parish—
in token, I suppose, of fealty.' *Communicated by the Rev. H. Caddell.*

[4] 'This annual payment of £100 would appear to confirm the supposi-
tion of Wayford's having formerly been a Chapelry of Crewkerne. When
it was made a separate parish, the tithes of a certain portion of the lands

consists of a nave and chancel, with a turret at the west end, containing two bells, and a porch, with stone seats, on the south side. [1]

The church is lighted by lancet windows, some of which are furnished with foliated head mouldings. These characteristics point to the thirteenth century as the date at which the church was in all probability erected. [2] The chancel fell down in 1846, and was rebuilt at the expense of Mr. Caddell. Under a cumbrous gallery, erected in 1800, across the west end of the church, and effectually concealing a pretty double lancet window, is placed the font, which is very large and of octagonal shape. At the same end of the church is also a clock, unfurnished with a dial, but striking on the turret bells. The pulpit and reading desk are in the chancel. There are a few monuments to some members of the Pinney family, one of whom, John Frederick Pinney, of Bettiscombe,

were still retained for Crewkerne, though the lands were included within the newly constituted parish.' *Ibid.*

[1] The Porch was formerly not confined in use to the protection of the door from the weather, nor was it regarded as a mere ornamental appendage only; but it was considered the appropriate place, and employed accordingly, for the performance of the early parts of the services of Baptism, Matrimony, and the Churching of women. A stoup, or basin for holy water, was frequently erected on the right hand side of the entrance; and large porches sometimes contained a confessional. Before the practice of interment in churches was permitted, it was customary to bury persons of rank, and of eminent sanctity, in the porch; and by the Canons of King Edgar it was distinctly ordered that the privilege should be allowed to such persons only.

[2] See page 66.

Esq., was member of parliament for Bridport, and died in 1762.

Dawbeny Turbervile, of New Sarum, Esq., bequeathed, in 1695, £100 to the second poor of Wayford. The money was invested in the purchase of twelve acres of land at Mosterton, the rent of which is distributed annually by the rector and churchwardens. Fifty shillings a year are paid out of Ashcombe estate for the instruction of eight poor children of the parish. The donor of this charity was Mrs. Elizabeth Bragge, of Sadborough, July 17th, 1719.

Very healthy and pleasant is the situation of this retired little village. It commands extensive views of the valley of the Axe, beyond which the eye ranges among the hills of Dorset on the one side, and far away into Somerset and Devon on the other. Looking down, as the spectator does, upon the woods in the vicinity of Ford Abbey, at the distance of about two miles and a half, and tracing the gradually widening stream as it glistens along its tortuous course, through luxuriant meads and amid a profusion of scattered trees, ' dropped lavishly, in nature's careless haste,' a scene is presented to his admiration to equal which he must journey far away from the limpid waters of the Axe. But beautiful though it be, it is greatly inferior to many other valley-peeps which we hope to enjoy as we ramble further down. The view of Wayford itself, from the meadows beneath, is delightful also. The picturesque old cottages among their blooming gardens,—the old rectory house, with its veranda festooned with the honeysuckle and the rose—and the stately manor house, with its graceful chimneys, standing crowningly over all—form a pleasing picture for the eye to gaze upon.[1] * * * * * * *

Four brace and a half of 'spankers,' have you, friend, and several 'losses' counting nothing. . . No, no, Piscator,—not upon the grass, although you say the dews have now been 'stolen away' by the day-god, there, 'Apollo!' That rail will suit us better for a lounging-place. Besides, we thence can contemplate Bere Chapel, just before us on the little eminence, and can also feast our eyes upon the lovely meadow scenery for which old England is unequalled in the world. The woods around us, too, are exquisite. That little dell here on our right, which opens from the hill side, seems a perfect fairy's paradise, where Oberon and Titania might fitly hold their revels in the moonlight, and Puck perform his gambols amid the cowslips and the blue bells.

What hast thou in that flask? Not a 'gurgle of the glenlivet' which poor old charming Christopher[2]

---

[1] The manor house, a fine old building in the Tudor style, has long been appropriated to the purposes of a farm.

[2] 'Christopher North' (Professor Wilson), for many years the presiding genius of Blackwood's Magazine, and author of the matchless papers on Angling for which that publication was so long renowned. The Professor still lives,—a mere wreck, alas! of his more youthful days, when

delighted in,—no ' dew of the mountain,' even. But, of a verity, it is a glorious distillation—meet beverage on such a morning. Our service to thee, friend! May thy toils be profitable and thy troubles few— thy wanderings pleasant in the valley of life, as well as in the valley of the Axe. Our service to thee. * * * There! another sandwich, and we will ' beguile thine ear ' with all we know of Winsham, as we fish our way towards that rural spot :—

Winsham is a very pleasantly situated village, on the right bank of the river, in the county of Somerset, the union of Chard (from which town it is distant about five miles),[1] and the electoral division of West Somerset, its polling place being Ilminster. The parish comprises 2958 acres, and the number of its inhabitants is 1062, fifty-eight being registered county voters. It is divided into two tithings, namely, Winsham tithing, comprising the village of Winsham and the hamlets of Purtington and Amerham; and Street[2] and Leigh tithing, comprising the rest of the parish. The village is large, consisting of three streets of considerable length—the principal street,

he was as potent with the pen, in the wide range of learning which distinguished him, as he was beloved for his genial qualities of heart, and acknowledged to be the best and most enthusiastic angler in Scotland.

[1] It is also about the same distance from Crewkerne.

[2] So called from the ancient fosse-way, which passed directly through it. See pages 10 and 13. The presence of the Romans in this immediate locality has been indicated by the Roman coins and other articles which have been found there at different times. 'In 1684,' says Collinson, 'an urn containing many Roman coins was found betwixt Street and Winsham.'

leading up from the river, being wide and straight. Many of the houses are newly built, the place having at different times, of late years, suffered very severely from fires. It has more the appearance of a decayed town than that of a rural village; and, in truth, its importance was formerly much greater than at present. In common with many other places in this part of the country, it was the seat of a considerable manufactory of the broad and narrow cloth for which the West of England was unrivalled before the application of steam to machinery transferred so large a portion of the trade to the north. No inconsiderable amount, however, of its former importance still exists at Winsham in the factories at Gay's Mill and Winsham Bridge—the former belonging to Mr. Chick and the latter to Mr. Bennett. [1]

The manor of Winsham, in the Saxon times, was originally vested in the church of Wells; but it appears that, ' by some sinister practice or other, it was alienated from it, and fell into the hands of one Elsi.' Bishop Giso, however, compelled him to restore it to its proper owners, and at the Conquest it was thus surveyed :—

[1] The introduction of the woollen manufacture into the West of England, and also into the West Riding of Yorkshire, took place about the year 1336, during the reign of Edward III. At Exeter, and many other towns of Devonshire, it was long the staple trade; but of late years it has become gradually attracted to the neighbourhood of the coal fields, and the principal seats of the manufacture in the west are now Trowbridge, Bradford, Stroud, and Frome. The establishment of Mr. Boon, at Uplyme, is the most extensive in this immediate neighbourhood.

'Osmund holds of the bishop, *Winesham*. Elsi held it in the time of King Edward, and gelded for ten hides. The arable is sixteen carucates. Thereof in demesne are four hides, and there are three carucates, and twelve servants, and fifty villains, with nine ploughs. There are two mills of twenty shillings rent, and six acres of meadow. Wood half a mile long, and a furlong and a half broad. It was worth six pounds, now ten pounds.

'Robert holds of William, *Lege*. Sirewald held it in the time of King Edward, and gelded for three hides. The arable is forty carucates. In demesne is one carucate, with one servant, and five villains, and two cottagers, and eight acres of meadow. Wood two furlongs long, and one furlong broad. It was formerly worth thirty shillings, now twenty shillings.

'Roger holds of William, *Strate*. Huscarl and Almar held it in the time of King Edward, and gelded for one hide and a half. The arable is two carucates. There are three villains, and one cottager with one plough, and one acre and a half of meadow. Pasture five furlongs long, and two furlongs broad. It was and is worth fifteen shillings.' [1]

The Conqueror presented the manor of Street and Leigh to his countryman, William De Mohun, or Moion, who had accompanied him from Normandy and distinguished himself greatly at the battle of

[1] See pages 44, 90, 91, and 116.

Hastings. [1]   These manors have long been in the possession of the Henley family, of Leigh, the present owner being Cornish Henley, Esq. Leigh House, the residence of this gentleman, is about half a mile from Ford Abbey, on the opposite side of the river. It is a fine old Elizabethan residence, delightfully situated on the hill-side, overlooking the river and the buildings and grounds of the abbey. The family seat was formerly on their property at Colway, near Lyme Regis. It was battered in the civil wars, when the family removed to the more secluded retreat of Leigh, and the mansion at Colway fell into decay. [2] As a proof of the terror of those 'troublesome times,' and of the anxiety about the security of property, may be mentioned the circumstance of finding, at subsequent periods, considerable sums of money in the gardens and other parts of the premises at Leigh. Mr. Bonfield, the obliging host of the Knap Inn, [3] whose larder we have proposed to attack, some

[1] No less than fifty-five manors, in the County of Somerset alone, were bestowed upon this distinguished personage, who fixed his residence at Dunster Castle, which he held of the crown by the service of forty Knights' fees and a half. [see page 91.] His posterity flourished for many generations—possessed of enormous influence and wealth. The family became extinct, in the male line, on November 15, 1712, when Charles Baron Mohun, of Oakhampton, was killed in a duel with the Duke of Hamilton, who also perished at the same time.—See an account of this powerful family in Mr. Davidson's 'History of Newenham Abbey.' See, also, our account of this Abbey in a subsequent page.

[2] See 'Roberts's History of Lyme.'

[3] The word *Knap* signifies, in the West of England, a little mound or eminence. The name of this snug little hostelrie, which was built about

two hours hence, Piscator,—will relate to us the story of his own success in discovering, beneath a laburnum tree in the garden, about thirty years ago, nearly three hundred gold pieces of the reign of Charles I; and also that of his still more interesting discovery, in the same garden, of a very ancient silver coin, which, as he positively avers, bore the image and superscription of Edward the Black Prince. [1]

The manor of Winsham [2] formed part of the endowment of the provostship of Wells; [3] and when that office was abolished, it was annexed to the deanery of Wells, and has so continued to the present day. [4]

twenty-two years since, was thus undoubtedly derived from the situation of the building. An inn is known to have occupied the same spot for at least a century.

[1] To the honor of the individual be it annoted, that the whole of the coins, with the exception of two or three of those of Charles I, with which he was presented, were immediately handed by Mr. Bonfield to the owner of the property in which they were found.

[2] A large estate in the parish belonged to the Abbey of Ford. It was valued, in 1293, at £22 11s. 8d.

[3] The business of the Provost was to take care and keep an account of the goods and chattels which were possessed in common by the canons.— *Collinson.*

[4] A.D., 1234, Joceline, bishop of Bath, having finished the ordination of the provostship in the cathedral of Wells, endowed that office with the manor and rectory of Combe St. Nicholas, as also with the manor and rectory of Winsham, and the rectory of Chard and Wellington, charged with the payment of the salaries of *the fifteen Combe prebendaries*, to each £6 13s. 4d. With reference to Winsham, it was decreed that he [the provost] shall leave to his successors 'the demesnes in a proper state of cultivation, without any fixed number of acres or measure: and of stock sixteen oxen, the price of each ox three shillings and sixpence; and one plough-horse, value three shillings; six sows and a boar, the price of all

A charter of free-warren was granted to it by King
Edward III. [1]

The church is situated about the centre of the
principal street. It is an interesting ancient structure,
in different styles, bearing evidence of the different
periods of its erection. Sufficiently conspicuous are
the tasteless patchings and unskilful repairs of modern
times. It is built of flint, with Ham stone dressings, [2]
and consists of a nave and chancel, with a tower rising
between them. Its total length is ninety-four feet.
The breadth of the chancel is seventeen and a half

four shillings; ewes and rams, in all one hundred and thirty two, the
price of each ewe or ram five-pence; and fifty-three lambs, the value of each
two-pence halfpenny. At Chard he shall leave the demesnes tillaged,
without number or measure, in the same manner as at Winsham, and the
fallow without any stock.' &c., &c.—Collinson's '*History of Somerset.*'

[1] Free-warren was a franchise granted, under the feudal system, for
the preservation of ' beasts and fowls of warren.' The beasts were hares,
conies, and roes; the fowls were either *campestres*, as partridges, rails, and
quails; or *sylvestres*, as woodcocks and pheasants; or *aquatiles*, as mallards
and herons. ' All these,' says Blackstone, ' being *feræ naturæ*, every one
had a *natural* right to kill as he could; but upon the introduction of the
forest laws, at the Norman Conquest, these animals being looked upon as
royal game, and the sole property of our savage monarchs, this franchise
of free-warren was invented to protect them, by giving the grantee a sole
and exclusive power of killing such game, so far as his warren extended,
on condition of his preventing other persons. A man therefore that had
the franchise of warren, was in reality no more than a royal gamekeeper;
but no man, not even a Lord of a Manor, could by common law justify
sporting on another's soil, or even on his own, unless he had the liberty of
free-warren. This franchise is almost fallen into disregard since the new
statutes for preserving the game, the name being now chiefly preserved
in grounds set apart for the breeding of hares and rabbits.'—Blackstone's
' *Commentaries.*'

[2] See page 34.

feet, and that of the nave twenty-three and a half feet. It has a porch on the south side, within which is an antique box for alms, placed upon a pedestal also of wood.[1] The earliest part of the church, as usual, is the chancel,[2] in which two of its five windows are lancets,[3] which, together with other indications of the Early English style, point to the thirteenth century, as the date of its erection. A miserable proof of the poverty of modern architecture is furnished by the east window, a description of which may be advantageously omitted. The nave is lighted by two principal windows on each side. They resemble the nave-windows of Axminster church, and, like them, their cusps and foliations have been chopped away, 'for the convenience, probably,' as Mr. Davidson humorously suggests, 'of the parish glazier.' Some of the other windows of the church are Perpendicular, and the rest, including a small square one in the dairy-house style, need not be more particularly referred to, with the exception of the west window, which is a chaste little specimen of the Decorated style.[4] What was

[1] By the canons of 1603 (James I.) a poor's box was ordered to be placed in every church—that receptacle for the unostentatious charity of the affluent having then disappeared from several churches. We need hardly state that in the present day such a relic of the 'benighted' past is very rarely to be stumbled upon.

[2] See page 143.

[3] See page 66.

[4] See our account of Axminster Church.

originally a door-way underneath this window, has been metamorphosed, by some versatile genius, into a Perpendicular *window*, with spandrils. [1]

The rood screen, of which a considerable portion remains, forms a very interesting feature of the interior of this church. It is of oak, very beautifully carved in the Perpendicular style. The remains of the rood itself (or rather of a painting which answered to the rood) may also still be seen in what is now a room in the under part of the tower in which the bells are rung. This room was formed, some years ago, by the erection of a floor across the tower, at the spring of the arches by which it is supported—thus entirely cutting off the view of the arches themselves from the floor of the church, where the bells were originally rung. The rood painting is on panel, and without the slightest pretensions to artistic merit. It comprises five figures :—the crucified Christ in the centre, the two Maries (or perhaps Saint Mary and Saint John), and the two thieves. The colors are still fresh and brilliant, notwithstanding that the picture was for years embedded in whitewash. [2]

[1] See page 55.

[2] The rood was an image of Christ upon the cross, with attendant figures, made generally of wood, but in small churches sometimes painted, as in the case of Winsham. The rood was placed in a loft, or gallery, between the nave and chancel. Beneath it was the screen, which divided the chancel from the nave [see page 39], and which was lavishly carved and adorned. Lights were kept burning in the loft, especially on festivals, and at one period the Epistle and Gospel were read from it. Rood lofts do not appear to have been in use in this country before the 14th

What appears to have been the doorway of the stair-case leading to the ancient rood-loft, may still be seen in the south western pier of the tower arches.

The seats in the body of the church are of very old carved oak, exhibiting the *linen pattern* so prevalent during the reign of Henry VIII. The font is octagonal, and very ancient. It is made of Ham stone, *painted to represent marble.* The church is much deformed by an immense gallery which stretches more than half way up the nave, with a second gallery of smaller size above it. The front of the lower gallery is of carved oak, *ornamented* in the centre with a rude painting, between sham organ pipes, of David playing upon the harp. The pulpit and reading desk are at the eastern end of the nave. A curious old black letter copy of the first edition of Fox's Book of Martyrs is chained to a pedestal in the nave. It is beautifully illustrated, for the time,

century, and they were not general until the 15th century. An order for the removal of roods was issued by Elizabeth in 1650. They had previously been removed by order of Edward VI, but were brought back again in the reign of his successor, Queen Mary. Some splendid lofts and screens remain to the present day. Those in the churches of Kingsbury Episcopi, Honiton, Uffculm, Cullompton, and Totnes may be mentioned as instances in this part of the country. At Sherborne, Dorsetshire, is a small sculpture of a rood in stone, inserted in a niche on the outside of one of the walls,— the work of the 12th century. The symbolism of the rood screen—for in ancient times every article in a church was symbolical—was death. The nave signified the Church Militant, the chancel the Church Triumphant. The rood-screen was the line of separation through which was a passage from one to the other, and it therefore 'appropriately supported the image of Him who by His death hath overcome death.'—See '*Handbook of English Ecclesiology,*' '*Glossary of Architecture,*' &c., &c.

AA

and is bound, literally, in boards, which are half an inch thick. In all probability it has occupied its present position since the days of Queen Elizabeth.

The tower, which has a turret at the south west corner, is square, embattled, and furnished with gargoyles. It is lighted in the bell story with four windows of two lights, cusped, and surmounted with a quatrefoil.[1] It contains a clock and five bells. Upon one of the bells is the date 1583, and the great bell bears the following inscription :—

'I to the church the living call,
And to the grave I summon all.'

In the church are monuments to some members of the highly respectable family of Henley, with their arms.[2] The latest monument is to the memory of 'Mary, widow of the late Henry Hoste Henley, Esq., who departed this life November 25th, 1836, aged 75 years.'

Tablets also record the death of some members of the family of Royse (a former vicar); and there is a neat Caen-stone tablet to the memory of the late wife of the Rev. George Ware, the present vicar.

The church is dedicated to Saint Stephen. The living is a vicarage, valued in the King's Books at £14 13s. 4d. The vicarial tithes are commuted for £400, and the rectorial tithes for £200 per annum.

[1] See pages 40 and 51.

[2] Azure, a lion rampant, argent, within a bordure of the second, charged with eight torteaux.

The vicarage house is situated on the south side of the church, and a capacious school room, recently erected, stands on the opposite side.

A small income arising from the rent of a meadow called Kingsfield, abutting on the river, in the parish of Thorncombe, is appropriated to the education of poor children of Winsham.

There is an Independent chapel in the village, erected in 1811.

The hamlet of Purtington lies north from Winsham village, at the distance of about a mile and a half. A brook which rises in this hamlet falls into the Axe at Amerham, on the south,—the other hamlet of Winsham before referred to.[1] It flows through a delightful little comb[2] in which are situated the mansion house and grounds of Lord Bridport. These are in the parish of Cricket Saint Thomas, which, for a short distance, abuts upon the Axe near Ford Abbey. Hence its claim upon our attention, which is increased by the interest which attaches to Lord Bridport's family and domain.

Cricket has received the adjunct Saint Thomas (the patron saint of its church) as a distinction from Cricket Malherbie, a parish in the valley on the northern side of Windwhistle.[3] Cricket St. Thomas

[1] See page 169.

[2] The name given, in the West of England, to a little valley which opens into a larger one.

[3] On the crown of the hill, in a field close to the Windwhistle Inn, was formerly a well, which for ages supplied the inhabitants of the locality with

is a small parish of 860 acres only, and the number of its inhabitants is but 69—a number considerably less than formerly. It is in the hundred of South Petherton and the union of Chard. Anciently it was held of the great barony of Castle Cary by military service.[1] In the 19th year of King Edward I (1290), Richard De Courtevyle held two knights' fees and a half in Cricket of Sir Hugh Lovel, Knight; and in the 2nd year of Edward III (1328), Walter De Rodney was Lord of the manor. Sir Peter Courney, Knight, held it in the 6th year of Henry IV (1405), and in 13th year of the same reign we find that it belonged to Margaret, widow of Sir John St. Hoe, who held it, with the advowson, of Lord St. Maur, as of his manor of Castle Cary. The subsequent owners were Sir William Botreaux, Bart., the Hungerfords, and, in the 31st year of Queen Elizabeth, John Preston. More recently, the property belonged to the Coxes, of Stone Easton, who sold it to the

water. On the day of the great earthquake at Lisbon (November 1, 1755) the spring ceased to flow, and the well has ever since been dry. We were once told by an old man named Chick, that his grandfather, then a boy, was present when the water went away, and that he described it as 'sinking through the bottom like cider through a tunniger.' The view from this hill is truly magnificent—extending entirely across the island, and also over a considerable portion of the county of Somerset northward. In clear weather the English channel at Seaton on the south, and the Bristol Channel near Burnham on the north, can be distinctly seen with the naked eye.

[1] Manors were formerly called Baronies, as they still are called Lordships. See page 92.

Bridport family. The present Lord Bridport is now the sole owner.

The mansion house was erected about sixty years ago, when the old house, which stood about two hundred yards to the north of the present building, was taken down. It occupies a low and sheltered situation, being completely shut in by hills on every side except the south, where the comb opens into the valley of the Axe. It is neatly built of stone, with extensive offices, and is surrounded by beautiful gardens fitted up with hot houses and conservatories. The park is delightfully laid out on the hill-side facing the south and east, and extending into the plain below. It is ornamented with large and beautiful trees of oak, elm, beech, and fir, scattered profusely over the ground; — here forming shady avenues along winding gravel walks, and there disposed into miniature woods in situations which command delightful glimpses of the surrounding country. Those glimpses are chiefly in the direction of the valley of the Axe, at the distant extremity of which are seen the romantic cliffs of Beer and the beautiful Seaton bay. The brook to which we just referred meanders through the park—broken frequently into picturesque little cascades, and imparting to the scene those indescribable charms which are peculiar to running water.

The family of Hood is of historical renown, and it received the title of nobility in reward for the important services to the country which were rendered by two of its members. It sprang originally from Mosterton, where it possessed an estate. The ancient residence of the family in that village is exactly opposite the new church, and is now a beer house. [1] About the middle of the last century, the Rev. Samuel Hood was instituted to the living of Thorncombe. Two of his sons entered the navy at an early age. Both became admirals. One of them was created Viscount Hood, and the other Viscount Bridport. They distinguished themselves in several brilliant engagements, indelibly recorded in the annals of the country which they served so well. Lord Bridport, who was created Viscount in 1794, died in 1814, [2] and was succeeded by his nephew's son, Samuel Hood, the present Viscount Bridport, who on July 3, 1810, had married Charlotte Mary Nelson, only

[1]   See page 65.

[2]   He was buried in Cricket Church, where a large and handsome monument is erected to his memory. Underneath the inscription are his lordship's arms, namely :—Azure, a fret, argent, on a chief, or, three crescents, sable. *Supporters* :—dexter,—Neptune, proper, mantled, vert, supporting with the left arm a trident, and resting the right upon an anchor, or. Sinister,—a sea lion, argent, supporting with the sinister paw an anchor, or. *Motto*, 'Steady.' *Crest* :—a Cornish chough, proper, supporting with the dexter claw an anchor, or. This monument was erected 'by his affectionate and afflicted relict,' Mary Sophia Bridport, who was his Lordship's second wife. She died February 18, 1831, aged 82, and has a monument by the side of her husband's. Her benevolence was extreme, and she is remembered with great respect. A tablet on the other side records the death, in September, 1786, of his Lordship's first wife, Mary, daughter of the Rev. Dr. West, and niece to Lord Viscount Cobham, of Stowe, in Buckinghamshire.

daughter of the Rev. William Earl Nelson, brother of the hero of Trafalgar and of the Nile. A numerous family is the result of this marriage.

The living of Cricket is a rectory, in the Archdeaconry of Taunton. The patron is Lord Bridport, and the present rector is the Rev. C. J. Shawe, of Seaborough. In 1292, the living was valued at three marks and ten shillings, and at the same time an estate in the parish, belonging to the Abbey of Ford, was declared to be worth twenty-one shillings. The living is valued in the King's Books at £9 17s. 6d., and the tithes are commuted for £87 10s. The church is a neat little structure, a few yards north of the mansion-house. It is surrounded by luxuriant laurels, which effectually conceal it from the gaze of the passer by, and impart a peculiar degree of solemnity and retirement to the building and its little grave-yard. The church consists of a nave and chancel, with a south transept appropriated to the use of the Bridport family, and a turret at the west end containing two bells. It has been so greatly and so frequently altered as to render unsatisfactory any attempt to fix the date of its erection from its architectural characteristics, the earliest of which, however, appear to belong to the Second-pointed, or Decorated style of the 14th century.[1] Tradition says, that it was originally only a domestic chapel,

[1] See our account of Axminster Church.

and that the parish church, *at Whitedown*, was accidentally burned. There is some show of probability in this account, for an annual fair is still held at Whitedown, on the hill near Windwhistle, about a mile from the present Church, and fairs were originally held *only in churchyards*. [1]

Besides the monuments which we have already described, there is a very interesting and beautifully executed one of white marble, against the north wall of the chancel, to the memory of the Rev. William Earl Nelson, Duke of Bronte, and father of the present Lady Bridport. It consists of a full-length reclining figure of the Earl, in canonicals, contemplating an ascending angel above, and holding, in one hand, an open book. The countenance is remarkably fine. An inscription sets forth that the Earl was born on April 20, 1757, and died February 28, 1835, and that his remains are deposited in St. Paul's Cathedral by the side of those of his brother, the celebrated Admiral. On the same monument is also recorded the decease of Horatio Nelson, son of Samuel Lord Bridport; of Charlotte Mary, his wife; and of his brother, Horatio Nelson, who was born April 27, 1826, and died January 2, 1832. The monument was erected by the present Lady Bridport.

But we have now fished our way to Winsham bridge, [2] and here we must reel up for awhile. A

---

[1] See page 122.

[2] This is a modern bridge of stone, consisting of only a single arch. Just below it, the Axe receives a tributary from the east, which rises near

walk through the principal street—across the church-yard—and through three or four lovely fields beyond it—will bring us to Knap Inn, about which a few words have been already said.[1]　＊　＊　＊　＊

There! the village is quickly passed, and we are fairly on our way to the Knap. How glorious are those teeming fields! The perfume of a thousand flowers—more grateful than the spices of Arabia—is borne upon the breath of the 'sweet south,' which the hummings of a thousand insect things combine to make melodious. Every lovely hue and every graceful form compose the unequalled picture. The starry daisy, the moon-like primrose, the golden buttercup, and the pendulous cowslip, bedeck in myriads the grassy earth; while the hedge-rows are all redolent of May-bloom, scattered wantonly by the bounteous hand of Nature as she hastens on to beautify the spring!

Pillesdon Pen, and flows by Race Down and Thorncombe. It is called the Synderford Brook, and is particularly valuable as a breeding-stream, on account of the proximity of its mouth to the Ford Abbey preserves, in which it helps most materially to keep up the supply of fish. The stream is small and woody;—not worth fishing with the fly, although a few parts of it are sufficiently open. The worm is the more appropriate bait. Being peculiarly a breeding-stream, it cannot be fished late in the season without material injury to the next year's stock of fish in the main river. Not a fish should be taken out of it after July. The same remarks apply also to the numerous other tributaries which we shall have to notice, and have already noticed; but there is little hope, alas! of their being heeded. The poacher's object is *fish*, at all times and in any way, and he is superlatively indifferent about the extermination of the species.

[1] There are two or three respectable 'publics' at Winsham—quite capable of gratifying a hungry angler's reasonable wants.

As to the river, friend, from Winsham to Broad-bridge,[1] about a mile below the Knap, we can only say that it abounds in fish, and that it is the perfection of a trout stream. It flows, however, through the private preserves of Leigh and Ford Abbey, and therefore is not open ground. There is also some restriction below Broad-bridge, in the property of Earl Poulett on the right bank, and that of Amos Barns, Esq. on the left. And this extends almost to Tytherleigh bridge, at least a mile still further down. Within the lengthened interval of more than three miles—that is, from Winsham to near Tytherleigh bridge—we must suspend our angling operations.[2] Delightful, though, will be our ramble through those charming velvet meadows; and abundant are the subjects for discourse in the matters antiquarian, which, to preserve the chain of our explorings, we can by no means skip so easily. *   *   *   *

And here, Piscator, is the Knap—our welcome halting place. Sitting as we do, friend, in its little parlor, what a treat it is to contemplate the view which it commands! Immediately below us is the stream, pursuing its winding course among the meadows, and gliding here and there beneath the fine old woods which dip into its crystal waters. Upon its

[1] Broad-bridge is situated on the road from Perry Street to Thorncombe. It is an ancient little structure, and interesting on that account.

[2] From Broad-bridge to Tytherleigh the river is also truly beautiful, and it produces abundance of the finest trout.

bank is reared the venerable Abbey, peeping out among the trees in all its picturesqueness and solemnity. The deer-park stretches up the opposite hill side, where many a noble tree presents itself to view in all the beauty and profusion of its early foliage. And the eye can wander, also, down the valley—more especially from the garden in the rear of our hostel,—and glimpses may be caught of its remote recesses, and of a few of the beauties and notabilities with which we have yet to become more intimately acquainted.

But, verily, here comes our luncheon! First, a brace of our largest trout—pounders—cooked *a la Soyer*. Next, a boiled capon, with cold tongue and etceteras. Then there are delicious potatoes, cauliflowers, and, by our holidam! some asparagus. Furthermore, we are gravely informed that there is pastry for the third course, and that preparations are advancing for the concoction of a certain favorite beverage of ours, which, out of compliment to its inventor, we have christened 'Akerman.'[1] The stock of cigars, too, it is satisfactory to be assured, is even

[1] It is made thus:—take two glasses of wine, one of port and one of sherry, two table spoonfuls of moist sugar, a quarter of a nutmeg, and a sprinkle of ginger. Fill up with a pint of *mild* ale over a piece of well-baked (but not burnt) toast. These are the proportions; and if you will make it with a *quart* of ale, you, of course, must double the quantity of wine, &c. *Any* wine will answer the purpose, but if of two kinds, the better. It should stand a quarter of an hour before it is drunk, that the flavor of the sop may be duly imparted to it. Akerman's '*Spring Tide; or, the Angler and his Friends.*' Page 114.

beyond *our* capability of very seriously reducing.

Let us first, however, while these tempting viands are in the course of being displayed for our especial demolition, take a momentary survey of our morning's sport:—Since leaving Bere Chapel, and during our chat about Winsham and Cricket—which, by the by, was often very agreeably interrupted by the landing of sundry glorious fish—we have managed to secure a dozen and a half of unexceptionables, besides the nine already mentioned. Four of them are hard upon four pounds, and the rest will average full half a pound apiece. The morning has been excellent. The clouds came on, as we anticipated. A shower fell, which made 'the face of nature gay,' and brought the trout 'upon the feed' voraciously. We were in a *deadly* mood;—in splendid *striking* order. Behold the successful result !   *   *   *   *

Come, join us, landlord; come,—begin at once,—no more apologies, we beseech thee. We have an hour only to indulge in these thy fascinations, and we must employ it, as well as the time which it will take us to reach Tytherleigh bridge,—another hour nearly,—in our historical discoursings about this interesting neighbourhood. The Abbey claims, of course, our first attention.

FORD ABBEY.

W Spreat lith. Exeter.

CHAPTER VI.

SEVEN hundred years have rolled away, since the sounds of labor, which proclaimed the erection of the Abbey of Ford, first broke upon the stillness of the valley—arousing the wild-fowl from the marsh below, and the fox and the badger in the lone woods around it! Seven hundred years have come and gone, since the passing traveller stopped to gaze in admiration upon the newly-reared and glorious walls, and since the earliest notes of praise were wafted from the sacred fane to the angler who sauntered, with his rude equipment, along the banks of the pellucid stream!

And the angler who saunters there to-day, can gaze upon no trifling portion of the stately fabric which has thus withstood the mighty changes of those departed and eventful centuries. He beholds in it a noble monument of the piety of our forefathers, and a proof of the wonderful architectural ability which they possessed. His mind is impressed with the solemnity of the associations, and looking back through

the long vista of the Past, he becomes aware of the
fleeting nature of the Present, and of the mockery of
man's fancied might.   For where are the generations
of those, who, century after century, have given
vitality to the spot, and have been associated with
it in the days of its greatness and its power ?

> 'Thou unrelenting past !
> Strong are the barriers round thy dark domain ;
> And fetters sure and fast
> Hold all that enter thy unbreathing reign.'

Ford Abbey is one of the most perfect of the
numerous remains of those magnificent conventual
establishments with which the country was anciently
studded—those much decried establishments, which,
to say the least, were at once the homes of the desti-
tute, the hospitals of the sick, and the sanctuaries of
learning and refinement.[1]   It stands upon the left
bank of the Axe, in the parish of Thorncombe, and
in the county of Dorset.[2]   Its foundation was singular, and to some extent accidental.   In the year

[1] Monachism is believed to have been introduced into Britain by
Pelagius, at the commencement of the fifth century. Egypt was the
great theatre of monastic establishments. At the close of the fourth
century it was computed that 27,000 monks and nuns were to be found
in that country.—*Phelps.*

[2] Prior to 1842, the parish of Thorncombe was in the county of Devon
and the hundred of Axminster. The inconvenience of its situation for
county business, led to the obtaining, in that year, of an act of Parliament by which it was transferred to Dorsetshire, while Stockland and Dalwood, two isolated Dorsetshire parishes north-west of Axminster, were
given to Devonshire in lieu. The distance of Ford Abbey from Axminster
on the south, and from Crewkerne on the north, is about seven miles.
From Chard, on the north-west, it is about four miles.

1132, Richard, Baron of Oakhampton and Viscount
of Devon, son of Baldwin De Brioniis, by Albreda,
the Conqueror's niece, founded a Cistercian abbey [1]
at Brightley, in the parish of Oakhampton. Twelve
monks, and an abbot named Richard, were received
from the abbey of Waverley, in Surrey. They entered
upon their new abode in 1136. In the following
year the Baron died, without issue, leaving his inheritance to his sister Adelicia, who resided at West Ford,
in the manor of Thorncombe. Abbot Richard also
died about the same time. [2] The monks suffered
great privations, on account of the barrenness of their
lands. All their associations with the new monastery
were also of a melancholy character. About five
years after the death of their abbot, they determined,
therefore, upon breaking up the establishment, and
returning at once to Waverley. Accordingly, they
set out upon their journey on foot, in procession,
preceded by Robert, their abbot, the successor of
Richard, who carried a lofty cross. Passing in this

[1] The order of Cistercians was founded about A.D. 1098, by Robert, a
Benedictine monk and abbot of Molesme, in Burgundy. Its name was
derived from the town of Citeaux, in that country, where its first abbey
was established. The order increased so rapidly, that within a century
after its institution it could boast of 1800 abbeys; and both in the civil
government and spiritual affairs of the chief European countries, its
influence was almost unbounded. There were fifty Cistercian abbeys in
England alone. The only order of monks in Europe before the Conquest
was that of the Benedictines, which was established in the sixth century.

[2] The bones of both the founder and the abbot were afterwards
removed to Ford Abbey and buried near the high altar.

order through the manor of Thorncombe, they attracted the attention of Adelicia. She heard with surprise the account of their misfortunes, and immediately decided upon a plan by which to prevent the frustration of her brother's intentions. The speech which she addressed to them has been handed down to us; and it shows, as plainly as anything, both the influence of the church at that period, and the spirit by which its faithful benefactors were actuated :—

'Far be it from me, my lords and most holy fathers, to incur the guilt of damnable scandal and ignominious danger. What my lord and brother Richard, out of a heart full of pure devotion, for the honor of God, and the salvation of us all, began so solemnly, shall not I, his sister and heir, into whose hands, before his death, he delivered all his possessions, be willing or able to accomplish? Behold my manor on which I now reside! It is sufficiently fertile—it is sheltered and shaded with woods—it is productive of grain and other fruits of the earth; behold we give it you in exchange for the barren land of Brightley, together with our mansion house for ever! Remain here till somewhere else in this possession you can have a more competent monastery. We shall not be wanting in respect; nay, we shall sufficiently help you to build it.'

The generous offer was of course accepted. A site was selected at a place called Harteschath, and the monks resided at the manor-house while the building

was in progress. In 1148 they took possession of
their new monastery, to which they gave the name of
Ford, from its situation on the stream, and they dedicated it to the Virgin Mary. Adelicia, however,
did not live to witness the realization of her design.
She died soon after the arrival of the monks (1142),
whose earliest duty it was, after the consecration of
their monastery, to afford a final resting-place for her
remains in the most sacred spot within its walls.[1]

In the reign of Henry II (1154-1189), the estates of Adelicia were brought, by the marriage of
her descendants, to the Courtenays, who thus became
naturally interested in the welfare of the Abbey, and
some members of their family, whose bones now
moulder in the vaults, were its munificent benefactors.[2] Among the most pious of this princely house,

[1] 'Now, for that ye shall meet with many Monasteries in the Itinerary
of this county (arguments of ancient piety), therefore know the manner of
ceremonies used at the foundation of such religious houses, and listen to
the Bishop Chadda, that lived in the time of Ediswold, King of Northum-
berland, who, at the founding of an Abbey, first purged the place with
prayer and fasting, craving leave of the King there to remain every day
of the lent fasting (Sundays excepted), only feeding on a little bread, a
hen egg, and a little quantity of milk mixed with water. Thus anciently
were all such places consecrated with prayer and fasting, which were ordained for Monasteries or Churches.'—Risdon's 'Survey of Devon.'

[2] 'Hawisia de Courtenay, descended from Adelicia, gave to the monks
of Ford certain land at Herteyne for the support of three poor persons
in the Infirmary of the Abbey. She died in 1209, and lies buried in the
chapel, on the south side of the chancel. Through the means of her son,
Robert De Courtenay, Geoffrey de Pomerai was induced to bestow upon
the monks the lands of Tale.' See Dugdale's 'Monasticon.'

was John de Courtenay, whose devotion to the monks of Ford was increased by an accident which may be related as follows :—

One night, at sea, he was overtaken by a storm, and the destruction of the vessel seemed inevitable. The sailors gave up in despair, expecting immediate death. Lord John exhorted them to take courage, assuring them that to weather the storm but an hour longer would ensure their perfect safety. 'By that time,' urged he, 'my monks of Ford will have risen to their prayers, and they will intercede for me to the Lord, so that no storm, nor winds, nor waves, shall be able to shipwreck us.' But his hearers were not greatly comforted by these assurances. 'What signifies talking of the monks,' said one; 'they are fast asleep, and will be asleep an hour hence. How can they think of you, when they have, in a manner, forgotten themselves?' The storm, however, abated about the time that Lord John had named, and the ship, with all on board, came safe to land. This deliverance was attributed to the prayers of the monks. Their monastery was further enriched, and Courtenay himself, at his most earnest desire, was admitted into their fraternity.[1]

His son and grandson 'walked not in the steps of

---

[1] 'He died happily in Christ, the fifth of the nones of May, 1273, (1 Ed. I.) and was buried by his father, Robert de Courtenay, before the high altar at Ford. He bequeathed, with his body, forty pounds to the said monastery, with his arms, and horse, and all other things belonging to his funeral paraphernalia.' Dugdale's 'Monasticon.'

their forefathers;' for instead of endowing the abbey with additional revenues or privileges, they greatly diminished those granted by their ancestors:—the son by charging the estates bestowed on the monks in free alms, with the service of carrying his baggage in time of war, and with the maintenance of dogs for the chase; and the grandson, in addition to these oppressions, by infringing their immunities in the manor of Tale, and obliging them to pay an acknowledgment of fifty shillings per annum to the church of Cruck.[1]

At least twenty abbots, including the two at Brightley,[2] presided successively over the convent.[3]

[1] Grose's *'Antiquities of Devonshire.'*

[2] It is now impossible to ascertain the exact number, which was probably twenty-four.

[3] The following were some of the officers belonging to an abbey in the 'olden time:'—The ABBOT was the governor of the convent. He was generally appointed partly by the king and partly by the election of the monks in chapter. He possessed absolute control over the establishment, in accordance with the rules of the order to which the convent belonged, and he was treated with profound respect, both by his own monks and by the community at large. The PRIOR was the second officer. He was the Abbot's deputy, and performed a great deal of the actual management of the abbey. He was assisted by a SUB-PRIOR, who had the especial charge of the infirmary, and watched over the conduct of the monks and servants. In smaller convents, the Prior was the principal, and his establishment was called a PRIORY. The SACRISTAN had charge of the plate and vestments, and it was his duty to prepare the church for service. He is the prototype of the modern *Sexton*. The ALMONER was the distributer of the abbey charities, by which great numbers of the poor were entirely supported—both poor-rates and *paupers* being then unknown. The CELLARER had charge of the 'victualling' department, and also of the sick; the PRECENTOR regulated the choral service, and took

The third abbot was the famous Baldwin, who, 'from the meanest origin,' rose to the highest ecclesiastical distinction.   He was born at Exeter, where, at an early age, his aptitude for learning attracted the notice of Bishop Bartholomew, who encouraged and assisted him in his studies.   He afterwards removed to Glastonbury abbey, where he made astonishing progress 'in learning and virtue.'   From a schoolmaster his patron made him archdeacon of Exeter; but he soon resigned that office, 'either,' says Prince, 'because he thought it too secular, and involved him too much in the affairs of the world, or else for some other reason,' and with 'great devotion, and a mind above these inferior things,' he became a monk in the abbey of Ford, and within a year was elected abbot of 'that noted convent.'   This office he resigned, in 1180, to accept of the see of Worcester, which he filled for about three years, when he was translated to the archbishopric of Canterbury.   Seven years afterwards he died in the Holy Land, whither he had accompanied Richard I[1] on one of the crusades with

charge of the books and archives of the establishment; the HOSPITALLER dispensed 'good cheer' to strangers and visitors; the BURSAR presided at 'the exchequer;' the MASTER BUILDER kept the magnificent structure in repair; the PORTER kept the gate; and last, not least, the CHARTULARIES were incessantly engaged in the transcribing of manuscripts, by which alone the mental productions of preceding ages have been preserved. Several 'lay brothers' belonged to every abbey, and, with the servants, they filled various offices in addition to those which we have enumerated.

[1] Baldwin had officiated at the Coronation of Richard, Sept. 3, 1189.

which the name of that heroic monarch is so roman-
tically associated. [1]

In 1190, the election of the fifth abbot fell upon
John of Devon, the friend and confessor of King
John. He was an eminent scholar, and greatly raised
the reputation of the abbey, which, during his abbacy, was said to have 'more learning in it than any
three convents of the same bignesse to be found in
England.' [2] He died in 1220, and was succeeded by

The Cistercian Roger, 'who took his name,' says
Prince, [3] 'not from his progenitors, who were, it
seems "*nullius nominis*," that is, had not at that time
any surname at all, ' nor from the place where he was
born (as was the practice of learned men in those
days), but from that religious order of which he was
in the church. He made this profession near the

---

[1] Risdon says, that 'by his preaching, liberal alms, and example of
life, he won many people to God,' and that ' he died in the city of Tyre.'

[2] Fuller's '*Worthies of England.*' See page 88.

[3] The Rev. John Prince was born at the farm-house which now occupies the site of Newenham Abbey, in the parish of Axminster, in 1643.
He was educated at Brazenose College, Oxford, and commenced his pastoral duties as curate of Bideford. He was afterwards elected minister of
St. Martin's church, Exeter. About the year 1675 he became vicar of
Totnes, and in 1681 was presented, by Sir Edward Seymour, of Berry
Castle, with the vicarage of Berry Pomeroy, where he remained till his
death in 1723, at the age of eighty years. He was the author of several
sermons and pamphlets; but his great work, by which he will ever be remembered, was '*The Worthies of Devon,*' which is a collection of
biographical sketches of the principal families in the county. It is regarded as a very valuable contribution to county and general history.

[4] See note at page 100.

place of his birth,[1] in the abbey of Ford, in the
easternmost part of this county (Devon)—a stately
monastery heretofore, standing on the river Ax, at a
place where it hath a ford or passage, which gives its
name to a healthy, clean, market town, four miles
distant towards the west, from which, and a certain
minster for four priests it sometime had, it is called
Axminster unto this day.[2]   Here he continued a stu-
dious and pious life, for many years, of whom,
notwithstanding (as it often happens by the best of
men), I find a very different account given by two
eminent authors, Bale and Leland.'   The latter speaks
highly in his praise, while 'Bilious Bale,' as Fuller
calls him, informs us, that 'he diligently apply'd
himself to fallacies and devilish impostures that he
might obscure the glory of Christ.'[3]   Prince, who
tells us that he is anxious 'to salve the reputation of
a worthy person long since in his grave, and so can't
defend himself,' thinks that Bale is unjustly severe,
as he was notoriously prejudiced against the Roman
Catholics ; and Fuller expresses his belief that 'he
(Bilious Bale) would have been sick of the yellow
jaundice if he could not have vented his choler in
such expressions.' 'Let the judicious reader, then,'
sums up Prince, 'climb up those two mountains of

[1] Fuller, page 263.

[2] See our account of Axminster in a subsequent page.

[3] 'Invigilavit fallaciis, atque imposturis diabolicis, ut Christi gloriam
obscuraret.'

extremes, only with his eye, and then descend into the valley of truth which lieth between them.'

'Our Roger' was a great traveller, and like some travellers of a later age, he saw 'very strange things,' which he related for the benefit of mankind. Among other productions was his account of Elizabeth, Abbess of Schonaugh, who, in 1152, made a great noise in the world by her 'visions and revelations from the Lord, which he was pleased to conceal from the rest of mankind,' and which she duly communicated, 'falling into strange raptures of mind, and suddenly uttering many divine expressions in the Latin tongue, though she had never learned it.' He also wrote an account of St. Ursula (a Cornish or Devonshire woman) and her eleven thousand virgins killed at Cologne. He resigned his office in 1236.

William de Crukerne, the ninth abbot, was excommunicated by Bishop Bronescombe in 1276. He had rebelled against, and even excommunicated, his bishop, because of the exercise of some episcopal authority, from which, the abbot contended, his convent was exempted by papal indults. Bronescombe solicited from the King (Edward I) the assistance of the secular power, and a special commission was accordingly granted. The judges were Walter Stamel, Dean of Sarum, and Thomas Weke, Archdeacon of Dorset, Professors of Canon and Civil Law. On October 22, 1276, the court sat at Westminster. The abbot expressed contrition, and offered to pay a fine of £500. But he was not to be let off so easily. The judge, after much deliberation, passed sentence that the fine should be one thousand marks,—that the abbot should recal his sentence of excommunication, and ' that he, his monks, and dependents should proceed, on the ensuing feast of the nativity of St. John the Baptist, from the gate of St. Peter's Cemetery, in Exeter, to the entrance door of St. Peter's Church, bareheaded, barefooted, and loosely dressed, and there receive a discipline either from the bishop or his deputy.' [1] The bishop, on his part, revoked his censures against the abbot and convent, and even remitted the greater part of the fine. The ' discipline,' however, was rigidly administered, and we suppose that it produced the desired effect, as we hear no more of William de Crukerne after his severe humiliation. [2]

Abbot Nicholas succeeded William de Crukerne. He was confirmed abbot on January 1, 1284, when he was solemnly blessed at Axminster by Bishop Quivil, who was then pontifically celebrating mass in the church of that town.

William de Fria, or Fry, became abbot soon afterwards. He resigned his office April 14, 1297, when he was elected Abbot of Newenham.

In 1388, during the abbacy of Walter Burstock, (?)

[1] Dr. Oliver.

[2] In 1276, during the Abbacy of William de Crukerne, the convent was called upon to pay the large sum, in those days, of £15 6s. 8d. on a subsidy raised by King Edward I to maintain his expedition against Llewellyn, Prince of Wales.

a commission was granted by the Bishop of Bath and Wells to shut up 'Master Robert Charde,' monk of Ford, in a solitary house on the western side of the parish church of Crewkerne, under the church-yard. We hear nothing of the doings of this pious anchorite, who duly took up his solitary abode; but we can well believe that he was regarded by the good people of Crewkerne in those days as a very desirable neighbour, and that he was treated by them with commensurate respect. [1]

The last abbot was Thomas Charde, alias Tybbes, a native of Awliscombe, near Honiton. He was appointed suffragan bishop, and became the coadjutor of Bishop Oldham. He was presented with the vicarage of Wellington, Somerset, and had some other preferments for the purpose of sustaining his episcopal dignity. In 1513 he was appointed warden of Ottery College. But he resigned all his appointments in 1520, became a monk at Ford, and was very shortly afterwards elected abbot. He appears to have been a man of great intellectual attainments, and was a munificent benefactor to various public institutions. St. John the Baptist's College, Oxford, [2] at

---

[1] Anchorites, when once inured, never left their cells. They were bound by severe rules and subsisted on the offerings of the charitable. 'They were supposed to hold direct intercourse with angels, and therefore were often consulted for their advice and blessing. They were denominated "Sir," as "Sir Thomas the Anchorite;" and the females "Mother."' —*Fosbroke.*

[2] Then called St. Bernard's College. Dr. Charde made extensive reparations and additions to this building, in memory of which his

which he was educated, and the hospital of St. Margaret, near Honiton, may be mentioned as two of the places which shared his liberality. He erected a considerable part of the buildings now remaining at Ford Abbey, including the cloisters and some other portions of the south front which our artist has so beautifully illustrated. Dr. Charde presided over the convent nearly twenty years. His government was judicious and his devotion to his duties great. But his career must have been an anxious and a troublous one. The approaching Reformation was indicated by repeated occurrences which must have kept him in a state of constant alarm; while the unscrupulous character of the monarch held out little hope of consideration or respect for the ancient faith and its institutions, should they prove impediments to his *kingly* purposes. With reason might the crosier tremble in the grasp from which it was destined to be speedily and rudely snatched. The blow, so long impending, fell at last with a fury which no foresight could prevent, and no arm could turn aside. In March, 1536, the act for the dissolution of ' the lesser monasteries '—that is, all those with an income below £200 a year—was passed. A similar act for the suppression of all the remaining religious houses was obtained during the following year, and within two years afterwards the possessions of 644 convents,

initials were painted on the glass of several of the windows, particularly in the large middle window on the south side of the tower.

90 colleges, 2374 chantries and free chapels, and 110 hospitals, were annexed to the crown.[1] Dr. Charde surrendered his convent on the eighth of March, 1539.[2] The annual revenues of the abbey amounted to about £380.[3] The abbot was allotted a pension of £80 and 'fourtie wayne loads of fyre wood' a year, and the monks received pensions varying from £5 to £8 each.[4]

The abbey, and some lands in its immediate vicinity, were given by the king to Richard Pollard,

[1] 'The clear yearly value of all these houses was, at the rents actually paid, only about £130,000, but Burnet affirms that their real value was at least ten times as much; and a vast amount of plate, jewels, and goods of all kinds must also have been obtained. To gain over popular feeling upon the subject, it was given out that its effects would be to relieve the people for the future from all services and taxes—that in place of the monks and nuns thus driven out, there would be raised and maintained 40 new earls, 60 barons, 3000 knights, and 40,000 soldiers;—that a better provision would be made for the poor, and that preachers should be handsomely paid to go about everywhere and proclaim the new religion. It is almost needless to say that these promises were wholly unfulfilled—that pauperism rapidly increased, education declined, proper preachers (owing to the scantiness of their stipend) almost disappeared, and that a great part of the money so iniquitously procured was turned to the upholding of dice-playing, masking, and banqueting.' *Eccleston.*

[2] Willis's *'History of Abbeys.'*

[3] Dugdale estimates them at £374 10s. 6¼d, Speed at £381 10s. 5d. The property of the abbey was situated at Thorncombe, Winsham (see page 173), Burstock, Hawkchurch, Tale and Payhembury, Lynton, Broadwinsor (see page 74), Toller Porcorum, Crewkerne, Bridport, Lyme Regis, Charmouth, and other places.

[4] Dr. Charde held the vicarage of Thorncombe till his death in 1543—four years after his surrender of the abbey which we can well believe was endeared to him by the most agreeable associations, and the glories of which he had outlived.

Esq.,[1] sheriff of Devon. His son, Sir John Pollard,
sold them to Sir Amias Poulett, of Hinton Saint
George, whose mother was Richard Pollard's sister.
Sir Amias's grandson, of the same name,[2] sold them
to William Rosewell, Esq., Solicitor General to
Queen Elizabeth, from whose son, Sir Henry Rosewell, it passed, in 1649, to Edmund Prideaux, Esq.,
second son of Sir Edmund Prideaux, Bart., of
Netherton Hall, near Honiton, still the seat of the
representative of that ancient and influential family.[3]
Mr. Prideaux spent immense sums upon the abbey,
imparting to it all the essential features of a private
residence which it possesses to this day. His architect was the celebrated Inigo Jones, who unfortunately destroyed the harmony of the magnificent
front by the introduction of a Grecian porch in the
midst of the Perpendicular work of Dr. Charde.[4]

[1] The manor of Thorncombe was given to the Earl of Oxford.—See
our account of Thorncombe.

[2] To this second Sir Amias Poulett was entrusted the care of the
unfortunate Mary Queen of Scots. He died in 1588.

[3] In 1649 Edmund Prideaux was Cromwell's Attorney General,—
a circumstance to which may very probably be attributed the preservation
of Ford Abbey from the fate of so many ancient residences during the
civil wars and the Commonwealth.

[4] The reason of the failure of Inigo Jones, Wren, and Kent in their
imitations of the Gothic, was simply their *classically* confined views of
architecture. They were unwilling to copy and unable to invent designs
in any degree analogous to original examples of the different *Gothic*
styles. [See Walpole's '*Anecdotes of Painting.*'] We fear that we should
be accused of severity if we were to attempt to account for the failures of
modern architects by going a great deal further than this; and yet it

The Duke of Monmouth visited Ford Abbey in ·
the time of Mr. Prideaux's successor, five years before the Duke's unfortunate rebellion. [1] He received
a princely reception, and slept there one night.
Jeffreys, when, a few years afterwards, he was let
loose upon the West of England, endeavoured, by
the bribery and intimidation of witnesses, to impli-
cate Mr. Prideaux in the rebellion.   Mr. Prideaux,
it was alleged, was well known to be an admirer of
Monmouth, and had once been his delighted host.
On the news being brought to him of the Duke's
landing at Lyme he had drunk to the success of the
expedition. [2] He was committed to the tower, and
after a harassing imprisonment of several months he
was '*given as a present*' [3] by King James to his
abominable judge, who thirsted for the life of his
victim and also for the possession of his delightful
residence.   Unable, however, to effect his purpose,
he at last consented to receive £15,000, of which he

is really difficult to know what to say of those who as often select for
imitation the *imperfections* of the ancient specimens as they do their
incomparable beauties.

[1] See pages 126 and 127.

[2] This was most emphatically denied by persons who were present on
the occasion referred to.   Mr. Key, a clothier of Ilminster, in spite of the
threats of Jeffreys, swore positively that this allegation was a malicious
falsehood.   But the most atrocious circumstance was the offer of a free
pardon to Mr. Charles Speke, who was under sentence of death, if he
would swear against Mr. Prideaux.   The offer was treated as it deserved.

[3] The meaning of this is, that Jeffreys was allowed to fleece him as he
could, and to appropriate the result to his own private use, instead of its
being handed to the king in the usual way of fines and confiscations.

was generous enough to return £240 in the shape of
discount, and Mr. Prideaux was ultimately par-
doned.[1] He died in 1702. His heiress, by Amy
Fraunceis, of Combe Florey, Somerset, brought Ford
Abbey into the possession of the Gwyn family of
Llansannor, Glamorganshire, in which it remained till
the death of the late possessor, John Fraunceis Gwyn,
Esq., in 1846, when the property was sold to ——
Miles, Esq., its present owner. Among the occupiers
of the Abbey we must not omit to mention the celebrated Jeremy Bentham, who, during the absence of
Mr. Gwyn on a continental tour, resided there from
1815 to 1818. He is still remembered with great
respect by some of the old people of the locality,
who enumerate among his eccentricities the habit of
frequently running up and down the walks with his
arms a-kimbo.[2] Sir Samuel Romilly, who visited
Mr. Bentham at this time, gives, in his Diary, the following account of the abbey :—' Our last visit was to
my old and most valued friend Jeremy Bentham, at
Ford Abbey—a house which he rents, and which
once belonged to Prideaux, the attorney-general of
the Commonwealth. I was not a little surprised to

[1] In the reign of William III he made an ineffectual attempt to recover this fine, which Jeffreys, who was then dead, had invested in
estates inherited by his family.

[2] The hostess of the Knap was in his service, and has a fund of anecdotes of the great philosopher, who, she will tell you, with extreme simpli-
city, ' did nothing, dear old man, but write, write, write, from day's end
to week's end.'

find in what a palace my friend was lodged. The grandeur and stateliness of the buildings form as strange a contrast to his philosophy as the number and spaciousness of the apartments—the hall—the chapel—the corridors and the cloisters—do to the modesty and scantiness of his domestic establishment.'[1] The same visit is also referred to by Sir Samuel in a letter to M. Dumont, dated October 2, 1817, as follows:—' Another of our visits was to Ford Abbey. I had heard of it only as a place that had fallen into decay, and whose gloomy appearance had produced such an effect upon the imagination of the servants that they never ventured into some of the apartments from terror of spirits, with which they supposed them to be haunted. I was much surprised, therefore, by the cheerfulness, and still more by the magnificence, of the house—a palace, I should rather call it, for it is much more princely than many mansions which pass by that name. The front of it extends no less than 250 feet. To the remains of the monastery, which are very considerable, and are of Gothic architecture, have been added, about the time of Edward VI, or Queen Elizabeth, a great pile of building, broken into different parts and very richly ornamented, which have a most striking and beautiful effect; and the pleasure grounds are rendered as gay as a great profusion of flowers can make them. The

---

[1] This is dated September, 1817.

rooms are spacious, and some of them splendidly furnished and enriched with tapestry, which is some of
the best that I have ever seen in England.'

Of the original building the little chapel is the
only remaining vestige, and that, as a whole, has been
greatly altered by modern reparations. It is, however, a sacred and an interesting spot, for within its
walls is the dust of Adelicia and that of many other
noble and famous personages who played an important part in the history of the abbey, and, more or
less, in the great world beyond it.   The chapel occupies the eastern end of the south front, from which it
projects, as our artist has depicted it, immediately beneath the bell-turret. It exhibits many of the peculiar characteristics of the Norman style of architecture
which prevailed at the time of the foundation of the
abbey. [1]   Behind the chapel, and extending towards
the west, is a range of ivy-covered building of a
little later date. It consists of two storeys, lighted
by several lancet windows. The under storey was part
of the ancient cloisters,[2] and contains some beautiful

[1] See our account of Thorncombe church. The eastern window of the
chapel, inserted, probably, by Dr. Charde, is Late Perpendicular, corresponding with the windows of the cloisters in the south front.

[2] The CLOISTERS were the place of promenade for the monks. They
usually surrounded a square court, or a garden, and connected the different
parts of the abbey. They were, indeed, an arcade, or a covered walk, supported with arches, forming windows. The lower orders of monks were
generally interred in the enclosed space. Over the cloisters was generally
the DORMITORY, or sleeping-place. The CHURCH always formed an important part of an abbey. In some places it served as the *parish* church,

Early English work. [1]   It is now appropriated partly to a school-room and partly to a cellar and other domestic offices.   Above is the ancient dormitory, now called the Monks' Walk.   These parts of the building are full of interest to the antiquary and the man of taste.   Indeed, there is no part of it which is not so.

The principal portion of the south front, as already stated, is the work of Dr. Charde.   It bears his

as at Bath, and in that case it was, at the Reformation, spared the fate of the other buildings.   The SACRISTY answered to the modern vestry. The CHAPTER HOUSE was generally an elegant part of the building.   It was the place in which the monks assembled to discuss the affairs of the convent, and to receive instruction from the abbot.   The REFECTORY was the great hall appropriated to the important business of eating.   It was fitted up with tables and benches in a set way, and with due regard to the different ranks of the brethren.   At one end was a desk at which a monk was stationed to read aloud during meals.   One William Tyler, of Axminster, Master of Arts, was granted an annuity, by Abbot Charde, of £3 6s. 8d., with a gown, ' at five shillings a yard,' and lodgings, in acknowledgment of his services to the abbey, and as a remuneration *for expounding the scriptures in the refectory*, when required, and for teaching grammar to the boys in the monastery.   The LIBRARY was the place in which the records preserved for us by the monks were carefully deposited. Many valuable manuscripts were wantonly destroyed at the Dissolution. Leland, who was appointed to investigate the literary treasures of the monasteries, found the library at Ford Abbey to contain only a dozen books.   The spoliation had of course been committed before his arrival. The INFIRMARY had separate chambers for the sick, and also a chapel. The FRATERY was an apartment for the novices.   In the LAVATORY, or Laundry, the clothes were washed; and in the COMMON-ROOM was always kept a fire at which the monks could come and warm themselves. The KITCHEN and BUTTERY were always well attended to, ' if ancient tales say true, nor wrong these holy men.'   The GARDENS were admirably cultivated, and furnished with fish-ponds; and the GRANGES were the farms of the abbey, sometimes situated at a considerable distance from it.

[1] See page 66.

initials in many places, and also the arms of the
Courtenays, Pouletts, the Bishop of Exeter, and
other influential personages connected with the abbey
in former times. Most of the more ancient fittings-up
are by Mr. Prideaux, and those of a more recent date
by Mr. Gwyn.   The great hall to the left of Inigo
Jones's porch, as shown in our illustration, is a magnificent apartment, lighted by four large transomed
Tudor windows. [1] It is the ancient refectory. Over
the porch, and reached in the interior by a staircase
designed by Inigo Jones, is the saloon, a large and
handsome apartment, remarkable for being adorned
with the splendid tapestry of the cartoons of Raphael
for which Ford Abbey has been so long renowned.
This tapestry completely covers the walls, and has
occupied its present position for about 140 years.
It is said to have been captured in a Spanish galleon,
during the reign of Queen Anne. It is the production of the celebrated looms of Arras, and was
intended for the King of Spain. Mr. Gwyn, the
owner of Ford Abbey, was secretary at war at the
time, and the tapestry was presented to him by the
queen. It is said that his son was offered £30,000
for it by the Empress Catherine of Russia. [2] In the
dining-room, on the left of the refectory, is some
curious and ancient Gobelin tapestry, [3] and in one of

[1] See page 55.

[2] Mrs. Allen's '*History of Ford Abbey.*'

[3] The subjects of it are, first,—Scipio Africanus leading Hasdrubal, the

the bedrooms, which was fitted up for an expected visit of Queen Anne, and called thenceforth by her name, is some tapestry in which the proceedings at a Welch wedding are minutely represented. The walls of some of the other apartments are adorned with valuable paintings. Indeed, in the metamorphosis of this ancient and sacred pile, nothing has been omitted which could assist in producing a truly magnificent residence, with which its park and gardens are justly commensurate. The park is about sixty acres in extent.[1]

The village of Thorncombe is at the distance of about a mile and a half south-east from the abbey. As we have already stated, it is now in the county of Dorset, although formerly in that of Devon.[2] It is in the union and magisterial division of Axminster—

last Carthaginian general, a prisoner to Rome; second,—A Roman Gladiator encountering a lion before the statue of Jupiter; third,—Cyrus, King of Persia, with the vessels full of silver and gold for rebuilding the Temple at Jerusalem; and fourth,—The Temple in progress.—Mrs. Allen's 'History.'

[1] Since the preceding pages were put to press, we have been favored with a communication from the Rev. Dr. Oliver with reference to 'the Cistercian Roger' (page 197), who, the Dr. states, although a *monk* at Ford was never *abbot* of that convent. The abbot who succeeded John of Devon was named Roger,—a different personage, however, from the Cistercian Roger, who flourished a few years previously, in the time of Abbot Baldwin and that of his two successors, Robert and John of Devon. To the Abbot Baldwin 'the Cistercian' dedicated some of his writings. The mistake has arisen partly from the similarity of the names of the two persons alluded to, and partly from an apparent confusion of dates in some of the records which we have consulted.

[2] See page 190.

from which town it is distant about seven miles—the
hundred of Hawkchurch, the diocese of Salisbury,
and the deanery of Bridport.[1] Its situation among
the hills which bound the southern side of the valley
is singularly sequestered, and the approaches to it
on every side are through narrow, steep, and intricate roads, in which the stranger finds it easy to lose
his way. The village bears evidence of an importance far greater than that which it now possesses.
A person visiting it for the first time could hardly
fail to be impressed with this idea, even if he were
not aware that it was formerly the seat of a considerable clothing trade,[2] hardly a shadow of which
remains,—that its churchyard is crammed with graves,
accumulated, chiefly, as the headstones reveal, during
the last and the preceding century,[3]—and that a meat
market was formerly held in a large market-house,
which, becoming no longer needful, was taken down
about eighty years ago.[4] The circumstance of Thorn-

[1] It was formerly in the hundred of Axminster, but a few years since
it was annexed to the newly constituted hundred of Hawkchurch.
Thorncombe was also formerly in the deanery of Honiton.

[2] See page 170.

[3] Mr. Chapple, speaking of Thorncombe church, about the year 1770,
says that 'it is not large enough to contain a *fourth part of the inhabitants*, though *rather large* for a parish church.'

[4] A market at Thorncombe on Wednesday (altered in more recent
times to Saturday), and a fair on Easter-tuesday, to last for six days, were
granted to the abbot of Ford, by Edward II, about the year 1312. The
fair on Easter-tuesday is still kept up, but of course for that day only,
and there is another fair held annually on October 20th.

combe's being situated in the immediate vicinity of a magnificent abbey, and of the seat, at Olditch, of a powerful baron, no doubt contributed essentially to its importance at an early period. And after the glories of the one had been swept away by a theological revolution, and the power of the other had been humbled by an insulted sovereign,[1] another, and a very different cause, but quite in character with the altered times, arose to maintain, in some degree, the comparative importance of the place. This was the introduction of the clothing trade into the West of England, the almost total loss of which, in the changes of years, has been already adverted to.[2] Thorncombe, shorn completely of its former importance, has now no pretensions beyond those of a quiet, retired village, the inhabitants of which are mainly engaged in agricultural pursuits. The parish, however, is extensive, containing an area of 5550 acres, with a population, in 1851, of 1317 souls.

Thorncombe, we are quaintly informed by Risdon, was 'no doubt so called from the situation and disposition of the soil; for as it is full of combes,[3] so it is subject to thorns and briars (if manurance did not prevent it), unto which it is naturally prone.'[4] Sir William Pole says :—' This place tooke his name of the Saxon names *Thorn* and *Cumb*, which is a fa-

[1] See our account of Olditch.
[2] See page 170.
[3] See page 179.
[4] ' *Survey of Devon*,' page 15.

miliar name in most parts and signifieth a bottome, or lowe grounde, subject unto thornes.'[1] Polwhele, who gives no opinion of his own, says that 'some attribute its name to one remarkable *thorn* near the *combe*.'[2]

The manor was given by William the Conqueror to Baldwin de Sap, or de Brioniis, of whom mention has been made at page 191. It is thus surveyed in Domesday Book:—'Rannulf holds of Baldwin Tornecombe. Edward held it in the time of King Edward, and gelded for two hides. The arable is twelve carucates. In demesne are two carucates, and two servants, and sixteen villains, and eight cottagers, with ten ploughs. There are eighteen acres of meadow, and thirty acres of pasture, and fifteen acres of wood. It was formerly worth four pounds, now one hundred shillings. Rannulf holds of Baldwin Forde. Alveva held it in the time of King Edward, and gelded for half a hide. The arable is four carucates. In demesne are two carucates, with one servant, and two villains, and five cottagers, with two ploughs. There is a mill which renders thirty-pence, and twelve acres of meadow, and one acre of pasture, and fifteen acres of wood. It is worth twenty-five shillings.'

The manor of Thorncombe became the property of the abbot and convent of Ford, as we have already seen, and it remained in their possession till the dis-

[1] '*Collections towards a Description of Devon.*' Printed copy, p. 112.
[2] '*History of Devon.*' Vol. II, page 289.

solution of the monastery, when it was given by
Henry VIII to the Earl of Oxford. It was pur-
chased, in the reign of Elizabeth, by an ancestor of
Colonel Bragge, its present possessor, who resides at
Sadborough House, a delightful mansion, about a
mile from the village to the south. [1]

Olditch, a manor, and one of the tithings of
Thorncombe, [2] is situated at a little greater distance
nearly west of the village, and within a mile of the
river from Tytherleigh Bridge. Its name is undoubtedly derived from its situation on the old
Roman road described at page 13. The manor of
Olditch 'was first belonginge,' says Sir William Pole,
from whom all the subsequent accounts have been
manifestly copied, 'unto the family of Flemynge, and
was by Richard Flemynge given in mariage unto
William la Sancer, a Norman, with Jone, daughter
of the said Richard, which William, with his wief
and children, revoltinge from Kinge John unto the
French Kinge, the saide manor was seized into the
King's hands; but the said Richard soe muche prevail'd with the said Kinge, that he restored it unto

[1] 'At Satburgh,' says Risdon, writing about the year 1650, 'dwelleth
Mr. Bragge, having a fair demesne improved out of the tenements of the
ancient manor. The fair demesne of Sadborow was purchased from the
crown, in the reign of Queen Elizabeth, by the family of Bragge, as a
barton, with the manor of Thorncombe annexed.' The ARMS of Bragge
are *argent*, a chevron, *vert*, between two bulls passant, *gules*. CREST, a
lion's head erased, *argent*, collared, *vaire*, *or*, and *azure*.

[2] There are two tithings in this parish, Thorncombe and Olditch.

him againe, and left it unto William Flemynge his
sonne, and hee unto William his sonne, which gave
it, and all other his lands, unto Reginald de Mohun.'
From him it passed to the family of Brook, afterwards Lords Cobham, in which it continued till the
first year of James I (1603), when it was forfeited to
the crown by the attainder of Henry Lord Cobham,
who, with his brother George, was concerned, among
other plottings against the royal succession, in what
was termed Raleigh's conspiracy.[1] It was bestowed by
the King, along with the other estates of the Brooks,[2]
to Charles Blount, Lord Mountjoy, whom he created
Earl of Devonshire.   It now belongs to Colonel
Bragge, having been purchased in 1714 by his ancestor William Bragge, Esq., from John Bowditch, to
whose family it had been conveyed by Blount.[3] The
Brook family resided for many generations at Olditch
Court, the ruins of which bear abundant evidence of
the extent and stateliness of the original building,
which, as usual at the time of its erection (probably
about the time of Edward III), partook of the com-
bined character of the fortified castle and the quiet

[1] The object of this conspiracy was to carry into effect the design of
Sir Walter Raleigh to place upon the throne Lady Arabella Stuart, or the
Infanta of Spain.

[2] See our account of Weycroft, which was also the property and one
of the residences of the Brooks.

[3] See Lysons's ' *Magna Britannia*.'   Chapple says, in his ' *Historic
Collections for Devon*,' that ' Sir Thomas Putt died seized of the manor
in 1686.'

country home. It was, in fact, a fortified manor house, in accordance with the necessities of the times.[1] The remains of this ancient building are the stone arch of the gate house, of depressed form and ogee moulding, and a much smaller arch, or doorway, by its side. These are worked into the front wall of the farmhouse which now occupies the site of the old mansion; or rather, perhaps, the modern additions were made to the old gate house, which was altered and adapted to its new position. Remains of extensive foundations are still to be traced, as well as those of some fish ponds; and the situation of the court yards, and of some of the outbuildings, is very evident. Two or three noble old fire-places have been retained in the modern building.

---

[1] Formerly, the landholders almost invariably resided upon their estates—a circumstance which accounts for the numerous fine old residences scattered about the country and now occupied as farm houses. The few *town* residences were almost invariably at the capital of the county; but, as a general rule, the landlords very seldom left their country homes, where they attended personally to the welfare of their dependants, and enjoyed themselves in rural sports. The government, even within a comparatively recent period, gave great discouragement to the residence in London of the country gentry, who, as they were once told by King James, 'did thereby, through the instigation of their wives, or to new model and fashion their daughters, neglect their country hospitality and cumber the city.' A proclamation, in 1617, commanded 'the swarms of gentry' to depart from London within twenty days, with their wives and families, for their country residences, there 'to perform the duties and charge of their several places and service, and likewise, by housekeeping, to be a comfort unto their neighbours, in order to renew and revive the laudable custom of hospitality in their respective counties,' &c.—See '*The Diary of Walter Yonge, Esq., of Axminster and Colyton,*' published by the Camden Society.

But by far the most interesting relic is the ruin of an old tower—a square flint building, with a circular turret at its western angle, up which the traces of a spiral stone staircase are discernible.   It is

[RUINS AT OLDITCH COURT.]

covered with a mass of ivy, and forms a very picturesque and interesting object;—a fitting habitation for 'the moping owl'—a thing impossible to gaze upon, in the loneliness of its crumbling decay, without its awakening, in the thoughtful mind, a train of profitable reflection on the fate of the proudest monuments of human skill,—on the change which

Time produces in a people,—on the romantic associations with the poetry and chivalry of a departed
age—and on the unsatisfying and transitory nature of
all merely conventional honors!

The village of Thorncombe is situated on a considerable acclivity, at the foot of which flows the
Synderford Brook already described. [1] The church
is in many respects an object of great interest, but,
in common with the majority of ancient churches, it
has, in the course of ages, become so patched and
mutilated as to leave room for little beyond conjecture as to its original design and character. Fortunately, however, in the case of churches in general,
the grounds upon which conjecture is formed are of
a much safer nature than those of many other
branches of antiquarian research. A natural feeling
of respect for the edifices set apart for religion, preserved them, in past times, from wanton mutilation;
and the science of ecclesiastical architecture, which
was fostered and kept alive by the devotion of the
people, attained to so much perfection, in the uniformity of its designs during the periods of the
different styles which succeeded and grew out of each
other, that in viewing an ancient church the experienced eye is seldom at a loss for a faithful version of
its architectural history as revealed by the mute walls
around it. [2] Nothing but the most inveterate 're-

---

[1] See page 184.
[2] 'When studying the architectural works of the Middle Ages, two

storations ' of modern times can produce any difficulty in such a revelation. Not, indeed, that the student is not often perplexed by works upon which time and national changes have been operating for centuries—especially in the remains which here and there are found of particular arrangements of the building and its fittings-up peculiar to the ancient modes of worship. These, however, instead of arresting an inquiring mind, serve only to stimulate it to renewed exertion, and thus to impart an additional charm to a study which abounds in interest.

curious circumstances force themselves on the attention. One is, the similarity apparent in the buildings of each particular period, although erected in various parts of Europe—the rapidity with which every alteration in style was made widely known; the other, the fact that many of these extraordinary buildings, which display the most lively imagination, sound judgment, and great mathematical skill, were erected at a time when the greatest ignorance prevailed—when kings were to be found unable to read, and men who knew a few physical truths were regarded as magicians. On inquiry, it seems tolerably clear that they were executed by bands of men bound together by certain laws in an association partly of a religious character, who were, to a certain extent, protected by the church, and known as freemasons. The early history of this extraordinary fraternity is obscured by fable. At the present time we know them simply as a body of individuals associated for social purposes, who meet at the freemasons' tavern, and elsewhere, to discuss a dinner and dispense charity. Originally, however, their proceedings were very different. Some masonic writers seek to trace them from a remote time, and endeavour to show a connection with the Eleusinian mysteries, and the Dionysiac artificers who possessed the privilege of erecting public structures in Asia Minor. Without entering here on this questionable ground, or even stopping to ascertain the earliest date whereat their presence in England can be proved, suffice it to say that they were the builders of many of our cathedrals and churches, and preserved within their lodges a great amount of scientific skill, greatly disproportioned to the general attainments of the time.'—' The Builder.'

Thorncombe church consists of a square embattled tower at the west end, containing a clock and chimes and five bells,—a nave, north and south aisles, and a chancel. The visitor, on entering the church, will be immediately struck with the two beautiful arches which divide the nave from its south aisle. These, if not Semi-Norman,—that is, the style which marks the transition from Norman to Early English—are certainly in the Early English style of the thirteenth century.[1] They are beautifully moulded, and rest upon circular piers with circular moulded capitals. The once corresponding arches on the opposite side

[1] The Normans introduced great improvements into the Saxon style of architecture which they found prevailing in this country at the Conquest—retaining, however, all its principal features, especially the rounded or semicircular arch. Their favorite ornament, the chevron or zig-zag moulding, was lavishly employed, especially in their doorways, which were generally highly ornamented. Specimens of this moulding, and of the semi-circular arch, may be seen in the doorway at the eastern end of the south aisle of Axminster church, [probably *Saxon* work, however,—see our account of that church] and also in the doorway opening into what is now a vestry on the north side of Axmouth church. But the finest specimen in this part of the country is the north doorway of Sherborne church, Dorset. The chief characteristics of the *Semi-Norman* style are increased and improved ornamentation, and the employment of the *pointed* arch upon the massive round and other piers of the pure Norman style. The surface of the walls of towers, and other parts of the building, was also enriched with a series of shallow arcades, the arches of which interlace, by springing from the centre of each other, and thus produce acute *lancet* arches—one of the chief features of the succeeding Early English style. The fine Norman towers of Exeter cathedral exhibit specimens of this characteristic ornamentation. The Norman style is generally considered to have prevailed from the Conquest till the death of Stephen (1135), when the Semi-Norman succeeded, and continued through the reign of Henry II, at whose death, in 1189, the Early English style commenced. See page 66.

have been *cut away* to make room for a gallery which rests upon the circular piers considerately allowed to remain for that purpose. This gross outrage of taste, and mutilation of workmanship which its mutilators could neither imitate nor understand, is of no very recent date, as is evidenced by the style of the gallery-carving—a miserable contrast to the exquisite work which was removed. Another gallery, of large dimensions, adds its deformity to the west end of the building; and beyond it, underneath, is the ground floor of the tower, forming an entrance to the church at the west end, through a pointed doorway. The side aisles are in the Perpendicular style, and were obviously added to the original building during the fifteenth century. They are finished externally with battlements disproportionately large. The chancel appears to be about the same date as the nave; or perhaps it is a little later. The east window, which contains stained glass, is composed of three lancet lights within a pointed arch, in the head of which are two elongated quatrefoils surmounted by a lozenge-shaped figure in the apex. What appears to have been the piscina may be detected in the *north* wall, almost concealed by the modern paneling of the chancel. [1] In the same wall, near its north-west end, is an aperture supposed by some to have been a place for confession. [2] It is, in reality, a squint, lori-

[1] The *usual* situation is in the *south* wall. See page 52.
[2] Many churches were anciently furnished with an aperture opening

cula, or hagioscope,[1] the object of which was to
enable the persons who occupied the eastern end of
the north aisle to view the elevation of the host at the
altar—an important object in Roman Catholic worship. There are similar apertures in the churches at
Musbury and Seaton.

The eastern end of the north aisle is divided by a
wooden screen containing carving of a contempora-
neous date with that of the aisle itself. It was not
improbably a chantry chapel; and there is evidence
of another chapel in the opposite aisle—a very small
and curious piscina being found in the easternmost
pier of the arches of that aisle. Against this pier,
and projecting into the nave, are placed the pulpit
and reading desk, of carved oak. The form of the
pulpit appears to have been originally dodecagonal,
or twelve-sided, but it now has only ten sides, two
of them having been cut away for the convenience of
erection. The form of pulpits, as well as that of
fonts and other objects in a church, is symbolical;[2]
but since the Reformation less attention has been

into the churchyard, for the 'outward confession of all comers,' intended
for the convenience of the passing traveller, who, although a stranger to
the officiating priest, could thus receive absolution upon his journey without much loss of time.—See the 'Handbook of English Ecclesiology.'

[1] The term *hagioscope* was introduced by the Ecclesiological (late
Camden Cambridge) Society, to replace the names *squint* and *loricula*
which were previously applied to such an aperture as that referred to in
the text.

[2] For a note on the symbolization of fonts see our account of Axminster church.

paid to such matters than previously, and many of
the subsequent forms are therefore the result of accident or caprice.

The font stands near the western doorway. It is
square and shallow,[1] on a high circular stem. It is
quite plain, and is probably ancient. The nave, we
have yet omitted to state, has a coved ceiling, which
is pierced with two dormer windows on each side.
There are some very old oak benches in the church;
and some new benches, carved with the linen pattern,
have just been erected in the chancel by Colonel
Bragge, the patron of the living. There are mural
monuments to some members of the Bragge family;
William Hood, Esq., 1814; the Rev. W. French,
vicar of the parish, 1760; and the Rev. Thomas
Cook, another vicar, 1747. Mr. Cook had possessed
the living for forty years, and was eminent for his
amiable disposition and numerous charities.[2] The

[1] 'Of other forms, less admissible, the *square* is the principal. This
was a favorite in Romanesque time, but evidently from the superior ease
only with which it is worked. It died out, as a use, in First-Pointed;
is scarcely to be found in Middle-Pointed; but was sometimes employed
in rude late work, as in S. Laurence, Telscombe, Sussex. It also occurs
in Cornwall churches, where old forms are strangely united with modern
details.'—'*Handbook of English Ecclesiology.*'

[2] 'The Rev. Thomas Cook, in 1734, gave to the parish a mansion, now
known by the name of the school-house; appropriating the great hall,
two butteries, and three chambers over them, with the orchard and garden,
for the occupation of a schoolmaster who should teach six poor children:
the remainder of the premises for the habitation of poor persons, to be
maintained out of the parish rates. Mrs. Elizabeth Bragge, in 1719, gave
a rent-charge of £2 10s. per annum to the school.'—*Lysons.*

most curious monument is a large brass on the floor
of the north aisle representing full length figures of
Sir Thomas and Lady Brook, of Olditch. The inscription, partly concealed beneath the pews on each
side, is beautifully cut in Old English, and gives the
date 'MCCCC & XXXVIJ, the XV yere of Kinge
Harry the VJ.' The church is dedicated to the Virgin Mary. The living is a vicarage, valued in the
King's Books at £15 18s. 9d., and the tithes are
commuted at £516.[1] The Rev. John Bragge is the
present vicar, and the Rev. John Marsh the officiating minister.[2]

Besides the school charities mentioned in the preceding page, there is an annuity of 33s. 4d. arising
from a spot of land called Mitchell's, in Thorncombe,
given to the poor in bread on the Sunday after
Christmas-day. It was left by John Rockett, alias
Wakely, by will dated November 7, 1615.[3]

We must not forget to state, in taking our leave

[1] 1847A. 1R. 26P. of land in the parish are tithe free (see page 163),
having belonged to the Abbey of Ford.

[2] We are indebted to Mr. Marsh for a copy of an original document
'of William by divine mercy the humble minister of the church at Exeter,' dated '1239, the fourteenth of the calends of January.' It recites
that 'after the death of Philip, the present vicar of Thorncombe, his
successors shall pay annually six marks out of the church of Thorncombe
to the church of Ford' [Ford Abbey] instead of two marks as previously.
This was done 'for the sake of increasing divine worship, that light might
not be wanting to those who labored in the vineyard of the Lord of
Sabaoth.'

[3] '*Report of the Commissioners of the Charities of Devon.*' Vol I.
page 142.

of Thorncombe, that, notwithstanding its comparative
seclusion, it was not without its active partizans in
the cause of Monmouth when that unfortunate personage made the West of England the scene of his
short-lived triumph. After Jeffreys' assize at Exeter,
in September, 1685, as many as thirty-three persons
belonging to Thorncombe were known to have been
concerned in the rebellion and could not be apprehended.   Their names were published, along with
those of more than three hundred besides belonging
to the neighbourhood, [1] who lived at hide and seek in
the woods and fields, and in the houses of such of
their friends as could be found willing to manifest
their dangerous sympathy.   ‘*The Western Martyrology*’ records that ‘Mr. Thomas Stayle, of Thorncombe, was severely whipped on the sentence of
Jeffreys.   His sufferings were so hard that it caused
many to pity him.   He was a good liver, well beloved
amongst his neighbours, and a true protestant.’

[1] Of these, 92 belonged to Axminster, 76 to Colyton, 34 to Axmouth,
6 to Combepyne, 18 to Membury, and 9 to Musbury.

CHAPTER VII.

WE have not yet, Piscator, reached the limits of the
' preserved ground' between Winsham and Tytherleigh Bridge. We can, therefore, say but very little
about the angling matters which must occupy our
attention when we get beyond the range of keepers
to the ground below, which is so liberally thrown
open to all who choose to ply their art upon the
' daynteous denisons' of this delightful stream. The
remaining distance, however, is not great, and while
we linger over it, let us, friend, indulge in some
discoursing about the town of Chard, which lies five
miles behind us. This may seem, perhaps, like travelling out of our way. But we must recollect that
although the town is so far off, we are now actually
walking in the *parish*, which the river bounds for a
considerable distance in the vicinity of West Ford. [1]

[1] The Axe separates the parish of Chard from that of Thorncombe
for about two miles, namely, from about a quarter of a mile above Broad-
bridge to the same distance above Tytherleigh bridge. At West Ford the
Axe receives a tributary which rises at Chard and flows by the hamlet of

But it is sufficiently distant from the river to warrant
us in being far more brief than the importance of the
town would otherwise justify,—especially since it
cannot be regarded as an angling station.

Chard, the most southerly town in Somerset, is
seven miles from Axminster, eight from Crewkerne,
and twelve from Taunton. It is situated on one of
the sides of the range of hills in which are seated
the villages of Combe Saint Nicholas, Buckland,
Chardstock, Yarcombe, and Membury,—the range
which for some distance separates the valley of the
Axe from that of its tributary the Yarty. The town
consists of three principal streets which cross each
other at nearly right angles. The front street, called
Fore-street, as far up as the intersection of the other
streets, and High-street above it, is wide and straight,
and about three-fourths of a mile long. It has been
greatly improved within a few years. Some shambles,
a market-house, and an ancient building[1] at the in-

Perry-street, from which hamlet the tributary derives its name—'the
Perry-street Brook.'. The brook contains a few trout, and would contain
many if the factory worthies would leave them alone, or else would fish
fairly. There are three factories driven by this little stream:—a lace
factory belonging to Mr. Payne, in which about 130 hands are employed;
a smaller lace factory belonging to Mr. Gifford; and a small cloth factory,
called Knap Mills, belonging to Mr. John Phillips.

[1] This was called the Guildhall, or 'the New Work.' It is said to
have been originally a chapel, but was used from time immemorial as the
Townhall. In a deed which we have consulted, dated 1570, it is described
as a building *considered* to have been formerly a chapel of ease, 'but
there is no evidence to prove it.' The old market-house was used as an
assize hall when the assizes were held at Chard. Among the cases tried

tersection of the three streets, formerly obstructed and deformed it. All these have been removed, and large and convenient shambles, over which are the townhall and other apartments, have been erected in a handsome building fronting the main street.[1] This street derives a considerable degree of picturesqueness from some ancient houses which have escaped the ravages of modern 'improvement,' and remain to link the associations of the present with those of the past. They are of squared flint, and were erected, probably, at some time during the sixteenth century. The grammar school, at the entrance of the town from Crewkerne, is in the same style and forms a very ornamental object.[2] The streets, which are well paved and lighted with gas, have a copious stream of water flowing through them.[3]

at Chard of which the records have been preserved, are those of some royalists in the time of Cromwell. But the most curious case is that related in Glanvil's 'Witchcraft' of Jane Brookes, who, in 1658, 'took her trial at Chard assizes for bewitching a boy named Richard Jones, and was executed.'

[1] The new market-house was opened on September 21, 1835.

[2] This school owes its origin to a deed poll dated May 24, 1671, signed by William Symes, of Poundsford, Somerset, Esquire, grandson and heir at law of John Symes. The said William, in consideration of the sum of £300, previously paid to John Symes, and of a piece of plate given to himself by the portreeve and burgesses of Chard, conveyed 'the burgage, messuage, and tenement,' now known as the school-house, to certain trustees, to be converted into a place for a grammar school and the residence of its master. The school is open to the sons of any of the inhabitants of Chard on a small annual payment, and the master has the privilege of receiving boarders. The present master is the Rev. Mr. Gould.—See 'Report of the Commissioners for the Charities of Somerset.'

[3] The editor of Camden's 'Britannia' annotates that 'this stream, by

That Chard was known to the Romans is evident from the coins and other remains of that people which have at different times been found in its vicinity. In 1810, a tesselated pavement, which has been often described, was discovered at Wadford, in the parish of Combe St. Nicholas, about a mile north-west of the town. A very short distance from this, in the parish of Chard, was found, a few years since, a silver coin of the Emperor Claudius, in beautiful preservation, representing, on the reverse, four horses abreast. It is one of the coins well known to have been struck in commemoration of the subjugation of the Britons. In 1836, as many as 300 Roman copper coins were found just within a field on the Axminster road, about a quarter of a mile from Chard church. They were in a heap, about twenty inches below the surface of the soil. At Southchard, also, near Saint Margaret's chapel, several Roman coins have been dug up, chiefly of the reign of Constantine. Tesseræ and pieces of Roman tile, exactly corresponding with those discovered at Combe Saint Nicholas, have been found at the same place; and the appearance of the ground would seem to indicate the

being turned, as it easily may be, north or south, will run, as is affirmed, either into the Severn or the South Sea.' 'A real fact,' adds Collinson, 'and hence it appears that it rises in the highest land between the vales which communicate with either sea.' A similar circumstance occurs at Roundham, Crewkerne, where, after a fall of rain, part of the water runs into the Parrott and the other part into the Axe. Those rivers empty themselves on opposite sides of the island.

presence of more important remains which a careful search might bring to light. Again, at West Ford, besides coins, a little vase of earthenware, apparently Roman, was discovered buried in a field.[1] A glance at the map will show that the places at which those articles were found are nearly in a direct line with each other and with the two important entrenchments of Neroche and Lambert's Castle, which, although of Ancient British origin, were undoubtedly occupied by the Romans. May the conjecture, therefore, be hazarded that a Roman vicinal way connected those entrenchments along the line which we have indicated, and that it fell into the road near Portway and Olditch which branched from the Fosse and led, as we have traced at page 13, to Weycroft and Lambert's Castle?

Chard, however, was undoubtedly a place of no importance in the time of the Romans, although its claims to antiquity are by no means inconsiderable. It is called in Domesday, *Cerdre*, a word which is said to have been derived from Cerdic, a Saxon, who, with his son Cenric, arrived in this country in the year 495.[2]

[1] Many of the coins and other articles mentioned in the text are in the possession of Mr. Arthur Hull, of Tudbeer, Chard, who has a considerable collection of old coins and other curiosities, found in the locality, and who has placed us under considerable obligations, not only for access to his museum and library, but also for the valuable information which he has orally communicated.

[2] 'He was a German by nation,' says William of Malmesbury, 'of the noblest race, being the tenth from Woden, and having nurtured his

Chard, in common with the entire hundred of
Kingsbury East, in which it is situated, [1] belonged,
from a very remote period, to the Bishop of Bath
and Wells, and it is thus surveyed in Domesday:—
'The same bishop holds Cerdre. He also held it in
the time of King Edward, and gelded for eight hides.
The arable is twenty carucates. Thereof in demesne
are two hides, and there are two carucates, and eleven
servants, and twenty villains, with fourteen ploughs.
There is a mill yielding thirty-pence, and twenty
acres of meadow. Wood two miles long and four

ambition in domestic broils, determined to leave his native land and extend his fame by the sword. Having formed this daring resolution, he
communicated his design to Cenric his son, who closely followed his
father's track to glory, and with his concurrence transported his forces
into Britain in five ceols.' He dealt fearful havoc among the poor Britons, quickly compelling them to fly, and founded the West-Saxon
kingdom, becoming king of Wessex in 519, and dying in 534, to be
succeeded by his son.' See ' *The Anglo-Saxon Chronicle.*'

[1] It is also in the Western Division of the County, its polling place
being Ilminster—in the diocese of Bath and Wells, and in the deanery of
Crewkerne. It is a county court division, and petty sessions are held
monthly. The sessions were formerly held at Crewkerne, as appears from
several entries in the Chard parish books. One entry, in 1738, is as follows:—'Charges at Crewkerne sessions, horse hire and expences, 3s.'
[See page 108.] Chard is likewise the centre of a union comprising the
following parishes:—CHARD DISTRICT—Buckland St. Mary, Chard
Borough, Chard Parish, Combe St. Nicholas, Wambrook, Whitestaunton,
Yarcombe. CREWKERNE DISTRICT—Chillington, Crewkerne, Cricket
St. Thomas, Cudworth, Dinnington, Hinton St. George, Lopen, Merriott,
Wayford, Winsham. ILMINSTER DISTRICT—Ashill, Broadway, Chaff-
combe, Cricket Malherbie, Donyatt, Dowlish Wake, Ilminster, Ilton,
Kingstone, Knowle St. Giles, Seavington St. Mary, Seavington St.
Michael, Shepton Beauchamp, Stocklinch Magdalen, Stocklinch Ottersey,
West Dowlish, Whitelackington.

furlongs broad; and as much of pasture. Of the same land a thane holds two hides, which cannot be separated from the church. The whole is worth sixteen pounds.'

The bishop obtained a charter of free warren in all his demesne lands within this parish, which were rated, in 1293, at £32 3s. 4d. The manor now belongs to Earl Poulett. The borough was incorporated by Bishop Jocelyn, who gave fifty-two acres out of his manor of Chard for the purpose of enlarging the town, which previously consisted solely of the part now called 'Old Town,' and which is not included in the modern borough. Its privilege of sending members to parliament was, however, of short duration, extending only from the year 1300 to 1329. The burgesses quarrelled among themselves, objected to the expense of *paid members*, and soon forfeited, by disuse, the privilege which has never been restored.[1] The town, however, continued till the passing of the Municipal Reform Act, in 1835, to be governed by a portreve and two bailiffs, chosen annually at a court leet.[2] By the act referred to it was

[1] The following were the representatives of Chard at the periods assigned to them. They constitute the entire list:—28 Edward I (A.D. 1300), John Benedict and Thomas Haville. 6 Edward II (1313), Peter Clark and William Sopere. 7 Edward II, John Longfarr and Stephen de Legh. 8 Edward II, John Benedict and Thomas Haville. 15 and 16 Edward II, William Sopere and John Benedict. 19 Edward II, Henry Corton and Henry Fabri. 1 and 2 Edward III (1327), John le Smyth and Richard le Dykere.

[2] The court leet is still held, though shorn of nearly all its original

given a town council, consisting of a mayor (chosen from the council), four aldermen, and twelve councillors. The mayor is a magistrate for the borough during his year of office, and also during the year which succeeds it. The borough and parish have separate churchwardens and overseers. They are, indeed, separate parishes, except only for ecclesiastical purposes. The parishes contain five tithings, namely :—Old Town, Crimchard, Forton, Tatworth, and Southchard. [1] These comprise an area of 5136 acres. The population of the borough is 2291, and that of the parish 3006, being a decrease, since 1841,

importance. The origin of leets is thus given in Wood's '*Institute:*'— 'In early times, the administration of justice was limited, in a great measure, to districts. The sheriff's court, or turn (from *tour*, a circuit), had jurisdiction throughout the county; but as the people were put to great trouble in travelling to the sheriff's turn, *leets*, or *views of frankpledge* (from *free-pledge*, that is surety for freemen—see page 63) were granted to the lords of hundreds, manors, and other franchises. . . . . . . The leet is a court of record held before the steward of the leet, that the king may be certified, by the view of the steward, of the manners of the people within that precinct, for the preservation of the peace and the punishment of several offences against the public. For this reason every one must belong to some leet.' (See page 63.) Courts leet, and many other of the old courts and customs of our noble Saxon ancestors, are very rapidly disappearing with the circumstances which called them into existence.

[1] At Southchard, three miles south of Chard, and about a mile and a half from West Ford Mill, is Saint Margaret's Chapel, [see page 230] now used as a meeting house for the particular baptists. It exhibits the remains of an ancient ecclesiastical edifice in the Early English style, and an old vault, approached by steps, was lately discovered in an adjoining garden. At Tatworth, near Southchard, and on the road to Axminster, a church, in imitation of the Early-English style, was erected in 1851. Nearly opposite this church is a handsome mansion called Parrock's Lodge, now the residence and property of J. C. Langdon, Esq.

of 491 in the whole. [1]   Several attempts have been made in former times to unite the parish and borough into one parish for *every* purpose.   At the county sessions at Ilchester, in 1667, it was ordered that they should be so united.   The order, however, was not acted upon; and, indeed, the two magistrates whose report in favor of the union had been confirmed at those sessions, signed *separate* rates almost immediately afterwards. [2]   The attempt at a union was renewed at the Bridgwater sessions in July, 1786, and the matter was left to be removed by certiorari into the court of King's Bench.   The parish, like a spirited young lady who found herself about to be forced into an objectionable alliance, was determined to resist; and the council for the borough, anticipating an

---

[1] The town languishes under the absence of railway accommodation from which (thanks to the jealousies of rival companies) this part of the country has so long been suffering. [See page 42.]   But it has the advantage of a canal to Creech Saint Michael, to join the Bridgwater and Taunton Canal.   Canals, however, can ill compete with railroads, and we hope that the *better things* now promised will in due time be realised in the whistle of the steam engine through the quiet recesses of the valley of the Axe.   We should state that an Act of Parliament has lately been obtained for converting the canal into a railway; but there appears to be no immediate chance of the desirable metamorphosis.   The reservoir of the canal, at Furnham, where there are extensive wharves, is a fine piece of water covering about seventy acres.   It contains some remarkable trout, of which mention is made in the ' *Vade Mecum of Fly Fishing for Trout,*' page 19.   The canal was opened for traffic in May, 1842.

[2] These rates are still preserved, and they are curious from their form, which is not that of a book, like the rates of the present day, but simply a long list of names—five or six feet in length; and they were evidently affixed to the church doors entire.

adverse decision, advised his clients to proceed no further. The matter was therefore dropped. Considerable ill-feeling, however, existed between the inhabitants of the borough and those of the parish, up to a recent period;—the former smarting under reflections near akin, we may imagine, to those of a foiled and unscrupulous lover, and the latter acting like an indignant damsel, proud of her escape and determined for the future to keep such admirers at a distance. But this ill-feeling is become a thing of the past, and the ancient dispute is forgotten. The great car of Time, as it rolls along its rugged road, smooths deeper ruts than those. So Chard and ' Chardland,' if not one in parochial matters, are now united in all that relates to the good of either and to the general weal.

Chard, from an early period, has possessed one of the best weekly markets in the West of England. The market, as usual, was originally granted for Sunday, [1] and is so mentioned by Dr. Stukely; but it has for generations been held, as at present, on Monday, though attempts have been made to alter the day. [2] In Collinson's time (1790) it was cele-

---

[1] See page 122.

[2] Collinson gives the following as a foot note:—' Whereas, since the determination of Mr. Baron Price on the late trial concerning the borough of Chard, in the county of Somerset, the market there is begun to be held on Mondays, as formerly: and whereas certain persons, falsely pretending themselves to be Mayor and Burgesses of the said borough, have lately set up a Tuesday's market, by virtue (as they pretend) of a

brated as the largest market in England for potatoes,
—'thirty waggon loads,' says he, 'being brought on
a market day, frequently, during the season, and
seldom less than twenty.' It has three fairs yearly,
namely, on the first Wednesday in May, August, and
November.

The manufacture of cloth was formerly the staple
trade of Chard, and on its extinction it was
succeeded by the manufacture of lace, which is
extensively carried on in two large factories, one
belonging to Mr. John Sherwood Wheatley, of
Nottingham, and conducted by Mr. Catford, and the
other belonging to Mr. James Hill.[1] Mr. Wheatley
employs about 300 hands, exclusively of 'menders,'
who work at their own houses. Mr. Hill employs
about 180, exclusively also of 'menders.'

'The fair town of Chard,' as Clarendon calls it,
was frequently occupied, during the civil wars of

charter from King Charles the Second. To all such persons as repair
to the Monday's market, this is to give notice, that by advice of council
such grant of a Tuesday's market is in itself void, and the said charter
long since determined ; and that the market of the said borough will, as
legally it may, be holden on Monday, notwithstanding the notice given
by the said pretended Mayor and Burgesses to the contrary. And we,
the members of the old corporation of portreve and burgesses, do, as
formerly, engage to bear all cost and damage that may accrue unto them
by reason of their repairing unto the said Monday's market. Dated the
2nd day of January, 1704. Nath. Pitts, Richard Legge, John Pitts,
John Newcomen, John Chapman, John Smith, Richard Ivery, John
Slater, George Selwood, George Strong.'

[1] Mr. Wheatley's Factory was burned down on the night of April
9th, 1825. It then belonged to Messrs. Wheatley and Risto, and was
immediately rebuilt.

King Charles and the parliament, by the troops of
both parties; and the king himself, who was with
one division of his army, took up his quarters there
for a week in the end of September, 1644, when on
his way from Cornwall and Exeter to his intended
winter quarters at Oxford.   His great object in halting at Chard was to obtain the supplies which the
Commissioners of Somersetshire had promised to
send thither.   He also issued a proclamation, dated
from Chard, inviting the 'speedy peace' which he
never lived to enjoy.   'It was on the last of September,' says Clarendon,[1] 'that the king marched
from Chard and quarter'd that night at a house of
the Lord Pawlet's [at Hinton St. George], where
Prince Rupert met him and gave him an account
of the unhappy affairs of the North, and that he had
left about two thousand horse under the command
of Sir Marmaduke Langdale, which *he might as well
have brought with him*, and then the king would have
had *a glorious end of his western expedition*.'[2]

Among the numerous plots and insurrections of
the defeated royalists, after the establishment of the
Commonwealth, the most formidable was the insurrection in Hampshire and Wiltshire which commenced

[1] '*History of the Rebellion*.' Vol. II, p. 117. Folio ed. Oxford, 1703.

[2] Mr. Hull (see note, page 231) has in his collection several tokens
coined at Chard during the rebellion, (see page 114).   The issurers were
'the Portrif,' 1669; Thomas Williams, 1656; George Bartly; William
Sayer, 1670; William Buridg, 1665; Humphrey Able; Peter Way; and
Henry Seldred.

on March 12, 1655. On that day the judges were seized at Salisbury, where the assizes had just commenced. They were brought out 'in their robes, and humbly produced their commissions.'[1] The gaol was broken open and the prisoners were liberated. The leaders of this insurrection were Sir Joseph Wagstaff, Mr. Jones, Mr. Penruddock, and Mr. Hugh Grove. Their followers were not more than two hundred in number. After proclaiming 'Charls Stuart' king they condemned the judges to be hanged; but afterwards 'poor Penruddock was so passionate for to preserve their lives, *as if works of this nature could be done by halves*, that the major-general (Wagstaff) durst not persist in it.'[2] The triumph was brief. The royalists went westward, and were pursued by Captain Crook and his troop, who defeated them at South Molton.[3] Upwards of sixty, including three of their leaders, were taken. Wagstaff escaped. Some of the prisoners were tried at Exeter, others at Salisbury, and the rest at Chard. Penruddock, Grove, and many others were executed. Jones was respited. 'Likewise at Chard,' says a writer of the time, 'were divers of those persons executed on May 17, 1655.'[4]

[1] Clarendon's '*History of the Rebellion.*'
[2] Ibid.
[3] Some accounts say at *Chard.*
[4] See page 229. Major Hunt, an ancestor of the well known late Henry Hunt, member of parliament for Preston, was condemned to death for having been concerned in this rising; but he escaped from Il-chester gaol disguised in his sister's clothes.

Chard was also the scene of some of the atrocities of Jeffreys with which the West of England was but too familiar after the failure of Monmouth's rebellion. Twelve of his victims, condemned at Taunton, were hanged at Chard upon an oak which, Tradition says, still stands at the cross road leading to the union-house at the foot of the town. It is known to this day by the name of Hangcross Tree.[1] Among the individual cases the particulars of which have been preserved, may be selected the case of Mr. Matthew Bragge, of Childhay, which is given at length in ' *The New Martyrology :* '—The Duke of Monmouth had arrived at Chard on Tuesday, June 16 (old style), having landed at Lyme on the preceding Thursday, and had sent a party of his horse into the country ' to search the house of a Roman Catholic for arms.' On their way they met Mr. Bragge on horseback, as he was returning home from a gentleman's house at which he had been transacting business as an attorney. They compelled him to become their guide, and urged him to join the standard of the Duke, which he positively refused to do. Arrived at the house, they proceeded to their search, while Mr. Bragge remained

---

[1] The names of the persons executed at Chard were :—Edward Foote, John Knight, William Williams, John Jervis, Humphrey Hitchcock, William Godfrey, Abraham Pill, Henry Easterbrook, William Day, Simon Cross, Edward Warran, and James Durnett. There is a field at Snowdon called Hanging Close, at which, when the new road to Honiton was cut, in the year 1827, some human bones were found. Perhaps to increase the interest in the *instructive* scene, some of the victims were executed at one place and some at the other.

outside without dismounting. The business over, they took him with them to Chard, where great persuasions were again resorted to, but with no better success than before. On the following morning he prepared to return home, when he was informed that his horse was seized for Monmouth's service. He therefore set out on foot, without having even seen the Duke. After the discomfiture at Sedgemoor, 'some busy person' lodged information against him with a justice—'the said justice accounting the matter in itself but trivial, and indeed all men did judge him out of danger.' He was tried at Dorchester, at the ensuing assizes, and with twenty-eight others, out of thirty, received sentence of death, 'the jury being well instructed by the Lord Chief Justice, who had been often heard to declare that no lawyer or parson ever coming before him should escape.' Two days afterwards the same town was the scene of his execution, in company with twelve other persons—the rest having been considerately distributed amongst other towns for the purpose of teaching the 'moral lesson' of the gallows with that of its demoniacal concomitants of 'drawing and quartering.' The only 'favor of this protestant judge,' concludes the writer of this awful history, 'was to give his body to his friends in order to its interment among his ancestors.'

Chard church is dedicated to Saint Mary. It stands at the entrance of the town from Axminster, at the extremity of Holyrood-street. In common with the great majority of Somersetshire churches, it is built in the Third Pointed or Perpendicular style of the fifteenth century. It is, however, rendered greatly inferior to many of them by the absence of a clerestory,[1] and also by the want of boldness in the ornamental details of the windows and other parts of the building. But the general effect of the exterior, notwithstanding, is a certain amount of *completeness*, which goes far to counteract the imperfections to which we have referred. It is surrounded by a churchyard, which, a few years since, was enclosed with iron palisades. The building consists of a chancel, nave and side aisles, transepts, and a tower. Projecting from the centre of each aisle are what might originally have been chantry chapels, of which there were several in connection with this church.[2] Perhaps the north transept was a porch, but a window now occupies the place of the doorway, if there ever was one, and it is entered only from the interior of the building. It is now used as a baptistry. The font and its stem are octagonal, and are

[1] See page 54.

[2] 'In this church were formerly several gilds, fraternities, and chantries, viz.:—I. The fraternity of the Blessed Virgin Mary. William Atkyns and others, wardens of this fraternity, were recorded for having purchased burgages in the town of Chard without the king's licence, 19 Ric. II. II. The chantry of the Holy Trinity. Robert Strange gave a rent and burgage in Chard to the use of this chantry, 19 Henry VI. III. William Peats, the last incumbent of a gild here, was, in 1553, allowed a pension of five pounds.'—Collinson's 'Somerset.' Willis's 'History of Abbeys,' &c., &c.

ornamented with quatrefoils and the Tudor rose. The uniformity of their date with that of the church is thus clearly indicated. The projection on the opposite side is used as the vestry. The tower, which stands at the west end of the church, is square, embattled, and furnished with buttresses, gurgoyles, and pinnacles, with a turret surmounted by a weather-cock. It has stone windows pierced for light and sound, and contains a clock and chimes and six bells.[1] The bell ropes in former times used to descend in every church to the ground floor, as they do in many churches at the present day. That they did at Chard is evident from an inspection of the floor above, to which the ringers are now elevated. The doorway opening into the ground floor of the tower, which thus answers to a porch, forms the principal entrance

[1] Upon one of them is this inscription:—'We were five recast into six, in the year 1790, by T. Bilbie, Cullompton, Devon. Rev. Thomas Alford, Vicar; William Read and Edward Tapp, churchwardens.' The personification of bells, of which an instance is afforded by the phrase 'we five,' &c., is very curious. It appears to have prevailed from very early times, and to have been universal in the christian world. The ancients, indeed, gave to their bells the names of men and women. In the tenth century they began the custom of consecrating them, by the act of sprinkling with holy water and other ceremonies, which were supposed to give them the property of driving away evil spirits [see page 49]. Bells are said by Du Cange to have been invented by the Italians. They appear to have been introduced into this country during the seventh century, and were at first rung by the priests themselves. In later times, bell ringing became a favorite amusement, and was carried to great perfection. Even the highest classes thought it no degradation. Sir Matthew Hale and Anthony Wood are mentioned, among others, as having been particularly attached to an amusement which is now hardly allowed the name.

to the church, through a second doorway underneath the flights of stairs which lead over it into the organ gallery at the west end of the nave. The eye is not particularly struck on entering the building, unless with the *neatness* of the church and the good order in which it is kept. There is none of the loftiness, grandeur, and elegance with which a visitor to Crewkerne church is impressed. The painted window at the chancel most likely first attracts attention, and therefore we will commence our brief description of the interior at this point. [1] The chancel is remarkably short—extending but a few feet beyond the transept. It is lighted by two side windows and the east window, which is of five lights, and contains a representation, in stained glass, of Christ in the garden. There is nothing else remarkable in the chancel, the modern paneling of which effectually conceals whatever traces there may happen to be of the piscina or other interesting remains. The south transept, which is entered beneath a beautiful paneled arch, is lighted by four windows. The south aisle has five windows in the side wall, each consisting of three lights with foliated headings and the usual tracery of the period in the head, and one window at the west end. The north transept has three windows and the north aisle five, with a transomed window at its west end. [2] At the western side of the exterior of the north transept

[1] This window was erected by subscription in October, 1829.
[2] See page 55.

is a turret containing stairs which lead to the leads. The nave is divided from its aisles by three pointed arches on each side. It has a coved ceiling, with no pretensions to elegance, divided into compartments by ribs of wood which cross each other at right angles. The ceilings of the aisles partake of the lean-to form of their roofs, and are also ribbed—the ceiling of the north aisle being considerably handsomer and of earlier date than that of the opposite aisle. There are galleries in both aisles, erected in 1828, when the church underwent extensive repair. They are lighted by dormer windows, embellished, outside, with pinnacles. In the gallery which crosses the entire church at the west end, is an organ, erected in 1814.[1] The pulpit and reading desk stand in the centre of the nave, at its western end; and behind them is a large stove, the pipe of which passes in an unsightly manner in front of the eastern window. Two chandeliers depend from the roof into the nave—the parishioners, in the lighting of their church, still patronising the tallow chandler in preference to the gas manufacturer.

There are but few monuments in the church, and those are far from being imposing. The records of the departed—the sad tales which tell so tritely, and too often so ostentatiously, of the end of all worldly

---

[1] The first organ in Chard church was erected in 1788. It was sold for the use of one of the dissenting chapels when the present organ was erected.

greatness—are appropriately inscribed upon plain mural tablets. There is, however, one exception in the curious old monument to the memory of 'William Brewer, of Chard, Phisitian,' his wife, and their children. The dates are 1614 and 1618, and the arms *gules*, two bends, wavy, *or*. It stands high up against the north-east angle of the south transept. It is of marble and porphyry, ornamented with angels and other figures, with Corinthian columns on each side supporting a cornice, beneath which, in arched recesses, are effigies of the deceased persons kneeling at an altar, one of the parents on each side, facing each other, and their children, size after size, kneeling in pairs behind them,—all in the quaint costume of the period.

The living of Chard is a vicarage, in the patronage of the Bishop of Bath and Wells. It is valued in the King's Books at £36 18s. 9d., and the tithes are commuted at £520 5s. per annum. The great tithes, with a small exception, are leased by Earl Poulett of the Dean of Wells.[1] The vicarage is vacant by the recent death of the Rev. W. B. Whitehead.[2] The

[1] They are disposed of thus:—Annual amount of tithes leased by Earl Poulett, £306 10s. Tithes of 'Overlands' (belonging to Earl Poulett), £12 11s. Lease from the Dean of Wells by the widow of the late Robert Cuff, Esq., £3 9s. Total great tithes £322 10s.

[2] The late vicar, the Rev. William Bailey Whitehead, died August 22, 1853, while this sheet was passing through the press. He had been vicar for twenty-eight years, and was much respected by his parishioners, whose welfare was his unceasing study.

officiating minister is the Rev. H. T. Thomson. The vicarage house and the school rooms are on opposite sides of the church.

There are four dissenting places of worship in Chard, namely:—an Independent chapel in Fore-street, a chapel for the Baptists, and one for the Particular Baptists in Holyrood-street, and a Wesleyan chapel.

Besides the grammar school already mentioned, Chard possesses a valuable charity in the shape of an almshouse, or a 'hospital'—a new and handsome building in High-street. It was founded by Richard Harvey, of Exeter, who, by will dated July 17, 1663, left for that purpose some lands and other property in Norfolk and Cambridge, after the death of certain of his relations who were first to enjoy them. 'The building was left by the will of a Mr. John Monday, the date of which has not been ascertained. From the time that Harvey's charity commenced, in 1698, the building began to be used for the purposes of that charity, as a hospital or almshouse for the poor people appointed by the trust . . . . . to receive relief from this benefaction;' namely, 'eighteen (men and women) residing in the house and eleven out of it, who receive from one shilling to three shillings and sixpence per week, according to their circumstances,' [1] besides occasional relief in the shape of

---

[1] Commissioners' Report of '*The Charities of Somersetshire.*'

coals, bedding, medicine, &c.; and they are buried at the expense of the charity.

From 'Coggan's charity' the poor receive fifty-two shillings a year divided amongst them; and from 'Eveleigh's charity' twenty poor widows receive the interest of twenty-two pounds yearly in bread. [1]

*   *   *   *   *   *   *   *

*   *   *   *   *   *   *

A leap over that bog at the style, Piscator, and here we are in 'Lady Meads,' [2] at the foot of which is Tytherleigh Bridge. [3]   Thence to the sea, through

---

[1] On a tomb on the north side of the church is the following inscription:—'Here lieth the body of Elizabeth Knight, widdow, who died the 2 day of August, 1644, and gave vnto the poore of the town of Chard 30 pound, to remain for ever; and ten pound to the church.'

[2] 'Lady Meads' are two beautiful meadows on the east bank of the river, the rent of which belongs to the 'second poor' of the parish of Chardstock.

[3] Tytherleigh bridge derives its name from the family of Tytherleigh to whom belonged the estate and manor of the same name, situated on the hill about half a mile west of the bridge, on the turnpike road from Axminster to Chard.   What remains of the original mansion is now a farm house.   At a very early period, William Tyderleigh held of the Bishop of Sarum, by knight's service, a hide and a half of land at Tytherleigh; and in 1400 (3 Rict. II) a person of the same name did homage to the bishop for lands 'held in the manor of Chardstock.'   Tytherleigh manor, in 1578 (20 Eliz.), was held by Robert *Tudderley*, at his death, together with 'a messuage, garden, and cottage, and ninety-two acres of land, of the bishop, as of his manor of Chardstock.'   The family of Tytherleigh is now extinct.   Its last member was living in 1741.   He had dissipated a fortune, and sold Tytherleigh to Mr. Pitt, of Chard.   [See Hutchings's '*Dorset*.'] The arms of Tytherleigh, which were not allowed till the time of Elizabeth, were:—*Ermine*, two glazier's cripping irons in saltire, *gules*.   These may

one of the loveliest of the lovely vales of Devon, and on the banks of one of the best and *most neglected* of its streams, is an uninterrupted range of *open* ground, in which the 'brother of the angle,' be his *caste* or clothing what it will, may wander as he listeth, uninterrupted and 'unforbidden.' [1]

Let us then, friend, at once resume our angling operations, and, commencing at the bridge, proceed along this western bank to fish our way to Axminster, some four miles down the stream. We shall have

now be seen in stone at the entrance gate, having been lately removed from a wall in the dwelling-house. Tytherleigh now belongs to J. C. Langdon, Esq., of Parrock's Lodge. A very comfortable and 'well conducted' inn stands near the farm-house, abutting on the road, about half way between Axminster and Chard. It is called 'Tytherleigh Inn,' and possesses peculiar attractions for the angling tourist.

[1] An excellent letter, signed 'D. L., Derwent Bank, Keswick,' was published in the '*Times*' newspaper of October 28th, 1851. The writer's object was that of inducing the anglers of Great Britain to combine for the purpose of obtaining an Act of Parliament for the better preservation of trout. 'By a legal enactment,' says he, 'which would summarily repress night poaching and the destruction of trout during the spawning season, and by the formation of Angling Associations in suitable districts, *all classes* would preserve the means of enjoying a healthy amusement, and the lesson of following his sport in an honest fashion could not fail to be applied by the *peasant or artisan* to his other relations in life.' The writer continues, with much good feeling and good sense, to urge the claims of the working man to a pursuit which too many absurdly fancy should be enjoyed only by the rich. Angling, in reality, is one of the few old English pastimes which was once pursued alike by all classes, and which had its share in the formation of the genuine *English* character as contradistinguished from that of all the other nations. A liberal encouragement of fair fishing among the working classes, divested of the spirit of *caste*, with which society is now so unfortunately pervaded, would do more, we think, than all the keepers, and all the restrictive laws, to extinguish poaching and to restore our rivers to their former condition.

abundant opportunities upon the way for discoursing
on the various localities which possess a claim upon
our attention. Almost every inch of the stream is
fishable. There is no intermission to the pools and
stickles which so uniformly succeed each other.
What a drawback to the charms of such a stream, that
so large a portion of it should be at the mercy of the
vilest poachers;—that an unaccountable indifference
prevails as to the fate of an invaluable breed of fish,
which, if it were not prolific in the extreme, must
have long since become extinct. [1]

Now try that run below the bridge, friend, carefully. The range at the turn beyond is ruffled by this
balmy breeze, and two or three goodly trout lie underneath the high bank opposite—especially at the
mouth of the tributary there. Well done ——— a
lively one and good! The fish, you see, already are
more shy than those above. We need not tell you
why. There!———basket him at once. The farm-
house in the third meadow below Tytherleigh Bridge,
on this western bank, is named from the river, 'Axe.'
We leave you, friend, to fish the river to the foot-
bridge opposite this farm, expecting it to yield you

[1] These remarks apply more particularly to the river *below* Axminster,
where the havoc of salmon and trout is incessant. One great evil is the
erroneous belief that the salmon and salmon-peal are *not* identical. Let
there be no salmon-peal killed for two years, and the abundance of *salmon*
at the end of that time would carry conviction, we think, to every unpre-
judiced mind. What a boon the river might be made to a neighbourhood
which need not *languish* if it did not, as it would appear, *prefer* to languish!—See *the Introductory Chapter*.

at least two brace of trout, while we say a few words about the tributary to which we have just referred, and tell a more lengthened tale about Hawkchurch—the village which you have been admiring upon the hill from which that tributary flows.

The tributary is called the Blackwater, and by no means inappropriately; for, from the nature of the soil over which it flows, and from its situation among the hills, it becomes foul after a comparatively light fall of rain, and often renders the Axe unfishable for some distance below its confluence. The Blackwater is very woody and of little account for angling, though valuable, of course, as a breeding-stream. It rises among the hills near Marshalsea, and, flowing through a combe below Hawkchurch, falls into the Axe, as we have stated, a few score yards below Tytherleigh Bridge.

Hawkchurch occupies an elevated and a delightful situation on the eastern side of the river, at the distance of about a mile and a half from its banks, and about four miles from Axminster, on the extreme verge of the county of Dorset. It is itself a prominent object from the valley, and is particularly distinguished by its lofty tower rising above a beautiful avenue of lime trees, about which we have a few words to say presently. The name Hawkchurch is significant of the situation of the place. It comes from the German *hock*, high. Heychurch, the common name, has a similar meaning, derived from the

Anglo-Saxon *heah.*[1] In the thirteenth century the
name was spelled *Avekchurch,* and also *Havekchurch.*[2]

Hawkchurch was formerly a tithing in the hundred
of Cerne, Totcombe, and Modbury, but it has within
a few years been constituted a liberty,[3] in which are
included the parish of Thorncombe and the adjoining
tithing of Beerhall, in the parish of Axminster.[4]
Hawkchurch is in the diocese of Salisbury, the
deanery of Bridport, and the union of Axminster,
to which it sends one guardian. The parish comprises 4030 acres, and its population is 773, of which
83 are registered voters. Its polling place is Beaminster.

No mention is made of Hawkchurch in Domesday
Book; but it belonged, at a very remote period, to
the abbot and convent of Cerne, and remained in
their possession till the Dissolution. The manor and
advowson were then given to John Leigh, who, in
1554, obtained a license to alienate them to Thomas
Moore, Esq., of Spargrove, Somerset. From the

[1] See Mr. Davidson's '*British and Roman Remains.*'

[2] Hutchins's '*Dorset.*'

[3] At page 212, Hawkchurch is erroneously spoken of as a *hundred.*

[4] Beerhall derives its name from the family of De la Beere, to which
it anciently belonged. By an heiress it came into the possession of the
Okestons, from whom it was sold to John le Jew. The daughter of Jew
married the Lord Chief Justice Hody, whose second son, Sir William
Hody, Chief Baron of the Exchequer, inherited the estate and settled
there. It is now the property of Sir Alexander Hood, and the dwelling-
house has for at least two hundred years been appropriated to the purposes
of a farm.—See Sir William Pole's '*Devon.*'

Moores they came, by marriage, about the close of
the reign of Elizabeth, or early in that of James I,
to the Wyndham family, of Trent, who sold them to
the Honorable J. Everard Arundell, of Wardour,
from whom the manor, as distinct from the advowson
and right of presentation, was purchased by the late
Admiral Lord Bridport, whose successor, the present
Lord Bridport, inherits it. A Mr. Hook bought
from Lord Arundell, for £1500, the then next right
of presentation to the rectory, and sold it, in 1800,
for £1800, to Mr. Newnham, of London, who subsequently purchased the advowson from Lady Caroline
Damer for £2000. [1]

Hawkchurch is divided into two tithings—Phillihome and Wylde Court. Of Phillihome there is
nothing worth recording. Wylde Court, now a farm-
house, is situated about a quarter of a mile west
of the church, which is approached through the
magnificent avenue of lime trees to which we have

---

[1] 'An advowson *(advocatio, jus patronatus)* is a right of presentation, or collation, to a church. Advowsons are of two kinds, *Appendant,*
and in *Gross.* I.—Appendant is a right of presentation dependant upon
a manor, lands, or tenements; and does pass in a grant of the manor as
an incident, without saying, " *with the appendants and appurtenances
thereunto belonging.*" But in the case of the king, though "*with the appurtenances,*" is added, an advowson will not pass without express mention of
it [See the 17 Ed. II, chap. 16]. II.—In *Gross,* is a right subsisting by
itself, belonging to a person, and not to a manor, lands, &c. So that
when an advowson appendant is severed by deed or will from the *corporeal*
inheritance [that is, an inheritance which can be touched or handled—
like franchises, privileges, tithes, &c.] to which it was appendant, then it
becomes an advowson in gross.'—Wood's *'Institute.'*

just referred. This avenue, and the field in which it is situated, are the appropriate scene of the annual festivities of the far-famed Hawkchurch Club, to which, for many years, the late rector, Dr. Rudge, so materially contributed. These festivities are the source of innocent recreation to many hundreds of pleasure-seekers in the neighbourhood, and also of much good-feeling among the members of the societies in honor of which they are held. The dwelling-house at Wylde Court was built by Mr. Leigh, its first possessor after the dissolution of the monasteries. He resided there himself, as did several of its subsequent owners. In the time of the civil wars, either Wylde Court or the rectory house (it is not certain which) is traditionally said to have furnished Charles II with temporary accommodation for a few hours on the evening of September 22, 1651. On the morning of that day he had set out from Trent for the purpose of reaching Charmouth, where arrangements had been made for his escaping to France, as already related. [1] There is no mention of the circumstance in the Boscobel Tracts, nor in any other of the authorities which we have consulted. Our authority is the late Rev. Dr. Rudge, who obtained his information from old inhabitants of the parish, with whom it was traditionary. [2] What gives the story an air of

[1] See pages 75—80.

[2] See the 'Mirror,' for March, 1837; the 'Literary and Pictorial Repository,' 1838; and 'the British Magazine,' for December, 1832.

probability, is the fact that Mrs. Moore, of Wylde Court, was a sister of Colonel Wyndham, of Trent, who took so active a part in the deposed monarch's attempted escape. One version is, that the rectory house was considered the preferable resting place, on account of the suspicion attached to all the members of the Wyndham family; and that the rector, Robert Jones, was afterwards deprived of his living because of his share in the transaction. This is not improbable, for the rector undoubtedly lost his benefice and was reduced to poverty. We should mention that the house at Wylde Court is built in the Elizabethan style; that the arms of the Moore family are carved in stone over the entrance, namely:—*Argent*, two bars engrailed, *azure*, between nine martlets, *gules;* and that on a lead pipe near the entrance are the Tudor rose, the date 1593, and the initials ' R. M.'

Tradition also tells of a sanguinary battle, in one of. the glebe fields, between the parliamentary forces and a part of the king's army under Prince Maurice, encamped on Lambert's Castle.[1]   Colonel Hellier,

[1] Lambert's Castle is a high hill, in the parish of Hawkchurch, upon which are the remains of an Ancient British entrenchment in connection with the chain of forts from Axmouth to Ham Hill about which we shall have a few words to say in our acccount of Musbury. The entrenchments consist of a triple vallum enclosing an area of about twelve acres, to which there are three entrances. In the year 1709 (7 Anne), a grant was obtained for holding a fair yearly on Lambert's Castle and Hawkdown, on the Wednesday before the feast of St. John the Baptist. The fair is still held, with races on the following day; and there is a fair, recently

the king's commander, was taken and hung upon the spot, and the field is called Hellier's Close to this day. The circumstance of arms and bones having some years since been dug up in this field, would seem to be confirmatory of this traditional account.

The Doctor mentions the superstition which lingers at Hawkchurch of turning the beehives when a corpse is carried out of a house for interment ;—it being thought that the omission of this practice would cause the bees to die, or some ill to befall the surviving relatives of the departed. The superstition, we may remark, is not confined to Hawkchurch. We have seen it practised near Colyton. On one occasion the bees resented the disturbance, and putting the funeral party and the bystanders to flight, imparted, very probably, a wholesome lesson of enlightenment. In this neighbourhood, also, as well as in many other rural districts, the custom of fixing a horse-shoe over the cottage door is still deemed necessary as a protection from ¬Witchcraft ! Verily ! 'the schoolmaster' hath no little work upon his hands, albeit ' the age ' professeth to be so ' enlightened.'

The church at Hawkchurch is one of the most ancient and interesting in the valley of the Axe, and perhaps in the West of England. It is difficult to

established, held annually on September 18th. Coker says that he never could ascertain the origin of the name of Lambert's Castle, and that ' many fables are related in the neighbourhood about a hole near the top of the hill.'

say that it contains remains of Saxon architecture,[1] but the probability of such a circumstance is very strong.[2] The piers and circular arches are unques-

[1] The Anglo-Saxons built their churches in imitation of the debased Roman Style which prevailed in Germany and France—the art of building, which had been taught the Britons by the Romans, having been lost in this country for about two centuries after the Romans had quitted it in the fifth century. Some of the Saxon churches were of considerable magnificence. The old York cathedral, which was built in 757, is described by Alcuin, one of its architects, as having 'pillars, arches, vaulted roofs, porticos, galleries, and altars.' The country churches were comparatively small, and were very generally enlarged after the Norman Conquest. The chief characteristics of Anglo-Saxon architecture are:—I. The masonry, —which consists chiefly of small stones, with occasional large ones, interspersed with Roman bricks, and the quoins exhibiting what is technically called long-and-short-work, from their being arranged with stones of equal size placed alternately in a vertical and horizontal position upon each other. II. The frequent use, in windows, of a peculiar kind of rude baluster instead of a column. III. Another kind of window, being a small one, of a single light, inserted in the middle of the wall and deeply splayed on both sides—unlike the Norman window, which is usually placed near the external face of the wall, and splayed only on the inside. IV. The rounded arch, occasionally ornamented with rough mouldings; and sometimes the triangular arch, formed simply of two straight slabs, placed upon jams and meeting at the top in an acute angle, like a gable. V. Reticulated towers, placed sometimes between the nave and chancel, and sometimes at the west end of the church, and formed, originally, without buttresses, pilasters, or staircases. The general character of the work is more massive and less ornamented than the Norman style which succeeded it, and which is really only an improved form of the Romanesque, or debased Roman style. See page 221.

[2] 'There are probably many vestiges of Anglo-Saxon architecture still preserved in churches, which have hitherto escaped observation; and this is not to be wondered at from the coats of plaster and rough cast, which, in many instances, are spread over the surface of the masonry, and thus conceal its rude yet peculiar features and construction. But yet, comparatively speaking, examples of this style are rarely to be met with. This may be partly accounted for by the recorded fact, that in the repeated incursions of the Danes, during the 9th and 10th centuries, most of the

tionably of very ancient date—especially those between the nave and its north aisle, the rude carving
on the capitals of which greatly resembles Saxon
work; while the carving on the capitals of the opposite piers is late Norman, or rather, perhaps, of the
earliest First Pointed or Early English period.[1] The
mouldings of the arches on the south side, also, indicate a more recent date than that to which the plain
arches on the north side can be assigned.[2] In each
aisle, a corbel-table,[3] composed of human heads and
other figures, of Norman, or perhaps of Saxon construction, runs along the wall of the nave above the
arches within, and extends beyond the eastern end
of the aisles along the wall of the chancel outside.
This curious circumstance undoubtedly indicates

Anglo-Saxon monasteries and churches were set on fire and destroyed; as
well as by the custom which prevailed in the 12th and following centuries
of rebuilding from the very foundation, in the style of the then existing
age, the earlier structures of rude masonry and design.'—*Bloxam.*

[1] See page 66.

[2] It is by no means improbable that the sculptures on the piers of the
south aisle were executed subsequently to the erection of the arches, as is
known to have been frequently done. See *Bloxam's ' Gothic Architecture,'* page 115.

[3] A *corbel* is a block of stone, or timber, projecting from a wall and
carved into some figure—very often a grotesque human countenance. Its
use is to support a weather moulding, a groining arch, or some other
object above. A *corbel-table* is a row of corbels supporting a parapet,
or, as in the case of Hawkchurch, a cornice. Some of the figures represented in the Hawkchurch corbel-table are very grotesque, displaying
some very curious specimens of the 'human face divine,' and also rams'
heads, two or three of which are exquisitely carved, and are apparently
of later date than the other figures.

(what, indeed, may be easily seen without such
indication) that the aisles are subsequent additions to
the more ancient body of the church. The chancel
window, no doubt inserted long since the erection
of the chancel itself, is of the Perpendicular period,
and contains stained glass. The windows of the
aisles are square headed, of two and three lights,
cusped,—some of them of the Decorated period.[1] At
the west end of the south aisle is a lancet window,
deeply splayed inside; and at the opposite end of the
same aisle are the remains of the ancient rood-screen.[2]
The ceiling of the nave is coved, and pierced for two
square windows on each side. The pulpit stands at
the south-east end of the nave, against one of the
piers of the chancel arch. The reading-desk is placed
against the opposite pier. A gallery occupies the
western end of the tower, and lately contained
a small organ. The font, which is square[3] and
mounted upon a circular stem, is evidently of great
antiquity, every indication of which, however, except
the shape, is carefully concealed by the whitewash
for which the majority of churchwardens have so
much affection.

The tower, at the west end, is elegant, and, from
the elevated situation of the ground, forms a conspicuous object from the valley beneath. It is in the

[1] See our account of Axminster church.
[2] See pages 176 and 178.
[3] See page 224.

Perpendicular style, square and embattled, with
angular pinnacles and an octagonal turret, and is
supported by buttresses. It is lighted by windows of
pierced stone, and rises to the height of sixty feet.
Over the doorway which forms the western entrance
to the church, is a handsome Perpendicular window.
The tower contains a clock and five bells, which
were cast at Cullompton in 1802. The total absence
of gurgoyles, both from the church and tower, is
remarkable.

Among the monuments within the building is one
against the south wall of the chancel to the memory
of the late Admiral Domett, who was a native of
Hawkchurch. It is of white marble, and bears an
inscription which embraces, in a few words, many of
the principal events in the life of the distinguished
subject of it.[1] Close to this monument is one to the

---

[1] The inscription is as follows:—'Sacred to the memory of Sir William Domett, G.C.B., Admiral of the White. He entered his Majesty's Navy in 1769, under his friend and patron Viscount Bridport, and was engaged in active service 46 years. He had the rare and distinguished honor of serving under the following naval heroes of England:—Lords Bridport, Hood, Rodney, Howe, Keppel, St. Vincent, and Nelson,—an eulogium on his character and talents more eloquent than words and more durable than marble. He was present in Lord Rodney's action, 1782. In the same year he commanded the Queen at the relief of Gibraltar, and the Royal George at the glorious victory of the first of June, 1794. For the style and gallantry with which he commenced the fight he was honored with a medal by his Majesty George III. He was appointed by the King, in 1801, Colonel of the Portsmouth division of Marines. At the battle of Copenhagen he acted as Captain of the fleet, by the particular request of Lord Nelson. On his return from the Baltic he was appointed Captain of the channel fleet by Admiral Cornwallis.

memory of the Admiral's sister, Ann, wife of Mr. George Templeman, of Middle Chinnock, who died at Westhay House on the 7th of October, 1844, in the 82nd year of her age.

There are also monuments to the memory of some members of the family of Barns, whose residence is at Tilworth, in this parish. One of them is to the memory of the late Thomas Barns, Esq., who died at the age of 60 years, on November 20, 1844. Some deceased members of the Moore family, of Spargrove and of Wylde Court,[1] have a handsome monument in the chancel. It was erected in 1840, and bears the date 1695. The inscription is in Latin.

The remains of the late Rev. Dr. Rudge are interred in the churchyard, on the north-west side, and the spot is marked by a neat coped tomb, of cruciform design, on one side of which is this inscription:—
' Here lieth also the body of the Rev. James Rudge, D.D., F.R.S., twenty-four years rector of this parish. He was born at Croomhall, county Glo'ster, 27th April, 1785, and died at the Rectory 11th July, 1852.' An inscription recording the death of one of

In 1804 he was appointed one of the Commissioners of the Admiralty, and in 1813 Commander in Chief at Plymouth; but in 1815 he resigned this command, in consequence of ill health, and retired to spend the remainder of his life on his estate at Westhay, in this parish, where he suddenly expired on the 19th of May, 1828, aged 76 years. A friend to the poor, a christian indeed, he died as deeply regretted as he had lived universally beloved.'

[1] See page 254.

his daughters occupies the other side of the tomb.
The Rev. gentleman was the author of several works,
including sermons, and was formerly domestic chaplain to the Duke of Kent.

The church was dedicated at different periods to
St. John the Baptist, All Saints, and St. Peter.[1]
The living is a rectory, valued in the King's Books
at £23 2s. 11d., and the tithes are commuted for
£536 per annum. The Rev. Edward Adams is the
present incumbent.

* * * * * *

About two hundred yards below Axe Bridge, the
river receives a tributary from the north-west which
is known by the name of the Chardstock Brook. It
rises near Whitestaunton, and flows near the village
from which it derives its name and which is situated
about two miles from the junction of the brook with
the Axe. The stream is small, and, like most small
streams, is very woody, and therefore useless for
the fly. But in days of yore it was much resorted
to by anglers. The late Rev. William Wills, to
whom we have before referred,[2] was formerly in the
habit of fishing it, and was wont to speak of his sport
as excellent. But there were few anglers who knew
so well as he the lurking-places of the 'oldsters,' or
knowing them possessed his skill. The brook is
shamefully poached, and great numbers of fish are

[1] Sarum Registers.
[2] See page 100.

taken in the field gutters into which the water is often diverted for the purpose of irrigation. We remember that thirty dozen of trout were thus destroyed in two days. The brook is *least* woody in the last meadow of its course, where a few fish may sometimes be taken.

Just cast your flies, Piscator, underneath those alders on the opposite side of the stickle in the Axe next above that at which the Chardstock brook disembogues itself! Nay, nay,—not into the bushes! But there you are, friend, fast enough. Behold a practical lesson on patience and command of temper. How gracefully your collar festoons about the branches to which your hooks so pertinaciously adhere! Take care. You must be gentle. You will lose a fly, no doubt. There is an anecdote about this very spot which we will relate for thy especial solace while engaged in repairing the mischief of that unlucky cast. That done, we beseech thee, friend, to hasten on, for the day begins to wear, and it is almost time to reach our quarters. But it is delightful ground to Axminster, deserving careful fishing. Our ramble since the sun rose has been a lengthened one, and we have a good mile yet to fish ere we shall arrive at Weycroft Bridge, where we mean to wind up and thence to trudge along the turnpike road to Axminster. Chardstock, and the sundry interesting spots along the stream, will afford abundant subjects for discourse. But first for our anecdote:—

As we have said, the first stickle above the mouth
of the Chardstock Brook is overhung, on the east or
Hawkchurch bank, with alders, which extend to the
pool below, and the roots of which, from the hollow-
ing of the bank by the action of the current, are
laid bare and shoot out into the stream beneath the
surface,—forming an impregnable hold for the large
fish which are generally 'in possession,' and also a
treacherous hitching-place for the flies of the unwary.
Axminster, some thirty years ago, could boast among
its numerous anglers of a noted wight whose opinion
of his own piscatorial skill was far higher than the
opinion of any other person. It had been confidentially
reported to him that a large salmon had taken up its
quarters in this pool, and had hitherto baulked the
ingenuity of all who had attempted its capture. [1]
Our friend resolved upon a triumph. Fate seemed
to have created for him an especial opportunity for
distinction. He passed a sleepless night. The morning found him early at the spot, provided with
abundant gear, and impatient for the crowning feat,

[1] Salmon, at the period referred to, were not confined, as at present, to
the part of the river below Axminster. They were very frequently
captured in the river between Coaxdon Mill and Tytherleigh Bridge.
The Rev. Mr. Wills once caught three large ones there in one morning,
with the fly. It is remembered that a very large salmon was once caught
as high up as Clapton Bridge, and one in Mosterton Meadow. The
weirs near Axminster now prevent the ascent of the few fish that would
ascend if they could;—or rather, we ought to say that the illegal closing
of the hatches at one time, and the fixing of a net across the only opening
at another,—taking every fish above the size of a minnow—are sufficient
to account for the present proscribed limits of the migratory fish.

the success of which he nothing doubted. Very
anxiously did he scan the dancing stickle on which
was floating a host of tiny flies, inviting the appetite
of 'the monarch of the brook,' and fancy pictured
to him the mighty fish already struggling on his
hook and yielding to his consummate skill. Pat, pat,
pat, beat his heart, when, after a few casts, a little
trout broke the surface but missed his fly. Another
cast.———What could *that* be? The fly was tugged
violently under the water. He struck, and it was
fast enough. Whiz from 'the active wheel' went
the tightened line. It *must* be the salmon. What
else, in the name of Izaac, *could* it be? Our hero
was in extacies—stamping, shouting for help, and
pitching stones into the water, in the orthodox
fashion, for the purpose of keeping the fish 'moving,'
—for it lay most provokingly quiet, and gave notice of
its presence only by a tug, which made the reel whiz
again as often as an attempt was made to get its head
against the stream. The noise and antics of the
angler soon brought from the neighbouring farms a
bevy of rustics — men and boys — who naturally
imagined, as they expressed themselves, 'that the
feller was maz'd, and gwine ta drownd eszull.' But
he quickly convinced them of their mistake, by
explaining his real situation and need of their assistance, when they all bolted back again for *poles* and
pitchforks with which to render it. During their
absence, as the 'salmon' still remained inactive, the

expedient of rousing it by sinking the butt of his rod in the water, and thus 'touching it up' at close quarters, suggested itself to the angler. No sooner was the idea conceived than attempted.to be acted upon. Our hero rushed to the brink and reached forward to effect his purpose, laying hold of an over-hanging branch for support. Misfortune dire! The branch gave way, and he pitched headforemost into 'the liquid element.' By this time the auxiliaries had returned. In their approach they had heard the flounce, missed the angler, and guessed the rest. Amid their coarse gibes and side bursting laughs, the unfortunate subject of them was soon dragged ashore, half drowned and drenched to the skin. Still the prize remained unwon. Had it escaped during the affray? The truth was quickly known:—a *salmon* had not been hooked! The fly had caught in one of the alder roots below the surface of the water, to which the current had imparted an undulatory movement which led to the deception and catastrophe described!

Truly delightful are the stickles and ranges which now, Piscator, successively present themselves to your attention; and not less delightful is the valley scenery, which begins materially to improve as we advance towards Axminster and the lower parts of the stream. There is something very picturesque, friend, in the mill below us—something very beautiful in the back ground formed by Cloakham and the other undulating hills, apparently one mass of wood—soft and silent in the setting sunlight. That mill is Coaxdon Mill, and the long range above it, to which we have now fished, is called by the same name. You may walk, Piscator, a hundred miles in any direction before you will alight upon a piece of river with better recommendations for all that relates to the perfection of fly-fishing, than the part of the Axe which you have just fished from Tytherleigh Bridge to Coaxdon Mill. Nay! we need not draw this limit, for the remark applies to the entire stream. You fancy this high praise, old friend. It is not higher than deserved.

Coaxdon Range is, in reality, the mill-dam. It is nearly a quarter of a mile in length. The water is very deep, and, when ruffled by a breeze, affords to the accomplished fly-fisher abundant sport—all other circumstances being favorable.[1] When salmon had a

[1] It must be distinctly understood that we expect none but the *accomplished* angler to be successful in the Axe in its present condition. The trout are very shy, and comparatively few. But there are not many parts of the stream in which a good dish of fish cannot even *now* be caught in a favorable day in spring or autumn. The banks of the stream are sometimes trodden by 'pretenders,' whose qualifications for fly-fishing consist in the possession of huge baskets, landing nets, and other gear which they never want;—in the knowledge of the *names* of a host of useless flies, and of a vast deal of absurd theory about the *proper times and seasons;*—and, lastly, in a remarkable readiness to discover that there are *no fish in the river,* and that nobody but themselves can be in possession of the *science* of sporting. But, ill-natured though it may appear in us to say so, these people are really *not fly-fishers* at all, and we must not be supposed to address ourselves to *them.* A good proof of a man's proficiency as a fly-fisher will be found in the circumstance of his being able to catch a dish of trout in the Axe. This is well known to all the old anglers of the locality, and will soon be discovered by the visitor.

chance of fair-play in their spawning season, it was a sort of resting place to which the salmon of the previous autumn fell back in the spring, after having deposited their spawn higher up the stream. Here they took up their quarters for some weeks, in order to renovate their strength before returning to the sea. In fact, the weir and mill-hatches prevented their return until a flood, for which they often had to wait till May. All this time they were gradually recovering from the effects of spawning, and often afforded splendid sport to the fly-fisher.[1]

The name of Coaxdon is obtained from that of the old residence which is visible among the trees on the western side of the river, at the distance of a couple of meadows from the range of which we have just been speaking. It is in the parish of Chardstock, and abuts upon the turnpike road from Axminster to Chard, at about a mile and three-quarters from the former town. Coaxdon, or Coxdon, was anciently a

---

[1] The condition of this part of the river in former times may be imagined, when we state that two salmon of ten pounds each, and one of fourteen pounds, with a cart-load of salmon-fry, were taken, about thirty-five years since, in a net, at one haul. This destruction of the fry was most unpardonable, and was just in character with the *present* mode of destroying this valuable breed of fish. The net was used for killing an immense otter which the hounds could not master on account of the depth of water. The plan resorted to was that of lowering the water by means of the hatches, placing a net at the lower end of the range, and dragging another net towards it. Two large old otters and their five cubs were killed on this occasion. Speaking of otters, reminds us that it may be worth while to state that the river is hunted every year by a pack of otter-hounds belonging to Mr. Collier, of Culmstock, near Cullompton.

manor; and it is now somewhat interesting from its associations with the past. Among other 'notabilities,' it is the birth-place, and afterwards became the property, of Sir Symonds D'Ewes—a celebrated puritan and antiquary, who was born December 18, 1602. He was the son of Paul D'Ewes, one of the six clerks in Chancery, by Cecilia, daughter and heiress of Richard Symonds, of Coaxdon Hall, Esquire. Sir Symonds passed his boyhood at Coaxdon, and went to a school at Wambrook. He received his college education at St. John's, Cambridge, and afterwards resided at Stow Hall, Suffolk. He had become possessed of Coaxdon at an early age, on the death of his grandfather. He ardently espoused the cause of the Parliament, and died in 1650. He had been made a baronet in 1641. His principal works are 'a Journal of all the Parliaments of Queen Elizabeth,' and an account of his own life in the Harleian Library.

But the most interesting story in connection with Coaxdon, is that of its having been the alleged scene of one of the romantic escapes of Charles II. We copy the story from Wilson's '*Memoirs of Daniel de Foe*,' the work in which it was first related :—

' The family of Cogan were originally from Ireland, where they possessed good property, which was much injured by the wars of Charles. Upon the Irish massacre they took refuge in England, and, with the wreck of their fortune, purchased Coaxdon and Lodge

—two estates situate between Chard and Axminster, the former of which is still possessed by one of their descendants. There they were seated at the time of the battle of Worcester, when the Royalists being entirely defeated, Prince Charles, afterwards King Charles the Second, escaped in disguise, and for some weeks eluded his pursuers, until he found means to depart the country. Having gone to Lyme for that purpose, the people, who were mostly disaffected to him, soon got scent of it, which obliged him to make a hasty retreat. Closely pursued on all sides, he took refuge at Coaxdon, and entering the parlour where Mrs. Cogan was sitting alone, threw himself upon her protection. It was then the fashion, as it was long afterwards, for ladies to wear large hoops, and as no time was to be lost, the soldiers being at his heels, she instantly concealed him under this capacious article of her dress. Mrs. Cogan was in her affections a royalist, but her husband belonged to the opposite party, and was then out upon his estate. Observing the approach of the soldiers, he made towards his house, and, entering with them, they all walked into the room where the lady was sitting, affecting surprise at the intrusion. The men immediately announced their business, stating that Prince Charles had been traced very near the house, and that, as he must be concealed upon the premises, they were authorised to make a strict search for him. Assenting with apparrent readiness to their object, Mrs. Cogan kept her seat, whilst her husband accompanied the men into every room. Having searched the premises in vain, they took their departure, Mr. Cogan going out with them. Being now released from their singular and perilous situation, the lady provided for the security of the fugitive until it was prudent for him to depart, and having furnished him with provisions, and a change of apparel, he proceeded on his journey to Trent, and thence to Brightelmstone, then a poor fishing town,—whence he embarked for France. Clarendon, who has given an interesting narrative of the Prince's peregrinations, has omitted the above adventure. But it is well authenticated. After he had reached the continent, Charles rewarded the lady's fidelity by sending her a handsome gold chain and locket, having his arms on the reverse. This relic was long preserved in the family, until the last possessor unfortunately exchanged it away for plate with a Jew at Exeter. Repenting of this step, an attempt was made, a few days afterwards, to recover it back again. But it was then too late, the purchaser having reported, whether truly or otherwise, that he had melted it down for the gold. The chain was long and massy, and is within the recollection of the family.' [1]

[1] The truth of this story is said to be questionable. It certainly cannot be reconciled with the accounts of Charles's adventurous journey from Trent to Charmouth and back which are given by Clarendon and other historians, nor with the account in the Boscobel Tracts which has formed the groundwork of our own account of this journey at pages 77 —80. Mr. Davidson, who disbelieves the story, suggests the probability

The parish of Chardstock extends along the river
from the termination of the parish of Chard, a
quarter of a mile above Tytherleigh Bridge, on the
western side, to near Weycroft Bridge, where the
parish of Axminster commences. The river, therefore,
divides for this distance (about two miles) the parish
of Chardstock from the parish of Hawkchurch in the
upper part, and from that of Axminster below. The
village is about two miles north-west from the mouth
of the Chardstock Brook, four miles north from
Axminster, and about the same distance south-west
from Chard. It occupies a secluded situation among
the hills, in the midst of extensive commons which
give an air of barrenness to the locality.[1] It is in
the county of Dorset, the diocese of Salisbury and
deanery of Bridport, the hundred of Beaminster
which is also its polling-place, and the union of
Axminster. The parish contains an area of 5800

of its origin in the following facts:—Sir Hugh Wnydham was an uncle of
Colonel Wyndham, one of the principal actors in the plans for the escape
of the Prince. This gentleman, who was of known loyalty, had a manor
and mansion at Pillesdon, a few miles north of Charmouth. On the hot
pursuit of Charles, after his leaving that place, this residence was strictly
searched. The soldiers opened even all the trunks and linen-chests, and
would scarcely be persuaded that a young lady whom they met in the
house was not the Prince in disguise. Gold pieces of money were given by
the Prince to several persons, who had them pierced and wore them
afterwards as lockets or medals—especially among the Wyndham family.
The family of Cogan, some of which were royalists, and compounded for
their estates, was connected by marriage with that of Wyndham.

[1] Arrangements are now (1853) in progress for the enclosure, by the
Ecclesiastical Commissioners, of about a thousand acres of these commons.

acres, and is divided into two tithings—north and south. Its population is 1387, of which 80 are registered county voters.

Chardstock signifies, literally, *Cerdic's Wood*—a name of the same origin as that of Chard, the two places having undoubtedly belonged to the same Saxon possessor.[1] Chardstock is thus surveyed in Domesday Book:—The same Bishop (the Bishop of Salisbury) holds Cerdestoche,[2] and two knights of him—Walter and William. In the time of King Edward it gelded for twelve hides. The arable is twenty carucates. Of these there are in demesne four hides, and there are four carucates, and six servants, and forty-five villains, and twenty-one cottagers, with seventeen ploughs. There are two mills, rendering twenty shillings, and ten acres of meadow. Pasture three miles long and one mile and a half broad. Wood two miles long and broad, and, in another part, three furlongs long of coppice wood and two furlongs broad. The total value is sixteen pounds.

In the middle of the thirteenth century, the right of the Bishop of Salisbury to hold the manor of Chardstock was disputed by one William Percy. He claimed the manor as the descendant of a former William Percy, its acknowledged owner, who, it was alleged on the part of the Bishop, had 'levied a fine

[1] See page 231.

[2] It is now vulgarly called *Chestock*.

NN

of it.' On Percy's side it was contended that the fine had been levied, not by his direct ancestor, but by another person of the same name and family, who had no right to the property. This plea, however, does not appear to have been allowed, for in 1293 the lands at Chardstock are found to be rated to the Bishop of Sarum at £36 15s. During the Commonwealth, the manor was possessed by Laurence Maidwell and Matthew Pindar, who, in 1645, had purchased it for £5242 9s. 7d.[1] After the Restoration, it reverted to its former owner, the Bishop of Sarum.[2] The liberty and manor are now held by Anthony Lord Henley, under a demise for twenty-one years[3] from the Bishop of Salisbury, with power to grant lands and tenements belonging to the manor for four lives.[4]

[1] In the same year, the impropriation of the church, value £160, belonging to Sir Simon Every, was sequestered.

[2] Six hides of land in this parish, together with land in several other places, were given to the church of Sherborne by the Saxon King Keneuulfus. Hutchins's '*Dorset*,' Dugdale's '*Monasticon*,' &c.

[3] By the '*Restraining Statute*' of the 1 Elizabeth, cap. 19, (made entirely for the benefit of the successor), all grants by Archbishops or Bishops of any manors, lands, &c., belonging to their bishoprics, or any charge or incumbrance out of them, shall be void other than for the term of twenty-one years, or three lives, from such time as any such grant or assurance shall be given, or without reserving the usual rent. See '*Blackstone's Commentaries.*'

[4] A curious custom exists in this manor, and also in the adjoining manor of Membury, that on the death of any tenant in possession, holding either for his own life or for the life of another, his widow is entitled to be admitted, for the term of her widowhood, to all the tenements in the manor held by her deceased husband at the time of his death—wholly irrespective of all his debts or responsibilities.

In ancient times, the Bishops of Sarum occasionally resided at Chardstock, where they had a seat and an extensive park.[1] Some impudent wights, not having the fear of the church before their eyes, and perhaps tempted by the fatness of the deer, broke into this park in 1298. They could not be detected; but, on the Bishop's order, the ban of excommunication was levelled by the Archdeacon of Dorset against 'some person or persons *unknown.*'

In 1219-20 (3 and 4 Henry III) a market at Chardstock was granted to the Bishop of Sarum; and in 1441 (19 Henry VI), the grant of a fair was also made to the same dignitary. The fair is still held on old Michaelmas day (October 11), but every trace of a market has long since disappeared.

The church, which is dedicated to Saint Andrew, stands towards the bottom of the steep village street. It is built in the form of a cross, with a tower at the west end. In common with many other country churches, it exhibits almost all the phases which ecclesiastical architecture has assumed, from the elegant Early English of the thirteenth century to the most recent modification of the Churchwarden style. The chancel, as usual,[2] is the oldest part of the church, and it exhibits the unmistakable effects of whitewashing, repairs, and Time. It was originally

[1] In the '*Register of Institution,*' at Salisbury, many instruments occur dated from Chardstock.

[2] See page 143.

Early English, and, judging from the arrangement of the base-course outside, it appears to have been lengthened in the fifteenth century, when the eastern Perpendicular window, and the one on the south side, were undoubtedly erected. The arches of the north and south transepts—plain and ill-wrought though they are—belong to the Decorated, or Middle Pointed style of the fourteenth century. The arches of the south aisle are Perpendicular, exhibiting the usual details. The windows of the body of the church are, without exception, poor. Some have the pointed heads of the fifteenth century, but the majority are straight-headed, with a few cusps to each light. The exterior is in no respect striking, and the tower, which contains a clock and five bells, possesses no feature of interest. The walls are of flint, with Ham stone dressings.

In the time of Henry II (1154-1189) the *prebend* of 'Cerdestoche' was presented by Gilbert de Percy to the church of Sarum, and it has ever since denominated a Prebend in that Cathedral. The prebend is valued in the King's Books at £18 16s. 8d. The vicarage was endowed at an early period, but there is no mention made of it in the 'Valor' of 1291. In 1506 it was endowed with the tithes of 'blade and hay' in the limits of the prebendal church, except in the chapelry of Wambrook.[1] The patrons were the

---

[1] Audeley Register.

Prebendary, his procurator, or lessee. Till the Reformation, the Bishops of Sarum collated to the living; but since that event the vicars have been presented by the dean. The living—a 'discharged' one—is valued in the King's Books at £14 2s. 6d. The great and small tithes are commuted for £490 each.[1] The Rev. C. Woodcock is the present incumbent. The parish schools are well conducted, and spacious school rooms have lately been erected.

A church, or rather a chapel of ease for both Chardstock and Axminster, was built in 1840 on the common, in Chardstock parish, near the hamlet of Smallridge[2] in the adjoining parish of Axminster. It is dedicated to All the Saints. A residence for

[1] The return to the Commissioners, in 1650, was, that the vicarage house and garden were worth £3 per annum. The tithes of wool, lamb, cow, wheat, hay, and orchards, £40. There was then no minister.

[2] 'This Smallridge,' says Prince, 'lieth on the north side of the pleasant river Axe, about a mile [it is two miles] from the church,—so called from its being advanced on the *ridge of a small hill*.' It was anciently a manor, and belonged, in the time of William the Conqueror, to Ralph de Pomeroy. It afterwards was added to the immense possessions of the Mohuns of Dunster Castle [see page 172]. In the reign of Henry III [1216-1272] it became the property of Sir Wymund Ralegh, a younger son of the Raleghs of Nettlecombe, Somerset, and ancestor of the celebrated Sir Walter Ralegh, whose grandfather conveyed the manor to John Gilbert, Esq. Ralegh Gilbert, great nephew of John, sold it to Chief Justice Hyde. Rawlin Mallock, of Cockington, Esq., afterwards possessed it, and sold it to Mr. Champion, by whom it was sold in parcels to the tenants. The original manor house was built by Sir Wymund Ralegh, whose posterity, for many generations, made it their principal residence. 'A sweet and delightful seat it was,' says Prince; 'but now there remain not so much as any ruins to testify the being of any eminent house in that place.'

the minister—now the Rev. J. G. Brine,—has also been recently built on a pleasant site near the turnpike road at Coaxdon, and within a few hundred yards of the church. A certain district of the parishes of Axminster and Chardstock is set apart, the tithe rent-charge of which supports the clergyman.

The parochial charities comprise one in which several of the parishioners, by deed dated March 24, 1625, and by a subsequent deed dated February 23, 1716, gave certain lands to the poor, for placing out poor apprentices, and for the repair of the church,—producing about £50 a year. Other donors to the poor are John Sampson, who, at a date uncertain, gave an annuity or rent-charge of 20s. a year from land supposed to be Baycroft, Membury; Richard White (1624) lands at Taunton, yielding about £6 a year; Henry Tucker (1631), 20s. a year from a rent charge out of a field at Axminster; and the parishioners, by copy of court roll, February 1, 1781, gave a house and orchard in Chardstock, held on *four lives*, to be inhabited by persons unable to pay house rent.[1]

Hutchins relates a story, originally published in the '*Philosophical Transactions*,' of the remarkable preservation of a woman of Chardstock, named Joanna Crippen. She was returning from Chard market, with some of her neighbours, on January 24, 1708. Finding the snow begin to fall heavily, she parted company

---

[1] Boswell's '*Charities of Dorset.*'

and applied at a cottage for shelter. The application was refused, and she set forth to overtake her companions. Night coming on she was unable to proceed, and lay down under a hedge. There she remained from six o'clock on Monday till the following Sunday afternoon, when she was discovered four feet deep in the snow. She was alive and almost naked, having *eaten* a considerable portion of her clothes. Mortification was found to have commenced on one of her toes, but she was perfectly sensible. It is not stated whether she recovered or not.[1]

*　　*　　*　　*　　*　　*　　*

There! Piscator. A brace and a half of trout, from Coaxdon Range, averaging half a pound a-piece, is not bad work, we think,—taking all things into consideration. Could you be here in a fine April morning, when the wind blows freshly from the south-west, and when, ever and anon, a stealing shower

> ———'is scarce to patter heard
> By such as wander through the forest walks,
> Beneath th' umbrageous multitude of leaves,'

you would kill three times as many over the same ground. You would also find some work in the weir pool, and likewise in the 'back stream.' We

---

[1] This is by no means a solitary instance. Several such cases are on record. We remember having once heard of a similar instance in the neighbourhood of Colyton. A woman was there buried under the snow for more than a fortnight, and subsisted upon the starch which she sucked from her handkerchief and clothes.

once had extraordinary sport at the weir with one of Mr. Allies' pectoral fin minnows. [1]

The water from Coaxdon mill to Weycroft weir—a few hundred yards below—is heavy, and may, generally, be passed over. Between Weycroft weir and the bridge are two or three delightful stickles; and the weir itself, notwithstanding its inconvenient landing-place, should be carefully fished. [2]

Weycroft Bridge—which is of two stone arches—is crossed by the turnpike road from Axminster to Chard. And here, old friend, we cease our angling for to-day. A goodly stretch of country, that between us and our starting-place;—twelve miles, at least, we warrant you! It is not ours to boast of the pleasures of the ramble. We must confess, however, that we are not sorry at the prospect of its speedy termination; for our labors, friend, have not been light. Bethink thee that we are indifferent to the consolation of the dinner table, presently? Indeed we are not. Bethink thee that we will not fill

[1] The Axe is not considered to be a good stream for trolling—perhaps because the fish, generally speaking, are not large. The minnow, however, in skilful hands, is undoubtedly a destructive bait. We hold Mr. Allies' 'pectoral-fin' in high esteem; but Mr. Pulman, of Totnes, has just invented an artificial minnow which possesses some peculiarities which, in many respects, render it superior to any of the imitations in common use.

[2] We once hooked two large salmon-peal *at once*, in the weir hole, and held them for half an hour. But the impossibility of lifting them from the water to the top of the wall on which we stood, and the absence of assistance, are sufficient to account for their escape with the collar and a considerable part of the line.

an extra glass to-night, and drink success to the labors which remain? Of a surety we will! For verily our work is far from ended yet. * * *

Now trudge we lightly on this pleasant road, and let us, as we foot the mile or so, fill up the gap from Weycroft down to Stony Bridge—which you can fish, Piscator, at your leisure,—for we mean to make a lengthened visit at the good old town. Come—step it out, friend;—we pray thee lag not now! The sun, you see, peeps out all gloriously beneath the clouds, which, fortunately for us, have obscured his brightness during so large a portion of the day; and ere he dips behind the old fir-crowned hills of Shute—away there undulating in the west—he paints the heavens with an inimitable hue, and sheds a flood of glory upon the earth, which thus is bathed in beauty and rejoiceth in it like a little child!

Overlooking Weycroft mill and bridge, from the crown of a considerable knoll, on the left bank, is a farm house erected on the remains of the ancient mansion of Weycroft. It is supposed to occupy the site of a small ancient Roman fort. Not the slightest vestige of such a structure can now be discovered, but there appears to be no doubt of the correctness of the opinion which has been advanced by Mr. Davidson, who thus speaks of the matter :—' Judging from its commanding situation as respects the road, its name, its striking appearance, and its form, there is good reason to conclude that it was one of the

oo

præsidia, or outposts, which the Romans usually
constructed in the vicinity of their larger stations.
These Castella were placed on the line of their military ways, frequently at the junction of the roads, and
especially at the crossings of rivers, to afford assistance
to the troops and convoys, to secure the necessary
supplies of provisions, and sometimes, in the lower
grounds, to protect their cattle in the neighbouring
pastures.   A more necessary, or a more eligible spot,
could scarcely have been fixed upon for the situation
of one of these forts, than that which this elevation
presented. Its name, "Weycroft," indicates its immediate vicinity to the Roman way, which it commands
very boldly, and from which a road leads up to its
area under the steepest part of the hill.[1]   Without
this it was accessible only on the eastern side; and it
is so formed by nature and art, being partially surrounded by a deep ravine, and supplied with water
by a well on its summit, that it must have been a
place of considerable security for its garrison.   The
ford of the Axe at this place was probably, in the
time of floods, both difficult and dangerous; for at
the present day, in spite of the limits which the
turnpike road has endeavoured to assign for it, the
river not unfrequently overflows its bounds to a considerable extent on the northern side.   Here, then,
was placed a fort, at the junction of the roads, which
could afford assistance in case of need.'

[1] See page 13.

In the reign of Edward the Confessor, the manor of Weycroft was valued at ten shillings per annum, and in the reign of the Conqueror at twenty shillings. From 1086—the time of Domesday Book—till the reign of Henry III, the owners of the manor are unknown, and from that time their names only are recorded till 1385, when the estate was purchased by Sir Thomas Brook, of Holditch and Holcombe Burnell. The mansion house was erected soon after 1400. It was in the castellated style, with octagonal turrets; and an oratory, or chapel, was attached to it. Traces of the spacious hall still exist. In 1416, the heir to the estate, being under age, was in the guardianship of the Duke of Gloucester, who obtained the royal license to crenellate the mansion and enclose a park of eight hundred acres, with a grant of free warren. During the formation of this park, a dispute arose between Sir William Bonville, of Shute, and Joan, the widow of Sir Thomas Brook, respecting the stoppage of several public paths through it. The dispute was referred to umpires chosen by the parties, one of which umpires was Nicholas Wysebeach, the abbot of Newenham. They decided in favor of Sir William Bonville, that all the paths should be thrown open, and directed that on a day appointed the knight and the lady should ride amicably together to Newenham Abbey, where they should exchange a kiss, in token of peace and friendship, and dine together at the abbot's table. The circumstances of this case

are recited at greath length in a deed—of which a
transcript has been preserved—dated at Axminster,
August 31, 1428.[1] The family of Brook were raised
to the peerage, with the title of Lords Cobham.
Weycroft was neglected; the park was thrown open
again to cultivation; and the house became ruinous,
'for want,' says Risdon, 'of a worthy dweller to
make his abode there.' A farm house now occupies
the site; but some remains of the ancient mansion
may still be traced. A few old trees, also, in the
field at the turnpike gate, show the traces of a
magnificent avenue which formerly led through the
park to the 'very pleasant seat over the river.' On
the attainder of Henry Lord Cobham, in 1603, the
manor and mansion were forfeited to the crown, and,
in the following year, were bestowed by the king on
Blount, the Earl of Devon.[2] This nobleman left the
estate to his second illegitimate son, and *his* son sold
it to Sir Thomas Bennett, whose son dismembered
the manor and sold the estate piecemeal. The principal portion is now the property of Henry Bilke,
Esq., of the Stock Exchange. Other parts passed
into the Mallock family. A portion belongs to W.
Tucker, Esq.; another to Henry Knight, Esq.; and
another to the Rev. Thomas Babb.[3]

[1] See Mr. Davidson's '*History of Newenham Abbey*,' page 91.

[2] See page 216.

[3] During a temporary relaxation of the persecutions of the Noncon-
formists, in the reign of James II, the dissenters of Axminster 'hired a

Towards the close of the last century, a public house stood on the spot now occupied by Weycroft mill, and was the rendezvous of the local sportsmen. A rude painting of a fish depicted its characteristic title, which was further explained by the quaint and needful line,—

'THIS IS THE SINE OF THE SAMMAN.' [1]

Sisterhood is the name of the farm among the trees, on the west bank of the river, a quarter of a mile or so below Weycroft bridge. Notwithstanding the expectations which may be raised by its attractive

house at Wykecroft for assembling together to worship.' The writer of the 'Church Book' in the Independent chapel at Axminster [see page 127] records, that 'during the space of about two whole years, an open door was continued to them in their public meeting house at Wykecroft, with much peace and liberty.' But towards the close of 1681, 'the clouds returned again and gathered blacknesse apace. A dreadful storm of persecution began to fall, and it prov'd to be a violent storm of some continuance—the Lord stirring up adversaries again to afflict the profess-ours of religion and to break the assemblies of the people of God, ranging up and down like roaring and ravening lyons, with fiercenesse and rage in many places; and about this time was this congregation constrained to leave their publick meeting house at Wykecroft. The violence of the adversary was so great that they could not assemble together in that place with any quietness or safety for a considerable space of time, but wander'd up and down, sometimes in one place or wood, sometimes in another, as in former daies. And thus they continued stedfastly in their assembling together, the Lord being as the shadow of a great rock to them in a weary land,—as the refuge from the storm even whilst the blast of the terrible one was as a storm against the wall.'

[1] A few years since, the title of an alehouse, at Perry Street, was set forth in the following business-like and yet poetical style:—

'The *Rising Sun and Evening Star;*—
Pay to-day and trust to-marr.'

name, we believe that there is nothing of consequence
to be said about this beautifully situated place. It is
believed to have been a barton, held under the manor
of Smallridge, and sold when that manor was dismembered,—about the year 1640.[1]

To the neighbouring estate of St. Leonard's, more
interest is attached. It was also a small farm and
parcel of the manor of Smallridge. It took its name
from a chapel which formerly stood there, and which
was erected by one of the family of Ralegh after an
event which is thus related:—An ancestor of the
family, at a period antecedent to the Norman Conquest, had been taken prisoner by the French.
Having found means to make his escape, he got into
a boat without sail or oars, and, committing himself
to the tide, was at length driven ashore at the mouth
of the Axe. In gratitude for his preservation, and
in remembrance of his escape, which took place on
St. Leonard's day, he built this chapel and dedicated
it to the saint, hanging up in it, like the votive offerings of the ancients, his fetters and a target of steel
gilt—all which, with the records of the foundation,
were given to his descendant, Sir Walter Ralegh, as
their rightful owner, by a priest of Axminster who
had been the officiating minister in the chapel. Of
this building not a vestige remains.

That mansion on the hill, friend, a little below

---

[1] See page 277.

Sisterhood, the glimpses of which excite so much your admiration, as we approach the town on our pleasant walk along the road, is Cloakham[1] House. Its situation is truly delightful — commanding a charming view of the town, the stream, the valley, and the distant ocean. The mansion was erected by Edward Smith, Esq., about the year 1732. His niece brought the property, by marriage, in 1773, to William Kennaway, Esq. It was afterwards the residence of James Alexander, Esq., whose widow continued to reside there till her death, in 1846. Its present occupier is Henry Knight, Jun., Esq. The river at the foot of the eminence on which Cloakham House is situated, is crossed by a bridge of a single arch. The road which passes over it winds through a lawn of considerable extent, which was laid out by the late James Alexander Frampton, Esq., and, with great liberality, thrown open to the public. It is a delightful spot, but now bears evidence of the incubus of Chancery, with which the manor of Axminster has so long been oppressed.

Stony Bridge is about half a mile below Cloakham bridge. The town weir, a magnificent range, and sundry unexceptionable stickles, occur in the interval. This range, which forms the upper part of the dam of the mill and factory[2] below it, resembles, in many respects, the famous Coaxdon range already described.

[1] Anciently, and more elegantly, written *Clocombe*.
[2] See the next chapter.

The river between Weycroft and Stony bridge is really beautiful, and forms an appropriate and a charming place for the saunterings of the summer evening angler who does not prefer a longer walk to shake off the lassitude of the day. He had need, however, be a skilful one, if he would be successful; for the river is greatly lashed, and the fish are knowing of the angler's wiles and eschew a bungler's fascinations.

* * * * * * *

Through the turnpike gate—past the lodge [1]—over Millbrook bridge [2]—up the hill—down Chard-street; ———and,—all hail to thee, old Axminster!

[1] Abutting upon the Chard road at the top of the lawn referred to in the preceding page.

[2] Mill Brook is a little tributary of the Axe which rises on Furzleigh farm, about two miles east of the town, and empties itself below Cloakham bridge. It receives its name from the old mill at Millbrook, which it drives.

AXMINSTER.

From the Meadows below Cloakham Bridge.

W Spreat Lith Exeter

CHAPTER VIII.

AXMINSTER is the largest and most important town upon the banks of the Axe,[1] and it is, without doubt, the principal angling station—commanding, as it does, the best of both the upper and lower parts of the stream, and also the largest of its tributaries. The town is situated in the eastern extremity of Devonshire, upon the immediate confines of Somerset and Dorset. It is twenty-five miles from the Station of the Great Western Railway, at Taunton; twenty-seven from Dorchester, the nearest Station of the South Western Railway; twenty-five north-east from Exeter; thirteen from Crewkerne; seven from Chard; and one hundred and forty-seven west-south-west from London.

Axminster is situated in the diocese of Exeter and archdeaconry of Honiton, and in the southern division of the county, its polling place being Honiton.

---

[1] Crewkerne and Chard, it must be remembered, are not upon the banks of the river, although both *parishes* are washed by its waters.

It is the capital of a hundred [1] and the centre of a union comprising seventeen parishes. [2] The union also forms a county-court district, and a petty sessions division. The parish of Axminster contains an area of 7640 acres, and a population of 2769, of which 107 are registered county voters. It is divided into ten tithings, namely:—Axminster town, Abbey, Beerhall, [3] Shapwick, [4] Smallridge, [5] Trill, [6] Uphay, [7]

[1] The hundred comprises Axminster, Axmouth, Coombpyne, Coombe Rawleigh, Dalwood, Honiton, Kilmington, Luppit, Membury, Musbury, Roosdown, Stockland, Uplyme, Upottery, and Yarcombe.

[2] Namely:—Axminster, Axmouth, Colyton, Coombpyne, Dalwood, Kilmington, Membury, Musbury, Seaton and Beer, Shute, Stockland, and Uplyme, in Devonshire; and Charmouth, Chardstock, Hawkchurch, Lyme Regis, and Thorncombe, in Dorsetshire.

[3] See page 252.

[4] Shapwick is an estate of about 480 acres, in the parish of Axminster, and about four miles from the town to the south-east. It is entirely surrounded by other parishes, but has from the earliest times formed part of the manor of Axminster. It was one of the granges of Newenham abbey, and was under the superintendance of a monk who resided at the dwelling-house on the estate. After the dissolution, the estate was given, with the other conventual property, to the Duke of Norfolk [see a future page]. In 1605 it was sold, with the rest of the manor of Axminster, to Lord Petre. In 1670 it was purchased by Solomon Andrew, Esq., of Lyme Regis, whose granddaughter excited the affections of the celebrated Henry Fielding, and was attempted to be carried off by him one Sunday on her way to church. His suit was unsuccessful, and he afterwards immortalised the lady in his character of Sophia Western. The subsequent marriage of this lady brought the property to the family of Rhodes, in which it still continues. The name Shapwick is derived from the Anglo-Saxon ' wic,' a home or dwelling, and ' scep,' a sheep.—See Mr. Davidson's ' History of Newenham Abbey.'

[5] See page 277.

[6] See our account of Ashe House.

[7] Uphay is situated on the hill near Cloakham, on the west side of the river, where, in ancient times, its owner had a mansion. ' It took its

Westwater, Weycroft, and Wick.¹ The town occupies a pleasant and healthy situation on the side of
the range of hills by which the valley is enclosed on
the east. The views in its vicinity are extensive and
beautiful, and it is itself a pleasing object from the
valley and the surrounding hills.²

All the principal entrances to the town are exceedingly good. Wide roads well lined with
trees, and handsome villas occurring frequently,

name,' says Sir William Pole, 'from its scite, and gave its name unto its
dwellers, for it appears that many of that name successively enjoyed the
same.' The family of Uphay were also the owners of the neighbouring
manor of Haccombfee, from 'the latter end of Kinge Edw. I unto Kinge
Rich. II. tyme,' when 'Sir William Umfraville enjoyed it [Haccombfee],'
after whose death Edmond Pyne, in right of Alice his wife, relict of Sir
William Umfraville, held both Uphay and Haccombfee. Lord Bonville
possessed them in the reign of Edward IV, and they descended from him
to the Duke of Suffolk, who sold them to Lord Petre, from whom they
passed with the other manor property, as hereafter described. The termination *hay*, we may remark, so common in this neighbourhood, is a
French word derived from the Saxon, and signifies a *hedge* or an *inclosure*.

¹ Wick (see page 15) is a hamlet in the parish of Axminster, about
a mile south from the town. It was anciently the property and residence
of the 'knightly family of Doune, whoe had alsoe land neere the sea'
[at Roosdown, &c.] The coheiresses of Hugh de Doune, the last of the
males, married Henry Ledred and John Holcombe. North Wick was
inherited by Ledred, whose heiress brought it by marriage to the Strodes,
of Parnham, by whom, after a few descents, it was sold in parcels.

² 'This parish is diversified with hill and dale, coarse and rich land;
and furnishes a variety of pleasant views. From the heights in the
neighbourhood of Axminster we are presented with noble prospects of the
British sea. Dr. Stukeley seems to speak with transport of his first view
of the ocean on his entrance into this county. "From the hill-tops about
Stockland," says the Doctor, "I first had sight of the southern ocean—a
most solemn view—a boundless extent of water thrown into a mighty
horizontal curve." '—Polewhele's '*Devonshire.*'

excite, in the stranger, ideas of the size and beauty of
the town itself, which, in all probability, he will not
realise. Not that it is by any means unhandsome.
Its streets, now lighted with gas,[1] and partially paved,
were formerly very narrow and intricate, bespeaking
the high antiquity of the town. But a series of extensive fires, within the last twenty years, afforded
an opportunity for improvement which has not
been thrown away. A large triangular space in
front of the church, in which are some respectably
built houses, may be mentioned as not the least of
these improvements. Trinity Square, as this open
space is called, was laid out after a fire on Trinity
Sunday, 1834, which consumed about thirty dwellings. But there is at least one dark cloud which
looms depressingly over the town, and manifests itself
in a declining trade and a corresponding lack of an
appropriate field, in these bustling times, for the
vigorous exercise of industry and talent. We allude
to the comparative isolation of the place from the
great railway thoroughfares,—to say nothing about
the manorial chancery suit, the influence of which
must be anything but beneficial.[2]

[1] The gas works were erected in 1838.

[2] These drawbacks to the prosperity of this delightfully situated place,
will, in all probability, be soon removed; for the 'broom' is at work in
Chancery, and the indispensability of at least a coast line of railway, on
national grounds, is admitted by the highest authorities. The only question is, who shall make it? See page 42. But, comparatively speaking,
there is still a great amount of travelling through the town, situated, as
it is, on the high-road from Exeter to Dorchester.

The antiquity of Axminster is beyond all question. The striking circumstance of its situation at the intersection of the two ancient roads which traversed the West of England,[1] is strong presumptive evidence of its being the site of an Ancient British settlement, which is further strengthened by its name, its form, and its situation between the two earthworks at Musbury and Membury which are undoubtedly of British foundation.[2]

The Ancient British forts and trackways were adopted by the Romans, after they had sufficiently subjugated the natives, as we have elsewhere shown; and abundant evidence of the occupation of Axminster by that wonderful people has from time to time been brought to light. But the industrious researches of Mr. Davidson leave nothing new to be

[1] See our Introductory Chapter.

[2] 'Strabo observes, that the Britons fence-in large circles with trees, where, having constructed huts, they and their herds dwell together. And we learn from Polybius and Cæsar, that before the Roman conquest their settlements were not surrounded by a wall, but, as already mentioned, were fortified by a ditch and a mound of earth. The Britons often placed their villages at the intersection of their roads, on the sides of which they threw up banks at the entrances, by way of defence. They were desirous, if possible, of settling near a stream, on a position defended by nature, and especially on a promontory having a gentle declivity to a river. Their earthworks were irregular in form, but generally corresponded in shape with that of the hill-side on which they stood. These are the principal known peculiarities of the British settlements; and it is impossible not to observe the remarkable agreement with these features which the site of the town of Axminster presents, especially if viewed on the approach to it from the west, and if the form of the declivity called the Castle hill be examined, with that of the ground upon which the town stands, sloping gradually down to the river.'—Davidson's *British and Roman Remains.*

said upon the subject.[1] That gentleman thus sums
up his elaborate essay :—'That the town of Axminster is the site of one of the hyberna castra, or more
important settlements of the Romans, will not be
maintained, as these usually present considerable remains to notice, are in general of greater extent, and
have in most instances risen into towns of consequence at the present day.   But it was, in all probability, one of the smaller stations, fixed at convenient
places on the roads for the temporary accommodation
of troops and passengers, and which were called
" mutationes," in consequence of horses being kept
there for the use of the couriers. For such a purpose its position seems peculiarly adapted, and the
numerous discoveries of Roman remains in the
neighbourhood prove the constant intercourse which
must have been maintained on the several roads
which concentre at this point ; while its intermediate
situation between the forts of Musbury and Membury, and its direct communication with them and
with the castellum of Weycroft, independently of its
own means of defence, would render it a position of
considerable security.'
   Coming down to the Saxon times, after the declining power of Rome had rendered it necessary for her
to withdraw her legions from the ' islands of the sea,'
we find ourselves treading upon more solid ground,
and in possession of something like the basis of

[1] See page 10.

AXMINSTER. 295

authentic history upon which to proceed. It happens that the Saxon period is exceedingly rich in events connected with this locality; and therefore we shall linger over it with some minuteness, believing that we can bring forward some peculiarly interesting facts, for the most part new to the majority of our readers. [1]

Axminster, Colyton, and Axmouth formed a part of the royal demesne, and so continued till after the Norman Conquest. [2] These places, with many others, are mentioned in the will of Alfred the Great. Axminster was a town of considerable consequence in those early times. [3] There is hardly any doubt, indeed, that it was one of the residences of the Anglo-Saxon royal family. It was certainly one of the places selected in various parts of the country by the princess Ethelfleda for the erection of castles or forts. This princess was Alfred's eldest daughter, and the

[1] We cannot write another sentence without an especial acknowledgment of our deep obligation to Mr. Davidson, who, with the greatest liberality, has not only thrown open to us his magnificent library, but also the still more valuable treasures of his manuscript collections relating to the locality. We need hardly say that we have not scrupled to avail ourselves of the opportunity thus afforded.

[2] See the extract from Domesday Book in a subsequent page.

[3] 'The origin of cities rested with the Romans; for the Britons had none, properly so called, and the Anglo-Saxons planted theirs, in the first instance, upon the sites of the Roman towns and stations. So rapidly did they spread, however, that, with very few exceptions, all our present towns, and even villages and hamlets, appear to have existed from the Saxon times.' [See page 63.] Eccleston's 'Introduction to English Antiquities.'

wife of Ethelred, who was appointed by her brother Edward to the earldom of Mercia. The selection of such a site was most appropriate, being on the great road across the valley, and near a part of the coast peculiarly liable to the predatory incursions of the Danes. The castle was founded in the year 916, on the spot now occupied by the market-house, and where the Ancient British fort had originally stood. [1]

No vestige remains of this ancient building; but what were undoubtedly some of its foundations have at different times been discovered. About twenty-

[1] 'We will now advert to an open space within the town, which bears the appellation of "the castle," though it has long ago been divested of the character of a military post. Towns among the Britons, as with the Gauls, were, in their origin, merely fortresses to secure the people and their cattle from sudden irruption or attack; but as the population increased, and civilization advanced, their fortified places were enlarged in compass, and were provided with market-places within their intrenchments. An area within the town of Axminster, which comprises the market-place, upon "the castle hill," appears to have been of this description. It is a projecting point or extremity of the natural declivity which defended the town on the north-western side; but there are marks of its having been an intrenchment, in the vestiges of a fosse, which may be distinctly traced. That it may be ascribed to the British period is extremely probable, when we consider not only its situation as respects the Ikeneld and the Fosse-way, which bend out of their course to reach it, but that it is immediately connected by ancient roads with the British forts of Musbury and Membury. With the last-mentioned intrenchment, also, there is a second communication, which seems to have been provided in case of the other road being in possession of an enemy. From the northern side of Axminster castle a narrow way winds along under the hill, and, crossing the river at the distance of half a mile, proceeds to a junction with Smallridge lane, which, as before stated, leads directly from the eastern gate of Membury fort. A parochial fortress having such a covert way to it is a known accompaniment to a British village.'—Davidson's ' *British and Roman Remains*.'

five years since, in digging a trench on the north-western side of Castle Hill, where the ground begins to slope abruptly towards the river—in fact, in the garden now belonging to Major Still,—the workmen struck upon some flint walls which were found to be ten feet thick, and of great firmness of structure. These could have belonged to no ordinary building, and it may with safety be inferred that they were the remains of the ancient castle, which appears to have been destroyed at some time previous to the four-teenth century. It is not easy to account for its destruction; for being on the king's demesne it can scarcely be supposed to have shared in the general demolition of castles in the reign of Henry II.[1]

The most extraordinary event in connection with Axminster in the Saxon times, was the celebrated battle of Brunenburgh, the scene of which, there is the strongest evidence to show, was the now peaceful valley of the Axe. All the old chroniclers speak in the most glowing language of this sanguinary battle. It was, indeed, of the greatest importance to the country, the destinies of which were materially af-fected by the triumphant result. Nearly a thousand years have passed, and yet to this day there is hardly a child, from Axminster to the sea, who does not prattle about *Warlake* and its once 'running

---

[1] Anglo-Saxon castles are supposed to have been mere enclosures of walls, having within the area, on one side, a strong and lofty tower, of square or circular form, called the *keep*.

with blood;'—hardly a full-grown man who would
not confess, if he could forget the 'weakness' of
such a confession, that he feels an involuntary thrill
of horror, and is oppressed, in spite of himself, with
all sorts of 'supernatural fears,' while he crosses at
night the little bridge over the same 'lake,'[1] at
'Kingsfield,'[2] on the turnpike road from Axminster
to Musbury. The still but impressive voice of tradition is indeed no trifling feature in the evidence in
favor of the valley of the Axe as the scene of this
famous battle; and we have other evidence to bring
forward, in the course of our annotations upon this
account, which, we think, will place beyond all
reasonable doubt a subject upon which so many
modern writers have disagreed.[3] But before pro-

[1] In the West of England the word *lake* is used synonymously with
brook. See '*Rustic Sketches*,' by the same author.

[2] The names of Kingsfield and Warlake are of obvious significancy.
The same remark applies to *Battleford*, two miles north-east from Axminster, to which the fight extended. And there are many other names
which might be added of undoubtedly a similar origin.

[3] Many of them, copying one from another, assert that the battle of
Brunenburgh was fought in the north of England. A few of them say
that it was somewhere in Cheshire. Three or four other places have also
been selected. But no *facts* have been brought forward in support of
any of them. The Anglo-Saxon Chronicle, one of the most authentic
and important of the ancient documents, gives no clue to the locality, but
speaks of Brunenburgh as a well-known place,—a place which we hope to
identify, in a future note, with Axminster. Mr. Davidson, to whose industrious researches we are so greatly indebted, and whose intimate
acquaintance with the locality has given him advantages and opportunities far superior to those of perhaps any other writer on the subject, has
long been satisfied that our valley was indeed the scene of this terrible
contest. He informs us that his conviction has been gained after a careful

ceeding to describe the battle itself, let us say a few words in explanation of its origin:—

Athelstan, the grandson of Alfred, was, after his great ancestor, the most famous of the Anglo-Saxon kings. 'He had appeared above the horizon,' says Mr. Turner, in his inimitable history, 'just before Alfred set; and a beam of this great radiating luminary lighted upon him.'[1] He was the illegitimate son of Edward the Elder, the eminent son of Alfred, and he ascended the throne on the election of the nobles, who passed by the legitimate children of the deceased king, on the ground of their extreme youth, —a circumstance by no means unusual in those early and unsettled times. This was in the year 925. After the suppression of an insurrection against himself, he found it necessary to direct his attention to the great enemies of his race, the Danes, who, in Northumbria, under Sihtric their king, had begun to manifest a degree of turbulence and dissatisfaction to which they were never strangers long together. It was the character of Athelstan to pursue a concili-

investigation and comparison of the statements made by all the ancient chroniclers and writers to whose works he could obtain access, and that these are *more than seventy in number.* We shall produce sufficient evidence, we think, to set the matter entirely at rest.

[1] Some of the old chroniclers consider Athelstan to be even superior to Alfred. Edgar, in one of his charters, says of him:—'Qui primus regum Anglorum omnes nationes qui Britanniam incolunt sibi armis subegit.' 'The truth seems to be,' says Turner, 'that Alfred was the first monarch of *the Anglo-Saxons,* but that Athelstan was the first monarch of *England.*'

atory policy whenever practicable,[1] and he accordingly propitiated Sihtric by the gift of his sister Editha in marriage. Sihtric embraced christianity on the occasion of the wedding, and entered into a treaty the basis of which was the admission of his fealty to the Anglo-Saxon monarch. But twelve months afterwards Sihtric died, having first renounced his religion and dismissed his wife. Immediately on his death, his two sons by a former marriage, Anlaf and Godefrid, took possession of the sovereignty as a matter of hereditary right. Athelstan, however, was already on his way with an army to revenge the insult to his sister and to punish the apostate to his faith. The result was, that the two usurpers were compelled to fly,—Anlaf to Ireland and Godefrid to Scotland, where the latter was protected by Constantine the king.[2] Athelstan's army accordingly entered Scotland, and, after ravaging the country, brought Constantine to subjection; while Godefrid, after various attempts to regain his position, had at last recourse to piracy, and died, after several years, with a dreaded name.[3] Anlaf acquired influence and dominion in Ireland. Constantine was smarting

[1] It is recorded of Athelstan that 'he nurtured and *enthroned* several kings in Europe;' that, among others, he 'returned to Howel the kingdom of Wales, and to Constantine that of Scotland, declaring that *he would rather bestow kingdoms than enjoy them.*' See '*William of Malmesbury.*'

[2] Matthew of Westminster.

[3] William of Malmesbury calls him 'an incorrigible pirate, accustomed to live in the water like a fish.'

under his humiliation. Certain Welch princes, also, were burning with revenge for a yoke which had been imposed upon them.[1] A combination, therefore, was entered into by those parties, which it was hoped would not only result in a satisfaction for their supposed injuries, but in the overthrow of the Saxon power. Europe beheld with astonishment the immense preparations which were made by the confederated powers, whose forces were swelled by fleets of warriors from Norway and the Baltic.

Athelstan, who was now in the West of England, regarded, with the firmness of a hero, the tremendous storm which was thus gathering around him. He industriously prepared for his defence, not only by the concentration of his own Saxon troops, but also by the offers of munificent rewards for assistance from the piratical adventurers who then roamed the seas in readiness for any profitable enterprise which might present itself. Egil and Thorolf are the names of two of the famous sea-kings, who, in sailing by Saxony and Flanders, had heard of the offers of Athelstan, and came, with three hundred companions, to proffer the services which were gladly accepted, and which proved to be so important and valuable.

---

[1] Among the allies of Anlaf, the Northern 'Saga,' which has afforded many of the materials for this account, names Hring and Adils as British [Welch] princes. Adils is supposed to have been the son of Anarawd, who was reigning in North Wales at this period; and Hring was most likely a Danish leader, the son of Harold Blaatand, or Blue Tooth. See Turner's 'Anglo-Saxons.'

The movements of Anlaf were as rapid as they were alarming. Before the Saxon monarch could have time to organise his defence, the invaders had entered the estuary of the Humber with a fleet of 615 vessels, carrying about 30,000 men. [1] They were immediately opposed by Alfgeir and Gudrekr, the governors whom Athelstan had left in Northumbria. But the scanty forces of the Saxons were no match for the hordes of fierce invaders, and the result of a battle was their total overthrow and the death of Gudrekr. Alfgeir fled with the tidings to Athelstan, who was already on his way with his army. But the invaders did not wait for his arrival. Their object was something beyond the mere pillaging and conquest of Northumbria. Accordingly, no sooner had they routed their opposers and found that Athelstan was marching towards them, than they put to sea again, with the intention of sailing southward and of landing at a far distant part of the coast in the rear of the Anglo-Saxon army. And now we come to the deeply interesting events which more particularly concern us with reference to the valley of the Axe.

Seaton, at the mouth of the Axe, was in many respects a tempting place for the grand descent of

---

[1] 'Mailros, 147, and Sim. Dun, 25. Hovedon, 422. The ship in which Egil afterwards left England contained 100 men, or more. [Egil's 'Saga,' page 55.] If Anlaf's ships were of this size, his army must have been 60,000. We may take 30,000 as a safer average.' Turner's 'History.'

the invaders. It was sufficiently distant from Northumbria and from Athelstan;—it was in the immediate
vicinity of the royal demesne;—and it was familiar
to numbers of the roving adventurers who formed so
large a portion of the invading army.[1] Seaton was
accordingly selected, and the landing was accomplished without a shadow of opposition.[2] Anlaf
fixed his camp upon *Hanna* hill, a commanding position within a mile of the landing place, and in view
of the fleet which was riding at anchor immediately
below. A detachment was probably sent on to
Danes' Hill, about seven miles up the valley, burning and plundering on the way.[3]

[1] The southern coast of the West of England was the frequent scene
of some of the most terrible descents of the Danes. Egbert, the Saxon
king, it will be remembered, had, a century before the battle of Brunenburgh, encountered a formidable band of these marauders at Charmouth.
See page 76.

[2] Among the evidence in favor of this landing having taken place at
Seaton, not the least conclusive is a curious document preserved in the
British Museum, that great store-house of historical curiosities. It is a
chart or plan, representing, on a large scale, the whole line of the southern
coast from Seaton to the Land's End, with views, extending several miles
inland, of towns, churches, rivers, castles, and parks. The date of this
document appears to be about the time of Henry VIII. Opposite to the
river Axe, it affords a memorandum, very much to our purpose, in the
following words:—'The entrie of Otterford and Seton ryvers, good londyng,
and in the tyme of King Athelstan there entrid at Seton dywse [divers]
strange nacions, who were slayne at Axmyster to the number of V Kings,
VILJ erles, a busshoppe, and IX score thousand in the hole, *as a boke
old written doth testyfye.*' [Cotton MSS., Augustus I. Vol. I., folios
25—28.] This plan is engraved, in part, in Lyson's ' *Devonshire,*' from
which it is copied into ' *the Western Miscellany,*' a late Exeter periodical.

[3] The name of Honey Ditches, at Seaton, as the remains of the encampment on Hanna Hill are now called, is probably a corruption from

Athelstan, although so distant, was not long in ignorance of the hostile occupation of the valley of the Axe.   The terrified inhabitants, unable to resist, had fled to seek his protection, and from every hill blazed forth the beacon-fire which conveyed, with infinitely greater rapidity, the startling and important news. [1]   The proceedings in Northumbria had also been communicated to him.   He lost not a moment, therefore, in retracing his steps.   A detachment of his army was sent southward in advance, and in all probability took up its position upon Membury Castle.   It was much too small to hazard an attack, and its leader, in order to gain time, resorted to the expedient of a delusive treaty with the invaders— offering them money to take their departure, while Athelstan was making every exertion to bring up the main body of his troops.   In a few days he arrived with a powerful host.   A division of his army pushed

Anlaf; while that of *Danes' Hill* seems to speak for itself.   Danes' Hill is in the parish of Dalwood, nearly west of Axminster.   Other camps in the neighbourhood, which are shown, from their remains, to be un- doubtedly of Saxon and Danish origin, were probably constructed on this occasion.

[1] The beacon-fire was in ancient times what the electric telegraph is at the present day.   It was in use, in a variety of forms, from the earliest period to the reign of Edward III.   The position of several beacons in this neighbourhood is still unmistakably indicated.   At *Beacon Hill,* near Chardstock,—the beacon connected with Membury Castle,—an urn containing the ashes, no doubt, of the Roman beacon-keeper, with the usual accompaniment of coins, was discovered a few years since.   The beacon of Musbury Castle, on Trinity Hill, also still retains its name. At one period the towers of churches were employed for beacons, and many of them to this day show the remains of the beacon-turret.

on to the entrenchments on Longbear Down, near Stockland, within sight of Membury Castle already in possession of his troops; another division, under the command of Alfgeirr, the Saxon earl, and Thorolf, the northern sea-king, appears to have occupied the immediate neighbourhood of the town of Brunenburgh;[1] while Athelstan himself, with the main body of his troops, descended into the valley below and pitched his tent there.

His arrangements being soon complete, all treaties with the invaders were at once broken off. Adils, the Welch prince, exclaimed against the artifice

[1] The town of Axminster was also called Brumby or Brunenburgh by the Anglo-Saxons. That people were in the constant practice of adding to or changing the names given to places by their predecessors. They adopted such terms of their own language as were applicable to the local circumstances, more especially in cases where an intrenchment had previously existed, and then the term *burgh* or *bury* was uniformly added or bestowed. The Ancient British name of the town was Axa [see page 7], to which the term *minster* was added by Athelstan when he so liberally endowed the church in commemoration of this famous battle. During the Saxon period the town is found to be called Axminster whenever mentioned in connection with civil or ecclesiastical matters; but in military affairs the term *Brunenburgh* is invariably given to it—a term which designates at once the river and the fortress upon it—*burn* or *brone,* a brook or stream, and *burg,* a place of retreat or defence. There is a great deal of circumstantial evidence in favour of this double name of Axminster, and the fact is expressly recorded in the ancient French Chronicle cited in Leland's ' *Collectanea,*' vol. i, page 202 :—' Ceste bataille commensa a Brunedune, pres de Coliton, et durai usques a Axminster, que adonques fust appellez Bronebyri, et la fust le grand occision et le ior devint adonques auoir nuit.' Translated thus :—'The fight began at Brundune, near Colyton, and extended as far as Axminster, *which before that was called Bronebyri,* and there was the slaughter which lasted from morning till night.'—Mr. Davidson's MS. ' *History.*'

which had been practised, and proposed that Hring
and himself should the same night make an attack upon that part of Athelstan's army which was under the
command of Alfgeirr and Thorolf. But Anlaf was
desirous of proceeding more cautiously, and in order
to become thoroughly acquainted with the disposition
of the Saxon forces, and to know where to direct the
attack with the best advantage, he resolved upon
an artifice resembling that of Alfred the Great
in the camp of Guthrum the Dane. Divesting himself of his warlike attire, and assuming the privileged
dress of a minstrel, he passed singing through the
Saxon camp and gradually approached the royal tent.
Athelstan, gratified with his performance, dismissed
the imaginary gleeman with a present of money.
Too politic to betray his disguise by refusing the
present, the noble Dane was also far too haughty to
retain it ; and as soon as he believed himself beyond
the reach of observation he buried it in the earth.
His movements were watched by a soldier of the
outer guard, who had once served under the banner
of Anlaf, and who, from the first, had suspected that
the minstrel was no other than his former chieftain.
With a true nobility by no means confined to mere
conventional 'rank,' he allowed the deceiver to depart,
and then hastened to communicate with his sovereign.
Athelstan, at first, was greatly displeased with the
soldier for allowing the escape of his enemy; but the
nobleness of the reply which his expression of dis-

pleasure elicited, produced feelings of an opposite description :—' O, King,' said the noble soldier, ' the oath which I have lately taken to you, I once gave to Anlaf. If I had been faithless to him I might have broken it to you! But deign to hear a servant's counsel, and remove your tent to another quarter.' The advice was unhesitatingly adopted. Werstan, Bishop of Sherborne, arrived soon afterwards with his troops,—for bishops, in those days, were in every sense *militant*,—and he pitched his tent upon the spot which the king had quitted.

Anlaf, on returning to his camp, gave a willing consent to the proposed attack. Adils and Hring, therefore, embodied their troops, and in the dead of night marched silently towards the Saxon position, intending to surprise it by a sudden advance from the woods on the southern side. But the cautious sentinels of Thorolf discerned the advancing enemy, and sounded an alarm,—not in time, however, to prevent a furious onset, which was so well directed to the former situation of the royal tent, that the Bishop of Sherborne was one of the earliest victims. Thorolf and Alfgeirr, who had quickly aroused their warriors, bravely resisted the assault. Thorolf was opposed to the advance of Hring, and Alfgeirr to that of Adils, who pushed forward with such impetuosity that he drove everything before him ; and Alfgeirr, unable to bear the mortification of a second defeat, [1]

[1] His first defeat, it will be remembered, was in Northumbria. See page 302.

fled at once from the field of battle and passed over
into Gaul. Adils, exulting in the advantage which
he had gained, now fiercely turned upon the other
Saxon troops. It had long been day-light, and there
was no impediment to his most energetic movements.
He found himself opposed by Egil, who, at the
desire of his brother Thorolf,[1] led on his troops,
exhorting them to stand close, and if overpowered to
retreat to the wood. Egil pushed forward, though
with an inferior force, and a direful conflict ensued.
Thorolf, animated to a furious pitch of valor, threw
his shield behind him, and grasping his huge weapon
with both his hands, cleared a way for himself through
the opposing ranks until he reached the standard of
Hring, which, with its bearer, he levelled with the
ground. Then, with a mighty exertion of strength,
he directed his weapon against the breast of the
leader. Piercing the coat of mail, and plunging
through the body, his javelin came out between the
shoulders, and thus the brave Hring breathed his
last. The success of Thorolf animated his followers,
and Adils, mourning the death of his friend, at length
gave way and retreated to the wood, accompanied by
his vanquished troops, whose numbers were greatly
reduced by the slaughter.[2]

[1] We have till now inadvertently omitted to state that Thorolf and
Egil were brothers.

[2] There is some reason to believe that this furious but merely *preliminary* conflict took place in the vicinity of the lower part of what is now
called Woodbury Lane, a short distance south of the town of Axminster.

The commanders of the hostile armies, now looking forward to a decisive engagement on the morrow, collected their forces during the day, and moved them forward towards the field which was destined to be the scene of a still more deadly conflict. Athelstan, who had previously removed his quarters from the plain below the town to a more distant spot, now again advanced, and gathering his troops from the several positions which they had taken up in the neighbourhood, led them into the valley further down, on the eastern side of the river. Anlaf, in the same manner, advanced to the ground which had been occupied by his allies before the attack. A night of repose preceded the eventful day. In the first flush of morning[1] the king commenced the arrangement of his troops. Nor was Anlaf behind with his preparations. Let us ascend, in imagination, the neighbouring eminence of Trinity Hill, and take a view of the hostile regions drawn up in the valley beneath :—

Well may we picture to ourselves the wolf-packs collecting in the dense sombre woods which clothe the hill sides far and near! Well may we fancy the kite and the raven in the grey morning sky, swooping ominously over the marshy plain and startling the red deer as he slakes his thirst in the as yet unbloodstained stream! *   *   * Athelstan has formed his arrangements, we perceive, by dividing

[1] It was in the month of July, 937.

his forces into two main bodies. [1]   The principal
body, commanded by himself, he places in the open
field towards the river, where there is ample room,—
it being more than two miles in length from the
town to Kingsfield, the centre of the coming conflict, [2] and about the same in breadth from the rising
ground towards Kilmington on the right.   To these
are joined the small but hardy band of northern
heroes under the command of the courageous Egil. [3]

[1]   Egil's 'Saga.'   Ingulf.   William of Malmesbury.   Matthew of
Westminster, &c., &c.

[2]   Sir William Pole, who died in 1635, after relating what he had read
'in an old chronicle' concerning this battle, viz., the landing of the invaders at Seaton,—their encamping on 'a little hill called Bremeldoune,'—
their 'marching neare unto Axminster,'—their fighting with Athelstan,
and the dreadful slaughter which ensued,—proceeds as follows:—'Holingshed doth somewhat agree with this, and Mr. Camden writeth, "Axanmin-
ster, a towne of the Saxon princes, which, in that cruel battaile at
Brunaburge, being slayne, were thither convayed, and with their tumbes
(famous in ancient histories) hath made the place famous." [See a future
note from Leland.]   This story beinge soe famous, and in and neere the
place of my dwellinge, hath made me the more curious and carefull in the
searchinge thereof out of the names of the places mencioned therein.
And first for theire landinge at Seaton, and the marchinge upp the bottome, and encampinge at Bremeldoune.   The name Bremeldoune doth
yeat remayne unto this day, and the hill lyinge East from Colyton (where
I dwell) retayneth the name of Est Kingsdoune unto this day, and the
place where the battaile was fought conserveth the name of Kingsfield,
being in distanc not above three myles from Kingsdoune.'—'Collections
towards a History of Devon.'   We may add to this, that the Chartulary
of Newenham Abbey, which was compiled about the year 1340, contains
a direct and positive statement that the valley of the Axe was the scene
of this battle.   [See a future note.]   Risdon, Polewhele, Lysons—indeed,
all the county historians—receive the claims of our valley as an established fact beyond all reasonable question.

[3]   A small valley a short distance east of Kingsfield, bore, early in the
fourteenth century, and for many years afterwards, the very significant
name of Egilscombe.   Davidson's MS. 'History.'

Here is also Edmund the Atheling, the king's brother, accompanied by Turketul, the brave and learned chancellor of the kingdom, who leads a numerous body of the citizens of London. Near these, on the left, are to be seen the Earls Elwin and Ethelstan, kinsmen of Athelstan, with a numerous body of Mercian troops, and a powerful force from Worcestershire, under the command of Singin. On the right of the valley across the river, and stretching along the sides of the hills all crowned with woods (where now are the smiling fields of Kilmington and Shute), are stationed a numerous body of West Saxons, which, with his own adventurous band, are to be led by the impetuous Thorolf, and guided by the brave but cautious standard-bearer Thorfidus.[1] But however numerous are Athelstan's troops, they are few compared with the host in array under the various banners of the allied invaders. Anlaf, observing the disposition of Athelstan's army, has followed the example by placing his main body in the valley, in opposition to the Saxon king,[2] taking its command himself; while Constantius, the son of Constantine, accompanies him with an immense number of Scottish troops under Inwood, their earl. These are supported by large bodies of Anglo-Danes and

---

[1] Egil's 'Saga,' 46, 47. In addition to the commanders whose names we have given, the old writers say that the Saxon party numbered more than eight earls among their leaders.

[2] Ingulf.

Cumbrians, under the Earl Eligenius; while Froda
and other leaders attempt the command of the
almost innumerable hordes of the uncivilized Irish,
Danes, Norwegians, Picts, and Islanders.[1]   A numerous body of Scots, with a band of Welch, led by
the sturdy Adils, extend themselves between the
woody hills of Colyton and Shute to the left, and
are destined to act against the right wing of Athelstan's troops under Thorolf.   *   *   *   *

The respective armies thus drawn up, the attack
was not long deferred.   While the main body of the
Saxons was advancing, Thorolf, impatient to begin
the battle which he loved, rushed forward with impetuous haste, intending to turn the enemy's flank.
His eagerness impelled him beyond his companions,
who were also pressing fiercely and blindly onwards.
Adils, who had penetrated the woods on the right,
rushed with his chosen warriors from their concealment, and taking Thorolf's men in the rear, quickly
overwhelmed them and their brave commander with
destruction.   Thorfidus, however, who bore the standard, threw himself back upon the main body.   Egil
perceived these movements.   Being alarmed for the
safety and honor of his brother, he flew to the
spot, and stimulating his troops to a rally fought his
way to Adils, whom he quickly sacrificed in revenge
of Thorolf's death.   The Scots and Welch, their commanders being slain, betook themselves to flight, and

[1]   Egil's ' Saga,' 47.

were pursued by Egil and his troops with dreadful slaughter. [1]

At this period, while the battle was raging in the valley between the opposing monarchs—when missile weapons had been mutually abandoned—when foot was planted against foot, and shield against shield, and manual vigor was exerting every energy of destruction—when chiefs and vassals were perishing in all the levelling confusion of battle, and the ranks mowed down were quickly supplied with new crowds of warriors hastening to become victims—the chancellor Turketul made an attack which influenced the fortune of the day. [2] Placing his vast muscular figure at the head of the citizens of London, with whose veteran courage he was familiar, and supported by the men of Worcestershire and their leader Singin, he chose a peculiar quarter of attack, and rushed impetuously forward. Piercing the ranks of the Picts and Orkneymen, and heedless of the spears and arrows which fastened in his armour, he penetrated to the Cumbrians and Scots. Beholding Constantius, he waded through the gory torrent to assail him. Constantius was too brave to decline the daring

---

[1] Egil's 'Saga,' 48, 49.

[2] 'Cessantibus cito ferentariis armis, pede pes, et cuspide cuspis, umbo que umbone pellebatur. Cæsi multi mortales, confusa que cadavera regum et pauperum corruebant.'—*Ingulf*, 37. Quoted in Turner's '*History of the Anglo-Saxons.*' The extent to which we are indebted to Mr. Turner will be at once apparent to every reader of the interesting portion of English History which relates to our noble Anglo-Saxon ancestors.

combat. And now every heart beat vehemently ;—
on one side every arm was impatient to rescue the
Scottish prince, and on the other side to take him.
Such was the fury of his assailants—so many weapons
surrounded the Saxon chancellor—that his life might
be said to tremble, and he almost to repent of his
daring. The prince was nearly released, when Singin,
leaping forward, terminated, with a fatal blow, the
contested life. New courage rushed into the bosoms
of the Saxons on this event. A panic as suddenly
seized their enemies. The Scots, in consternation,
took to flight, and Turketul, with triumphant shouts,
pursued them. [1]

During these events, Athelstan and his brother
Edmund were engaged with Anlaf. Watching the
battle from one of the neighbouring eminences was
the Archbishop Otho, who had accompanied Athelstan, not, like his brother of Sherborne, as a warrior,
but perhaps in the capacity of chaplain. Prayer and

---

[1] Turner follows William of Malmesbury and some other historians,
in asserting that Constantine himself was slain in this battle. The Saxon
Chronicle distinctly states that it was his son who fell, and that the father
escaped :—

> 'Here was his [Constantine's] kindred band
> of friends o'erthrown
> on the folk-stead,
> in battle slain ;
> and *his son* he left
> on the slaughter-place
> mangled with wounds,
> young in the fight :
> he had no cause to boast,' &c.—'*Anglo-Saxon Chronicle.*'

intercession on behalf of the Anglo-Saxons appear to have occupied his time. The king, while in the hottest of the fight, had the misfortune to break his sword. He was immediately supplied with another, and some of the old chroniclers gravely assert that it was by no less an agency than that of a miracle produced by the invocations of the pious Otho. [1] Greatly were the Anglo-Saxons stimulated by this event. So signal an instance of the Divine favor, as it was considered, had doubtless no little share in the result of the conflict. That result was now at hand. Egil and Turketul, who had returned from the pursuit of the fugitives, charged suddenly upon Anlaf's rear. Athelstan exhorted his men to profit by the auspicious circumstance. He commanded his banner to be carried into the midst of the enemy. A deep impression was made upon their front, and an awful slaughter thinned their ranks. The rout began, and far and wide the air was rent with shouts of victory from the Anglo-Saxon troops. The soldiers of Anlaf

---

[1] William of Malmesbury's version of this story is somewhat different, but if possible still more curious. Thus saith the quaint old chronicler:—'His (Athelstan's) sword fell by chance from the sheath; upon which, while all things were filled with dread, and blind confusion, he invoked the protection of God and of Saint Aldhelm, who was distantly related to him; and replacing his hand upon the scabbard, he there found a sword, which is kept to this day, on account of the miracle, in the treasury of the kings. Moreover, it is, as they say, chased in one part, but can never be inlaid either with gold or silver,' &c. We must not be too severe with this supernatural story. Many a pretended 'miracle,' both ancient and modern, has been manufactured out of far less rational materials.

fled on every side, and the valley was strewn with
the bodies of the slain.[1] The river, made turbid with
the blood-stains, flowed horribly along.   Bearing, as
it did, the fountain of life upon its bosom, it might
be taken as an emblem of the Dread Angel himself
hurrying the spirits of the debased of God's image
into the great ocean of Eternity looming near!

It was night when the battle ended, and the conquerors, exhausted with the fatigues of the day, were
unable very long to continue the pursuit. Anlaf and
a few of the other leaders, with a remnant of their
troops, regained their vessels, effected an embarkation, and three days afterwards succeeded in reaching
Ireland.[2]

Athelstan, having left his people in pursuit, returned to the town of Brunenburgh, where he passed

[1] 'There lay many a warrior
        by javelins strewed;   *   *   *
        West-Saxons onwards
        throughout the day,
        in bands,
        pursued the footsteps
        of the loathed nations.
        They hewed the fugitives
        behind, amain,
        with swords mill-sharp.'—'Anglo-Saxon Chronicle.'

[2] On the south side of Axmouth churchyard, near where the allied
invaders landed and embarked, there is found a stratum of human bones
of considerable length and breadth. Unless these are the remains of the
victims of this battle, it is difficult to account for so extraordinary an accumulation ; for if this was the common burial-place at any period when
the plague was raging, the population of this now little village must
have been exceedingly numerous, or bodies must have been brought
from a long distance to this remote churchyard.

the night in mourning the death of his relations; for his victory had not been gained without the loss of Elwin and Ethelstan, the sons of his uncle Ethelward, besides the Bishop of Sherborne and another prelate whose name is not mentioned, his ally Thorolf, seven of his earls, and many other Saxons of distinction, with the flower of his troops. On the other side the loss was immense. The old writers differ in their statements respecting it—varying the number of the slain from 3,000 to 20,000; while the leaders, Constantius, Eligenius, and the Welch prince Adils, Hring, and five Danish princes, twelve earls, and several other nobles of various nations, were numbered with the dead.

> 'Carnage greater hath not been
>   in this island
>   ever yet
>   of people slain,
>   before this,
>   by edges of swords,
>   as books us say,
>   old writers,
>   since from the east hither
>   Angles and Saxons
>   came to land.' [1]

The body of Thorolf was, after a long search, discovered. It was buried on the spot, after having been washed and prepared in the manner customary, with a golden bracelet placed by his brother Egil upon each arm. The grave was covered with stones, and a

[1] Song in the 'Anglo-Saxon Chronicle.'

mound of earth was raised over it.   His brother, in
the manner of the ancients, concluded the ceremony
with a mournful song :—

'He who nothing feared has passed away,
   And valiantly has he departed—
The slayer of earls.
With the heart of the brave he fell—
Thorolf, in the battle fray of Odin.
May the grass grow green upon the woody hill over my illustrious
      brother's grave !
But we (how bitter is the presence of death to the soul!)
Are weighed down with grief of heart.' [1]

Having thus performed the last ceremonies over
the dead, Egil repaired to the town and sought the
presence of Athelstan.   He found the king in the
midst of his friends, who were now celebrating the
victory with floods of wine and boisterous mirth.
His reception was of course most cordial.   The
grateful monarch loaded him with presents.   Among
other articles of value he gave him as much silver as
two men could carry, and offered him lands and
goods, and the warmest personal friendship, if he
would remain and settle in this country.   But Egil
had determined upon a speedy return to his native
land, and after a few days he took his departure.

Athelstan collected the bodies of the slain earls
and other great men of both armies, and caused them
to be buried in a manner suitable to their rank.   The
bodies of his kinsmen Elwin and Ethelstan were conveyed to the abbey of Malmesbury, and those of the

---

[1] 'Saga,' 19.

two bishops to the churches of their respective sees. Five Danish princes and seven Saxon earls were buried, by the king's command, in the cemetery adjoining the castle of Brunenburgh. [1] A church already existed there, and the king endowed it with the manor of Prestaller, [2] out of the royal demesne in the parish of Axminster,—appointing seven priests to pray continually for the souls of the slain. [3] After the lapse of nearly a thousand years, the manor remains attached to the church of Axminster to the present day.

Most important, to Athelstan and to England, was the result of this famous battle. The power of the northmen was crippled for a time ;—Athelstan found himself an object of respect among the powers of Europe ;—and his country began to assume a far higher position among them than that to which it had previously attained. Great were the rejoicings

[1] 'In the year 1780, the skeleton of a man was found in digging to an unusual depth towards the west end of the north aisle of Axminster church. The hair was undecayed. It was long, and light yellow, and arranged in the style which prevailed among the Anglo-Saxons of distinction at the period of this battle.'—*Mr. Davidson.*

[2] A term which signifies *belonging to the priests.*

[3] The chartulary of Newenham Abbey informs us that 'King Athelstan gave the church of Axminster to seven priests, who should there for ever serve God for the souls of seven earls and many others put to death in battle with him against foreign invaders, *which fight began at Calix Down, in the parish of Colyton, and extended to Colecroft,* below Axminster, on which spot they were slain, A. D., 937.' Leland says :—'Axeminster church is famose by the sepultures of many noble Danes slain in king Athalstone's time at a batel *on Brunesdown thereby;* and by the sepultures likewyse of sum Saxon Lords slaine in the same field.'

of the Anglo-Saxons on the occasion. Their poets
sang the praises of the monarch and his deeds; and
by many a Saxon fireside were they repeated for
generations afterwards—even when the Saxons themselves had become a conquered race. [1]

Nothing further of importance is recorded of Axminster until we come to the time of Domesday
Book, in which it is thus surveyed :—[2]

'The King holds the manor called Axminster,
which King Edward also held during his life. The
number of hides which it contains is not known, as
it never paid the geld. The arable is forty plough-
lands, of which the King holds in demesne two
plough-lands, and the villains eighteen. There the
King has thirty villains, twenty-five boórs, and four
bondmen, with two beasts, fifty sheep, and two mills
which pay ten shillings. There are one hundred acres
of coppice, thirty acres of meadow, and one hundred
acres of pastures. The rental is twenty-six pounds
of full weight and value per annum, the same as
when B. [3] received it.

[1] One of these popular songs is preserved in the Anglo-Saxon Chronicle, and has been often translated. It simply describes the battle in the
peculiar style of Anglo-Saxon poetry. We have given, in the course of
our account, a few brief extracts from this curious composition.

[2] Our extract is from the 'Exeter Domesday,' which is more circumstantial, and therefore more interesting, than the Exchequer Domesday,
while its authority is in every respect equal. See page 36.

[3] Baldwin de Brioniis, sheriff of Devon, and a kinsman of the Conqueror. [See page 191.]

'To this manor another is added called Deneord, [1] which Ailrich held in the time of King Edward. It paid the geld for two virgates. The arable is a plough-land and a half. There the King has two villains and one boor, and they pay ten shillings to the manor aforesaid.

'In that of Axminster itself is another manor called Odesclive, [2] which Edric, a lame man, held by the charitable gift of King Edward. It is now held of King William by Edward, the son of Edric, and pays the geld for one virgate of land. The arable is one plough-land. Here Edward has two villains and one boor, who hold one plough-land. It is worth five shillings per annum.

'The church of Axminster has half a hide adjoining the manor. [3] The arable comprises two plough-

[1] There is reason to think that this was Uphay.

[2] Lands now in Membury.

[3] Now called the manor of Prestaller, which was granted by Athelstan. See page 319. 'Before the reign of king Edward II, and probably soon after the Conqueror's grant, the lands of Prestaller were erected into a manor, which, by an admeasurement taken in the year 1821, was found to comprise 402 acres, 1 rood, and 36 perches of land, dispersed throughout the three parishes in the following proportions, viz. :—in Axminster 312A. 0R. 36P., in Membury 52A. 3R., and in Kilmington 37A. 2R. The largest estate, which is at Wick, in Axminster, extends only to 56 acres; and a very humble dwelling, which is called the manor house, stands about half a mile east of the town. The lands in Membury form two little estates called Parslands (Parson's or Parsonage lands), with a small plot of ground, where the tithe barn is supposed to have formerly stood, on the south-western side of the church-yard. Those in Kilmington are divided into several fields.'—Davidson's ' *History of Axminster Church.*'

TT

lands. There are twelve boors, and it is worth twenty shillings.

'The Earl of Moreton holds a manor called Honiton, which was accustomed, in the time of King Edward, to pay thirty-pence a year to the royal manor of Axminster. But before the Earl obtained it this rent was witheld. Drogo holds it of the Earl.

'Ralph de Pomerai holds a manor called Smallridge, which in the time of King Edward paid thirty-pence annually to the royal manor in farm. But it has been witheld by Ralph for twelve years past, as it was before he received the manor.

'William Capra holds a manor called Membury, which also, in the time of King Edward, paid thirty-pence annually to the said royal manor. But William has witheld it for twelve years past.

'The Bishop of Constance holds a manor called Charlton, [1] which also, in the time of King Edward, paid fifteen-pence annually to the aforesaid royal manor. But before the bishop received it the rent was witheld.

'The Canons of St. Mary of Rouen hold a manor called Roridge, [2] which paid thirty-pence to the said royal manor in the time of King Edward. But the canons have witheld this customary payment for eighteen years past.'

The manor continued to be held by the kings of

[1] Lands in Axmouth, not now a manor.
[2] In the parish of Upottery.

England until the reign of John, who gave it to his
favorite counsellor William Lord Brewer, together
with the grant of a weekly market on Sundays,[1] and
an annual fair on the feast of St. John the Baptist.[2]
Alice, one of the co-heiresses of this family, brought
the manor to Lord Reginald de Mohun, of Dunster,
who gave it to the Abbey of Newenham, with which
it remained till the Dissolution. It was then granted
to the Duke of Norfolk, by whose family it was sold,
in the time of James I, to John Lord Petre. It remained in the possession of the Petre family till the
year 1824, when it was sold for £43,000 to the late
James Alexander Frampton, Esq., of the New Inn,
London. This purchase is stated to have been made
by Mr. Frampton on the joint account of himself
and the late William Knight, Esq., of Axminster,
although the conveyance, it appears, was executed to
Mr. Frampton alone, by private arrangement. A
large portion of the property, including the Westwater and Hunthay estates, was thereupon sold to

[1] After the suppression of Sunday markets (see page 122), Saturday
was selected, and the market continued for many centuries to be held on
that day. It has for more than ten years been held on Fridays, after having,
for a short time previously, been held on Thursdays. There have long
been three annual fairs:—on the first Wednesday after October 10; the
first Tuesday after April 25; and the 'charter-fair' on the first Tuesday
after June 24. The present market house was erected in 1826-7, on the
site of an old brick building, which, whatever might have been its defects
in other respects, was superior to the present building in having the accommodation of a second storey containing a large room for public purposes, the want of which is now greatly felt.

[2] See page 172. See, also, our account of Newenham Abbey.

the late William Tucker, Esq., of Coryton, and the estate of Nower was at the same time sold to Henry Knight, Esq., of Axminster. The division of the rest of the property between Mr. Frampton and Mr. W. Knight was never effected, and it therefore remained vested in Mr. Frampton alone by the original conveyance. Mr. Frampton, it appears, mortgaged the property for £18,000, without the knowledge of Mr. W. Knight, who, however, after the death of Mr. Frampton, and on becoming aware of the existence of this mortgage, took a transfer of it, as well as an assignment of £2800 then remaining a primary charge on the property for the benefit of some younger members of the Petre family. He thus became, independently, the mortgagee of the manor and estates. The affair of his joint purchase, owing to the informal manner in which it was conducted, and to subsequent transactions, is now, and has been since the year 1836, the subject of a suit in chancery.

CHAPTER IX.

AXMINSTER, from its vicinity to Lyme Regis—'the key of the West'[1]—had an abundant share of the troubles and vicissitudes which characterise the seventeenth century in the annals of England. In the great civil war which ended with the death of Charles I and the substitution of a Commonwealth for the ancient monarchy thus temporarily extinguished, the feelings of the great bulk of the people of the West of England, especially the trading classes, were on the side of the Parliament—estranged from the monarch as they had been by his unconstitutional exactions and arbitrary rule. Lyme, from an early stage of the quarrel, had assumed an imposing attitude. It was strongly garrisoned for the Parliament, and its inhabitants were enthusiastic in the cause which they had espoused. Hence the necessity, on the king's part, for the presence of counteracting forces in the neighbourhood, and hence,

---

[1] See page 125.

also, the excited state of the people, and the unhappy
scenes of violence and bloodshed which they were
destined to witness;—for the garrison of Lyme, historians tell us, 'gave the king much trouble,' and, at
one time, often made excursions even 'to the walls
of Exeter.'[1]

Axminster contributed its quota to a band of mi-
litia-men which was levied for the king in East
Devon and placed under the command of John
Drake, Esq., of Ashe.   The town was constantly
occupied by soldiery, and, with the surrounding
country, suffered greatly from the exactions and
immoralities which are inseparable from such an occupation.   A large body of troops and artillery,
under Prince Maurice, took up their quarters at Axminster in April, 1644.   They were intended for the
siege of Lyme, and had been compelled to leave
Beaminster, their previous quarters, by the fire which
nearly destroyed that town on the 19th of the same
month.[2]   The siege of Lyme was prosecuted until
the 15th of June, when the prince withdrew his
troops and retreated to Exeter, on hearing that the
Earl of Essex was marching from Dorchester to the
relief of the town.   The earl advanced, on June 23,
from Bridport to Crewkerne and Chard, and, on the
30th, to Axminster, whence he passed through Honi-

---

[1] Clarendon's 'History of the Rebellion.'

[2] See page 46, in which, in some copies, the date 1645 is misprinted
for 1644.

ton, Cullompton, and Tiverton, to Cornwall, where he was obliged to surrender to the forces commanded by the king in person. A regiment of the royal army, in passing through this part of the country towards Cornwall, took possession of Colyton on July 28th. They marched to Lyme the same night, and after 'threatening' the garrison there, fell back again to their quarters at Colyton. The Lyme party, however, at once returned the visit,—sending a force of 126 horse, commanded by Captains Pyne, Erle, and Bragge, who not only took a great number of prisoners, but completely dispersed the royal regiment. It was when on his way from Cornwall to the more eastern parts of the kingdom, that Charles halted at Chard and issued the proclamation referred to at page 238.

This short outline of these exciting events, will suffice to convey an idea of the condition of the locality at this eventful period. So alarming was the state of things, and so insecure were the lives and property of the people, that a few of the more wealthy townsfolks who were attached to the cause of the king, petitioned that a royal garrison should be placed at Axminster. The petition was granted, and 300 men, commanded by Sir Richard Cholmley,[1] took

[1] Sir Richard Cholmley, knight-banneret, of Grosmont, Yorkshire, married Margaret, daughter of Lord Poulett, of Hinton St. George. Camden says that there are twenty-five ways of spelling the name of Cholmley; and another writer adds that there is but *one way* of describing that ancient family, viz., as was said of the Lucas's, that 'all the daughters

up their quarters in the town and its surrounding
villages. Mr. Henry Hutchings, an inhabitant of
Axminster, was entrusted with the construction of
some works for the defence of the place, and also
with the office of receiver of the money brought in
by the county.[1] The primary object of the force
thus stationed at Axminster was the subjugation of
Lyme; but the indefatigable and courageous defenders
of that now 'loyal' borough neither waited for the intended visit nor gave their opponents sufficient time
for preparation to *receive* a visit. On October 25,
their brave commander, Colonel Ceeley, led a force to
Axminster. An action took place which resulted in
the capture of many prisoners by the Lyme party,
the total rout of the royalists, and the death of Sir
Richard Cholmley, their commander, who was shot
in the shoulder with a musket bullet. Sir Richard
was succeeded in the command of Axminster by Ma-

are beautiful and all the sons are brave.' The name is derived from
Chaumont-des-lis (village of 'lilies'), a place in Normandy, whence the
original family came with William the Conqueror.

[1] On the establishment of the Commonwealth, Mr. Hutchings was
one of the persons selected for punishment for the part which he had
taken on behalf of the king. The first article of delinquency against him
was, 'that he was one of them who had signed a petition to bring a garrison into Axminster, which was the overthrow of the town, and the un-
doing of many hundreds of people.' He was punished with a fine. Among
the other 'delinquents' were Sir William Pole, of Colcombe, fined in
£2855; George Southcott, of Kilmington, in £270; Thomas Coggan, of
Sadborough, in £206; John Harvey, of Chardstock, in £12; John Burnard, of Colyton, in £243; Richard Whitty, of Thorncombe, in £31; and
William Croft, Miller, of Thorncombe, in £25.—*Mr. Davidson.*

jor Walker, who, on November 15, was killed, with many of his men, in an attempt to surprise the ever-watchful garrison of Lyme. The conquerors pushed on to Axminster, where they found that the main body of the garrison, which had fallen back to the town, had taken refuge in the church, from which they could not be dislodged. The disappointed besiegers, therefore, set fire to several houses, and the greater part of the town was soon reduced to a heap of smoking ruins.[1] After this event the cause of the Parliament, in this locality as well as in other places, progressed amain. The garrison of Lyme had completely crippled that of Axminster, and soon possessed itself of most of the other royal stations in the neighbourhood.

Fairfax, when, in the following year (1645), he came on his great expedition into the west, made Axminster and the neighbouring villages the head quarters for a detachment of his troops on October 13th. The king's forces, under Lord Goring, were then near Exeter, endeavouring to force themselves eastward and to attack the army of Fairfax on their way. Accordingly, Lord Goring, Lord Wentworth, and other leaders, with a body of cavalry, passed over the Blackdown hills in the night of the 13th-14th, and surprised a small parliamentary force at Mem-

---

[1] A very interesting letter, written by a soldier who was present on this occasion, has been published by Mr. Davidson, who accidentally discovered it among the tracts in the British Museum.

bury [1]—taking prisoners forty foot and twenty dragoons, and making off before the intelligence could be conveyed to the head quarters at Axminster. No general engagement between Fairfax and the king's forces took place in the neighbourhood of Axminster, but those forces received a signal defeat at Torrington, and the result of the parliamentary commander's expedition was the reduction of several towns in Devonshire, and the ultimate dispersion of the royal army in that part of the. kingdom. The general issue is familiar to every reader of his country's history, and it would be foreign to our purpose to dilate upon it. [2]

The Commonwealth passed away without anything of public importance occurring in Axminster and its

---

[1] Sprigge's '*Anglia Rediviva.*' The historian does not distinctly say that this surprise was at Membury, but uses the phrase 'an outlying village near Axminster.' 'There can be little doubt,' says Mr. Davidson, 'that it was the village of Membury, as its situation coincides with the description, and the parish register there records the burial of a soldier on the 14th of October, who was killed near the church.' A skirmish had previously taken place at Membury on February 13, 1645, in which Sir Shilston Calmady was killed in the gateway of Ford House. He was buried in Membury church, where a monument is erected to his memory.

[2] Axminster followed the example of many other places in issuing tokens during this exciting period. Many of them are at this moment preserved in the cabinets of the curious. From one of the many specimens which have fallen under our notice, we copy the inscription, as follows:—*Obverse*—'Thomas Whitty in,' *Reverse*—'Axminster, mercer,' surrounding the initials 'T. $^{W \cdot}$ D.' The following appears among the Colyton tokens.—*Obverse*—'Benjamin Massey,' surrounding an anchor impaling a heart.—*Reverse*—'of Colliton, mercer,' and the initials 'B.M.' in the area.

neighbourhood. The following extracts from the parish books will serve to give an idea of the state of the town, and, to some extent, of public affairs, after the death of Cromwell :—

	£	s.	d.
Paid for meate and drinke for the ringers and others when the king was proclaimed	1	2	6
For two new bell ropes, and wire for the chimes ...	0	8	6
For the Book of Common Prayer	0	14	0
To Robert Knight for saxon's wages, keeping the clock and chimes, ringing the curfur,[1] looking to the bells, and maintaining the ropes	4	0	0
To Leonard Peream for painting the kinge's armes	3	10	0
To Robert Knight, the 5th November, in meate and drink for the ringers	0	10	0
To Leonard Peream and Thomas Poole for setting up the font, and lead, and soder, and labor[2]	2	5	0
For writing the ammunition rate and Autry [Yarty] Bridge rate [3]	0	10	0
To five watchmen for watching Mr. Carew	0	3	6
Paid for sending Hue and Cryes by night, this year...	0	3	2
Paid for carrying the disbanded men's armes to Exeter	0	16	0
Paid for conveying prisoners which were committed to the gaol *for conscience sake*, at two severall times [4]	0	11	0

[1] The custom of ringing the curfew at eight o'clock every evening during the winter season, had existed in this parish from time immemorial till 1840, when the parishioners, adopting the hint of the vicar on another parochial matter, refused to allow any part of the church-rate to be appropriated to the time-honored purpose, and the salary being no longer forthcoming, the custom, as a matter of course, was discontinued. See our account of Axminster church.

[2] 'The font had no doubt been thrown down during the rebellion, and its lining of lead converted into bullets.'—*Mr. Davidson.*

[3] The expences of erecting and repairing the bridges were not then, as at present, defrayed by the county at large; and there were also local rates, it appears, for the defence of the town and for the service of the constituted authorities in the state.

[4] See future pages for extracts from the ' *Church Book of the Axminster Independent Chapel.*'

	£	s.	d.
Paid men for help searching for armes	0	5	0
Paid for the muster-master's fee [1]	0	8	0
Paid the foot-post for travelling this yeare [2]	1	5	10
Paid Francis Parrick for travelling about the pha- naticks	0	1	0
Paid Leonard Peream for bread and beere when the quakers were taken up [3]	0	1	0
1664.—Paid Mr. Nicholas Fry (solicitor) for apearing in the crowon office about the bridges	2	16	8
For a bridge rate	0	5	0
1665.—Paid for a collation when the bishop past	0	6	4
Paid to the ringers the Thanksgiving-day for the victory against the Hollanders	0	10	0
Paid for furze faggots when the soldiers were here, to make a bonfire	0	2	0
Paid for oops [bullfinches], grays [badgers], oters and hedgehoggs' heads this yeare [4]	0	14	3

[1] The 'mustering' of men for the defence of the coast, and the inspection of their arms, were matters of great importance at that period, as they had been for a long time previously.

[2] The post office had been established in England twenty-six years previously (in 1635), but the payment of so small a sum for the year's services of a 'foot post' shows that his travelling could not have been very extensive. Perhaps, however, the 'foot post' had no connection with the post office, and was merely a parish messenger to and from the villages and other places in the neighbourhood which the post office had not then reached—confined as it was to the principal towns on the great lines of road.

[3] The quakers at that time, in common with other dissenters, were greatly persecuted in the West of England. John Whiting, a quaker, who was imprisoned at Ilchester 'for conscience-sake,' wrote a curious book on the subject of the persecution of his sect. See Saville's ' *History of the Society of Friends.*'

[4] The old parish books show the expenditure every year of considerable sums in the shape of bounty for the destroying of certain birds and animals which were supposed to be injurious to the agriculturist—an expenditure still kept up, to a less extent, in many rural parishes. Most of the creatures against which this war of extermination was carried on have been found, in reality, to be not only innocuous but of positive benefit to man. Such, for instance, is the hedgehog, which was absurdly

	£	s.	d.
1666.—Paid for lying in the town shutts [water courses]...	0	7	8
Paid for the bookes for the Fast for the burning of London, and the Thanksgiving for the overthrow of the Hollanders	0	6	0
Paid Mr. Crabb to make up his pay of £80 [1] ...	5	0	0
1667.—For a new tackle for the chimes and putting of him in, and getting of them in order	0	6	6
1669.—Paid for the Book of Articles and Peter's Pence [2]	0	8	0

supposed to have a *penchant* for cows' milk, and to be in the habit of anticipating the dairymaid in her morning's avocations. The same animal was, with equal absence of truth, believed to be an orchard robber—rolling itself among the fallen apples and walking off when a satisfactory load had become attached to its spines. It is now well known that a more innocent creature does not exist, or one more likely, from its feeding on destructive insects, to be of greater use in the fields. The same remark applies almost invariably to all the other creatures which have been ignorantly persecuted, and many of which are even now too often the objects of persecution. Notwithstanding an entry in the Axminster parish books on July 29, 1702, to the effect that no more money should be paid out of the rates for 'killing any sorte of birds,' &c., it is only within a very few years that the practice has been wholly discontinued in that parish.

[1] The amount of the vicarial tithes at the time Mr. Crabb was vicar (1662 to 1699) appears to have been but £75, exclusive of the sum which he allowed his curates at Kilmington and Membury. The sum of £5 to make his stipend 'four-score pounds,' was yearly paid by the parish as appears by the several entries.

[2] Peter's Pence was a tax of a penny upon every house, originally instituted by Ina, king of the West Saxons, for the support of an establishment at Rome for the reception of English pilgrims and the education of English youth. The tax was also called 'smoke-silver,' and it received the name of Peter's Pence from the circumstance of its being paid on St. Peter's day. Is was enforced, with occasional interruptions, till the time of Queen Elizabeth, when it was suppressed by law. This entry of its payment by the worthy old Axminsterians so long afterwards, is therefore curious, and induces a suspicion of the honesty of the archdeacon's official by whom the tax was collected. See Mr. Davidson's '*History of Axminster Church*.'

	£	s.	d.
1671. [1]—Paid for uncovering the cherubims and for cleaning the church	0	6	0
To the ringers when his Majestie passed through the towne—the 24th July	0	10	0
For a new book to register certificates of strangers residing in the parish	0	2	0
1675.—Paid for sending Aaron Enticott before Sir Courtnay Pole, by a warrant, &c., granted about catching a salmon [2]	0	0	6
For a warrant to ly against the scoulds [3]	0	1	0

It was in 1669 that Cosmo de Medicis, Grand Duke of Tuscany, undertook his famous travels in this country. [4] The following extract from his curious account of those travels will convey an idea of the state of the town, and be interesting in other respects :—'On the morning of the 8th [of April] his highness sent Platt to present his compliments to the mayor [of Exeter]. Towards noon, Mr. Kirkam and the Messrs. Rolle came to wish him a good journey ; after which, having dined, he got into his coach and departed for Axminster, where he arrived at an early hour. The road was through an uneven country, divided into fields under the plough, and spacious

[1] In this year, Sir John Drake, Mr. Thomas Bunstone, and Mr. Barnard Prince were 'returned into the ecclesiastical court' for refusing to pay their church-rate.

[2] It is much to be regretted that entries of a similar character cannot be found in the parish books of the present day. A rigid prosecution of the poachers of salmon would result in a reduction of the parish rates by the influx of respectable residents which so delightful a stream, if only taken moderate care of, would be sure to attract to the locality.

[3] See page 96.

[4] See page 124.

AXMINSTER, AS IT APPEARED IN 1860.
(FROM BELOW STONY BRIDGE.)

W. Spreat, lith. Exeter

meadows for feeding cows, in which this district abounds. At first we suffered a good deal of inconvenience, becanse we had to travel *a road full of water, and muddy, though not deep.* We passed through Honiton, a small but populous village, [1] situated in a valley, and having ascended a hill, from which we could see the sea, we arrived at Axminster, where we found the master of the horse of Henry Howard, brother of the Duke of Norfolk, and of my Lord Philip, grand almoner to the queen, who delivered to Colonel Gascoyne a letter from his master, in which he excused himself for not coming in person to pay his respects to his highness, in consequence of his approaching departure on his embassy to Fez; and informed him that he had sent his carriage to Salisbury, to be at the service of his highness. The master of the horse was admitted to an audience by the serene prince, and departed that same evening for London. His highness then went out to walk, and passed the evening in seeing some ancient medals [coins] which had been dug up in this neighbourhood, and were brought for his inspection by the minister of the church [the Rev. J. J. Crabb]. Axminster is a collection of two hundred houses, many of which are made of mud [2] and thatched with

[1] See page 124.
[2] Locally called 'cob,' that is, unburned clay mixed with straw—the material, it is supposed, of which the houses of the Greeks and Romans, even when in their highest civilization, were constructed. As the town had been burnt during the recent civil war, many of these houses were

straw. It contains nothing remarkable, except the parish church, which has a tower in which are bells so well tuned that their sound is exceedingly harmonious and agreeable. The trade of the inhabitants consists in the manufacture of woollen cloth. On the 9th, having travelled twelve miles through a country more cultivated, pleasanter, and more fertile than on the preceding day,[1] we arrived at Hinton St. George, a villa of my Lord John Paulet,'[2] &c. &c.

Monmouth's rebellion, and the circumstances in which it had its origin, are matters of general history into which it is not our province to enter fully—confining ourselves, as we obviously must, to a relation of none but the most striking events in immediate connection with the locality of which we have undertaken to treat. A vivid idea of the state of things at Axminster at the period of Monmouth's ill-fated

probably intended only for a temporary purpose, while houses of a more comfortable kind were in the course of erection; for many of the inhabitants were engaged in the staple clothing trade, which was then in a flourishing state, and they undoubtedly lived in a style more commensurate with their circumstances than a hut of clay could afford. The view of the town which we copy from Cosmo's work, shows that at the time of his visit, the tower which no doubt had been battered when the church was attacked by the troops from Lyme, was still remaining unrepaired. The entries in the parish books, indeed, prove that it was then in a state of reparation. Perhaps there is not at the present time a single house in the town which was standing at the time of Cosmo's visit. The date on a stone house on Castle-hill is twenty years later, namely 1689.

[1] A statement which the traveller of to-day, over the same ground, could not truly make. It is difficult to find a drive through a more delightful country than that between Exeter and Axminster.

[2] See page 124.

expedition, may be obtained from a contemporary manuscript preserved in the Axminster Independent Chapel,[1] to the pages of which we have been before indebted. We shall, therefore, extract a few of its most interesting passages, which will be new to the majority of our readers, and, we are sure, will afford them more gratification than any account that could be drawn up by ourselves, notwithstanding the *ex parte* character of the extracts. Due allowance must of course be made for the prejudices of the writer, and for his *characteristic* phraseology, and especially must it be borne in mind that he was smarting under a sense of the unrighteous persecution of his sect :—

'Now the Lord stirred vp James, Duke of Monmouth (reputed son of the former king C. II.), who had bin in an exile state for some time, and on the 11th day of the 4th moneth[2] of this year, 1685, he safely and peaceably landed at the haven of Lyme Regis with a small number of men, about eighty, having their ship laden with armour and ammunition, who, immediately vpon his landing, gaue forth his declarations to restore liberty to the people of God for the worship of God, to preserue the rights and

[1] *'Ecclesiastica, or a Book of Remembrance.'*—See page 127.

[2] That is, June 11th, (old style). The 25th of March had not at that time *generally* ceased to be considered as New Year's Day. In all legal instruments, indeed, the beginning of the year was dated from that day up to 1752. The alteration to January 1st had *commenced*, in England and France, about the year 1580.

priviledges of the nation, &c. Tydings of his landing were spread abroad far and near, very speedily,
and divers persons from severall quarters hasted to resort to him. Now were the hearts of the people of
God glad-ded, and their hopes and expectations
raised, that this man might be a deliverer for the nation and the interest of Christ in it, who had bin even
harrous'd out with trouble and persecution, and even
broken with the weight of oppression vnder which
they had long groaned. . . . . And now was
the sounding of trumpets and alarm for wars heard.

'On the 15th day of the moneth they began their
march from the town of Lyme, with much dread and
terrour, to the amazement and wonder of many what
the Lord had wrought. A great number of sober
and pious men marched forth with the army. The
first day of their march they came into the town of
Axminster, where some companies of souldiers came
towards them on each side of the town. [1] So that it

---

[1] The Duke's Army had gone through the narrow lane by Hay Farm,
and crossed Uplyme Common, by the old road, to a point where a fine
view is obtained, from above the present Hunter's Lodge Inn, of Shute
Hill and the valley of Axminster, here distant two miles. From this
high ground of south-east Devon, the Duke of Monmouth discovered the
Devonshire Militia marching towards Axminster; and on the other side,
when at the distance of two hours' march from Lyme, the Somersetshire
Militia hastening to form a junction with them. The scouts of the latter
force had entered Axminster, but retired upon the forces of Monmouth
hastily marching in, having doubled their pace. The Duke took possession
of Axminster and seized on the lanes leading towards each of the opposing
forces, which, from their being so narrow, and the hedges so thick, were
very favorable for being secured with cannon and musqueteers.—Roberts's
'Life of Monmouth.'

was supposed by some there might be a battle. But the Lord eminently appeared, filling this new army with wonderfull courage, and sending an hornett of fear amongst those that came to oppose them, so that a dreadful consternation of spirit ceized on them, that in some places they fell one vpon another, in other places some ran away with amazement, some were so stricken with terrour that they were even bereft of their reason and like distracted persons, others threw away their weapons of war and would take them vp no more, and many watched opportunities to leave their colours and old officers and came and joyn'd with this new company; and, as they marched on from town to town, the army increased dayly. [1] In a

---

[1] 'Four thousand men of the trainbands were actually assembled under his [Monk, Duke of Albemarle's] command. He seems to have thought that, with this force, he should be able at once to crush the rebellion. He therefore marched towards Lyme. But when, in the afternoon of Monday the fifteenth of June, he reached Axminster, he found the insurgents drawn up there to encounter him. They presented a resolute front. Four field pieces were pointed against the royal troops. The thick hedges, which on each side overhung the narrow lanes, were lined with musketeers. Albemarle, however, was less alarmed by the preparations of the enemy than by the spirit which appeared in his own ranks. Such was Monmouth's popularity among the common people of Devonshire, that, if once the trainbands had caught sight of his well known face and figure, they would probably have gone over to him in a body. Albemarle, therefore, though he had a great superiority of force, thought it advisable to retreat. The retreat soon became a rout. The whole country was strewn with the arms and uniforms which the fugitives had thrown away; and had Monmouth urged the pursuit with vigour, he would probably have taken Exeter without a blow. But he was satisfied with the advantage which he had gained, and thought it desirable that his recruits should be better trained before they were employed in any

few daies the number was jncreased to severall thousands. Divers, also, of the brethren belonging to this church marched along with them. And as this army went forward, so companies of souldiers belonging to King James pursued after, but durst not overtake them. There was likewise another army sent by the king to meet them. About four or five daies after they [Monmouth's party] marched out of Axminster, whiles they lay in the town of Taunton, some few persons were chosen out of the companies and sent to view the motions of the enemy that was behind them. Amongst which one of them was a member of this society, a faithfull brother named Samuel Rampson. Those persons, riding forth to descry the enemy, met with a party of them, and, engaging with each other, had a very smart battle, in which a great person belonging to the enemy was slain, and in this sore skirmish Samuel Rampson was mortally wounded, who, endeavouring to get to an house not far from the place, to seek some help and relief, but finding none to relieve him, lost his life also. After a few daies, as the army marched onwards, and meeting with the enemy, there was a more sharp battle and greater slaughter, in which one Henry Noon, a pious and liuely christian, a vsefull member related to this body, was also slain. . . . . And this

hazardous service. He therefore marched towards Taunton, where he arrived on the eighteenth of June, exactly a week after his landing.'— Macauley's 'History of England,' vol. I, page 175.

church began to be diminished, and their communion was much interrupted in regard both the pastor, the ruling elder, and severall of the brethren, were with the army.'[1] * * * * * * *

After briefly referring to the decisive battle of Sedgemoor, and to the subsequent execution of the unfortunate hero of the expedition, the narrative thus proceeds :—

'A little before this dreadful battle [of Sedgemoor] some of the brethren of this church were inclin'd to leaue the army, and if by any means to return back to their own habitations, [2] and, by the good providence of God, some of them returned home in safety,

---

[1] Monmouth's party, on their march from Axminster to Taunton, encamped for the night 'on a strong post beyond Axminster towards Chard.' [Wade's '*Confession*.'] This 'strong post' is considered by Mr. Davidson [MS. '*History of Axminster.*'] to be Membury Castle and Baaley Down. One of the skirmishes referred to in the text took place between Axminster and Chard, and the other, perhaps, at Ashill. The opponents of the Duke's forces were a party of the Somerset Militia, under Colonel Lutterell, who had the worst of the encounter. There is a tradition that a party of Monmouth's followers were entertained on the lawn in front of Coaxdon House, under the avenue of trees of which traces still remain. This is not improbable, for Mr. Richard Cogan, who then resided there, was a rigid dissenter, and, after the battle of Sedgemoor, a warrant was issued for his apprehension. Being closely pursued, he took refuge in the Green Dragon Inn, at that time one of the principal inns in Axminster. The landlord's daughter, Elizabeth Grey, concealed him in a bed;—so effectually that his pursuers were unable to discover him, although they searched the room more than once. Mr. Cogan, in more settled times, united himself in marriage to his deliverer. [See pages 269-271, in which a still more remarkable preservation, by a former Mrs. Cogan, is related. Both anecdotes are given for the first time in Wilson's '*Life of De Foe.*']

[2] Concurring in opinion, perhaps, with Falstaff, that 'the better part of valor is discretion.'

amongst whom Mr. Towgood, [1] pastor, and Thomas
Lane, elder. Of those that endeavoured to return
back were Mr. John Ashwood (son of the former
pastor, Mr. Bartholomew Ashwood [2]), who had for
some time before addicted himselfe to the work of
the ministery, and Thomas Smith, a very pious christian. These, being on their way returning, were
apprehended and imprisoned. Such as tarry'd with
the army were preserved from the power of the
sword, though afterwards some of them were exposed
to no small trouble. Another of the brethren, named
John Spiring, being taken by the rude souldiers, after
the battle was past, was stript of his rayment and
barbarously vsed by their hands, and imprisoned, as
divers other of poor christians were.   *   *   *
'About the beginning of the seventh moneth

[1] A relative, no doubt, of Micaiah Towgood, the eminent presbyterian minister and writer, who was born at Axminster in 1700, and became
master, in 1761, of an establishment at Exeter for the education of presbyterian ministers. At the beginning of the present century a similar
establishment was conducted at Axminster by the late Rev. Mr. Small.
Mr. Towgood was eminent as a preacher, and wrote several works which
are in great repute with the members of his sect. This mention of one
of the 'worthies' of Axminster reminds us that we might as well finish the
subject in this note by stating that Axminster has the honor of being
the birth-place of Dr. Buckland, the celebrated geologist and Dean of
Westminster. He was born on March 12, 1784, in the house which stands
on the eastern side of the entrance to Stony Lane on the Lyme Road.
We have before spoken of a third eminent native of the parish—the
county biographer, Prince. See page 197.

[2] Mr. Bartholomew Ashwood was vicar of Axminster from February
13, 1660, till August 24, 1662, when he was ejected by the act of uniformity, and joined the Independents, and founded a congregation at Axminster. See a future page.

(September—see page 337), the judges of the land came in circuit into the western parts. The great work that lay before them was to call forth, sentence, and condemn those poor prisoners that had lain in bonds for the late rebellion, as they term'd it. Those judges exercised great severity, especially one of them named George Jeffreys, who was Lord Chief Justice—a man of violence and blood, who, with madness and rage, caused great cruelty to be exercised on the bodies of many poor innocents, and whose infamy will not be wip'd off to the latest posterity—being the principal person in the management of those bloody assizes. And now was a time of sore distress and perplexity, for multitudes were involved in the ensnaring dangers of the day. . . . . Ah! what an heart-affecting sight it was to behold the blood of many to be spilt as water upon the ground, and their dead bodies hung up in the open aire, and none permitted to bury them! * * * And now were the brethren of this church (which had bin shut vp for some time in one prison and another) brought forth before man's judgement seat. The afore-named Mr. John Ashwood was sentenc'd to die as a traytor, and the place of his execution appoynted by the judge. But the blessed Lord, in whose hands are the lives of all persons, so overruled this sentence, that, by endeavours vsed, a reprieue was granted him and afterwards a pardon. As for Thomas Smith, he was sentenc'd also to dye, and the time being come to be led forth of the prison-house to execution, another prisoner, standing forth in his name, was carryed out of the prison in his stead, and the said Thomas Smith, continuing in the prison a little time longer, having a fitt opportunity, made his escape. . . . Concerning the said John Spiring, he was sentenc'd for banishment, and accordingly was carry'd captive into the Isle of Barbadoes, where he was sold as a slave once and again. And after some time was past, a door was open for his redemption by paying a sume of money which was collected of christian friends. But in returning home, whilst he was on the seas, both the ship in which he sailed, with the persons and wares in it, were cast away and drowned [1]

'There was also another brother of this society, named William Comb, who suffer'd imprisonment at the same time. . . . Notwithstanding all the menaces of a severe neighbouring justice of the

---

[1] Nearly 1000 of the unfortunate followers of Monmouth were sentenced to transportation and given *as presents* to favorite courtiers and soldiers, by whom *they were sold as slaves* to the West India planters. [See pages 130 and 205.] Among those unfortunate persons was Azariah Pinney, Esq., of Bettiscombe, son of the rector of Broadwinsor during the Commonwealth, and ancestor of W. Pinney, Esq., M.P. for Lyme Regis. Mr. Azariah Pinney, with 98 other persons, was presented to Jerome Nipho, who sent him to the island of Nevis. He was soon afterwards ransomed for £65, and ultimately became an important personage in the island, of which his son was made Chief Justice. The sufferings of the poorer slaves were most intense. An account of the slavery of John Coad, a 'God-fearing' carpenter of Stoford, near Yeovil, has been published by Mr. Roberts, along with other similar cases, in a small paper on this subject—and a truly heartrending account it is.

peace he could not sin against his conscience. . . . . Wherefore, by reason of the violence and rage of the said justice, he was constrain'd to abscond, and on a day as he was in a retired place alone, some informers, or petty officers, rushing in vpon him, apprehended him, and carried him before that magistrate, who immediately sent him to prison. But no matter of fact could be charg'd against him as having an hand in the late rebellion (as it was term'd), so was he afterwards acquitted by the judge.

'These were the only persons belonging to this congregation that suffered bonds and imprisonment at this time. The rest that escaped the edge of the sword and the hands of cruell enemies, were constrained to lurk in holes and to hide themselves in secret corners. . . . . O the breaches that were made in many families! What hanging of husbands and sons! How many places even soakt with blood! What imprisoning of divers persons, and others wandering about in holes, in secret corners, and caves of the earth! O the violence and spoiling that was in many places—the dreadful oppression and cruelty! What an vngodly generation swarm'd vp and down, full of malignity and all manner of wickedness!'

Axminster was the scene of the execution of one of the unhappy persons who was sentenced by Jeffreys at Dorchester. 'His name,' says the writer of the '*New Martyrology*,'[1] 'was Mr. Rose, a gunner,

---

[1] The author of this melancholy record was 'Thomas Pitts, Gent.,'

who landed with the Duke of Monmouth. He
had a great resolution, and was not started with the
fear of death. He said that he defy'd death and all
them that were the occasion of it. He was very courageous, and died so. He spent some time in private
prayer, but was not allowed long because there was
to be an execution at Honiton.'[1] The spot at which
this execution was performed is traditionally said to
be in Stony-lane, at the entrance to Love-lane, where
the old people still remember a decaying stump which
was said to have been the remains of the gallows.
Love-lane was formerly called 'Spinning-lane,' from
the circumstance of its having at one time been used
for a rope-walk.[2]

whose real name was John Tutchin. He was the author of several
political publications, and was tried by Jeffreys for having been concerned
in Monmouth's Rebellion, and sentenced to a heavy fine, with seven years'
imprisonment, and severe whipping once a year through all the market
towns in Dorsetshire—a sentence, however, which was afterwards reversed.
All the writers on the subject of Monmouth's Rebellion have been much
indebted to the pages of 'the New Martyrology,' and yet, strange to say,
some of those who have borrowed most liberally, affect to pronounce it
a work of no authority !

[1] Great was the odium which naturally attached to all the instruments
of these revolting executions. The hangman Ketch, who travelled in the
train of Jeffreys, and whose hands, from morning till night, were employed
in launching the victims into eternity, has transmitted his name to every
successor to his odious office. The unfortunate rustic who was compelled
to steep the mangled remains in pitch, after the hangman had done his
work, was ever afterwards called 'Tom Boilman;' and a farmer named
Raphael, of Grendon Farm, near Lidgate, Coombpyne, who sold furze
with which to burn their entrails, was known by the name of 'Burn-guts'
and shunned by every one.

[2] The following entries in the parish books, under the date of 1685,

The successful 'expedition' of the Prince of Orange, in the ever memorable year 1688, is thus referred to in the 'Book of Remembrance:'—'But the public affairs of the nation continued not long in

corroborate the statement in the text of this execution having taken place at Axminster, and will, therefore, be interesting to our readers.

	£	s.	d.
Nov. 3.—Laid out about the execution of John Rose ...	2	18	10
Paid for building the gallowse	0	16	0

From the numerous other characteristic entries during the eventful year 1688, we select the following:—

	£	s.	d.
Paid for building a stage to proclaim the king on ...	0	6	0
Paid for whipping a man who threatned to burn our town, and for a passport for him	0	2	0
Paid for a mettimus for six rebells, and for carrying four of them to the goal	0	6	0
Laid out in expences when we went two days to take the rebells, by the Justices' order	0	11	0
For making or casting 250 pound of Bullets	1	0	10
For 160 pound of powder	6	5	6
Paid for four Carts to go to Chard to attend on the Lord Churchill [afterwards Duke of Marlborough] and guides and other expenses	1	11	0
For one Cart and five Pack Horses to convey Captain Churchill's troope of Dragoones to Crewkern ...	1	2	0

[Considerable sums are charged for guides for the soldiers, for the 'judge's troope,' and for others in the service of the king; and especially remarkable are the numerous charges for horse hire 'to Crookehorn,' showing that the intercourse between the two towns was considerably greater than at present.]

	£	s.	d.
Nov. 6.—Paid Hugh Wise for whipping of two men brought from Exon	0	3	0
Paid for a wooden horse	0	5	0
Paid for taking and carrying to prison Caleb Bragg, John Beere, Ric. Tamson, Jo. Hamling, Ric. Backaler, Math. Roe, Jo. Variard, and Jo. Sweetland	8	0	0
For corde to binde the prisoners	0	0	5
Paid for a new pair of Stocks	1	5	6

a settled state under this government [James II], for lo! anno 1688, about the 8th moneth [October] there were great rumours of warrs and tydings of the nation's being *invaded by forreigners*. Great preparations, therefore, were made for war, and great thoughts of heart in many what the issue of these rolling Providences might be. Wherevpon, an vngodly generation of men began to perk up again, hoping, by the revolutions that were at the door, to get the day once more and hector over the people of God, as they had formerly done, for they *held a confederacy with the invaders*.[1] . . . . On the 5th day of the ninth moneth [November] the land was invaded [at Torbay] by a vast body of men of a strange language, having for their general the Prince of Orange, who, in a few daies marched through the land with vaste preparations for warre. A popish army was sent down from the king to meet him, and many of the king's officers and souldiers that favoured the protestant interest, dropt away from the king and joyn'd in with the invaders; and after some few daies' march the armies met. The popish army, through a spirit of fear and consternation, were totally

[1] The dissenters were at first exceedingly shy of the Prince of Orange, and the people generally, in the West of England, having so recently experienced the terrible results of Monmouth's expedition, hesitated to espouse his cause. But on becoming better acquainted with his principles and objects, and finding him supported by influential persons, the protestants of every sect and rank soon hastened to his standard and carried him in triumph to the throne.

routed, scattered, and subdued, insomuch that the Prince of Orange, with his army, came to the great metropolitan city of London with little effusion of blood.[1] In the mean while the churches of the people

[1] The Prince remained several days at Axminster, on his way to London [see Macauley's '*History of England*,' vol. 2, page 508]—putting up at 'the Dolphin,' then the principal inn in the town. It stood on the eastern side of the market-place, and had previously been the mansion-house of the influential family of Yonge. [See our account of Colyton.] The following are among the entries in the Axminster Parish Books at the exciting period of this 'glorious revolution:'—

	£	s.	d.
Paid John Whittey for an horse, and Edward Pike for riding a guide at Sherbourne, when the Prince was here	0	5	0
Paid for wood and candle for the guard	0	2	0
Paid Thomas Turner for two horses, to goe to Crookehorn with Colonel Lutterell's Regiment...	0	2	6

[There are entries of payment for twenty-three other horses for the same service, including 'an horse from Honiton prest to Crookehorn.']—

	£	s.	d.
Paid for a spleen plaister for a sick man, (soldier of the Duke of Bolton's)	0	1	6
For a shag to make a swather to bind him	0	0	8
For apples for them to roaste	0	0	6
Paid Hamlyn and Dight for keeping prisoners at the Bel	0	2	0
Paid Abraham French for carrying bulletts to Chard after the army	0	2	6
For a guide and an horse for the Lord Cornbury to goe to Honiton [See Macauley's '*History of England*,' vol. 2, page 496-7.]	0	1	6
Paid Richard Turner for a man and two horses to carry three sick soldiers to Crookehorn	0	2	6
Paid Daniel House for writing two rates for the officers' pay	0	4	0
Paid James Seward for riding to Exon for the concerns of the Prince	0	5	0
For a hogshead of cyder when King William was proclaimed	0	17	6

of God held their assemblies very peaceably—this
church enjoying the same priviledge, even while multitudes of souldiers lay in the town of Axminster and
march'd along by the pvblic Meeting-house. . . .
In a few daies divers of the great men of the nation
who had bin for the promoting of the popish interest,
were apprehended and closely secured, and the king,
qveen, many popish lords, and others, fled and hid
themselves.' &c.

A century after these events, the town of Axminster was again the scene of military occupation
for many years, and the inhabitants were in a state
of extreme anxiety and alarm, not, happily, on account of domestic warfare, but on account of the
fears which were universally entertained of an invasion by the French. Old men still tell of the excitement of the people in the early part of the present
century, and thousands are living who at that time
never heard the name of Buonaparte without a shud-
der. Very easy, therefore, is it to imagine the condition of the inhabitants of this locality, for the landing
was expected to take place upon the south-western
coast. Great were the preparations, both local
and general, for the anticipated event. Companies of
volunteers and of the militia, with some regular
troops, were stationed in Axminster and the neighbourhood, under Lieutenant-General Simcoe, who
had the command of the western district, and who fixed
his camp upon Woodbury-hill, near Honiton. Guns

bristled along the coast, which was closely guarded, and the old telegraphs, upon the highest hills, formed a chain of communication from the coast to the interior of the country and to London, by which information was constantly and expeditiously conveyed. Arrangements were duly made at Axminster for the removal of the women and children in carts and waggons impressed into the service, and 'First Combe' was appointed as the place of rendezvous whenever the alarm should be given that the dreaded landing had indeed been effected. The woods and coppices behind Cloakham were selected as the best and most available places of refuge. [1]

Fortunately these preparations were never called into requisition; but no one can adequately picture to himself the state of terror and alarm which had led to their adoption. The overthrow of Buonaparte upon the plains of Waterloo removed all cause for continued apprehension; and a more satisfactory state of public affairs restored peace and confidence, not to Axminster alone but to the country at large, and laid the foundation of the blessed results which a more fortunate posterity enjoys.

[1] The following is a copy of a card which was issued on this occasion:—'Axminster District. Card No.——. Place of Meeting——. In case of an Enemy Landing in this neighbourhood, or orders being received for the removal of the inhabitants, places will be allowed for your family in Mr. ——— waggon, No. ——. On your arrival at the place of meeting you are to deliver this Card to Mr. ———, conductors. You will be allowed to take with you only —— day's provision, and one Blanket (marked) for each person. Should the places allowed for your

Having thus presented a tolerably copious sketch of the history of Axminster from the earliest period to the present time, it remains for us to conclude with some other matters connected with the parish:—

The church, as a matter of course, is by far the most ancient and most interesting building in the town. Situated, as it is, in a large open space formed

[AXMINSTER CHURCH.]

on the site of some narrow and crowded streets which were swept away by one of the fires to which we have before referred, and being partially surrounded, in the churchyard, by elms and lime trees, the building

family not be sufficient, those that can walk may attach themselves to the same Waggon or Cart and take their turns to be assisted, and must bring provisions and blanket as above. R. Hallett, agent for Axminster Parish. Bull, Printer.'

presents a striking appearance on its northern side, which is by far more ornamented than the southern side.[1] It consists of a nave and chancel, with a tower standing between them upon very massive arches; north and south aisles to the nave; and a porch with a parvise[2] on the north side. It exhibits several styles indicative of the various dates of the different parts, and of the alterations made from time to time. The lower part of the tower, and perhaps a small part of the chancel, are, with the exception of a doorway to be referred to immediately, the most ancient portions of the church, and were probably erected during the thirteenth century. The nave and greater part of the chancel are in the Decorated style, and,

---

[1] Many of the trees, the whole of which, we are informed by Mr. Davidson, were planted about the year 1760, have been cut down at different times, and on various pretences. It is a positive duty of the parishioners to see that no old tree be in future allowed to be removed on any account, except that of natural decay, and that, if so removed, a young one be immediately planted in its place. Our ancestors, we may be assured, had a wise purpose in their encouraging the growth of trees in churchyards, and also in the fields; and we have but little doubt that they were right, in spite of the notions of improvement-mongers in this self-styled 'more enlightened age.' The yew tree on the north-western side of the churchyard, is one of the largest and most beautiful in this part of the country. The reason why the yew is so universal in churchyards is most probably to be found in the circumstance of its solemn and funereal character—like the cypress in eastern countries. But some writers say, that it is on account of the protection which its massive and perennial foliage affords to the building; and others, that it was anciently regarded as the common source whence the parishioners derived the material for their bows, in the use of which the *yeomen* [hence the word yeomen] were so expert, both in war and in the chase.

[2] See page 140.

therefore, date about a century later. [1] The north aisle is in the Perpendicular style of the fifteenth century, and is elaborately ornamented, externally, with a parapet of Ham-stone sculptured with a series of quatrefoils containing foliage, and with shields bearing the arms of Courtenay, the Stafford knot, and other devices belonging to families connected with the locality, and who were, perhaps, contributors towards the erection of the aisle. The parapet is ornamented, also, with gargoyles and crocketed pinnacles. [2] The aisle is supported by buttresses and

[1] The Decorated, or Middle Pointed, style of Gothic architecture, was formed, like all the other styles, by gradual and successive transitions from the style which preceded it,—namely, the Early English. [See page 66.] It prevailed, in all its distinctive developments, during the reigns of the first three Edwards—from about the year 1272 to the year 1377. Its windows—the feature by which it can most easily be distinguished—consist of several lights divided by mullions, which, unlike the mullions of the succeeding style, [see page 54] are never carried perpendicularly through the head of the window. Indeed, there is no indication of perpendicularity in the tracery of *pure* Decorated work. It is manifest, however, in the transition work from Decorated to Perpendicular. In *early* Decorated designs, the head of the window is filled with geometrical figures, such as circles, trefoils, quatrefoils, &c., very elegantly disposed; while later tracery is distinguished by beautiful *flowing* lines, without any geometrical form—as in the eastern window of Axminster Church, which, although not an elaborate specimen of the style, is not without its beauties. The windows of Exeter Cathedral, with the exception of the east window, are delightful examples of Decorated work. The same glorious building also exhibits numerous *flying buttresses*—another characteristic of this style. The *ball flower*, and a flower of four leaves, in a deep moulding, are ornaments peculiar to this style—a style, we may observe, not always so profuse in ornamentation as its name would seem to imply. Many high authorities consider the Decorated style to be the *perfection* of Gothic architecture.

[2] *Crockets* are the bunches of foliage and flowers with which the *sides*

lighted by five windows, each of which has three lights. Perpendicular tracery once occupied the heads, which have been mutilated into plain sexagonal compartments. The south aisle was erected in 1800, in the style of the Churchwarden-Gothic with which we are only too familiar in these 'enlightened' times. It is entered at the eastern end by a doorway which is not only by far the oldest portion of the present building, but is, in all probability, a vestige of the minster founded by Athelstan after the battle of Brunenburgh, already described. At all events it bears every appearance of Anglo-Saxon work, which is very strong presumptive evidence.[1]

The nave is divided from its aisles by four lofty and beautiful arches on each side, resting on moulded piers, and springing from capitals which were formerly beautifully sculptured with foliage and devices. The piers, arches,—indeed, all the stone facings in the interior of the building—are enshrouded in *blue paint*, carefully jointed with white!

of pinnacles are adorned. The ornament which crowns the apex of pinnacles is called a *finial*.

[1] It is well known to have been the custom to preserve, in the walls of churches, some relic—such as a doorway—belonging to a more ancient building on the same site, as exemplified in the present instance. This doorway had for centuries occupied a position in the south wall of the nave, till the erection of the south aisle, when it was carefully removed to its present position. We may here observe that the church was formerly furnished with transepts. The north transept contained a chapel. It was called Yonge's aisle, and was removed when the north aisle was extended to the west end of the church, in the sixteenth century. The south transept was called the Trill, or Drake's aisle, and remained till the year 1800.

The church is devoid of imposing monuments, but in the chancel there are two very ancient stone effigies lying within recesses which bear the well-known characteristics of the thirteenth century. One of these represents a female, who is supposed to have been Alice, daughter of Lord Brewer, and wife of Reginald de Mohun, lord of the manor of Axminster.[1] She appears to have been a munificent contributor to the fund for erecting the church of the twelfth century, as well as the chapel at Membury, in which there is a monument precisely similar.[2] The other monument is, by the same authority, assigned to Gervase de Prestaller, who held the living when the church of the twelfth century was in the course of erection. He had been chaplain and steward to the father of Alice de Mohun, and was really the first *vicar* of the parish. In the south wall of the

[1]   See page 323.

[2]   Mr. Davidson supposes that the first church at Axminster was founded during the eighth century, by Cyneard, an Anglo-Saxon prince, whose remains, in the shape of bones filled with lead, were discovered in digging a vault within the present building, near the western door, in the year 1748. [See his ' *History of Axminster Church.*'] The burial of Cyneard at Axminster, in 784, is thus recorded in the Anglo-Saxon Chronicle :—' And Cynewulf reigned thirty-one years, and his body lies at Winchester, and the ethling's [Cyneard] at Axminster; and their right paternal kin reaches to Cerdic.' Mr. Davidson very justly concludes that there must have been some very powerful reason for this interment at Axminster, Cyneard having died at Merton, in Surrey. That reason he considers, from other evidence, to be the fact of his having founded the church—the burying of persons in the churches which they had founded being a custom hardly ever departed from under any circumstances.

chancel are three sedilia and a piscina, under beautiful arches.[1]

The pulpit and reading desk stand in the centre of the nave towards its western end. They are of black oak, with carved panels, and were erected in 1633. In front of the pulpit, and of course out of its proper place,[2] stands the ancient font, which is large and of octagonal shape.[3]

[1] Since the publication, in 1835, of Mr. Davidson's '*History of Axminster Church,*' which contains a complete list of the monuments, tablets have been erected, or inscriptions added to tablets previously existing, to the memory of the following persons :— The Rev. Charles Steer, late Vicar died November 12, 1835, aged 79 years.—(Chancel.) The Rev. Edward Cook Forward, M.A., of Axminster, late Rector of Coombpyne, died November 11, 1836, aged 55 years.—(North Aisle.) William Knight, Esq., of Hilary House, Axminster, died December 3, 1839, aged 77 years; and Sarah his widow, January 19, 1851, aged 94 years.—(South Aisle.) Thomas Whitty Hallett, Esq., died January 29, 1848, aged 78 years; and Ann his wife April 14, 1851, aged 75 years.—(Chancel.) Thomas Northmore, Esq., M.A., F.A.S., of Cleve, Devon, died at his residence, Furzebrook House, Axminster, May 29, 1851; and his wife died July 21, 1850.—Arms:— *gules,* a lion rampant, *or.* Crest:—a lion's head erased, charged with a cinquefoil and crowned with a radiant crown, *argent.* *Motto:*—'Nec elata, nec dejecta.'—(Nave.) See page 52.

[2] It formerly occupied its *proper* place, just within the western doorway, from which it was removed when the singing gallery was reduced to its present dimensions, in 1834.

[3] The particular form in which different fonts are made is not the result of accident or caprice. In common with almost every object in the furniture and building of an ancient church, the shape of fonts, like their position (page 83), is symbolical. The octagon, which is the most common form of fonts, particularly in the period of the Perpendicular style, symbolises *regeneration,* ' for as the number seven is typical of the seven days' creation, so eight symbolises the new creation in Christ, who rose the eighth day from the dead.' (*'Handbook of English Ecclesiology.'*) The sexagonal shape refers to the death of Christ at the sixth hour of the sixth day. For this reason the *chalice* is almost always sex-

The church is deformed by galleries, one of which fills the whole of the north aisle; another nearly the whole of the south aisle; and a third stretches across the western end of the building. In the last is an organ, which was erected in 1800. [1]

The tower is square and massive, with battlements and buttresses, and a very graceful turret at the south-western angle. The tower, rising among the trees above the surrounding houses, forms a beautiful object from the valley for a long distance downwards. In the belfry are a clock and chimes and six bells. [2]

agonal. The heptagon symbolises the seven sacraments, or the graces of the Holy Spirit; and the circle, a form hardly ever used so recently as the Perpendicular period, is intended to signify perfection—the state in which *imperfect* man was supposed to be made by baptism.

[1] The organist's salary of twenty guineas a year, was defrayed out of the church-rate, by the unanimous consent of the parishioners, until 1849, in which year some proceedings with reference to the situation of organist, unparalleled, perhaps, in the history of such appointments, were attempted to be terminated by the vicar's actually putting himself to the trouble and expence of obtaining Counsel's opinion as to the *illegality of such an appropriation* of any part of the church-rate!—even after he had himself presided at a vestry meeting almost unanimous in favor of the re-election of the organist who had held the situation for ten years, and who subsequently polled the votes of the parishioners in the proportion of ten to his opponent's one. The vicar had, indeed, declared the whole of the proceedings to be 'perfectly regular,' mistaking, as he did, the feeling of the parish towards his *unpopular* nominee. An account of these scandalous proceedings has very fortunately been preserved in a pamphlet published by Mr. W. Pulman—a pamphlet which those of our readers who feel an interest in parochial affairs will perhaps not regret the trouble of perusing.

[2] The inscriptions upon the bells are as follow:—First bell—'All glory be to God. Anno Domini, 1718.' ['Paid Thomas Worth for casting the bells, £36 6s.'—'*Parish Books*,' 1718.] Second bell—'Matthew Liddon, Richard Haycraft, churchwardens. Cast by Thomas Bayley, Bridge-

The churchyard, which has been in use for many centuries, is greatly overcrowded, and it is earnestly to
be hoped that the time is not far distant when a more
enlightened method of disposing of the dead than
that of interring them in masses in the midst of the
living will be adopted, not only in Axminster, but in
every town and city in the kingdom.[1] The church,
we have as yet omitted to state, is dedicated to the
Virgin Mary. It is 114 feet long by 49 feet wide
across the centre of the nave and aisles, and the tower
is 77 feet high from the top of the turret.

The particulars of King Athelstan's endowment of
Axminster church with the manor of Prestaller, and
of his forming it into a collegiate establishment by
the appointment of seven priests to pray for the souls
of the slain in the battle of Brunenburgh, have been
given in the preceding pages.[2] The vacancies caused

water, 1765.' Third bell—'John Hoore, Barnard Prince, C. W. William
Pvrdve cast mee, 1647.' ['Paid Mr. Nicholas Fry, for law about the third
bell, £4 17s. 7d.'—'Parish Books,' 1664.] Fourth bell—'Benjamin
Woolly, Richard Haycraft, churchwardens. Cast by Thomas Bayley
Bridgewater, 1760.' ['Paid the bell-founder, £65.' 'Parish Books,' 1758.]
Fifth bell—'Matthew Liddon, Thomas Cook, churchwardens. Cast by
Thomas Bayley, Bridgewater, 1762.' Sixth bell—'Rev. Charles Steer,
vicar. Mr. James Lendy, Mr. William Bond, churchwardens. "Lo! I
come to do Thy will, O God." William Pannell, fecit, Cullompton, 1821.'

[1] See a pamphlet on this subject, published by Mr. William Pulman,
Axminster.

[2] See pages 319 and 321. The following, from the chartulary of
Newenham Abbey, relates to King Athelstan's grant:—'Rex Athelstan
dedit eclm de Axmister, septem sacerdotibus, in eâ ppetue celebrarent di-
vina p animabz septe comitu cu ipso occisor apud Calipsdoan et ibi incepit
bellu semp pseverans bellandi usq' ad Colecroft subtus Axmister in qo

by the successive deaths of the first seven priests appear not to have been filled up, and the duties
devolved, in time, upon a single incumbent. The
Conqueror, however, endowed with the church of
Axminster the prebendaries of Warthill and Grendale in York cathedral. A century afterwards it is
found that one, if not both, of the York prebendaries
at that time officiated at Axminster. One of them,
who had been confessor to Queen Maud, on leaving
his post for another appointment, nominated as his
successor one Gervase de Prestaller, of whom mention has been already made. The conditions were that
the prebendary should receive a certain annual pension from his nominee. We must refer our readers
to Mr. Davidson's '*History of Axminster Church*'
for the subsequent proceedings, and especially for
those which relate to a law suit between the king
(Edward I) and the abbot of Newenham, who claimed
the living as a gift, with the manor, by Reginald de
Mohun. [1] The result was that the abbot's claim was

---

fuerunt occisi. Et voluerit dictus rex ut de ecla semp sustinar tot' pres-
piteri celebrantes. Morientibs aute prespiteris qi tunc erant, cum nullus
curaret de aliquibs instituendis, non remansit ibi nisi unus. Nullus aute
a tempore conquestus tre Anglie dedit ipsa eclam quamdiu Maneriu de
Axmister in manu regu fuit.' Translated, in part, at page 319.

[1] See also Dr. Oliver's '*Ecclesiastical Antiquities in Devon.*' The
Doctor says, that 'soon after the Conquest the foundation was restored to
its primitive form,' but was soon reduced, by death, from seven priests to
two, and afterwards to a single vicar, when vicarages were instituted, in the
twelfth century. The Doctor proceeds to contend that the abbot was
right in his claim, but was obliged at last to succumb to the overwhelming
influence of the crown.

negatived, and the advowson restored to the prebendaries of York. 'From an early period to the
present time,' says Mr. Davidson, ' the entire rectory
has been let to farm. In the fifteenth century it was
held by the noble family of Brooke, of Weycroft,
and it was afterwards in the hands of various tenants
until the beginning of the seventeenth century, when
it was purchased by the Drake family, of Ashe, who
held it in separate moieties, on leases terminating
with different lives, and renewed from time to time.
In their hands it remained until the 24th December,
1766, when the last Lady Drake sold her remaining
interest in both moieties to Joseph Banks, Esq.,
chancellor of the diocess of York, on whose death,
about the year 1786, it became the property of
Colonel Henry John Kerney, in right of his wife
who was the only child of Mr. Banks. On the 30th
May, 1812, the Rev. Samuel Smith, D.D., prebendary of Grendale, purchased one moiety, and, on the
13th June, 1831, conveyed it to the Rev. William
Daniel Conybeare, rector of Sully, in the county of
Glamorgan. The other moiety, on the expiration of
the lease, became the property of the Rev. John
Josias Conybeare, prebendary of Warthill, whose
widow, on the 17th June, 1831, conveyed it also to
the Rev. W. D. Conybeare, who thus became the
owner of the entire rectory. The two moieties are
held on leases terminating with three lives, and are
each charged with a reserved rent of £20 a year, pay-
able to the prebendaries.'

The rectory of Axminster, with its chapelries of Kilmington[1] and Membury, is valued in the King's Books at £40 6s. 8d. The rectorial tithes were commuted, in 1838, for £607 10s., and the vicarial tithes for £607 1s. 3d. per annum.

The congregation of Independents at Axminster was founded in 1660, by Mr. Ashwood,[2] as thus recorded in ' *The Book of Remembrance* : '—' Now the Lord was pleased to engage the hearts of some serious pious christians of the neighbouring villages, to attend frequently on the ministry of this holy man, who got into an intimate acquaintance with him, and also with those few souls in the town of Axminster (whose hearts the Lord had wrought vpon by his word and spirit) who likewise resolved to joyn in and walk with them in the same order and fellowship of the gospel. And foreseeing clouds to gather blacknesse over these nations, and the Lord, in the way of his Providence, to threaten his churches and interest with a flood of trouble and persecution, both Mr. Ashwood, with the rest, endeavoured to incorporate themselves into one body before the storm did fall. And in a short time after, calling in the assistance of other churches, by the hands of Mr. Benn, pastor of a church of Christ at Dorchester, and Mr.

---

[1] ' Kilmington (albeit nowe in reputacion a parish of itself) is a member of Axmynster, where, in ancient tymes, their dead corpses were buried, and where they paye their tithes.'—*Sir William Pole.* See our account of Kilmington.

[2] See page 342.

Thorn, pastor of a church of Christ at Weymouth, on a solemn day of prayer . . . . were embodyed and constituted a church of Christ. . . . . . Mr. Bartholomew Ashwood was chosen by them to be their pastor ; who immediately, by the consent of the church, and his readily accepting their call, in the presence and by the assistance of those worthy pastors before named, was ordained and set apart for the pastoral office in this little sister church, whose foundation was now laid, the number of the names being but few, about twelve or thirteen.'[1] The old chapel, which still stands in Chard Street, was erected in 1698; the new one, close by, in 1828. The Wesleyan chapel, near the market-place, dates from the year 1796, and the Roman Catholic chapel, near the eastern turnpike gate, was opened on August 16, 1830, when the sermon was preached by Bishop Baines.

Axminster is rich in parochial charities, the principal of which we enumerate in a foot-note.'[2] In few

[1] Shortly afterwards Mr. Ashwood was imprisoned at Exeter for nonconformity, and the congregation suffered great persecution, being driven to assemble in woods and secret caves, in which they were more than once surprised and severely treated. As stated at page 285, they assembled for some time at Weycroft.

[2] Alexander Every, in 1588, left £100, the interest of which was to be laid out yearly in bread for the poor. He left, also, £50 to be *lent*, on proper security, to deserving young men of the parish. Deeds dated 10th December, 1621, and February 10th, 1679, show that these sums formed part of the purchase-money of a close in Woodbury Lane, containing two acres, also 'New Close' (one acre and two roods), and five closes and an orchard, containing fifteen acres—in all eighteen acres two roods, producing £29 yearly, distributed in bread at Christmas. In the same deeds, also,

towns, perhaps, are such charities more needed; for
the manufactories which formerly afforded employment to considerable numbers of the population are
no longer in existence, and the only labor-market is
now the overstocked one of agriculture, except the
trifling *casual* employment to be found in a non-

are included a tenement at Honiton, two houses, with a garden and an
orchard attached to each, in Axminster, 'one other house in Back-lane
(which afterwards fell down!), 'and another house in the same parish;'
another house and garden in Chard-street ' (afterwards formed into three
tenements inhabited by poor people), 'and another house and garden in
South-street.' Some of these houses were given by Walter Yonge, in
1613, and on the site of one of them was afterwards erected the old
Workhouse, on the western side of the church. John Sampson, in 1618,
gave 20s. a year out of lands in Membury, called 'Bathcote,' or Ridge
Farm. John Yonge, in 1612, gave a yearly rent-charge of £5, out of
Ham-close, Colyton, to be distributed in shirts and shifts. For a similar
distribution annually, to twenty poor persons, Leonard Peream left £100,
in 1711. Of this legacy £60 was laid out in the purchase of Stagmore or
'Brickfield,' near Cloakham Bridge, producing £4 a year. The remaining
£40, with £5 left by Ann Scriven, in 1727, were invested in the Bridport
Turnpike Trust. John Ellard, in 1816, left the interest of £100, also for
shirts and shifts to the poor; Anne Palmer, in 1815, a rent-charge of £6
out of 'ten or twelve acres of land at Wick,' for bread; and Thomas
Whitty, May 11, 1713, a rent-charge of 20s. on a piece of land at Will-
hay for the same purpose. The free school, for twelve poor boys and girls
of Axminster, and two of Kilmington, is endowed with six acres of land in
Kilmington, purchased, in 1746, for £160, made up with £100 bequeathed
by Penelope Saffin, of Exeter, and £60 from sources which the Commissioners were 'unable to discover.' The school is further endowed
with two acres of land given by the parishioners of Kilmington, on condition
that they should send two free Scholars. *See the 'Report of the Commissioners of Public Charities in Devonshire.'* Mr. Robert Bull, who died
August 11, 1830, left two fields at Musbury, and a rent charge of £40 a
year on the estate of Furzley, Axminster, a portion to be applied yearly
to the support of the Methodist cause, a portion to the repairs of the
Methodist chapel, at Axminster, and £5 a year to the poor of the parish
in bread or clothes at Christmas.

manufacturing town untouched by railways. Formerly
the town was the seat of an extensive clothing trade,
and more recently of a carpet manufactory, which
had a world-wide celebrity. It was established in 1755,
by Mr. Whitty, whose descendant carried on the
business until 1835, when it was abandoned, and the
looms were removed to Wilton. In 1759, the proprietor was rewarded by the Society of Arts with a
premium of £30 for the largest and handsomest
carpet which at that time had ever been made in this
country. Subsequently some truly magnificent car-
pets were made at Axminster for various sovereigns
and public bodies. Among them, was one for the
Sultan of Turkey, which cost more than a thousand
pounds. The manufacture of tape, and the preparation, by machinery, of flax for cordage and sacks,
were also carried on in the town until within a few
years. The 'tow factory,' at the foot of Castle-hill,[1]
has recently been taken by Mr. Lawton, of Rick-
mansworth, Hertfordshire, a silk-throwster, and it is
now in process of being fitted up for the purpose of
carrying on his business. It is not more a matter of
surprise than regret, that a town in which water-
power is so abundant and labor so cheap, should, in
these busy times, ever cease to be without some
extensive and profitable branch of manufacture.

[1] See page 287.

CHAPTER X.

LET us carry ourselves, in imagination, back to the beginning of the sixteenth century, and fancy an individual upon one of the hills which bound the valley of the Axe on the west, in the immediate vicinity of Axminster;—upon the hill, if it please you, reader, where now are situated so delightfully the mansion and grounds of Cloakham. [1] He has strolled out from the town to enjoy a ramble in the fields, and to view the beauties of nature, after the toil and lassitude of the long summer's day. The sun is just about to sink behind the old wood-crowned hills of Shute and Colyton,—the birds and the bees are serenading him on every side,—and the murmur of the stream below is wafted to him on the 'breath of the sweet south,' which is scented by the violet and the woodbine. He gazes with rapture upon the scene which is spread so magnificently before him. Within a mile across it, to the eastward nearly, is the old

[1] See page 287.

town upon the hill-side, looking quaintly enough
with its comfortable thatched-covered dwellings clustering around its ancient church. The valley stretches
southward. It is bathed in the last rays of 'bright
Phœbus,' which are reflected from the glowing red
and golden clouds in which he is about to be cradled.
Here and there is seen a marshy spot among the
fertile meadows, which are crowded with the delightful hedge-row elms which modern 'wisdom' (?)
panteth to destroy. The hill-sides, too, are clothed
with timber, far and near. The oak, the elm, the
sycamore, and the beech, spread high and wide their
umbrageous arms, contributing greatly to the attractions of the landscape, and affording a welcome shelter
to the lowing tenants of the fields. An opening here
and there among the trees reveals the windings of the
crystal stream, which the gazer traces downwards till
his eye beholds the ocean, glistening, like a streak of
burnished silver, between the cliffs and crags of Beer
and Axmouth. But the object which arrests his
gaze most forcibly is one which will never be gazed
upon again. Beyond the southern outskirts of the
town, amid the quietude of the greenest fields, and
within the sound of the rippling waters, are looming
the masses of magnificent building which constitute
the Abbey of Newenham. He looks upon pile beyond pile of wonderful masonry;—upon towering
roof, and sweeping arch, and ornamented buttress,
and ranges of 'storied windows richly dight,' very

marvellously wrought; while crowning all, so high
and so exquisitely fashioned that it soars into a mere
point against the sky, rises the graceful steeple
from which the pealing bells are making eloquent
each dell and dingle through the vale, and spreading,
far and near, the sounds of happiness and joy.   And
he knows that that peal is a faithful index to the
condition of many of the inhabitants of that transcendent home.   He knows that the immense riches of
the convent are gathered for no selfish purpose—that
its charities are as boundless as they are ungrudged—
that even at that moment, as at almost every other
moment of the day, the poor and needy are faring
sumptuously within its hallowed walls—that the naked
are clothed, and that the sick, no matter who, are
healed and cared for;—and all without the most
remotely compromising the independence of the re-
cipients of this disinterested bounty, or damaging in
the least their sense of self-respect.   Long does the
gazer revel in the contemplation of the scene before
him, and numerous and grateful are the reflections
which rise spontaneously in his mind!

He who gazes to-day from the tasteful grounds of
Cloakham, beholds no considerable change in the
natural features of the landscape.   Cultivation has
progressed, perhaps, and much of the timber has been
removed—although a great deal still remains to beautify and protect the innumerable inclosures.   The
river, still, is traceable among the meads, and the sea,

as heretofore, still glistens in the distance, as it will continue to glisten when the eyes which now behold it shall for countless ages have been closed for ever. But man is not conservative, as nature is. Many are the changes which his hand has wrought, and one, at least, is not a landscape-change alone. The eye which now beholds the scene, no longer includes within its range that splendid specimen of architectural skill which was once the pride and glory of the valley. It rests, instead, upon the bald and white-washed walls of *a union workhouse*, which stands at no great distance from the ancient abbey-site,—a perfect contrast to the once splendid pile. Each of these important institutions is a faithful indication of some of the most striking characteristics of the two widely different eras. The obvious inferiority of modern architecture—the principle of separating, in what ought to be called *dis*union houses, those 'whom God hath joined together,' and who for years and years have been battling with the demon Poverty, into whose clutches they at last have fallen—the doling out of *measured* food provided by *enforced* contributions—the deprivation of that personal liberty which ought to be a sacred thing to all but criminals;—these are a few of the very striking changes which a little more than three hundred years have brought about, and which, in the minds of the thoughtful, rise in solemn contrast to 'the olden time,' when, both in poetry and fact, there was a nation in the world called 'merrie England.' [1]   *   *   *   *

A few old crumbling walls among the buildings of a modern farm-house, on the eastern side of the river, and at the distance of a mile below Axminster, are all that remain of the once famous abbey of New-enham,[2] which was founded, in 1246, by Reginald de Mohun, Earl of Somerset, then lord of the manor of Axminster.[3] A colony of twelve monks, with an abbot named John Godard, was obtained from the Cistercian abbey of Beaulieu, in Hampshire. On the sixth of January, 1247, the monks passed through the town of Axminster, and took possession of their monastery. They had rested the preceding night at Ford Abbey. Reginald de Mohun accompanied the procession, attended by a numerous retinue, and great were the rejoicings of the townsfolks on the occasion. Of the comparatively humble building then erected, the eastern window of the chapel still remains, and forms the subject of our illustration on the opposite page.[4]   The buildings soon increased in size and

[1] In these remarks we must be understood as referring exclusively to a social question, altogether distinct and separate from questions of theology. The history of the Monasteries, says D'Israeli, 'has been written by their enemies.'

[2] Originally written Nyweham, *the new home, or dwelling.*

[3] See pages 172 and 323. Some writers, adopting the authority of '*The Annals of the Two Houses of Parcolude and Chester,*' give the year 1241 as that in which this abbey was founded. But this is undoubtedly a mistake. See Dugdale's '*Monasticon,*' page 690, and Tanner's '*Notitia Monastica,*' xxxiii.

[4] This window is composed of three lancet lights within a pointed arch,

RUINS OF NEWENHAM ABBEY.

Spreat. Lith.

splendour as the wealth of the community became rapidly augmented by the liberality of successive donors. The first stone of the magnificent conventual church was laid on July 6, 1250, in the time of the third abbot, John de Ponto Roberti. 'It was about thirty years in building,' says Mr. Davidson. 'The ground was opened for the foundation in the year 1248, and it was finished about 1280. Bronescombe, bishop of Exeter, contributed no less than six hundred marks, or £400, towards the erection—a munificent sum in those days; and a hundred marks were paid annually by Sir Reginald de Mohun, the founder of the abbey, during his life.[1] The stone

and may thus, from its style alone, independently of any other evidence, be confidently assigned to the period of the foundation of this abbey. See our account of the Early English style, at page 66.

[1] The Chartulary of Newenham Abbey, a most valuable and interesting document, records the particulars of a remarkable vision which was said to have preceded the death of Reginald de Mohun, an event which took place at Tor, Devonshire, on the 13th of the calends of February (January 20th), 1257-8. Mr. Davidson has translated the passage in his History of the Abbey (pages 211-214). The body was interred in the abbey church, 'near the officiating deacon's station.' 'When the pavement of the sanctuary of our conventual church was relaid, in the year of our Lord, 1333,' says the registrar, 'the body of the said founder, seventy-five years after its interment, was found in the sarcophagus perfectly incorrupt and uninjured, and exhaling a fragrant odour. For three days it lay exposed to public view. I saw it and felt it. Quod quidem corpus vidi, palpavi, et per triduum puplice coopertum jacuit, anno Domini M.CCC.XXXIII.' Various sums of money have at different times been found among the ruins, and the skeleton of an infant was some years since discovered in the centre of one of the walls. The abbey was the burying-place of many influential families, including the Bonville family of Shute.

was a free gift from the quarries of Sir John de
Staunton.[1]   The dimensions also attest the consequence of the edifice.   Its total length was 280 feet,
of which the nave was 200 and the choir 80, while
the transepts measured 152.[2]   If we would indulge
the imagination with a picture of this building
in its perfect state, we may judge of the style in
which it was erected by a reference to the noble
structure of the cathedral church at Salisbury, or to
the interesting remains at Letley, afterwards called
Netley, abbey in Hampshire.   These buildings were
of the same period.   Letley, a monastery of the
Cistercian order, founded in 1232, was, like Newenham, an emanation from Beaulieu, and beautiful as
are its remains at the present day, it may be observed
that not being so rich, it had not the resources for a
magnificent erection which were possessed by Newenham.[3]   On comparing the abbey church of the
latter with the cathedral church at Salisbury, we may
reasonably conclude that although on a far inferior
scale as to its dimensions, in its style of building it
assimilated, in a great degree, to that noble structure.'[4]

[1]   Situated, as Mr. Davidson supposes, at Churchstaunton, Somerset.

[2]   'Longitudo ecclesiæ de Newnam continet 100 steppys, et ejus lati-
tudo, videlicet brachiorum, continet 76 steppys, et longitudo chori continet
40 steppys.'—'Itinerary of William of Worcester.'   It has been ascertained that one of his steps was equal to two feet.

[3]   The possessions of Letley were valued, at the Dissolution, at
£160 2s. 9¼d. per annum.

[4]   'History of Newenham Abbey,' page 145.   Mr. Davidson has treated

During the abbacy of Walter Houe (1338-1361), the abbey was visited by the plague, which, for a long time, raged with frightful violence in several countries. No less than twenty of the monks, three lay brethren, and twenty-eight secular persons who lived in the abbey, were numbered among the victims—leaving the abbot and two of his monks the sole survivors.

In the time of the twenty-third abbot, whose christian name of John is only known, the abbey was visited by King Henry VII, when on his way to London from Exeter, whither he had gone on the affair of Perkin Warbeck. He arrived at Newenham on the 4th of November, 1497, having slept at Ottery St. Mary the preceding night. He remained at the abbey until the 10th—occasionally visiting the Marquis of Dorset, who then resided at Shute.[2] It is not difficult to imagine the rejoicing of the old Axminsterians in honor of the presence of their sovereign. The bell-ringing, the archery-feats, and the more boisterous amusements of the period, we may be sure were enthusiastically indulged in;

so fully and so satisfactorily of this celebrated abbey, that we shall confine ourselves to a very brief account of it.

[2] In the time of Henry VIII, Henry Marquis of Dorset, afterwards Duke of Suffolk, rented the fishery of the Axe at forty shillings per annum, and that of the Yarty at six shillings and eightpence. He appointed conservators of the fish in the Axe. It may be as well to state in this place, that the right or royalty of the lord of the hundred or manor of Axminster, as regards the fishery of the Axe, is *traditionally* said to extend from the spring head to as great a distance at sea as a lighted tar-barrel would be visible.

while the ale-can and the trencher played no secondary part!

Richard Gyll was the twenty-sixth and last abbot. He was confirmed in his dignity by Veysey, bishop of Exeter, on the 3rd of February, 1530,[1] and surrendered his monastery on the 8th of March, 1539. Shortly afterwards the building was demolished. Dr. Oliver, writing in 1820, says :—' From a careful inspection of the ground, of the ruins, and dismantled remains of this interesting abbey, I think it easy to trace out the site of the church, the chapter house, and the cloister quadrangle.'[2] Even in the time of Prince, who, as before stated [see page 197], was born in the farm house on the site of the abbey, in 1643, a very small portion of the ruins only was standing. A ground plan of the building, however, completed, as we can easily believe, with ' some time and labor,' is given by Mr. Davidson in his ' History.'

The revenues of the abbey, at the Dissolution, were estimated at £227 7s. 8d., arising, among other sources, from the manor of Axminster and the various estates, in that parish, of Furzleigh, Bevor, Shapwick,[3] Bovaria (lands around the abbey, comprising about 347 acres), and Breweshayes, in the western part of the parish; the manors of Plenynt

---

[1] Mr. Davidson's ' History.' Dugdale and Dr. Oliver say February 12.

[2] See our account of Ford Abbey (pages 189-211) for an explanation of the different parts of an Abbey and of the duties of the different officers.

[3] See page 290.

and Norton in Cornwall; the fishery at Axmouth; and the rectories of Plenynt and Luppit. The abbot and nine monks were pensioned off, for their several lives, with various sums, amounting, in the aggregate, to £91 13s. 4d. per annum. [1]

The site of the abbey, and part of the demesne lands, were given by King Henry VIII to the Marquis of Dorset, afterwards Duke of Suffolk, who was executed for high treason in 1551. They were granted by Queen Elizabeth, in 1563, to Thomas Duke of Norfolk, owner of the manor of Axminster. [2] His son, Lord William Howard, disposed of them to John Lord Petre, in whose family they continued till 1824, when they passed into the hands of the late J. A. Frampton, Esq., with the rest of the manor property now in chancery, as stated at pages 323-4.

*   *   *   *   *   *   *

Seated snugly among the trees on the hill-side, exactly opposite the ruins of Newenham, and at the distance of a little more than a mile across the valley, is the pleasant village of Kilmington. The great London road passes through it, at a little more than the same distance west from Axminster. Its name is derived from the Anglo-Saxon, and signifies *the village of the common meadow*. So say the antiquarians.

---

[1] After the Dissolution, the abbot was indicted at the Star Chamber for having been a party to the forging and ante-dating of certain leases, with the view to become possessed of some of the property which had belonged to the abbey. The result of the trial is unknown.

[2] See page 323.

Tradition, however, which is seldom wholly wrong, [1] gives a different explanation of the euphonious name. It says that Kilmington was the scene of immense carnage when the Saxons pursued their enemies at the battle of Brunenburgh, and that its name is a corruption from *Kil-maen-ton, the town at the stony burial-place.* [2]

The parish is in the union of Axminster. [3] It comprises 1760 acres, and a population of 533—forty-five being registered voters for the county. A considerable part of the parish which was formerly common, has been enclosed within the last ten or twelve years. [4]

The manor belonged, in ancient times, to the barons of Torrington, and was divided among the five co-heiresses of Matthew de Toriton, the last baron.

---

[1] However true might be Mr. Hunter's opinion of the comparatively unreliable character of tradition, and however lightly its mysterious voice may be regarded by those who prefer their own fanciful theories, it must not be forgotten that to tradition we are indebted for the discovery of many of the most interesting events of history, which have subsequently been confirmed by indisputable evidence. Among these may be mentioned the spot where Harold fell at the battle of Hastings.

[2] Sir William Pole, Polewhele, Risdon, &c., &c. The names of Membury and Musbury are also traditionally said to have a similar origin.

[3] To avoid useless repetition, it may be mentioned here that the whole of the parishes which we have yet to describe are in the Southern division of the county of Devon, the deanery of Honiton, and the union of Axminster; and that Honiton is the county polling place.

[4] On Kilmington Hill grows that interesting plant, *Lobelia urens,* which is perhaps peculiar to the locality. On the same hill, too, is found the *Illecebrum verticillatum.*

Those ladies carried their separate portions, by marriage, into the families of Merton, Humfraville, Martyn, Bryan, and Sully. Merton acquired, by purchase, the second sister's share. His two shares passed, in the time of Richard II [1377-1399], to Nicholas Kirkham, of Blagdon, and were sold into the Haydon family, of Hill, by whom they were enjoyed in the time of Sir William Pole, who died in 1695. Martyn's share descended to the Audeley family, and, by the attainder of Lord Audeley, in the reign of Henry VII, became forfeited to the crown. It was afterwards purchased by Sir Thomas Dennis, of Bicton, Devon. [1] The fourth share passed to the Goldes of Seaborough, [2] and Sully's share to the Prous family, of Tiverton, and the Warres of Hestercombe. The principal landowner is William Tucker, Esq., of Coryton Park; [3] but the manorial

[1] Sir Thomas Dennis was appointed steward of the manor, hundred, and town of Axminster, at a salary of forty shillings a year, and a reversion to his son Robert. On October 26, 1537, he obtained from the abbot and convent of Newenham, the absolute grant of all their estates and rights in Kilmington, with the reversion of Brodemede, and other lands, then in the life-tenure of John Stephyns. Sir Thomas was to pay one penny to the abbot and convent, at Michaelmas, 'si debito modo petatur pro omnibus serviciis exactionibus et demandis.' John Newton, of Kilmington, left to certain trustees, by will dated June 6, 1598, his house called 'Weeke Chappell,' in the parish of Axminster.— See Oliver's 'Ecclesiastical Antiquities in Devon.'

[2] See pages 92-95.

[3] The family of Tucker was originally from Exeter. It has been settled in the neighbourhood of Axminster for about two hundred years. William Tucker, Esq., purchased Coryton of the family of Warren, in 1697. The ancient family mansion was at 'Old Coryton,' now a farm-

rights are virtually lost, by reason of the dismemberment of the estates in demesne.

Dulcis, in the parish of Kilmington, was for many generations the seat of the ancient family of Doville, or De Oville, from which its ancient name of Dovils-hayes (corrupted into Dulcis) was obtained. After the attainder of Sir Thomas Doville, in the reign of Edward III, the property came to Sir William Bonville, of Shute. From him it descended to the Duke of Suffolk, on whose attainder it was purchased by Lord Petre. It afterwards belonged to one of the Fryes, of Yarty, from whom it was brought, by an heiress, to George Southcott, of Calverleigh, Esq.,[1] from whom it passed, by marriage, to the Halletts.

house. The present mansion, a few hundred yards to the south of it, was erected in 1756, by Benedictus Marwood Tucker, Esq., grandfather of the present owner. It was greatly enlarged about twelve years since. It stands in a pleasant deer-park, and commands some extensive views of the valleys of the Axe and Yarty. The name of Coryton is derived from the Cory, a little stream which rises at Coryfortice, near the Devonshire Inn, and falls into the Yarty near Yarty Bridge, after flowing for some distance, in the lower part of its course, through Mr. Tucker's property. This pretty little stream is, speaking generally, too small for the fly, although in the vicinity of Dalwood some tolerable sport may be had at the proper time. The worm, however, as usual in small streams, is the more destructive bait. [See page 185.] The arms of Tucker are:— *Azure*, on a chevron, embattled, between three sea horses, *argent*, as many hearts, *gules*. CREST: A demi sea horse regardant, *argent*, holding between his paws a heart, *gules*. MOTTO: *Auspice Teucro*. [Taken, no doubt, from the line in Horace—' *Nil desperandum Teucro duce, et auspice Teucro.*']

[1] Judge Southcott, or Southcote, who lived in the reign of Elizabeth, was a member of this family. A monument to the memory of Thomas Southcott, who died at Dulcis, December 31, 1715, is erected in Kilmington church. Arms:—*Argent*, a chevron, *gules*, between three coots proper.

It is now the property of the Rev. W. Heberden, of Broadhembury, Devon.

The estate called *Hill's Farm*, on the road to Colyton, either gave its name to the family of De la Hill, its owners in ancient times, or else received it from them. The Haydon family, lately mentioned, afterwards possessed the estate, and it is now the property of William Tucker, Esq. [1]

In the fourteenth century, the estate of *Ballehayes* was sold to Sir William Bonville, of Shute, by one of the De Balls, into whose family it had been brought, by marriage, in the reign of Richard I, from the barons of Torrington. [2] From the Bonvilles it passed, by marriage, to the lords de la Warre, and afterwards, by successive purchases, to the Drakes of Ashe, and the Fryes of Yarty. [3]

[1] The view of the valley from Hill's Farm is delightful, but not equal to that from the summit of the range of hills at the back of the neighbouring farm of Woodhayne, in the parish of Shute, which is also inferior to the view from Musbury Castle, on the opposite side of the valley—of which more hereafter.

[2] A family of the name of Ball anciently flourished in Axminster, 'near the way,' says Prince, 'that leadeth to Musbury, where it enjoyed a pleasant seat and a fair demesne, called Balls, unto this day. Richard Ball, with some others, was a witness to a deed of Rosel de la Gate, to William his son, of a certain place called the Castle of Axminster. an. 23. Edw. fil. R. Hen. 1295.'—' *Worthies of Devon.*' Balls is now a farm belonging to the manor of Axminster, but held on lease, for a life, by Miss Metford, of Bristol. It formed part of the ancient demesne-lands of Newenham abbey.

[3] Yarty is now a farm house, on the eastern bank of the river Yarty, near Beckford bridge, in the parish of Membury, three miles and a half from Axminster. It was anciently the residence of a family of the same

Kilmington church abuts upon the turnpike road leading from Axminster to Colyton. Among the mass of *modernisation* which it exhibits are traces of an ancient origin. The chancel, for instance, is lighted by two lancet windows, with foliated headings. These are, no doubt, coeval with the oldest part of the chancel of Axminster church. The building, as it now appears, consists of a tower at the western end, a nave, and a chancel with an aisle, or a chapel, on the northern side, divided by a paneled arch.[1] The chancel is, as usual, by far the most interesting part of the church. A portion of an ancient screen divides it from the nave. The style of the whole of the *ancient* parts of the building, including the tower, is Perpendicular, with the exception of the lancet windows just referred to. The nave, which in 1832 was greatly altered and liberally whitewashed, is lighted by flat headed windows of three lights, with foliated headings. It is entered by doorways on the north and south, besides the principal entrance

name, whose heiress, in the reign of Henry IV [1399-1412], brought it to the Fryes, who had branches at Dulcis [see page 378] Wood, and Deer Park. Robert Frye, the last of the Yarty branch, died in 1726. His heiress married Lord King, in whose family it remained till about the year 1838, when it was sold to Samuel Newbery, Esq., its present owner. The greater part of the dwelling-house was destroyed by an accidental fire about three years ago. The neighbouring farm-house of Waters gave its name to the family of De la Water, who resided there in ancient times.

[2] 'Unless I mistake, the northern aisle was the chapel of St. Christina, which Thomas Vivyan, bishop of Megara and prior of Bodmin, blessed on the 18th of January, 1509.'—*Dr. Oliver.*

through the ground floor of the tower. Over
the doorway on the south are carried, externally,
two flights of stone steps, which do not contribute
to the beauty of the building. They conduct to a
gallery within. Another gallery runs along the western end of the church. An elegant paneled arch
supports the eastern side of the tower, opening
into the church. The tower, of three storeys,
is square, embattled, and has a turret on the south-
eastern side. It is supported by buttresses, has
pinnacles and gargoyles, and contains five musical
bells. The principal monuments within the church
are those of several members of the Tucker family, [1]
and that of Mr. Southcott already alluded to. The

[1] Among them are the following:—I—William Tucker, Esq., of Westwater, Axminster, buried at Dalwood, March 9, 1691, aged 73 years.
II—His son, William Tucker, Esq., of Westwater, buried at Dalwood,
March 15, 1733, aged 70 years. III—William Tucker, Esq., of Coryton
Hall, son of the last named, buried in Kilmington church, November 11,
1748, aged 57 years. IV—His son William, April 8, 1740, aged 19 years.
V—Benedictus Marwood Tucker, Esq., of Coryton Park, brother of the
last named William, September 17, 1779, aged 48 years. VI—William,
son and heir of Benedictus Marwood Tucker, Esq., died September 2,
1841, aged 79 years. VII—Mrs. Agnes Tucker, November 21, 1788.
A proof of the salubrity of this delightfully situated village may be found
in the number of aged people who are now among its residents, and also
in the ages which are recorded upon the tombs in the churchyard.
Of these there are several above four score years, and the tomb of the
late Mr. Thorn records the patriarchal age of 96. The yew tree is very
old. Within its hollow trunk are twisted stems, thrown up from the
roots, through which the sap is conveyed to the branches—a curious effort
of nature to supply the place of the decayed trunk. Tradition says that
this yew was planted, long before the church was built, to mark the spot
at which vast numbers of those slain in the battle of Brunenburgh were
buried. See page 376.

church is dedicated to St. Giles. It measures fifty-four feet by thirty-one feet. Kilmington, although in every other respect a separate parish, is ecclesiastically dependent upon Axminster, which is also the case with the adjoining parish of Membury. In all probability, the three parishes were originally united.

The only other place of worship is a Baptist chapel at the upper end of the village. The chapel of Loughwood, within a mile of Kilmington, is in the parish of Dalwood. We should state that an annual fair at Kilmington is held on the 3rd of September.

*   *   *   *   *   *   *

*   *   *   *   *   *

But verily, Piscator, it is high time to be ' once more upon the waters.' The notabilities of Axminster, as we foretold, have proved a lengthened, and, we fear, a tedious theme. We arrived, friend, at the ancient town when the dainty Spring was ripening into full-blown Summer; and there have we been lingering while the weeks and months have rolled along, and brought us fairly to the eve of autumn, with its mellow fruits and ripened corn. We are early up, and gazing anxiously, this chilly ' rosy morn;' upon the winding vale and its enshrouding hills,—intent upon the ' outward aspects,' and eager for the pilgrimage which to-day we must resume. The stream below is hidden by the morning mist; but it is in famous ' tune,' we may be sure,—for the floods, a week ago, which filled the valley like an inland sea, subsided as rapidly as they had risen,— and even yesterday the 'tinge' was but a shade too dark.[1] A western breeze, unless that weather-cock be rusted on its pivot, makes music in these lofty elms, and whirls the dying leaves aloft—betokening clouds, by and by. Those flocks of swallows on the house-tops, too, are a certain indication that 'the year grows ancient.' Their twitterings are, for aught we know, about the orange groves of sunny lands, in which they soon will be luxuriating. Associated in our minds with those autumn swallow-flocks are silvery peal and the more richly marked sea-trout. We will try, anon, old friend, to realise the fancy! Be certain that our collars are well tied, and that our duns and palmers are the best and strongest! Not a moment must we waste at breakfast, for at nine o'clock—armed cap-a-pie—we hope to trudge down

[1] The Axe in a heavy flood is a truly imposing sight. Since land-draining and tree-destroying have become so general, a hasty fall of rain fills every ditch, brook, and draining pipe, and the mass of water thus carried at once into the river, swells it rapidly beyond its banks, and rushes into the adjacent meadows—leaving, far and wide, the trees and hedges only visible. On the same principle the flood subsides almost as soon as the rain which has caused it ceases. The river, in its ordinary state, is of less volume than it was before the days of excessive draining, when the land at the river-head, and around the sources of its tributaries, was in a more marshy state than now. This principle is well illustrated by Sir Humphrey Davy, who compares the soil in its undrained state to a thatched roof, which continues dropping long after a shower; while the land in a drained state resembles a slated roof, which is dry almost as soon as the shower has passed. See 'Salmonia,' pages 64 and 65, first edition.

Anchor Hill,[1] upon our way to where the fish are rising.

* * * * * * *

This brisk three minutes' walk has brought us, friend, to Bow Bridge, a short distance lower down the stream than Stony Bridge, at which we last wound up.[2] Behold, once more, the limpid stream mean-

[1] Anchor Hill is on the western road leading from Axminster towards the river. It derived its name from the circumstance of an anchorite's cell which stood, in ancient times, at the south-western corner of the church-yard. See page 201.

[2] See page 280. Stony Bridge is at the foot of Castle-hill, on the road from Axminster to Membury. The bridge over the mill stream, a hundred yards from Stony Bridge towards the town, was formerly called Ducking Stool Bridge, from the circumstance of the proximity, in ancient times, of that indispensable instrument of punishment. [See page 96.] A man named Butcher, it is remembered, was the last victim. He had applied the *argumentum baculinum* to his offending *cara sposa*, and his indignant female neighbours inflicted the humiliating punishment. This was at the close of the last century, when the bridge was constructed of wood. Stony Bridge was erected about fifty years ago, when a previous bridge was removed in consequence of its dilapidated condition. The old bridge crossed the stream a few yards below the present bridge, and the road on the western side passed *in front*, instead of at the back, of the row of cottages there. It is recorded, that in 1334 the principal bridges over the Axe (Stoford, now Bow Bridge, and Woford, now Stony Bridge,) were washed away by one of the heavy floods which, in that and the following year, caused immense destruction in different parts of the country—breaking down 'the sea bankes or walles' of the Thames, drowning 'infinite numbers of beastes and cattaile,' and converting 'fruitful grounds and pastures into salte marshes;' whereupon 'ensued morraine of beastes,' and a defective harvest, 'so that a quarter of wheate was solde at fortie shillings' [Chronicles Ed. 1577, page 897.] As bridges were not then erected or repaired at the public expense, no exertions were made for a long time to rebuild those which had been washed away at Axminster. A long series of inundations completely cut off all communication between the town and the parts of the parish

dering through that lovely vale, which is spreading like a scene in fairy land! A six-miles' ramble down to Axmouth is before us. We pray thee hasten to prepare thy tackle, and to lend thine ear, meanwhile, to what tradition saith in explanation of the name of Bow Bridge :—

There lived at Kilmington, in days of yore, a famous 'medicine-man' called Bow, who possessed the secret of a never-failing antidote to reptile poison. Among the means adopted to proclaim his healing skill, was one as horrid as it was attractive and successful. At fairs and wakes it was his wont, when vending from a stage his famous nostrums, to allow himself to be stung by infuriated adders to the extreme of vital endurance, and in a few minutes, to prove the efficacy of his marvellous antidote, by appearing safe and sound before the wondering and delighted crowd. His fame spread far and wide, and very envious were his less successful rivals. Now it came to pass, upon a wake-day at Axminster, that while the 'doctor' was engaged in preparation for this crowning feat, some heartless rascal picked his

lying on the western side of the river, so that the dead could not be brought to the churchyard for interment. At length the vicar, by the exercise of church censures *('per censuram ecclesiasticam'),* compelled his parishioners to contribute to the repair of the bridge. The rectors of the church, also, and the abbot and convent of Newenham, to whom the lordship of the hundred and manor belonged, acting by their stewards, imposed a tax upon their tenants for the same purpose; and the work was committed to Robert de Uphay, who, with his men, completed the new structure.

pocket of the precious antidote. The disgusting
exhibition soon commenced. Some vipers were applied to his bare neck and arms, and they soon
performed their part. The poor wretch prepared to
apply the sovereign remedy. Horror of horrors!—
it could not be found; and at his home alone, a mile
and a half away, was there a store of the abstracted
preparation. Too well he knew his dreadful fate,
unless that home could be very quickly reached.
His desperate situation gave him courage. Shriek-
ing fearfully, he pushed aside the astonished crowd,
and started, at his topmost speed, for Kilmington.
But the poison gained upon him. It rushed through
his boiling veins—it mounted to his brain—and while
in the act of crossing Stoford bridge, he dropped, in
awful delirium, upon a spot from which he never rose.
The bridge, so saith tradition, received its name,
thenceforth, in commemoration of this event. [1]

But you are impatient to begin. There! send
your flies into the stickle just below the bridge, and
fish rapidly along, a mile or so, to the junction of
the Yarty; for this portion of the stream is lashed

---

[1] Mr. Davidson does not think so, and all we can say is, that the story
must be taken at its worth. Mr. Davidson conjectures that the name
was suggested by the bow-like form of one of the bridges in ancient
times, as is known to be the case with Bow Bridge over the Lea, near
Stratford, Essex, erected by Maud, the queen of Henry I. The Register
of Newenham Abbey (now in the British Museum) speaks of a bridge
over the Axe, near the site of the present Bow Bridge, in the time of
Edward III. The name of the bridge in ancient times was *Stoford*, as
mentioned in the text.

incessantly, and some of the Axminster craftsmen
will soon be on the water to forestal us, if we lag, in
some of the less frequented spots below.   But you
will find the water *perfect*—pool, and stream, and
shelving bank, in just the places you would have
them, with hardly a bush to intercept your freest
movements.   Not, indeed, that these are anything but
characteristics of the lovely stream from rise to
mouth—with trifling exceptions, as regards the
bushes, in a few spots above Winsham.[1]   Alas! for
the abandonment of such a stream to the undisturbed
possession of the prowling poachers who infest it
night and day! . . . . . But look!   You have a
rise———and have missed your fish, man, unmistakably! So much for eager striking.[2]   Immediately
below you, in that gentle eddy, there at the commencement of the range which is rippled finely by
this piping breeze, a fish came up this moment, and
———— Bravo!   You have him, fast enough,—a
peal, as sure as we are sons of Zebedee!   You can
tell that by his even steadiness of pull—his less activity—less muscular power—than a trout of the
same weight; for he is a good one, of a verity!   But
now he rushes gallantly.   Give line—give line.   Now
run, as he drops down the stream.   Enough!   He

[1] See pages 70, 101, and 163.

[2] See the '*Vade Mecum of Fly-fishing for Trout*,' a work in which,
we may be pardoned for repeating, will be found a list of flies for the Axe,
and every other river in the kingdom, with ample instruction for their
successful use.

slackens, and is on his side. Wind gently up, and
we will help thee land the silvery beauty [1] * * *

'Twas bravely done, old friend. You handled him
like a Master of Arts. Such a prize may well be
taken as an omen of the sport in store for us to-day.
The autumnal dun will soon appear in myriads, and
bring the fish upon the feed,—so that we are pretty
sure of *something*, if the wind and clouds continue.
At present we must hasten to the heavier water lower
down, although it is a sin to pass so carelessly those
glorious pools and stickles. We ought not, verily,
to miss an inch. But there are reasons why we think
it necessary to proceed, and one is the movements of
that 'fashionably'-clad rod-man who, for the last five
minutes, has been watching us from Bow Bridge, and
who, if we mistake not, intends to get ahead of us,
if possible, by walking to the Yarty, and fishing to

---

[1] The valuable fish which is locally denominated *the peal*, as we have
before observed, is undoubtedly the *salmon* after its *first return* from the
sea to the river in which, a few months before, it was a *smoult*. The
poachers, of course, affect to disbelieve this truth, which has often been
proved by indisputable experiments; or rather, they are indifferent as
to *what* the fish may be, so long as it 'brings grist to their mill.' We can
hardly too often or too emphatically repeat our conviction that the Axe
would swarm with splendid salmon and sea-trout if the fence-days commenced earlier in the autumn [see page 22]—if the young fish, in their
various stages, were not killed by wholesale, and the old fish killed in the
act of spawning—if the nets were of the legal mesh;—in short, if only
ordinary care were taken of the stream. We live in hopes that a more
rigid salmon-law will be enacted before the princely breed becomes quite
exterminated. As far as the Axe is concerned, it requires not, even now,
the aid of artificial propagation. Nature alone would furnish an abundant supply, if man were not short sighted and would cease to thwart her.

its mouth that pretty stream—not quite a mile,—to get upon the Axe at ' the Old Water,' and thus to forestal us in that noted range,—and, moreover, to fish the lower ground before us. [1]   Now we, Piscator, must counteract those movements, for that fashionable 'gent' is not a true brother of the craft ;—he is a mere 'pretender' only — a mighty prater about wonderful flies, and fine gut, and all the quackery of angling. He is a boaster of his feats, forsooth,—and will condescend to fish for nothing less than salmon— a sufficient reason in itself for our wishing to get below the water disturbed by his enormous flies. Besides, we never hold communion with such crea-

[1] It will be understood from this, that the Yarty joins the Axe about a mile below Axminster, which it does not far from the ruins of Newenham abbey—and also that it is crossed by a bridge on the turnpike road beyond Bow Bridge. It is our *usual* plan, especially with a westerly wind, to commence at this bridge (called Yarty Bridge), on the western bank of the stream, and to fish down to the confluence with the Axe, as the 'fashionable' person in the text intends to do. The Yarty is one of the most important tributaries to the Axe. It is a favorite resort of peal, and, more particularly, of sea-trout. It rises at Staple Hill, Neroche, in the parish of Otterford, Somerset, about a mile from the source of the Otter, and becomes fishable near the village of Yarcombe, whence to Beckford Bridge [See page 379] a good day's sport may be relied upon in spring, although, in many places, it is much encumbered with wood. At Westwater Moor, the stream enters the property of Mr. Tucker, of Coryton, who preserves it from poachers. It contains great numbers of small delicious trout, and would abound in the migratory *Salmonidæ* if they had a chance of coming up from the lower parts of the Axe. Mr. Tucker's property extends to Yarty Bridge. From this bridge downwards the stream is open to all anglers, and although incessantly fished, possesses undeniable claims upon the angler's attention. Yarty bridge, at the close of the last century, was built, on the site of a former bridge, by John Sweetland, of Axminster. Its precise cost was £537 17s. 6d.

tures, for they have no fellowship with *anglers*. The
'brotherhood' is composed of different materials altogether.[1] .... Yea—let us hasten to the 'meeting of the waters.'   *   *   *   *

And here we are, trying well 'the Cupboards,'[2]
from which we have already managed to extract a
brace of goodly trout,—the little Yarty rippling
along at a few yards' distance only. We ought to
devote some hours to the Axe from Bow Bridge, and
to the Yarty from Yarty Bridge.[3] It is a very convenient *beat*, you see, Piscator, for the angler who is
limited to time, or is incapable of the fatigue of a
long walk; for it presents a considerable extent of
water within a very short distance.

But we are becoming uneasy about the movements
of the 'fashionable' would-be angler, whom we
fancy we discern among the trees, a mead or so above,
and whom we are determined to disappoint. Well,
what on earth is he about? He seems like one 'possessed;'—rushing headlong, with his hat off, among
those herds of great fat bullocks, which are cutting
curious capers also! Why, if our eyes deceive us
not, his salmon fly is fast into the flank of one of
those bovine monsters, which is leading him a dance,

---

[1] See page 267.

[2] The odd name given to the beautiful range on the Axe into which
the Yarty empties itself—a name suggestive of very tantalising ideas to
the hungry angler when plodding his homeward way after a day's fishing
in the lower ground.

[3] Some of the land between the two rivers is called 'the Isle of Man.'

at a swinging pace, around the field; and all the said
'bovine's' companions are manifesting their sympathy
by joining in the exciting run. Look how they all
plunge along—roaring and throwing up their heels,
as if in full appreciation of the joke, while Mr.
Would-be follows at his line's length;—like an Indian
with his lasso, among a herd of buffalos. In truth
he has a curious *fish!* But he is chary of his tackle,
and would rather run than break it,—regardless of
his polished boots, and of his shining hat, through
which one of the excited animals has already pushed
a hoof or two. * * * As we are alive, the
salmon-man has left one of his fancy boots in the
midst of that bog through which the whole racing
party dashed amid a cloud of mire, with a damaging
effect upon the exterior of the unfortunate biped!
See, see, Piscator, the herd have actually taken
to the river—salmon-man, and all! Oh, no, he
is too wise for that. He lets them go alone, and,
gazing from the bank, beholds his highly varnished
rod left in fragments among the alders opposite, while
his silken line he fancies he discerns in graceful folds
upon the grass, and his collar dangles ———— but no
matter where.[1] We may now proceed in peace.
Our salmon-friend has other things upon his hands
at present, and will be anxious to hasten home and
entertain his marvelling friends with a graphic story

[1] See '*Rustic Sketches,*' by the same author, in which this story
(founded on fact) is attempted in a different form.

of his glorious *sport* to-day—another proof of his transcendent skill at all times!

The Old Water is the name of that part of the river which flows through the large and beautiful meadow, on the eastern side, commencing a few score yards below the mouth of the Yarty. The long range with which it commences, and which stretches away to the west, is a favorite resort of the race of *Salmo*, and seldom disappoints the angler who fishes it, in Spring or Autumn, during a stiff breeze, and under other equally favorable circumstances. [1] Deep placid pools, which would harbor princely salmon, if the poachers pleased, occur alternately with *trouty* stickles, as the river winds and wantons through those 'flow'ry meads.' The farms next below the Old Water ground are Slymlakes, on the eastern side of the river, and Oxenlears [2] on the opposite side.

That was a goodly brace of trout, Piscator, which you took just now from underneath the high bank, at the turn nearest to the Oxenlears farm-house! A very prolific *turn* it is, or our note-book lacketh verity! *   *   *   *   Leaving Slymlakes ground, in which we have been lingering—for the

---

[1] We once caught thirty-nine large trout and three peal, in an April morning's fishing from Weycroft Bridge [see page 280] to the foot of the Old Water range. The range itself furnished the peal, one of which was considerably over two pounds; and we might have caught many more trout could we have provided *stowage*. But this was in days of yore.

[2] Corrupted from Oxen-*leaze—pasture land for oxen*. Slymlakes is in the parish of Axminster, and Oxenlears in that of Kilmington.

trout seemed in conspiracy against our rapid progress
—(our creels can testify to that)—we anxiously approach the Hampton Common range and stickles. [1]
Now steady, friend. Try every inch of those delightful curls and eddies under that high western
bank. Gracious—what a flounce! Beware of that
sunken bush—beware! Alas! the fish has made to
its secure retreat, and notwithstanding all your pelting and pulling, we suspect that you will have to
submit to the loss of both fish and fly.   *   *   *
What mean those stentorian shouts, which make the
welkin ring and startle us from our poetic musings?
Nay, nay, friend—you need not be alarmed. The
shouts are not those of a surly keeper, nor even those
of a greedy churl who would drive an unoffending
angler from his *preserve.* By neither of those unhappy beings is this glorious scene defiled. We may
wander at our will, old friend, and fish till we are

---

[1] So called from the neighbouring farm, in Shute parish, on the western side of the river. Lower Hampton bears evidence of having been
itself a residence of some note. Over a large and once handsome fire-
place is the following inscription, in old Roman characters, cut in the
stone:—'WHO SO FEARETH THE LORDE SHALL PROSPERE, AND IN
THE DAY OF HIS ENDE HE SHAL BE BLESED.' Running along three
sides of the cornice, in one of the bedrooms, is another inscription in the
same characters:—'HE THAT STOPPETH HIS EARE AT THE CRYENGE
OF THE PORE HE SHALL ALSO CRIE AND NOT BE HARDE. PROVERBS
——— KEPE BAKE THINE TONGVE AT MEATE AND MEALE.' The
inscription on the fourth side of the room is obliterated. The characters
are in relief, and highly ornamented. Should the tourist wish to pay a
visit to this interesting old place, he must be careful to inquire for
Yamp'n, or he will very probably not be understood.

tired of it, without a frown or murmur from the
liberal souls who own and rent the land. And best
of all is the gratifying fact, that this ' toleration' is
enjoyed alike by the ' squire of high degree' and the
clown in his homely fustian ! [1] Oh! no. They are
not the shouts of an enemy. If we mistake not they
proceed from a well-known form upon the hedge
yonder ;—one who farms no trifling slice of the rich
alluvial around us, and who, if we understand him
rightly, is desirous that we should become acquainted
with his ' mahogany,' and, among other favors, should
vouchsafe an opinion upon his newly tapped cider ;—
a butt of the richest, we shall find. No just cause or
impediment can there be to our reeling up forthwith,
striding across the two or three intervening meadows,
and accepting of his offer of a luncheon in the old
manorial hall of Ashe.

*   *   *   *   *   *   *

Delightfully situated, on the eastern side of the
valley of the Axe, is what remains of a once famous
residence with which is associated the name of one of
the greatest military heroes of England—one, moreover, who played a conspicuous part in the political

[1] See page 249. The property of Sir John George Reeve de la Pole,
Bart., commences near the spot at which we are now supposed to have
arrived. In common with the other landed proprietors on this glorious
stream, from Tytherleigh bridge downwards, he places no restriction upon
the fair angler. A tacit permission is given to 'one and all.' This is a
striking and most gratifying contrast to the selfishness exhibited by the
landed proprietors on the streams in many other parts of the country.

W. Spreat lith. Exeter.

ASHE HOUSE, MUSBURY.

THE BIRTH PLACE OF THE DUKE OF MARLBOROUGH.

affairs of the eventful period in which he lived—

   ——— 'The man to distant ages known,
   Who shook the Gallic, fix'd the Austrian throne.'

Years and years have passed since the splendour of
the old manorial state was rife at the 'antient and
gentile'[1] seat of Ashe. Long, long is it since the
old brocaded dames walked proudly through the
stately halls;—since trains of gallant knights and
high born damsels, swept, with hound and hawk,
into the marshes. Long, long is it since the oak
beams rang with 'Sir John's' loud laugh, while the
yule log blazed upon the enormous hearth, and the
boar's head smoked upon the groaning tables. The
Past is verily but as a dream; and men now gaze
upon the quiet home-stead, and ask, incredulously, 'Is
this the birth-place of the Duke of Marlborough?'

Ashe House is situated in the parish of Musbury,
hardly a stone's throw beyond the parish of Axminster.
It is close to the turnpike road, at the second mile
stone from Axminster to Musbury and Seaton. It
was from very early times the residence of a family
of some distinction. The persons to whom its first
ownership can now be traced, were the family of De
Esse or De Ashe, to whom it was given by John
Lord Courtenay, Lord of the manor of Musbury.
Henry De Ashe gave it to Julian, his daughter, wife
of John de Orway, of Orway, Kentisbeare, Devon,
from whom it came successively, by marriages, into

     [1] Prince.

the families of Stretch, or Street, and Hampton. [1]
Alice, daughter of Warran Hampton, carried it, by
marriage, to John Billett, whose heiress, Christiana,
married, first, John Drake, of Exmouth, and afterwards Richard Frankcheyney. A son was the result
of each marriage. Frankcheyney, the issue of the
second marriage, took possession of Ashe on the
death of his father; but a law suit, which terminated
in 1526, established the priority of right to John
Drake, his half-brother, to whom Ashe was accordingly given up, and his descendants resided there for
many generations. [2]

Sir Bernard Drake,—a very prominent character
in naval and military affairs, during the reign of
Elizabeth,—was born at Ashe. Prince speaks with
rapture of his many admirable qualities, and of his
courageous bearing in 'the long and glorious wars
with Spain, when the English gave the haughty Don
such knocks about the ears as made him stagger and
then go stooping ever since.' An extraordinary
scene at Court between Sir Bernard and Sir Francis

[1] On the 21st of April, 1387, Brantyngham, bishop of Exeter, granted
the privilege of a chapel at Ashe to John Stretch, its owner. The old
chapel, of more recent date, however, than that mentioned, still stands at
the distance of a few yards from the dwelling-house. It is now used as a
cider cellar and granary. The piscina may still be seen, together with
some of the old oak pewing, and the arms of Drake are carved in
stone over the doorway. The possession of a chapel in connection with
the mansions of the country gentlemen, was very common in Roman
Catholic times. There was a chapel in the old mansion at Uphay, and
also one in that of Wyke, Axminster. See pages 290 and 291.

[2] It is somewhat remarkable that the heir of this family was called
John, with one exception only, for ten generations.

Drake, which has been often related in a variety of forms, is thus given by Prince for the first time, on an authority which cannot be questioned : [1]—'About this time it was that there fell out a contest between Sir Bernard and the immortal Sir Francis Drake, chiefly occasioned by Sir Francis his assuming Sir Bernard's coat of arms, not being able to make out his descent from his family ; a matter, in those days, when the court of honor was in more honor, not so easily digested. The feud thereupon increased to that degree, that Sir Bernard, being a person of a high spirit, gave Sir Francis a box on the ear, and that within the verge of the court. For which offence he incurred her Majesty's displeasure, and most probably it proved the occasion of the queen's bestowing upon Sir Francis a new coat, of everlasting honor to himself and posterity for ever, which hath relation to that glorious action of his, the circumnavigating of the world, which is thus emblazoned by Guillim :—Diamond, a fess, wavy, between the two pole stars, arctick and antarctick, pearl, as before. And what is more, his crest is a ship on a globe, under reef, and held by a cable rope, with a hand out of the clouds ; in the rigging whereof is hung up by the heels a wivern, *gules* (Sir Bernard's arms, but in no great honor, we may think, to that knight, though so designed to Sir Francis). Unto all which Sir Bernard

[1] 'This relation I had,' says he, 'from Sir John Drake, of Trill, Knight and Baronet, my honorable god-father.'

boldly reply'd, that " though her Majesty could give
him a nobler, yet she could not give him an antienter
coat than his." ' [1]

The eminent services of Sir Bernard, however, in
time propitiated the queen, who knighted him in
1588. His end was a melancholy, but by no means an
uncommon, one at that period. He had captured, and
brought into Dartmouth, a Portuguese ship, the crew
of which were lodged in Exeter castle. 'At the'
next assizes,' continues his biographer, 'held about
the 27th of Queen Elizabeth, when the prisoners of
the county were brought to be arraigned before Ser-
geant Flowerly, there arose such a noisom smell from
the bar, that a great number of people there present
were therewith infected; whereof, in a short time
after, died the said judge, Sir John Chichester, Sir
Arthur Basset, and Sir B. Drake, knights and justices of the peace, then sitting on the bench, and
eleven of the jury, &c. . . . . . Sir B., it seems,
had strength enough to reach home to his house at
Ashe, but not enough to overcome the disease; for
he died thereof soon after, and was buried in his
church of Musbury, in 1585, in an isle of which are
several monuments, but, I think, no epitaphs. His
effigy is there in statue.' [2]

[1] The ARMS of the Drakes of Ashe, were:—*Argent*, a wyvern, with
wings displayed, *gules*. CREST, on a wreath, a spread eagle, *gules*. [The
old crest was an arm issuing from a wreath, proper, holding a battle axe,
sable, helved, *argent*.] MOTTO: *Aquila non capit muscas*.

[2] The inscription on a brass underneath the effigy is as follows:—
'Heer is the monvment of Sr. Barnard Drake, kt., who had to wife,

Elizabeth, great-granddaughter of Sir Bernard Drake, married Sir Winston Churchill, of Minthorne, Dorsetshire, knight, who, for his adherence to the cause of Charles I, was greatly harassed in the time of the Commonwealth, and remained for some time at the house of his father-in-law, at Ashe. There, on the 24th of June, 1650, the lady gave birth to a son, who became the celebrated Duke of Marlborough —the great soldier and statesman of his day and generation. [1]

Sir John Drake was created a baronet in 1660. Ashe had been burned to the ground during the civil war, and was long in ruins. The family, therefore, re-

Dame Garthod, the davghter of Bartholomew Fortescue, of Filly, Esq. by whom he had thre sonnes and thre davghters, where of whear five living at his death, viz:—John, Hvgh, Marie, Margaret, and Helen. He died the X of Aprill, 1586, and Dame Garthod, his wife, was here bvred the XII of Febrvarie, 1601, vnto the memorie of whome John Drake, Esq., his sonne, hath set this monvment, Anno 1611.'

[1] The bedstead upon which the confinement took place, is now in Shute House. The sister of the Duke, Arabella Churchill, became maid of honor to the Duchess of York, and afterwards mistress to the Duke of York. The following entries occur in the Register of Axminster Church;—'1650. John, the sonne of Mr. Winstone Churchill, was Baptized att Ash ye 28 Daye of Jun, in the year of our lord God.' 'Arabella *Churchwell*, daughter of Mr. *Weston Churchwell*, and Elizabeth his wyfe, was Baptized in *Aish Haule*, the 28th day of February, Anno Dom. 1648.' The words in *italic* are evidently misspelt, and a memorandum to that effect is prefixed to the register, in the handwriting of a subsequent vicar. A fac simile of the Duke's autograph, for which we are indebted to the kindness of J. C. Dale, Esq., of Glanville's Wootton, near Sherborne, will be found at the end of this chapter. The Duke's grandfather lived at Glanville's Wootton, and one account says that Sir Winston Churchill himself was born there. But of this there appears to be some doubt.

moved to the neighbouring residence of Trill, in the
parish of Axminster.[1] At length the second baronet,
Sir John Drake, 'who was,' says Prince, 'a sober,
serious, and prudent person,' sat about rebuilding the
mansion house. He 'enlarged and beautified it to a
greater perfection than it was before; enclosed a park
adjoining to the house, with a good wall; made fish-
ponds, walks, gardens well furnished with great
variety of choice fruits, &c., so that now it may
vye, for beauty and delight, with most other seats in
those parts.'[2] The owner's enjoyment of the residence
which he had rebuilt with so much expense and care,
was very brief. He died almost as soon as he had
taken possession of it.[3] With the death of Sir William, the fifth baronet, in 1733, the title became
extinct. His widow, Dame Anne, survived him
nearly half a century. He had left the whole of his

[1] Trill was anciently a manor, the property and residence, for many
generations, of a family of the same name. In the reign of Edward III
[1327-1377] it was sold by John de Trill to Sir Thomas Fitchett, of Somersetshire, from whom it was carried, by successive heiresses, into the families of Hill, Cheiny, (of Pinho) Walgrave, Hussey, and Clopton. It
was purchased by the Drakes, who formed a park there, and it descended
with their other possessions, till the death of Lady Drake, in 1782, when
it was purchased by the late Rev. George Tucker. It is now the property
of John Gregson, of London, Esq., the owner of the adjoining estate of
Little Trill, and of other property in the neighbourhood.

[2] There is no doubt that the ruins of the neighbouring abbey of New-
enham supplied a considerable part of the stone for the new residence.
A former John Drake, had, on November 8, 1533, been appointed by
Abbot Gyll to the stewardship of the conventual estates.

[3] 'He lies buried in Axminster church, with several other members of
his family. See Davidson's 'History of Axminster Church.'

property to her free and absolute disposal, and to the exclusion of his own family.   Four years after Sir William's death, she married Colonel Speke, of Dillington, by whom she had an only daughter.   This daughter married Lord North, the celebrated minister of state, and the ceremony was performed in the chapel, at Ashe House.   His lordship, during harvest time, in 1765, happened to be on a visit at Ashe, in company with Sir Robert Hamilton, the husband of Lady Drake's sister.   The ministers were extremely unpopular in the West of England, in consequence of a tax upon cider then recently imposed, and Lord North had been afraid to venture into Devonshire. Lady Drake, however, after some difficulty, had succeeded in allaying his fears.   But he was one day thrown into great alarm by a large party of reapers, who, having finished cutting the wheat on the estate, approached the house with their hooks in their hands, shouting the usual cry, 'We have'n—we have'n!' These portentous words Lord North applied to himself, and, pale with terror, considered himself a dead man.   Sir Robert Hamilton seized a sword, and was sallying forth to repulse the visitors, when, meeting her ladyship's steward, an explanation took place, by which the fears which had been so unconsciously excited were soon removed.

After the death of Lady Drake, the estate was sold and the mansion let to Sir John William Pole, baronet, who came to reside there in 1778, while the present Shute House was in the course of erection. On the 25th of September, in that year, at two o'clock in the morning, a fire broke out which entirely consumed the offices and stables, with thirteen coach horses and hunters. The dwelling-house was not materially injured. Ashe, with a great deal of other property in the neighbourhood, belonging to the late George Tucker, of Axminster, Esq., was sold, in 1799, under a decree of the court of chancery. It now belongs to John Marwood Woolcott, Esq., of Knole House, Salcombe.

Musbury village lies a mile to the south of Ashe, further down the valley, and immediately at the foot of the eastern range of boundary hills. It is a pretty specimen of an old English village, with its ancient church, its fine 'mansion,'[1] its alehouse, its blacksmith's shop, and its detached cottages in the midst of rose gardens—forming a congenial resting-place, in the evening of life, for the lover of nature, of angling, and of rural retirement. The parish contains an area of 2178a. 1r. 10p., and a population of 506. It was formerly included partly in the hundred of Axminster and partly in that of Axmouth, the two hundreds having been divided by the brook which flows through the village. But the

---

[1] Called Mountfield House, delightfully placed on the hill-side, and commanding views of some of the most beautiful parts of the valley. Its present occupier is William Hallett, Esq. 'In this parish,' says Risdon, writing about the year 1630, 'lieth Mount Drake, a mansion built and baptised by that name.'—'Survey,' page 24.

hundred of Axmouth has long been absorbed by its more important neighbour. The name of Musbury, like that of Kilmington, has a *traditional* origin associated with the sanguinary battle of Brunenburgh, already described; but it was most probably derived from the Anglo-Saxon, *maest*, greatest, and *beorg*, a heap or mound. [1]

In the time of the Conqueror, Musbury formed a part of the immense possessions of Baldwin de Sap, or De Brioniis, baron of Oakhampton. Ailmer, an Englishman, had possessed it previously, when it paid the geld for seven hides, cultivated by sixteen ploughs. Baldwin had in demesne four hides and three ploughs; the villains, three hides and six ploughs. There Baldwin had sixteen villains, and four cottagers, and eight servants, and eighteen wild horses, and sixteen oxen, and sixteen swine, and one hundred sheep, and thirty goats, and forty acres of wood, and a mill rendering five shillings, and forty acres of meadow, and fifty acres of pasture. Its value, formerly sixty shillings, was then eighty shillings. [2] From Baldwin the manor descended to the Courtenays, some mem-

---

[1] Membury, also (in Domesday Book, *Maneberie*), is thought by Mr. Davidson either to come from the adjective *meinin*, the Welch for stone, or from the Anglo-Saxon *maegen*, or *maen*, strong; and *beorg*, as in the text. 'Musbery,' says Risdon, 'anciently Muchbery, doth not now answer its name; for it is as little as it seems some time to have been great.'—'*Survey of Devon*,' page 23.

[2] From the '*Exeter Domesday*.' In the '*Exchequer Domesday*' many of these particulars are omitted.

bers of which family appear at one time to have fixed their residence at this pleasant village.[1] Upon the attainder of Henry Courtenay, Marquis of Exeter, the manor was given by King Henry VIII to Sir Edward North, who sold it to Sir John Drake, of Ashe, in whose family it remained till the death of the last Lady Drake, in 1782, when the various estates, with the advowson, were sold to different purchasers. The manorial rights were bought, a few years since, by the late William Payne, Esq., who was also the owner of considerable estates in the parish, the whole of which are now the property of one of his younger sons, the Rev. John Vaughan Payne. This gentleman, also, is the possessor of the advowson and right of patronage, his father having purchased them from the present incumbent, the Rev. George Tucker.[2]

[1] At all events, this was done by Sir William Courtenay, a younger son of Robert Lord Courtenay, Baron of Oakhampton. He married Joan, daughter of Thomas Bassett, lord of the manor of Colyton, and had with her one moiety of the manors of Whitford and Colyton. On February 19, 1262, he presented to St. Alun's Church, Cornwall, in right of his wife.—*Dr. Oliver.*

[2] Musbury anciently contained a manor called Ford, on which was a mansion, inhabited by a family of the same name. Of this family it is supposed that John of Devon, one of the abbots of Ford Abbey, [see page 197] was a member. By an heiress, the estate was brought to the Bonvilles, of Wiscombe, and afterwards, by another heiress, to the Poles of Shute, with whom it still remains. The arms of Ford—*sable*, a poppy, with root and fruit, *or*,—are quartered by the Poles, as descendants from the heir general of Ford. We are unable to ascertain the site of the ancient mansion.

Musbury church is situated on the hill-side, near Mountfield House, overlooking the village and the charming valley. It is dedicated to Saint Michael, [1] and consists of a chancel, nave and aisles (the south aisle extending to the full extremity of the chancel), a vestry on the south side, and a square embattled tower at the west end, containing a clock and five bells, and rising to the height of fifty feet. The north aisle is divided from the nave by two acute arches springing from octangular piers. They point to the early part of the thirteenth century as the probable date of their erection. The south aisle is more modern. There is no chancel arch, and the roof throughout the nave and chancel is of the same uniform height. [2] The pulpit and reading desk are in the chancel, where the font is also oddly placed. [3] In the wall against which the pulpit is placed are the remains of what appear to have been the rood-loft stairs; [4] and in the opposite wall is an ancient

[1] A fair is still held at Musbury on the first Monday after Michaelmas day. See page 122.

[2] As the oldest parts of the church appear to be Early English, its foundation, therefore, may be assigned to the date which we have given. The building, as a matter of course, bears abundant evidence of subsequent repairs and mutilations, at different times. About fifty years ago, the east wall of the chancel, which extended about ten feet further into the churchyard than the present wall extends, fell down, and the chancel was reduced to its present dimensions.

[3] See page 83. The font is *painted*, and has carved upon it the date 1562.

[4] See pages 176 and 177.

hagioscope.[1]　The windows are very poor.　The entrance to the church is across the ground floor of the tower, passing under a gallery in which there is a small organ.　In the south or Drake's aisle, are monuments to some of the Drake family, of Ashe. They consist of full-size kneeling figures, male and female, in three pairs.　The males are painted in full armour, and the females in the peculiar costume of the period.[2]

The living of Musbury is valued in the King's Books at £19 11s. 8d., and the tithes are commuted for £435 per annum.　There is neither rectory house nor glebe.

Crowning the eminence behind the church are the

[1] See page 223.

[2] These are, according to the inscriptions:—To the memory of John Drake, who died October 4, 1558; and his wife Amie, daughter of Sir Roger Graynfield, died February 18, 1577.　Sir Bernard Drake (copied at page 398).　John Drake, buried April 11, 1628, and Dorothy his wife, buried December 13, 1631.　Sir John Drake, buried August 26, 1626, and Dame Mary Rosewell, wife of Sir Roger Rosewell, Knt., buried November 4, 1643.　On a highly ornamented marble tablet, in the chancel, are the names of Walrond Drake, second son of Sir John Drake, Bart., by Jane his first wife, daughter of Sir John Yonge, of Colyton, born at Trill, February 14, 1649, died at Exeter, April 5, and buried April 9, 1674; Sir John Drake, his elder brother, born at Lyme, January 13, 1647, died at Ashe and buried here March 13, 1683; Elizabeth his sister, wife of Sir John Briscoe, of Boughton, Northamptonshire, died November 9, 1694; and Dame Judith, wife of Sir William Drake, died May 8, 1701.　In the chancel is also a monument to the Rev. William Salter, forty years rector of Musbury, died March 17, 1770; and one to his wife and daughter. Against the western wall of the south aisle is a tablet to Nathaniel Gundry, Esq., Lord Chief Justice of the Common Pleas, who resided at Maidenhayne, which he held on lease from Lady Drake.　He died on circuit, at Launceston, of gaol fever, March 30, 1754, aged 53 years.

remains of the very ancient and interesting earthworks which are known by the name of Musbury
Castle. We have already alluded to them in our account of Axminster.[1] They are supposed to have
formed one of a chain of hill fortresses extending
many miles inland from the sea at Axmouth, and
including the earthworks on Hochsdon Hill, at Axmouth, the fortress at Axminster, Membury Castle,[2]
Lambert's Castle, Pillesdon Pen, Wynniard's Gap,
and Ham Hill,[3] with numerous outposts and smaller
stations,—the whole connected with each other by
means of trackways running along the eastern side
of the hills. The most satisfactory account of these
intrenchments is that of Mr. Davidson, who argues,
with great show of probability, that they were constructed, at a period long prior to the Roman invasion,

[1] See pages 293-294. At page 8 the ancient hill fortresses in the
neighbourhood of the valley of the Axe are, in some copies, spoken of as
'*mural* fortifications.' We do not pretend to account for so absurd a
mistake, and hardly deserve the reader's pardon for it.

[2] Membury Castle, easily distinguished by its crown of firs, lies to
the north, three miles beyond Axminster. The intrenchments are of less
extent than those of Musbury, and consist of a single vallum only, with
an entrance on the eastern and western sides. The view from this elevated position, though very extensive, is not equal, either in picturesqueness or extent, to that from the sister intrenchment at Musbury. Southward, it includes the town of Axminster, and the lower part of the valley,
with the sea in the distance. In other directions, are Danes' Hill, and
the hills of Yarcombe; Whitedown, and the famous intrenchment of
Neroche, in Somersetshire; and the hills of Tollardown, Blackdown,
Lambert's Castle, and others, in Dorsetshire.

[3] For remarks on these intrenchments respectively, see pages 14, 34,
76, and 255.

by the Morini, a powerful tribe which inhabited
Dorset, for the purpose of defence from the Danmonii, a tribe which possessed the counties of Devon
and Cornwall. [1] The Romans, on their landing, took
possession of most of these intrenchments, which no
doubt proved highly useful in their conquest of the
aboriginal inhabitants of the island. They have left
abundant proof of their having not only occupied
but adapted them to their peculiar system of castra-
metation. [2] 'The West of England,' says Mr. Davidson, 'is thickly scattered with hill-fortresses of
this description, and in no part of it, perhaps, are
these ancient earthworks more numerous than in the
district surrounding the town of Axminster. Within
the distance of twenty-five miles from that place, no
less a number than thirty may be pointed out, and
traces of many more might probably be discovered.'
Among those not already enumerated are Sidbury,
Woodbury, Belbury, Dumpton, Blackberry, and
Hembury, in Devonshire; and Neroche between

---

[1] 'Upon the top of the hill,' says Risdon, 'there is a strong castle,
and the entrance very narrow to come to it. Somewhat nearer the sea,
is another of like strength [at Hochsdon], which I suppose were the holds
of the Saxons over against the Danes, where they first encamped when
they landed hereabouts. This I leave to the liking of others.' Since
Risdon's time considerable light has been thrown upon the interesting
subject of our aboriginal antiquities, and the peculiar forms adopted by
the different occupiers of the country in early times are now known with
a great degree of certainty. By far the greater number of these wonderful fortifications were undoubtedly constructed at a period long ante-
rior to the times of the Saxons.

[2] See our Introductory Chapter.

Chard and Taunton, These, with some others, formed the frontier line of defence of the Danmonii. The intrenchments at Musbury consist of a single vallum, with well-protected entrances, and the area enclosed is about six acres.

The view of the valley of the Axe from Musbury Castle, is one of the most delightful that can be obtained of it, and the eye ranges far beyond the limits of that lovely tract. Standing on the crown of the hill, with his back to the little valley of Coombpyne, [1] the spectator beholds a glorious panorama, composed of hill and dale, of water and of wood —of all the accessaries, in short, of a perfect rural landscape. To the north his range is bounded by the undulating hills behind the woods of Cloakham and the looming haze of Axminster. Along the broad expanse before him winds the glittering stream among the elm-crowned hedge rows and the verdant meads. Across the valley are the Stockland hills and the hills of Shute, with the fir-embosomed mansion, while the western horizon is marked by the hills of Honiton and Ottery and the highlands of more

---

[1] The parish of Coombpyne is between Musbury and Uplyme, about two miles eastward from the valley of the Axe. It contains 800 acres, and a population of 138 only. It anciently belonged to the family of Coffin, and was called Comb-Coffin. This name was altered when it afterwards passed into the family of Pyne. It came by marriage to the Bonvilles, and having passed to Grey, Duke of Suffolk, was forfeited by attainder. It afterwards became the property of Lord Petre, and now belongs to Henry Knight, Esq., of Axminster. The village consists of a few houses only, and the church is proportionately small.

central Devon. Far away, in every direction among those eminences, is the eye allured into the innumerable combs which wind and wanton in the dark recesses, and pour their limpid treasures into the lap of fair Alænus.[1] Towns, and villages, and quiet homesteads, and all the paraphernalia of rural occupation, impart variety and animation to a picture which is made complete by the romantic cliffs of Beer, and the extensive Seaton bay, which lie in sunshine at his left !

[1] See page 7.

Marleborough

[AUTOGRAPH OF THE DUKE OF MARLBOROUGH.]

CHAPTER XI.

Woodhayne Bridge is the name of the railed plank which crosses the stream some five hundred yards below the Hampton Common eddies. Three ranges and four stickles—all really unexceptionable—occur within this interval. You must fish carefully, Piscator, the pool immediately below the bridge itself, casting your flies well underneath the western bank;[1] and almost impossible will it be for you, at this autumn season, and on this glorious day, to fish the next half a mile of water without finding frequent use for that capacious pannier of yours. * * *
Yes!—call it Millands range, since it is opposite the farm of that name,[2] and if you really *must* have some especial designation of the lucky spot! As sure as fate, old friend, it was a *salmon* which took your leader so *upheavingly*, half an hour ago, and which you

[1] This bridge derives its name from the farm on the western hill-side, in the parish of Shute.

[2] A quarter of a mile below Woodhayne Bridge, on the eastern bank. —some magnificent ranges, pools, and stickles intervening.

cannot, with the utmost of your manœuvring, induce
to show himself at the surface. Gently, gently, with
those volleys of stones upon the water. He begins to
move—slowly, at first, like a starting railway train,
but increasing rapidly, till————Run with him, run!
—your line is nearly out. All right! There—there
—he springs above the surface—once—twice. Give
him your top—be quick!—lower—lower—a monster,
friend, he is. Why you fairly tremble with excitement! Be cool—be patient, as you love your angling
reputation. There, that will do. But see—see—
that sunken bush, below, will settle all, unless————
'Twas glorious friend—'twas glorious! That timely
check and gentle handling of the rod, have brought
the fish well out of danger. Breathe freely now. . . .
But no—he grounds again among the gravel;—

> ' The wily fish is sullen grown,
> And, like a bright embedded stone,
> Lies gleaming at the bottom.'

We fear the pelting system must be tried again—a
dangerous one, forsooth, it is! Reel up—keep tight.
He moves—he runs—he rushes madly! * * * *
The game is nearly up, at last. We plainly saw his
pectorals, as you so cleverly diverted him again from
the sunken bush. A few more active turns will
bring him on that sand-bank, and the glorious trophy
will be won! * * * * 'Tis over. And thus
doth *salmo* lie upon the turf, and thus we gaze in
transport on his silvery tints, and feel that we have

fought no paltry fight and gained no paltry triumph—
for he weighs at least a dozen pounds, and we have
landed him *sans* gaff! [1]

Two hundred yards or so below us, friend, is
Whitford Bridge, and goodly are the eddying turns
and gentle ripples within the interval. We cannot
condescend, immediately, to trout, of course, but
prefer, for the nonce, an adjournment to the ' timely
inn,' where the blue smoke wreaths so gracefully
among the orchards over there. [2]   If the celebration

---

[1] We once had the good fortune to kill a salmon of this weight, with
fine trout tackle, in Millands range. It was on April 4, 1837. We were
quite alone, and without a landing net. The fish gave us *four hours'*
vigorous play. Twenty yards of line and a ten feet rod were sorry
implements for such a capture.

[2] At the hamlet of Whitford, in the parish of Shute. Whitford was
anciently a manor, and formed part of the royal demesne, having, with
Shute itself, been included in the parish of Colyton. It belonged, at an
early period, to the family of Basset [See our account of Colyton] from
whom it passed, by marriage, to the Sandfords, and, in the fourteenth
century, to Brewose. About the year 1342, a market was granted to
Peter de Brewose, to be held on Wednesday, within his manor of
' Wytteford,' and a fair for four days at the festival of St. Peter, *ad vincula.*
Four years afterwards he obtained another fair for five days at the festival of the Assumption. There is still the shadow of a fair held annually
in September. The manor was held by the annual render of an ounce
of silk. It was afterwards re-united to the manor of Colyton, which
belonged to the Courtenays, with whom Whitford remained until the
extinction of the elder branch, when it was divided between the four heirs
general. One fourth part belonged to the Poles, and, in 1787, Sir John
William Pole had acquired by purchase the three other shares. The
name of Whitford is traditionally said to be a corruption from *White-
friars-ford.* The more likely primitive, however, is simply *Wide-ford,*
for it was certainly never the residence of a religious community, although
the ancient records tell of a chapel there of which no traces now remain.
[See Bacon's ' *Liber Regis,*'] Robert Ottleigh, its last incumbent, was

of this unusual capture of ours cannot be made to include a little *quaffing* at the very first opportunity, we deserve not the name of anglers. Besides, we are nothing loath for half an hour's rest, and, if the truth must out, we have a sneaking desire to exhibit our prize to the admiring gaze of the denizens of that rural retreat. Furthermore, we can avail ourselves of the opportunity to say a few words about the history of the parish. *   *   *   *   *   *

Shute is situated between Colyton and Kilmington, and a great part of the parish is on elevated ground, commanding extensive and delightful views of the valleys of the Axe and Colly. Shute House, the mansion of the Poles, which has an exquisite position on a hill, contributes, in no small degree, to the beauty of the valley scenery from all the points of view below.

The parish contains a population of 597, on an area of 2450 acres. Its owners, in the time of Henry III, were the de Schetes, so called from the name of the place itself—a name suggested by its situation 'on the side of a hill,' as Risdon hath it. From the Schetes the manor came to Sir Thomas Pyne, from whom it was inherited by Sir Nicholas Bonville, whose family, for many generations, made Shute their principal residence. The manor was

living in 1553, on a pension of £5 per annum. The village Inn affords excellent accommodation, and is a favorite refreshment-house of the local anglers.

brought, by marriage, to Thomas Grey, Marquis of Dorset. It descended from him to Henry Duke of Suffolk, upon whose attainder, in 1553, it was forfeited to the crown. The queen (Mary) granted it to her principal secretary of state, Sir William Petre, of whose descendant it was purchased, in 1787, by Sir John William de la Pole, baronet, in whose family it still continues—its present owner being Sir John George Reeve de la Pole, baronet.[1]

Shute House, as before stated, was built in 1787-8. It stands in a beautifully wooded lawn, on an eminence which commands an exquisite view of the sea and of the lower parts of the valley. The plan of the building is that of a square body with two handsome wings connected with the body by corridors.

---

[1] Long before 1787, the Pole family had made Shute their residence—holding it, we presume, on lease. Sir William Pole, Knt., the historian of Devon, who died on February 9, 1635, says that his father had the house and park from Sir William Petre, 'and dwelled there during his life, and left it unto me; and my eldest son, John Pole, holdeth it from me.' The family of Pole, to use the words of Prince, 'is both ancient and honourable;' and he informs us that 'Pole, in the parish of Tiverton, was the seat and possession thereof from the time of the Norman Conquest for several generations.' The head of the family was William De Pole, or Pulle, of Pole, or Pulle, in Cheshire, and the two branches intermarried. Sir William, the historian, was the fifteenth in descent in the Devonshire branch. His eldest son, John, was created a baronet on September 12, 1628. The present is the eighth baronet. In 1838, he assumed, by royal license, the additional name of Reeve, and succeeded his father, the late highly respected Sir William Templar Pole, Bart., on April 1, 1847. The ARMS of Pole are:—*Azure*, semée of fleurs-de-lis, and a lion rampant, *argent*. CREST: a lion's gamb, *gules*, armed, *or*. SUPPORTERS: *dexter*, a stag, *gules*, attired and unguled, *or; sinister*, a griffin, *azure*, gorged with a ducal coronet, proper, armed and beaked, *or*. MOTTO: '*Pollet virtus*.'

The entrance has a portico, with Doric columns. Old
Shute House was a few hundred yards west of the
present building. It was an ancient castellated mansion, in the early Tudor style. The fine old gatehouse, and a few other parts of the interesting old
place, remain to show its former extent and consequence. The deer-park is about half a mile west of
the mansion house. It comprises about 150 acres,
and is charmingly situated upon a knoll. Delightful
are its extensive views, its picturesque glades, and its
noble and venerable trees. It formerly contained a
heronry, omitted in Mr. Yarrell's list of heronries in
Britain; but within a few years the herons have left
their old resort and adopted a new home among the
woods of Stedcombe. The village of Shute, which
consists of about fifteen houses only, lies in front
of the old gatehouse, among lofty trees and a profusion of roses. [1]

---

[1] Upon the highest point of Shute Hill, about half-a-mile north of the
mansion, is an ancient beacon house in admirable preservation. It is of
circular shape and composed entirely of stone, the roof being arched like
a bee hive, which it resembles in other respects. There is an aperture in
the centre of the roof. In the walls are slits commanding views in
various directions, and also the remains of a fire place. The situation
commands a great extent of country, but the beacon house has, within
a few years, become surrounded with trees which completely shut out the
view, and it is itself almost buried beneath a mass of underwood and ivy.
We do not presume to fix the date of this interesting structure, but it
may be mentioned that the Axminster parish books contain an entry
respecting the erection of a beacon on a neighbouring eminence which
may have some relation to the date of the beacon on Shute Hill,
although the *site* of a beacon on such a prominent point cannot be
supposed to be of modern selection [See page 304]. It is as follows:—

GATEWAY OF OLD SHUTE HOUSE.

W Spreat Lith. Exeter.

The ancient and beautiful little church is dedicated to Saint Andrew. It consists of a chancel with a north aisle or chapel, containing monuments to various members of the Pole family,[1] and divided by two arches with foliated capitals; a nave and north aisle, separated by three arches; north and south transepts, with a square embattled tower, rising, at their intersection with the nave, to the height of about forty feet, and containing five bells. There are also a porch on the south side, and, at the west end, a door

'1679—Imprimis. Paid to the building of Trinity Beacon and Beacon House (being our parish proportion) £08 03s. 06½d.' The remains of this beacon are still to be seen upon Trinity Hill, at a point which commands an extensive view over a picturesque and fertile country.

[1] The most striking monument in the church is a marble statue, in this chapel, to Sir William Pole, Bart., master of the household to Queen Anne. It represents a life-size figure, on a handsome pedestal, attired in full court costume, with the wand of office in the right hand. The countenance is beautifully expressive, and the drapery very skilfully arranged and exquisitely sculptured. This Sir William died at Shute, December 31, 1741, aged 63. The tablets in the same chapel are the following:— A marble tablet, upon which is sculptured the figure of an ascending angel, to the memory of Sophia Anne, first wife of the late Sir William Templar Pole, Bart., and mother of the present baronet, died March 17, 1808, aged 20 years. A tablet to John George Pole, Esq., August 26, 1803, aged 10 years; and one to Charles Bulford Templar, Esq., who perished in the Halsewell East Indiaman, during the night of January 6, 1786, aged 16. The tablets in the chancel record, amongst others, the deaths of:—Sir John William de la Pole, Bart., Lieutenant Colonel of the Royal East Devon Cavalry, &c., November 30, 1799, aged 42. [The rather lengthy inscription is ably drawn up.] Jane Maria, youngest daughter of Sir W. T. Pole, Bart., and second wife of Edward Wyndham Harrington Schenley, Esq., judge at the Havannah in the mixed commission for the suppression of the slave trade, died April 23, 1837, aged 22. Anne, widow of John William de la Pole, the sixth baronet, died February 12, 1832, aged 81 years.

HHH

within a pointed arch of numerous mouldings. The
oldest parts of the church appear to date from the
early part of the thirteenth century—the four beautiful arches which support the tower, and a few other
parts of the building, being in the Early English style.
The greater part of it, however, is in the Perpendicular style of the fifteenth century. Most of the
windows are good. Some, however, are only flat-
headed, and others contain stained glass, exhibiting,
among other subjects, the arms of Pole and those of
other families in connexion with that ancient house.
But the western window is an obvious exception.
Under a lofty and graceful arch, once containing elegant tracery, no doubt, are three plain mullions
running from the bottom to the top. Fortunately,
this window is partially hidden by a gallery, which
runs across the western end of the church. The
elegant mahogany pulpit, which is surmounted by a
canopy, is placed at the eastern end of the nave. The
south transept is fitted up as a pew for the Pole family.

Shute, although in every other respect a separate
parish, is, like Monkton, a perpetual curacy dependent upon Colyton.

*   *   *   *   *   *   *

One of the best stickles in the river, Piscator, is
the delightful one along which your flies are floating
so temptingly, immediately below Whitford Bridge.[1]

---

[1] Whitford Bridge is of wood, and for foot-passengers only; but there
is a *ford* for vehicles and horses. It is the longest bridge upon the stream,
and is situated in one of the most beautiful spots in the valley.

If you do not·raise a peal in the pool below, under that very high western bank opposite, it will be an unusual circumstance at this season and on such a day!

Nunsford Bridge, a foot plank leading from Mus-bury to Colyton, over Kingsdown, is about half a mile below.[1] The river between those bridges is generally *heavy*, although broken by two or three stickles of surpassing excellence.[2] From Nunsford Bridge the river assumes a different character from that which distinguishes it in the portion higher up —a character which has been gradually developing itself from the Old Water downwards. The stickles now become less numerous, though by no means 'few and far between,' and the pools and ranges are more extensive. The coy stream, indeed, seeks the embraces of rude Neptune in a gentle style—as if unwilling

---

[1] The name of Nunsford has beguiled some writers into the idea that there was once a nunnery in the locality. There appears, however, to be no foundation for that belief.

[2] We crave the reader's indulgence for the introduction of the following little story in connection with Nunsford Bridge:—Many years ago, a near relative of our own, while crossing the bridge one morning in autumn, noticed that the fish were rising well in the stickle above. He was not on an angling excursion, and had no tackle with him, except flies and a collar; but the temptation to have a cast was so strong, that he was induced to cut a willow switch from a neighbouring hedge, fit it up with a whipcord line, and attach his collar in the usual manner. To work he went, and, with these rude implements, soon landed several brace of noble fish. Some weeks afterwards, he set a springle in a ditch of one of his fields, which was haunted by a woodcock, and it so happened that he used for the bow the identical switch that had served him for a fishing rod. A woodcock was caught, the switch was left in the ground, it took root, sprouted, grew, and is at this moment a flourishing tree.

.to leave the verdant meads through which she has so
long and so wantonly been straying.

The stream between Nunsford Bridge and the first
turn below it—two hundred yards or so,—is generally prolific of sport, and it should be fished from the
western side. The first pool below the bridge—about
half way to the turn—is called by the net-men
'Miraculous Hole,' from the circumstance of its having been the scene of a 'draught of fishes' so large
as to astonish its capturers almost as much as the
sons of Zebedee were astonished by the 'miraculous
draught' in the sea of Galilee.[1] Dace are very plentiful in most of the deep ranges, and in summer
evenings they afford very pleasant sport, when more
noble game cannot be obtained. Often a large trout
—delicious as the large trout in this part of the
stream proverbially are—surprises the dace fisher by
seizing his fly, and *insisting*, as it were, upon 'making

[1] An Exeter Paper of October 3, 1789, records this circumstance as
follows:—'On Saturday last, Messrs Isaac and George Tucker, with
James Benaville, Esq. (from London), and many friends of the town
and neighbourhood of Axminster, took a day's diversion of fishing on the
river Axe, in order to take salmon, and other fish, and had excellent sport.
But what exceeded every thing that can be remembered, and what must
be acknowledged to be something very extraordinary, they caught at a
single haul, in one pool, a salmon weighing upwards of twenty-two pounds,
two brace and a half of fine salmon peal, and more than three hundred
trout, roach, and dace, many of which weighed a pound, and a pound and
a half each. The sight was such as, it is supposed, hardly ever had its
equal, with a net of the same size, in any river of the kingdom, being a
trammel not forty feet in length. The parties gave upwards of twenty
dozen of the fish to the poor inhabitants of Musbury.' See page 25,

one' among the more scaly occupiers of his creel.[1]
Nunsford Hole, the deepest and most extensive in
the river, is the name of the still and gloomy looking
stretch of water at the turn below Miraculous Hole.
On the western bank, it is, as Pope says,

'With silver alders crowned,'

and there are also lofty trees upon the same bank,
which of course contribute to the sombre character
of the hole. The netters find it a profitable place,
but it is almost useless to the fly-fishers. Below,
however, succeed some magnificent stickles, which
make an ample compensation. Other stickles, with
Gin Bottle Hole, Newberry's Hole, Cownhayne
Range, and other famous pools and ranges, make up
some glorious fishing ground to the Iron Bridge at
Colyford, called Axe Bridge, friend.[2]   *   *   *

[1] Upwards of seven hundred roach and dace were once landed in a
trammel, at one haul, near Bow Bridge; and a few years since, a friend of
ours caught with the fly, at one standing, in a stickle near Millands
Range, more than fifty large dace in less than an hour. In the upper
parts of the river, a dace is hardly ever seen. We do not refer to roach
and dace as a valuable *acquisition;* neither, on the other hand, do we
think that the claims of a *trout* stream are much affected by their
presence in some of its heavy portions. *Ne quid nimis* is a motto which
even a trout and salmon angler would be foolish to despise.

[2] This iron bridge was erected in 1837, on the site of
'An auncient bridge of stone,
A goodly worke when first it reared was'—
a very picturesque object, with its ivy and its nooks. It was very steep
and narrow, resembling, somewhat, the present Beckford Bridge over the
Yarty. [See page 379.] It was very old, and the workmen were surprised at the immense labor which its removal cost them. They were

And there we are at last—the marsh extending itself before us—the valley widened greatly, very glorious to behold—the hills becoming more cliff-like, cliffs in reality a mile or so below, where the sea is glistening in the rays of the sun, which begins to struggle through the clouds, intending to have a cheerful peep at the world before he sinks, by and by, into the empurpled west. As for ourselves, Piscator, our ramble is about to end. Below the bridge we may have a few farewell casts, and even try the foot of the Coly, if we like, awhile; but we have arrived within the influence of the tide, and may as well, considering all things, devote no great amount of time, for we begin to be fagged.[1] There is, besides, a pleasant walk before us of a mile or so to Axmouth,[2] where, having seen the exit of the stream along the banks of which we have wandered from its source—we must

at once convinced that lath and plaster building, and similar 'shams,' are *modern* characteristics.

[1] The holes below the bridge are sure to afford peal in the spring months—sometimes salmon, and often large trout. The Bridge Hole, Hope, Clatty, and Hedge Corner Holes, are the principal *habitats*. A bright red palmer, a march brown, and a blue upright, are the best flies for use. Peal should be fished for in deep water, under high banks, and also in *the slack water*, or eddies, between two currents formed by an obstruction in the stream. The flies should be allowed to *sink* more than in trout fishing, and they are taken eagerly. A good wind is of course necessary.

[2] Truly delightful is the road to Axmouth—not only from Axe Bridge, but from Axminster—running parallel with the river, and commanding some exquisite peeps of the valley scenery. The wooded hills near Stedcombe, and the bare cliffs nearer Axmouth, are delightful objects, in charming contrast with the soft, rich, quiet valley.

PROTESTANT KIRCHE OFFEN...

W. Sprat Lith.

part, old friend, must *part*. Nay, nay—it *must* be so, however painful. Why we live in a world, as some one says, of meetings and farewells; and what exception can *we* claim? Even the *last*, long, sad parting must take place some day—we know not when, alas! alas! There remains, however, dear old friend, a great deal yet to talk about—abundance to beguile the way, when we are trudging Axmouth-ward. The good old town of Colyton, which looms away a mile to the north, its graceful tower harmonizing with the mass of embrowning leaves which cover the delightful landscape, demands no trifling notice. Yea we have a long and pleasant labor yet.

*　　*　　*　　*　　*　　*　　*

Colyton is a small and ancient market town, in a delightful valley, five miles south-west of Axminster. Along this valley, which opens into the valley of the Axe, flows the sparkling little stream which gives its name to the town, and which is an important tributary to the Axe.[1] The views from the heights around

[1] 'Colyton,' says Polwhele, 'signifies a town upon the hazel brook—*Collh-y-tun.*' The Coly is formed by the junction of several rivulets which rise in Colwell wood, near Offwell, and of others which flow from the hills near Farway. Near the turnpike gate at the eastern entrance to the town of Colyton, it receives the Shute Brook, called, also, the Umborne, which rises among the Stockland hills, near the source of the Cory, and flows by Ford, and thence to Willmington, watering the domain of Sir Edward Marwood Elton, Bart., and passing on the western side of Shute Park. It is preserved in these localities, and abounds in trout. The Coly, also, is a prolific little stream. The bridge at the turnpike gate before alluded to, is called Umborne Bridge. There is a stone bridge, also, called Chantry Bridge, over the Coly, on the Honiton road. The

the town are as extensive as they are diversified and beautiful.

Colyton is the capital of a hundred comprising the parishes of Branscombe, Colyton, Cotleigh, Farway, Northleigh, Southleigh, Monkton, Offwell, Seaton and Beer, Shute, and Widworthy. Being out of the way of railroads [1] and even of the great turnpike thoroughfares, it is of little importance in a commercial view. But it formerly had a share of the clothing trade, and even boasts at present of a manufactory of paper, and of an extensive tan yard. Considerable quantities of the celebrated Honiton lace are also made in the parish. The town is very irregularly built, and most of the streets are very narrow and intricate, bespeaking high antiquity. Some extensive fires, however, within a few years, have resulted in a great improvement in the streets and houses, and consequently in the general appearance of the place, which wears an air of respectability, repose, and comfort. It is, moreover, an excellent angling station.

united streams form a tolerable body of water from Colyton to Colymouth—a few score yards below Axe Bridge, at Colyford. Leland, speaking of it, says:—'Coley river renneth under the rote of an hille that this town standeth on. This broke riseth, as I could esteme, by west-northwest a . . . . . . miles from Colington, by the which it renneth, and then, as I marked, it passeth by Colecombe Park, hard by Colington, lately longginge to the marquisse of Excester, and thens, going on mile and more, enterith betwixt Ax bridge and Axmouth towne, into Ax river.' The Coly greatly resembles the Yarty, and, like it, is a favorite resort of peal. It is particularly valuable for early spring fishing, the fish being generally in a forward condition.

[1] See pages 42 and 235.

Leland, who visited the town in the time of Henry VIII, and who certainly was not greatly disposed to flattery, describes it, in his quaint way, as 'no very notable thing.' The parish, which is famous for its dairy produce and delicious cider, is very extensive—comprising rather more than 7200 acres, with a population of 2503. It is divided into six tithings, namely, the Town, Colyford,[1] Farwood,[2]

[1] Colyford is a hamlet about a mile from the town, in the direction of Seaton. It is built upon the Roman road which led along the coast to Exeter [see page 11], and is undoubtedly a place of high antiquity. It was constituted a borough by a royal charter obtained by one of the Bassets, the ancient lords of Colyton, and was governed by a mayor, elected annually, who had the profits of the fair. The form of mayor-choosing is still kept up, and the fair is of some consequence. Certain privileges and liberties of the burgesses were confirmed by a charter obtained by Hugh Courtenay, Earl of Devon, in 1340. [See Risdon's 'Survey.'] Colyford was the birth-place of Sir Thomas Gates, a 'valiant soldier' who was knighted by King James, about the year 1609, and made governor of Virginia, under the Earl of Southampton. He set sail for the colony with 500 men, in nine ships, and was accompanied by Sir George Somers, a native of Lyme. [Fuller's 'Worthies.'] They suffered shipwreck, and being cast upon the Bermudas (called afterwards the Somer's Islands), took possession of them for the king. On the incidents of this shipwreck, it is said that Shakespeare founded his play of 'the Tempest.' Sir Thomas afterwards reached Virginia, and ruled it with great ability till his death, in 1620. A family of the same name was re-siding at Axminster so anciently as the time of Henry III. Sir William Pole gives an extract from a deed in which occurs the name of 'Laurence de la Gate.' The Wesleyans have a small chapel at Colyford, and the visitor may be glad to know that there are two public houses there.

[2] Farwood was a manor belonging anciently to Henry Tracy, baron of Barnstaple, who gave it to the abbey of Quarrer, in the Isle of Wight. After the Reformation, it was purchased by the Haydon family. It now belongs to the Rev. Mr. Hunt, of Sidbury. Farwood is part of the Duchy of Lancaster, and the tenant, in consequence, enjoys the privileges of the Palatinate, which include exemption from tolls in all fairs and

Watchcombe, Tudhayes or Minchingholm,[1] and Woodland tithings.[2]

Colyton, as we have stated before, formed part of the Anglo-Saxon royal demesne. It is thus surveyed in Domesday Book :—The King holds Culitone. In the time of King Edward it gelded for one hide. The arable is sixteen carucates. In demesne is one carucate, and three servants, and twenty-one villains, and ten cottagers, with fourteen ploughs. There is a mill rendering forty pence, and thirty-six acres of meadow, and two hundred acres of pasture, and ten acres of copse wood. It is worth eleven pounds and ten shillings. To the church of this manor belongs half a virgate of arable, and it is valued at five shillings.

Colyton was bestowed by William the Conqueror

markets, and freedom from arrest. This is the case, also, with the tenants at Axmouth, Coombpyne, and Little Musbury. .

[1] Minchingholm belonged to the nunnery of St. Katherine, at Polsloe, near Exeter. It consists of several farms, and belongs to the Dean and Chapter of Exeter.

[2] There were formerly three more tithings :—Whitwell, Stowford, and Gatcombe—now merged into the others. Whitwell anciently belonged to the Lutterells, and afterwards to the Earls of Devon. It was at one time the property of the Fryes, of Yarty, who sold it to the Willoughbys, whose representative, Sir John Trevelyan, Bart., sold it to the Poles. Stowford was the property and residence of a family of the same name, whose heiress, in the reign of Edward I, married into the family of Walrond, from whom the property was purchased by Sir John de la Pole. It afterwards went to the Eltons, who sold it to Mr. Loveridge, of Chardstock. Gatcombe, a dismembered manor, was successively the property of the Hillions, Prouses, Stowfords, and Wises. Sir Thomas Wise disposed of it in parcels. The principal farm is now the property and residence of Mr. Thomas Salter.

upon Robert de Mount Chardon. Reverting to the crown, in the reign of Henry II, it was by that monarch given to Sir Alan Dunstanville, whose son, Sir Walter, caused it to be conveyed to Sir Thomas Basset,[1] his nephew, together with the manor of Whitford. By marriage of an heiress of Basset, in the reign of Henry III,—about the year 1250—it came into the possession of the noble family of Courtenay. It remained their property until the attainder of Henry Courtenay, Marquis of Exeter, in the reign of Henry VIII. It was restored to the family, along with other property, by Queen Mary, and, failing the male line, descended to four heiresses, whose husbands sold the manor to Lord Petre, Sir John Pole, Bart., and Sir John Drake, Bart.,[2] of

---

[1] The family of Basset (afterwards created Barons of Dunstanville), was descended from Osmond Basset, who accompanied William the Conqueror from Normandy. A branch of the family was settled in Devonshire at an early period.

[2] A branch of the Drake family resided at Yardbury for several generations. It sprang from William, brother of Sir John Drake, Knt., the father of the first baronet. The property was brought to the Drake family by the marriage of this William with Margaret, daughter and heiress of William Westover, of Yardbury. The Creditors of Francis Horatio Nelson Drake, Esq., disposed of the property, a few years ago, to Clifford Sherriff, Esq., its present owner and occupier. The fine old mansion was destroyed by fire during the night of February 23, 1853, and a new house has just been erected on its site. The earliest known possessors of Yardbury were the Baucheins, one of whom, Sir Stephen Bauchein, its owner in the time of Henry III, was 'skilful in feats of arms,' as Risdon tells us, and 'served very valiantly against the Welch, winning many victories;' but in the first year of that king's reign, he was slain by Rees Vuchan, a Welch Captain. It was possessed by the Bonvilles

Ashe. The whole has now become, by purchase, the property of the Pole family. [1]

in the reign of Edward III, and afterwards passed to the Coplestones, who sold it to Sir William Pole, Knt., from whom it was purchased by the Drakes.

[1] It may tend to elucidate this account of the descent of the manor, and to explain some of our allusions to the Courtenays elsewhere, by giving a brief sketch of that noble family—a family which played so important a part in the affairs of the county, and of those of the kingdom at large:—Its name is derived from the town of Courtenay, in France, and the founder of the English family, Reginald de Courtenay, came over to this country with King Henry II, in 1151. He married the heiress of Robert de Abrincis, or Averinches, Baron of Oakhampton and hereditary sheriff of Devon. Robert, the eldest son of this Reginald, married the heiress of William de Redvers, Earl of Devon, and inherited the title and honors of his maternal grandfather—which descended to his son and grandson. His great grandson, Hugh, was summoned to Parliament, in 1335, as Earl of Devonshire, on account of his descent from the daughter of William de Redvers—a title which had not been enjoyed by either his father or grandfather. Two of the sons of the second earl became famous military commanders, and the eldest, Sir Hugh, was one of the original Knights of the Garter. Their brother William became archbishop of Canterbury, and Chancellor of the University of Oxford. Thomas, the sixth earl, was taken prisoner at the battle of Towton, and beheaded at York, in 1462; and four years afterwards his brother Henry, the seventh earl, was attainted and beheaded at Salisbury. John, a younger brother, was restored to the title in 1470. He took a prominent part in the wars of the roses, on the Lancastrian side, and was slain at the battle of Tewksbury. Leaving no issue, the elder branch of the family became extinct. But the title was restored, in 1485, in the person of Sir Edward Courtenay, grandson of Sir Hugh, a younger brother of the third earl. William, Sir Edward's son, the tenth earl, married Catherine, youngest daughter of King Edward IV. [See our account, in a future page, of the monuments in Colyton Church.] His son Henry, the eleventh earl, was, in 1525, created Marquis of Exeter, and, in 1538, was convicted of high treason, and beheaded, as we have more than once stated in the text. In 1553, his son Edward was restored to the earldom, and to all the estates which remained unsold. He died without issue, in 1556. The four sisters of Edward, the ninth earl, became heirs general. Matilda, the eldest, married John Arundell, Esq., of Talverne, Cornwall;

King John, about the year 1208, granted a fair at Colyton, to Sir Thomas Basset, to be held for seven days, 'beginning on the octave of St Michael.[1]' There are now two annual fairs—one on the first Thursday in May, and the other on the Thursday after October 14th. The markets, now inconsiderable, are held on Tuesdays, Thursdays, and Saturdays.[2]

Elizabeth married John Trethurfe, Esq., from whom the Vyvyans of Trelowarren, and the Bullers, are descended; Isabella married William Mohun, Esq., and Florence one of the Trelawneys. In 1603, Charles Blount, eighth Baron Mountjoy, was created Earl of Devon, and dying without issue, left the earldom extinct for the sixth time. It has only recently been restored. Sir William Courtenay, of Powderham, was created a baronet before the Restoration, but never assumed the title. His immediate ancestor was said to be Sir Philip Courtenay, sixth son of Hugh, second Earl of Devonshire. Sir William, the third baronet, was, in 1762, created Viscount Courtenay, of Powderham. In 1831, the late Viscount succeeded in establishing his claim to the earldom, by the decision of the House of Lords, as heir of Edward, who was created Earl of Devon in 1553. He died in 1835, and was succeeded by his nephew, the present Earl and Viscount, who is the eldest son of the late Bishop Courtenay. He was born in 1777. [See Cleaveland's '*History of the Courtenay family.*'] The ARMS of Courtenay, Earl of Devonshire, are:—*Or*, three torteauxes with a label of three. CREST: a plume of feathers, *argent*, one, two, and three, issuing from a ducal coronet. The ARMS of Viscount Courtenay are:—Quarterly 1 and 4, *or*, three torteauxes, 2 and 3, *or*, a lion rampant, *azure*. CREST: a dolphin naiant, *argent*. SUPPORTERS: two boars, *argent*, bristled, tusked, and hoofed, *or*.

[1] Cart. Rot. 9 John. No. 67.

[2] The shambles are commodious, and stand in the centre of the town. The late Sir William Templar Pole, whose kindness and generosity were unceasingly manifested in his regard for the well-being and happiness of those around him, at one time took some pains to improve the Colyton fairs and markets, which were formerly much more considerable than they have been of late years; but without success. There was a time when Colyton could boast of a large pitched corn market, and of a good show of cattle at its fairs. But *tempora mutantur!*

COLYTON.

The immensely important proceedings in the seventeenth century, were not without their influence upon the rural town of Colyton. We have, in our ninth chapter, endeavoured to give an outline of the state of affairs in this part of the country during the wars between Charles and his Parliament. The result of an attack upon the garrison of Lyme, by one of the royal regiments, in July, 1644, is related at page 327. That regiment was commanded by Lord Henry Percy. Early in the preceding March, a similar event had taken place. A party of the King's forces had been successful in a surprise of Captain Weare and his troops, in a sally which they had made from Lyme, and a great many prisoners were carried for security to the royal quarters, at Colyton. But during the night, while in the midst of celebrating their triumph, the parliamentary leader, Captain Pyne, unexpectedly appeared with a gallant band. He overpowered the revellers, almost without resistance, rescued his own men, and retaliated by taking prisoners more than sixty of the royal troops, including their Colonel and several of the officers. The effect of this decided triumph was sought to be counteracted by the sending of a strong body of troops from Prince Maurice's division at Beaminster. They accordingly fixed their head quarters at Colcombe Castle.[1] On March 22nd,

---

[1] In a lovely situation among the trees upon the northern hill-side beneath which the little Shute-Brook ripples along, are the ruins of Colcombe Castle, partly converted into a modern farm-house. This

they marched to Stedcombe House, Axmouth,[1] which then belonged to Sir Walter Erle, who had garrisoned it for the Parliament. After an active assault, and a fight of three hours, they succeeded in gaining possession of the house, which was afterwards burned to the ground. Five captains, sixteen other officers, one hundred and fourteen soldiers, and *one seditious lecturer*, were made prisoners. A considerable quantity of arms and ammunition, six colors, a cannon, and two '*murtherers*,'[2] became also the prize of the conquerors.

But the royal cause gained no permanent strength at Colyton, and the majority of the townsfolks were not desirous that it should; for there existed a close

mansion was of great repute in the 'olden time.' Often have the old walls glittered with the grandeur of which they were the abode;—often have they rung with the shouts of revelry and mirth in the days of chivalry;— and once, at least, were they the scene of less agreeable proceedings, when the cannon balls, which are now kept as curiosities at the farm, were discharged from the opposite height by the troops of Cromwell. Hugh Lord Courtenay built the first mansion at Colcombe, in the reign of Edward I, about the year 1280. He made it his residence, and it continued to be the residence of his posterity till the attainder of Henry Courtenay, Marquis of Exeter, in 1538. It was intended by that nobleman to have been rebuilt in a style of great magnificence. He left it unfinished, and after a time it fell to ruins. It was purchased by Sir William Pole, the celebrated historian, who rebuilt it about the year 1600, and resided in it till his death, in 1635. His posterity adopted the neighbouring residence of Shute, and Colcombe fell into decay. A small park was attached to the mansion, and there is now a very interesting relic, a few hundred yards north of the ruins, in a pleasant field, of a well, under a beautiful recess with a Tudor arch.

[1] See our account of Axmouth.

[2] A certain kind of artillery.

political sympathy between them and the inhabitants of Lyme, who were so conspicuous on the side of the Parliament.[1] This congeniality of sentiment also accounts for the enthusiasm of the people of Colyton in the cause of Monmouth, and for so many of them flocking to his standard immediately on his landing at Lyme.[2] Of· these conscientious, but perhaps misguided men, some fell upon the field of Sedgemoor, and others, by far less fortunate, were reserved for a more cruel fate at the hands of Jefferys. We are indebted to Mr. W. H. Rogers for the following painfully interesting account of some of the terrible proceedings at Colyton at this awful period. Mr. Rogers has manifested great industry and care in the obtaining of his information. His chief informant was a gentleman of Colyton, far advanced in life, whose great-grandmother was living at the time, and whose very aged grandmother used often to relate the particulars :—

'In an old house that used to stand in the front street of Colyton (recently burnt down)—an ancient building, having a double gable in front, and familiarly known by the name of " the Bird-cage," there lived a man, in the time of the rebellion, named Clapp, a

[1] Monmouth, when on his famous 'progress' throughout the West of England, in 1680, had visited Colyton, and was hospitably entertained at 'the Great House,' by its owner, Sir Walter Yonge.

[2] Murch's *History of the Presbyterian Churches in the West of England.*

partisan of Monmouth. After the Duke's defeat at
Sedgemoor, the soldiers in the service of James II,
came to Colyton, as they did to other towns, in search
of such as had been favorable to Monmouth's cause.
They searched this house, and Clapp was in bed at
the time of their arrival. Hearing their approach he
had barely time to escape through a trap door into
the roof. This trap door was in the ceiling of the
passage leading to his bed room. The soldiers entered
the room, and remarked that he could not be gone
far as the bed was warm. They did not notice the
trap door in the passage, and he most fortunately
escaped. The bed, an antique piece of furniture,
is in the possession of a gentleman residing in the
neighbourhood. Another man, residing at the lower
end of the town, now known as 'Bull's Court,' was
surprised in the midst of his family, and had just
time to run into his garden and throw himself down
among some cabbages, when the soldiers entered his
house. They inquired of his children where he was,
and they innocently told them. Having found him
they took him out before his own door, and executed
him on the spot. They then quartered him, and
drove off one of the quarters in a wheelbarrow.[1]
Upon a little rising ground in the centre of the town,
now known as the Dolphin Hill, there lived, just on
the brow, a shoemaker, himself implicated, and being

---

[1] This was rather sharp practice, and may very probably be an
exaggeration.

fearful of his own fate, called out to the soldiers as they passed, "ah! you have caught one of the rascals," or words to that effect. They immediately ordered him out, and compelled him to drive the portion of his unfortunate neighbour round the town himself, as a warning to others. A third, living at the higher Paper Mill (since pulled down), hid himself under the water wheel. The soldiers searched the premises, but did not find him. However, in passing out, one of the soldiers noticed something white floating under the wheel, and thus discovered the poor fellow, his shirt sleeve having attracted their observation.

'Two others were more fortunate. On Chantry Bridge two dragoons were stationed to prevent any suspected person from leaving the town. A man went over the bridge—a "delinquent,"—although not known to the soldiers as such, and having made some common observation, passed on. His anxiety, however, was so great, that as soon as he had passed them, he ran off as fast as he could. The dragoons instantly gave chase, striking at him with their swords, just as he jumped over a gate and escaped. The other was chased round the back street, and he hid himself under some straw in a narrow court, where some persons were thatching. The dragoon repeatedly thrust his sword down through the straw, and once it passed completely through the man's thigh. The dragoon, however, did not discover him, and he also escaped. A man named Speed, who carried on the wool trade at the lower end of the town, is said to have been boiled in his own furnace. This, however, may not be correct. In the "*Western Martyrology, or Bloody Assizes*," mention is made of Joseph Speed and George Steward, who were tried at Dorchester and executed September 7, 1685. Two men, named John Sprague and William Clegg, were tried at Exeter and executed at Colyton, They were attended to the place of execution by the vicar, who prayed with them. They made a long speech, which is given in the before-named work. A place called "The Elms," is supposed to be the spot where they suffered. It is now occupied as a shrubbery, in the possession of Captain Powell. An old inhabitant, recently dead, recollected when the elm trees were standing there. Some large iron staples were affixed to them, which she was told were put there for the purpose of executions. Richard Hall and John Savage, two other inhabitants of Colyton, were executed at Sherborne; and a Mr. Roger Satchell, a very active partisan, for whom great application was made to Jeffreys to save his life, but without avail, suffered at Weymouth.'

Colyton church (St. Andrew) is a large, and, in some respects, an interesting structure, standing in the centre of the town. It measures 113 feet by 61 feet. A considerable part of it is comparatively modern, bearing evidence of the decline of architecture since the Reformation. The chancel is very beautiful, and the same may be said of the somewhat peculiarly

formed tower. The church was once furnished with
transepts, which were absorbed into the body of the
church when the aisles were added to the nave. Other
alterations and additions have completely changed the
original character of the edifice.[1] The chancel has
also aisles. That on the north, once the burying-
place of the Yonge family, was no doubt a chapel,
for the piscina still remains there. It has for some
time been used as the parish vestry, and not long
since, during a crowded meeting, the floor gave way
and sent a few of the weightiest of the parishioners
into the vault beneath. This vault was afterwards
filled up, as the family is now extinct. Mr. Rogers,
feeling anxious that all traces of a once influential
family should not be lost, removed the brasses from
some of the lead coffins, and, after carefully cleaning
them, attached them to the wall, where it is hoped
they will long be permitted to remain. They record
the deaths of Dame Gwen Yonge, November 11,
1729, aged 65; The Right Honorable Sir William
Yonge, K.B. and Baronet, August 9, 1755; The
Honorable Ann Lady Yonge, September 1, 1775,
aged 62; and Sir John Yonge, Bart., K.B., died at
Hampton Court, September 26, 1812, aged 80 years.[2]

---

[1] The south aisle was rebuilt in 1769, and the north aisle considerably
enlarged in 1818.

[2] The Yonge family were of great respectability and influence, in this
locality. Their principal residence was at Colyton, but they had also a
mansion at Axminster, as stated at page 349. The 'Great House,' as
what remains of their residence at Colyton is still called, has long been

The south aisle of the chancel is appropriated as a mausoleum for the Pole family. It is enclosed by an elaborate screen, erected by Canon Brerwode, whose initials it bears, and who was vicar of the parish from 1524 to 1554. The monuments are very imposing, and record the deaths of William Pole, Esq., August 15, 1587, aged 'LXXII yeares and vj dayes;' Katherine, his wife, daughter of Alexander Popham, of Huntworthy, Somerset, Esq., October 28, 1588; Mary, 'late the wife of Sir William Pole, of Shote,

---

inhabited as a farm-house. It became the property of the Poles, of Shute, in 1790, in exchange with Sir George Yonge for lands at Tallaton. It is an interesting old building, built of flint. In one of the bedrooms is a quantity of wainscot, with Corinthian pilasters; and in the garden is a curious old summer-house. The Yonges sprang from Berkshire, and one of their ancestors represented Bristol in Parliament, in the thirteenth century. They settled in Devonshire in the reign of Henry VII. Sir John Yonge, knight, was created a baronet in 1661. He had been knighted in 1625, and was member for Plymouth in 1640. His father, Walter Yonge, Esq., a rigid puritan, was the first member for Honiton, with Sir William Pole, after the privilege of being represented in Parliament had been restored to that borough, in 1640. Walter Yonge was the author of a curious diary, discovered accidently, in MS., a few years ago, by Mr. Roberts, and published by the Camden Society. The last two baronets, Sir William and Sir George, were both members of the Privy Council, Knights of the Bath, and held the office of Secretary at War. Sir William had also been one of the Lords of the Treasury, and one of the Lords of the Admiralty. Sir George, the fifth and last baronet, was M.P. for Honiton from 1754 to 1796. He held several high offices in the state, and, in 1799, was appointed Governor of the Cape of Good Hope. Some 'defalcation' there resulted in his disgrace, and his princely fortune became absorbed by electioneering expences, and the 'honors' of a borough. He died in poverty at Hampton Court. The ARMS of Yonge were:—*Ermine*, on a bend between two cottises, *sable*, three griffins' heads erased, *or*. CREST:—on a wreath, *argent* and *sable*, a boar's head erased, bristled, *or*, mantled, *gules*, doubled, *argent*.

Kng., beinge ye eldest daughter and one of the foore
heires of Sir W. Periham, of Folford, Kng., Lo.
Chief Barron, of ye King Majesties Exchequer,' she
had 'three sones at one birth, and perished by an
unfortunate fall,' May 2, 1605; and Sir William Pole,
Bart., Master of the Household to Queen Anne,
December 31, 1741.[1]

The arches which divide the chancel from its aisles,

[1] See page 417. Among the other monuments in different parts of
the church, are the following:—In the chancel, transepts, &c.:—a recum-
bent effigy of a girl, wearing a coronet, and with a dog at her feet, under
a canopy of stall work, with this inscription:—' Margaret, daughter of
William Courtenay, Earl of Devon, and the princess Katherine, youngest
daughter of Edward IV, king of England, died at Colcombe, choked by
a fish-bone, A.D., MDXII, and was buried under the window in the
north transept of this church.' William Westofer, [of Yardbury—see
page 427], 1622. William Drake, of Yardbury, buried in the Temple
Church, London, died March 6, 1680, aged 51; and three of his children.
Elizabeth, wife of John Pole, Baronet, April 16, 1628. An inscription on
the pavement marks the burying-place of Sir William Pole, of Colcombe,
the historian of Devon. Rev. George Rhodes, late vicar of Colyton,
March 15, 1798. Captain Piper, 6th regiment foot, July 17, 1801. Captain John Batut, 14th regiment foot, January 2, 1788. Mrs. Elizabeth
Bours, of Newport, Rhode Island, North America—'eminent for her
goodness and misfortunes,' February 27, 1806. In the north aisle are
several tablets to members of the Sampsons, a family who have been in
possession of the Grove House, Colyton, for upwards of two centuries.
John Sampson, Esq., is its representative. The arms of Sampson are:—
argent, a cross moline, azure. In the same aisle is a curious old brass
with this inscription, in black letter:—'Here lieth John Strobryg, the
elder, late of the pisch of Collyto., mchand, which John decessyd the xj
day off September, in the yere off owr Lord God, A thousand, cccccc,
xvj, on whois soule jhu have mercy. Amen.' [He was the donor of some
lands to the poor of the parish.] ' Capt. Henry Wilson,' who commanded
the Hon. East India Company's Packet, the Antelope, when wrecked on
the Pelew Islands, in August, 1783, 'died May 11, 1810, aged 70 years.'
There are many other inscriptions upon tablets, and on the floor.

and from the portion of the nave-aisle which once
formed the transepts, are very beautiful, springing
from moulded piers, with capitals ornamented with
foliage, like those in the chancel of Shute church.
The chancel windows are very beautiful specimens of
the Perpendicular style, with the exception of the
central eastern window, which is of five lancet lights,
the mullions intersecting each other in the head.
This window has evidently had its share of alteration
at different times; but it not improbably still retains
the characteristic features of its original design, which
is that of the Early Decorated style, in the first half
of the thirteenth century. It contains some beautiful stained glass, exhibiting the arms of Courtenay,
Strode, Yonge, and other families, with the cross in
the centre, and other subjects, and an inscription at
the bottom to the effect that the restoration of the
window was the gift of the vicar, the Rev. Dr. Barns,
in 1829. The architecture of the chancel, as well as
that of the tower, is Early Perpendicular, and may
therefore be assigned to the fourteenth century. [1]

[1] In the year 1383, when Hugh Bridham, Archdeacon of Totnes and
Canon of Exeter Cathedral, held the vicarage of Colyton, the living was
sequestered by Bishop Brantyngham, on account of the dilapidated state
into which the chancel had been allowed to fall—the vicar alleging, in his
defence, the serious drain upon his income which his annual payment of
£10 to the Dean and Chapter of Exeter occasioned. As the sequestration
was withdrawn soon afterwards, we may reasonably conclude that the
repairs had been effected to the bishop's satisfaction, and it is not improbable, therefore, that on this occasion the greater part of the present
chancel was erected. See Dr. Oliver's '*Ecclesiastical Antiquities.*'

The nave exhibits a striking contrast to the beauty of the chancel. It is sufficiently lofty and spacious; but its details strike the most indifferent observer with a sense of their inferiority. Windows with plain sexagonal figures in the head, and flimsy piers supporting *circular* arches, are sufficient to mark the style of architecture (if *style* it can be called) which succeeded, in *enlightened* times, the magnificent productions of our forefathers, who,—poor miserable souls!—were content to grovel out their lives in the ages which we so complacently denominate ' dark.' The western window, however, no doubt the work of the fifteenth century, is striking, from its immense size. It is thirty feet high and twenty feet broad, and consists of nine lights, divided by transoms into two stages, with tracery in the heading, above. It was formerly much more elaborate than now—most of the featherings and other ornaments having been destroyed. A door in the centre of the lower part of this window forms the western entrance to the church. There is another entrance through a porch on the south side, and a third entrance through a small doorway in the chancel. The porch has a parvise[1] which now forms the entrance to the gallery in the south aisle from without. A gallery also runs along the opposite aisle. The pulpit and reading-desk are placed at the western end of the nave.[2] The

---

[1] See page 140.

[2] The reading desk in churches is an innovation upon the ancient

tower rises from the centre of the building to the
height of ninety-five feet, and is supported by massive piers and arches. It consists of two parts—the
lower part square, with battlements and angular
pinnacles, and the upper part octangular, with battlements also, and surmounted by a well-planted
weathercock. The upper part is lighted by a window
of two lights in each of its eight sides, and it is supported by flying buttresses.[1] It contains six bells,
which have long been famous for their quality of tone
and for the style in which they are generally rung.[2]

usages which date from the reign of Queen Elizabeth. But it had not
the semblance of sanction till 1603, when it was ordered by a canon that
'a convenient seat shall be made for the minister to read service.' The
choir was anciently regarded as the only proper place at which the service should be read, and a lectern, often made of brass, and exquisitely
designed, was used for resting the books upon. There is still a lectern in
the neighbouring church of Yeovil. Sermons, too, in early times, were
delivered from the steps of the altar—the pulpit itself having been
introduced in the fourteenth century. But in the middle ages, preaching
was not regarded as an indispensable part of the service. In time, however, as it became more in vogue, pulpits were often erected outside the
building. The famous St. Paul's Cross is a familiar example. The general adoption of preaching as a liturgical act, was the effect of the spread
of Lollardism, which it was thus endeavoured to combat by its own
weapons.—See the '*Handbook of English Ecclesiology.*'

[1] See page 54. The opinion that this very handsome tower is a mere
piecemeal structure, erected at two different times, would seem hardly to
be borne out by a careful inspection of the masonry in the interior.

[2] The inscriptions on the bells are as follow:—1.—'This bell was put
up at the expense of the parish, anno domini 1772. William Hatherly,
vicar; Thos. Bilbie, fecit.' 2.—'When I call, follow me all. John Abbet,
J. P., 1667.' 3.—'O Lord, how glorious are thy works, Ao. Di., 1611.'
4.—'William Drake, gentleman, churchwarden, J. P., 1667.' 5.—'Mr.
William Uicary and Mr. James West, churchwardens; Thomas Bilbie,

The under part of the tower contains a clock with two dials.

The parish registers, which have been admirably kept, commence with the year 1538. [1]

The living of Colyton is a vicarage in the patronage of the Dean and Chapter of Exeter, who are the appropriators of the great tithes, commuted for £584 10s. The vicarage is valued in the King's Books at £40 10s. 10d., and the tithes are commuted for £372. The Rev. Frederick Barns, Canon of Christ Church, Oxford, has held the living since March 3, 1807.

---

fecit, 1775.' 6.—'Thomas Mears, Whitechapel foundry, London. Sum vitæ, mortis, temporis, atque tuba. A. D. 1711. Recast A. D. 1837. F. Barns, D.D., vicar; Charles Northam, James Loveridge, church-wardens.'

[1] They are headed as follows:—'The Booke of Mariadges (Christen-inge, Buryalls) take his begynnynge the XVIIJ daye of October, in the yere of our Lorde God 1538. Given and commanded by the injunctions of our moste soureinge Lorde, Kynge Henry the Eyght, and in the thirtye yere of his most noble raygne.' Under the date 1654, during the Com-monwealth, when matrimony was regarded simply as a civil contract, and not a religious ceremony, is the following entry:—'John Gerard was married to Ann Bagwell the 19th September, 1654, by Thomas Drake, Esq., one of the justices of the Peace for the County of Devon, accord-ing to an late act of Parliament, in the presence of Tho. Drake, Edward Washer, Bernhard Pinhay, Peter Bagwell.' A still more curious entry occurs under the date 1660, more than a century after the Reformation:—'It having been certified by two approved physicians of the necessity of Sir John Yonge eating flesh, upon which, having granted him a former license (so farre as in mee was) the same distemper again continuing (as is certifyed by one of the said physicians) his need of flesh being ye same, I do, as much as in mee is, give ye said Sir John Yonge license to eat flesh, having ye said necessity. In witness whereof I have subscribed my name this eighth day of March, 1660. John Wilkins, vic., in the pre-sence of John Whicken, one of the churchwardens.'

The vicarage house stands on the south side of the churchyard. It was built during the first half of the sixteenth century by Dr. Brerwood, the vicar, whose taste and liberality were so strikingly displayed in the erection of the screen which encloses the burying-place of the Poles, in the parish church. Repairs have greatly changed the appearance of a building which Leland designated a ' fair house.' The front gable, however, underneath which is the principal entrance, under a Tudor arch, remains unaltered. Underneath the battlement is an inscription, in old English letters, as follows:—' *Meditatio totum; Peditatio totum*,' which, being freely interpreted, may signify that as meditation is of the first importance to the mind, so walking is of the first importance to the body—a proposition to which every angler will very heartily assent. The date MCCCCCXXIX is also given, together with the initials ' T. B.' and the arms of Bishop Veysey.

There were several ecclesiastical establishments connected with Colyton before the Reformation. We have already alluded to the chapel at Whitford. In the year 1348, Hugh Courtenay, second Earl of Devon, converted the ancient domestic chapel at Colcombe Castle into a chantry, which he endowed with seventy-eight acres and three quarters of land,[1] and furnished with the church plate, vestments, and other necessary articles. It was dedicated to St. John

---

[1] Bishop Grandisson's ' *Register.*'

the Evangelist. At the suppression of chantries, in 1547, it was valued at £6 13*s.* 4*d.*, and Walter Este, its last incumbent, was living, in 1533, on a pension of £6 per annum.[1] The chantry estate was purchased of the crown by Walter Erle, Esq., whose descendant, Sir Walter Erle, sold it, about the middle of the sixteenth century, to the Sampsons, of Colyton. There was also a chapel in Colyton parish dedicated to St. Kalixtus, with a chamber for a recluse adjoining it.[2] At Sparkhayne, the seat of the Bittelisgates, a chapel was licensed by Bishop Brantyngham, on October 16, 1381—probably for domestic uses only. The mansions at Leigh and Gatcombe were also provided with chapels; and at Colyford, near the bridge,[3] was the chantry of St Edmund, the foundations of which are said by Mr. Stirling to have been discovered, a few years ago, in a field belonging to Captain Powell, of Colyton.[4] Its last incumbent, Peter Honeywood, enjoyed a pension of £6 a year, and was living in 1553.

[1] Dr. Oliver.

[2] Bishop Grandisson's '*Register*' (A.D. 1332). Vol. 2., fo. 151. Dr. Oliver asks, 'Can this have been "apud Kalestynesdoune," or "Almunt Seynt Kalyst," mentioned in the Newenham Register [See page 319]? In the charter of King Henry VIII, dated June 6, 1546, to the parish feoffees, express mention is made of "our chapel called Calesdoun chapel, alias Calesdown chapel, with other appurtenances situate and being within the parish of Colyton." '

[3] The bridge at Colyford, over the Coly, is of stone and has been erected within the last ten years. Upon the bridge which preceded it was carved the date 1681.

[4] Stirling's '*Beauties of the Shore,*' page 70.

The Unitarians, Independents, and Methodists have their respective places of worship in the town. [1]

Colyton is rich in parochial charities. Most of what are called the Parish Lands formed part of the forfeited estates of Henry Courtenay, Marquis of Exeter,[2] and were granted 'by letters patent bearing date January 6, 1546, in the thirty-eighth year of the reign of King Henry VIII,' in consideration of the sum of £1000 paid, principally, by the family of Strowbridge. They are vested in a corporation composed of twelve feoffees and twenty freeholders, called 'the twenty-men of Colyton,'—who are nominated by the majority of the parishioners. The property consists of the farm of Lovehayne and Buddleshayes, comprising 229A. 2R. 13P., houses and lands at Colyford, Ottery Saint Mary, and Alphington, sixteen acres of land at Hampton, in the parish of Shute, the profits of the markets and fairs, and other property, producing, in the aggregate, an annual income of £221 10s. 10d. Out of this sum are

[1] John Wilkins, vicar of the parish during the commonwealth, not taking the oaths of supremacy at the Restoration, was ejected from the living and became minister of the Presbyterian congregation which then assembled in what is now the Unitarian chapel. He died on October 9, 1667, and was buried in the vestry which he had built in the south aisle of the church.

[2] It will be seen that this property was not included in the estates which were restored to the Courtenays, along with their title, in the reign of Queen Mary. This restoration did not, of course, extend to such of the forfeited property as had been sold while in the possession of the crown. See page 428.

defrayed all the expenses of the town water, including a small salary, the repairs of the market-house,
and a salary of £30 a year to the master of the
free school for the instruction of twenty boys in
reading, writing, and arithmetic—the master of which
is provided with a dwelling-house erected in 1612.
The remainder of the income is distributed among
the poor who are not in the constant receipt of parochial relief.   The other charities are:—an annual
distribution of bread to the amount of £3, arising
from a rent-charge upon Rowlandsham farm, bequeathed by Thomas Holmes, in 1670; the dividend
of £100, three per cent. stocks, left by Isaac Grigg,
in 1812, and distributed in bread; and the dividend
of £200 stock in the five per cents. to the Colyton
Sunday schools, given by the Rev. James How. [1]

[1] '*Report of the Commissioners of Public Charities in Devonshire.*'

CHAPTER XII.

Two miles to the south of Colyton, and seven miles from Axminster, is the united parish of Seaton and Beer, which abuts upon the English channel and lies upon the western side of the Axe. It comprises 2766A. 2R. 5P., and a population of 2047, according to the census of 1851. Seaton, the principal place in the parish, is delightfully situated on the shore, between the cliffs of Beer on the west, and those of Axmouth, at the distance of rather more than a mile, on the east. [1]

The town has no pretensions to elegance or size, but it has, within a few years, become much more resorted to than formerly by summer visitors, as a bathing-place; and some handsome shops and newly built villas are the result. If the beauties of the neighbourhood and the salubrity of its air were more

---

[1] The views from these eminences are of a magnificent description—including, seaward, the extensive and romantic line of coast from Portland to Startpoint, and, inland, the lower part of the valley of the Axe, with a vast extent of country, in different directions, beyond it.

generally known, there can be little doubt that it
would soon arrive at considerable importance in this
respect—'provided always' that it became accessible
by railway, a circumstance, it would seem, almost
beyond hoping for.   The village—we beg pardon,
town,—consists of two principal streets—very clean
and cheerful—running nearly north and south, almost
parallel with each other, and meeting near the beach.
Many of the lodging houses are pleasantly situated
and well fitted up; and there is an establishment at
which hot and cold baths may be obtained at all seasons.[1]   The beach is hardly equalled by any other
beach upon this far-famed and delightful coast, and
within a few years it has been greatly improved by
the formation of a walk which extends from the
town nearly to Axmouth harbour at the mouth of

[1]   There was formerly a Billiard Room upon a mound upon the beach,
called the Barrow. This Barrow was the remains of some fortifications
which were commenced at Seaton in 1627, 'for the defence of the place
against pirates and other enemies,' there being 'a difference between this
state and France.' Sir Walter Yonge, from whose 'Diary' [see page
437] we make these extracts, says:—'There were, by consent of Sir
Edmund Prideaux, baronet, Sir William Pole, Mr. John Drake, Mr. Fry,
and myself, [Mr. Yonge] warrants granted out for assistance in the said
fortification: viz. the first week Colyton hundred to send 30 men for every
day; the next week Axminster hundred were to send 30 men for every
day; the third week Hemyock hundred 20 men for every day; the fourth
week Halberton hundred were to send 20 men for every day; and the
fifth week Bampton hundred to send 20 men for every day; but for those
which would not or could not come conveniently, being far distant, that
they send after the rate of 8d. for every man per diem; and we of these
parts would procure men in their places.' Mr. Roberts, in a note on this
passage, says that the cost of the 'Barrow' was £24.

the Axe. But it is a place of very little trade. Considerable quantities of fish, however, are caught there, and coal and culm are imported; but for want of a harbour the vessels are obliged to be anchored off the shore, and to discharge their cargoes in barges. This was not the case in ancient times, when Seaton could boast of a 'very notable haven.'[1] Leland, writing three centuries ago, describes his visit to the town as follows:—'From Colington to Seton, now a mene fisschar toun, scant two mile. I passed over Cole water again at Coliford, or I cam to Seton. Ther hath beene a very notable haven at Seton; but now ther lyith between the two pointes of the old haven a mighty rigge and barre of pible stones in the very mouth of it; and the river Ax is dryven to the very est point of the haven, caullid Whitclif, and ther, at a very smaul gut, goith into the se; and ther cum in smaul fisschar boates for soccur. The toun of Seton is now but a mene thing, inhabited with fisschar men. *It hath been far larger when the haven was good.* The abbate of Shirburne was lord and patron of it . . . . The men of Seton began of late dayes to stake and to make a mayne waulle withyn the haven, to have diverted the course of the Ax ryver, and ther, almost

---

[1] In 1346, Seaton furnished two ships and twenty-five men as its quota towards the expedition against Calais. About seventy years previously it had received the grant, from Edward I, of a market and fair. All traces of a market have long since been lost, but there is still a fair—if fair it can be called, at which the chief attraction is a row in a pleasure boat—held annually on Whitsun Tuesday.

in the middle of the old haven, to have trenchid through the chisille, and to have let out Ax and receyvid in the mayn se.   But this purpose cam not to effect.   Me thought that nature most wrought to trench the chisille hard by Seton toun, and ther to let in the se.'[1]   Risdon says of Seaton that 'it is memorable for the Danish princes' landing there in 937, as also for the attempt of the inhabitants of Colliton to make an haven there, which they had solemnly named Colliton Haven, and procured a collection, under the great seal of England, for the levying of money to effect the same; of which work there remaineth no monument—only a remembrance of such a place among strangers that know not where it stands, and is at this day [1630] a poor fishing village.'[2] The money collected for this desirable undertaking was, as Sir William Pole informs us, 'converted to worse use.' We shall return to the subject of the harbor in our account of Axmouth.

Seaton was long supposed by antiquaries to have been the Roman station Moridunum,[3] on the Ikeneld

---

[1] Leland's 'Itinerary.' See page 118.

[2] 'Survey of Devon,' page 31. Polwhele adds to this, 'it is, however, a remarkably neat village. The houses are thatched in a style superior to that of Devonshire cottages in general; and every house has a finished air.' Polwhele seems to have paid particular attention to the 'roofing' department of his domiciliary investigations, for in speaking of Colyton and Colyford, he gravely assures us, that 'in these towns, or villages, the *neatness of the thatcher* is shown to great advantage.'

[3] 'Moridunum,' says Polwhele, is 'from *mor-y-dun—oppidum magnæ undæ sive maris*, to which the present name Seaton, exactly corresponds;'

way which led from Norfolk to the Land's End. But more modern investigators have, with far greater probability, assigned that station to Hembury Fort, near Honiton. [1]

but Mr. Davidson derives it from the Gaelic, in which it signifies 'the hill-fortress,' which is quite inapplicable to the situation of Seaton, but applies exactly to that of Hembury Fort, to which he gives the preference.

[1] Lists of all the towns and stations on every road in Roman-Britain, with the distances, were provided for the guidance of travellers and for military purposes—somewhat in the manner of the modern railway tables. In the 'Itinerary' of Antonine, which was compiled about the year 320, and of which copies have been handed down, Moridunum is placed, in the fifteenth 'Iter,' between Durnovaria (Dorchester), and Isca Dunmoniorum (Exeter)—some other stations intervening, the names of which are now lost. The distances given, are thirty-six Roman miles from Durnovaria, and fifteen from Dunmoniorum, and there are nearly similar entries in the Itinerary of Richard of Cirencester, a monk who flourished in the 14th century, and who is regarded as an authority, having, it is supposed, obtained his information from an older Itinerary or map. Now, this line of road was the Ikeneld, the main line of which, as we have shown in our Introductory Chapter, passed from Dorchester, through Bridport and Axminster, to Honiton and Exeter. A branch of it, as we have also shown, passed within a mile of Seaton, diverging from Morcombelake to connect Lyme and Colyford with Exeter—Axmouth, undoubtedly a place of importance, being also directly connected with it. The preference has been given to Hembury Fort, among other reasons, because its actual distance from the two other stations corresponds almost exactly with that laid down in the Itineraries, while that of Seaton does not;—because it was almost close to the main line of road, whereas Seaton was seven miles from it;—because other important roads led directly to it, or were connected with it by branches, one from Colyford among the number;—and because Roman remains have been discovered there. We must observe, however, that the last reason gives Hembury no advantage, because Roman coins and other remains are said, by Mr. Chapple, to have been discovered at Seaton. Among the modern writers who do not give the preference to Hembury Fort, must be mentioned the bishop of Cloyne, who contributed the valuable chapter on the British and Roman roads in Devonshire to Lysons's 'Magna Britannia.' His reasoning, however, is not so conclusive as that of Mr. Davidson, nor are his facts so striking.

We have, in our account of the famous battle of Brunenburgh, enumerated all, perhaps, that can be said about Seaton in the time of the Saxons. Let us come, therefore, at once to Domesday Book,—that ancient and invaluable record. At page 104 of the printed copy of the Exchequer Domesday, we find the manor thus surveyed :—The church of Horton [Dorsetshire] holds Bere [in which Seaton appears to have been included]. In the time of King Edward it gelded for half a hide. The arable is seven carucates. In demesne is one carucate, and two servants, and six villains, and twenty cottagers, with five ploughs. There are seven acres of meadow. Pasture one mile long and half a mile broad. It is valued at sixty shillings. From this manor the Earl of Moriton has taken one furlong of land and four salt pans (salinæ) which are held of him by Drogo.

In the reign of King Henry I, all the possessions of the church of Horton were merged into the abbey of Sherborne, and in a bull issued by Pope Eugenius III, in 1145, reciting the property of this abbey, especial mention is made of 'the fisheries and salt ponds[1] of Bere and Seton, three cart loads of hay

[1] The salt works, in Seaton marsh, all traces of which have disappeared for many years, were formerly of an extensive character, and they had been in existence, as is evident from the extracts in the text, for many centuries. We have before us a copy of a lease, dated July 2, 1709. It relates to the sale of lands in the 'large field or parcel of land or Marrish Ground commonly called Seaton Marsh,' &c., 'all which premises are therein mentioned to have been antiently the *Comon*, or waste of the said *mannor*, and to have been, sometime before that, parcelled out, taken

yearly in Bere, and the ville of Stockland, with woods, meads, and two mills.' And again, in a bull of Alexander III, in 1163, are enumerated 'Lime and Seton, with their churches, chapels, and tithes, and Bere, with its appurtenances.' [1]

After the dissolution of the monasteries, the manor was given by Henry VIII to his last wife, Catherine Parr, as a part of her dowry; and three years afterwards, in 1546, the reversion of the manor, with the rectory and church, were granted by the same monarch to John Frye, of Gray's Inn and Yarty.[2] In Sir William Pole's time [about the year 1620] Seaton

in, and enclosed . . . . . . and banked out and fenced against the overflowing of the sea and the river Axe, there neare adjoyneing, and in some measure fitted and prepared for making of Salte thereon—and also the toft of a ruined or deserted cottage, situate on the premises, commonly called Lee's Cottage, and all mounds, bends, bankes, hedges, fences, inclosures, ditches, aqueducts, canalls, gurts, [dykes, in some parts called rhines], ponds, pools, salteworkes, salterns, cisterns, boyleinghouses, saltehouses, cellers, storehouses,' &c., &c, and proceeding, with great stringency, to enforce the 'preserving of the said marsh and premises from being overwhelmed by any of the waters of the sea, or of the said river,' by the erection of 'mounds, bankes, and other necessary fences.' The marsh has long been completely drained, and is therefore in a very different condition than in former times, when the mephitic vapors continually rising from its stagnant pools and damp decaying vegetation, produced their natural effect upon the health of the inhabitants of the locality, and, in the form of what was called 'the marsh fever,' sent hundreds, every year, into untimely graves. The registers of all the neighbouring parishes furnish abundant evidence of this melancholy fact.

[1] Hutchins's 'Dorset,' Dugdale's 'Monasticon,' Dr. Oliver, &c., &c.

[2] The manor and rectory were then valued, together, at £23 2s. 0¼d., and were held 'by the service of a fortieth part of a knight's fee, [see page 92] and the yearly payment, for the manor of Seaton, of £1 12s. 2¼d., and for the rectory 14s.' Oliver's 'Monasticon.'

belonged 'unto John Willoby, Esq., by the purchase
of his grandfather from John Frye.'[1] The marriage of
the heiress of Willoughby brought it into the family
of Trevelyan. In May, 1788, Sir John Trevelyan sold
the manor, with Seaton House, one of the family seats,
to Thomas Charter, Esq., his solicitor and steward;
but, in 1826, the validity of the proceedings was called
in question, and a chancery suit ensued. A decree of
the court, in 1835, declared that the conveyance of
1788 ought to be set aside, and directed a reconvey-
ance to the executor of the vendor (then dead) of all
the lands not disposed of by the purchaser previously
to the filing of the bill in chancery. This decision
was confirmed on September 5, 1844, on an appeal
to the House of Lords, and the present Lord of the
manor is Sir Walter Calverley Trevelyan, Bart., of
Nettlecombe, Somerset, and Wallington, Northum-
berland.

In a sequestered spot near the northern entrance to
the town, stands the ancient parish church. With
no pretensions to beauty of detail or to harmony of
design, it is still not without its attractions to the
student of ecclesiastical antiquities. The obvious
effect of subsequent reparations in every conceivable
style, is that of rendering it somewhat difficult to
fix the date of its erection, and quite impossible to
judge of its original size and character. The beautiful work of the early part of the thirteenth century,

[1] Sir W. Pole's ' Collections,' page 140.

is, however, unmistakably manifest in the chancel, which, almost as a matter of course, is the oldest part of the church.[1] It is manifest, also, in the eastern extremity of the south aisle. These, in all probability, are the only parts which remain of the original building. The north aisle was enlarged in 1817 by the late Lord Rolle, for the accommodation of his tenantry at Beer. The rest of the building, including the tower at the west end,[2] appears to have been erected about the middle of the fourteenth century, exhibiting, as it does, the prevailing characteristics of late Decorated work—or rather those of the transition from Decorated to Perpendicular. A gallery deforms the western end of the church, and the arches of the nave have been considerably *cut away* to make room for it. Some members of the ancient family of Walrond are buried in the church, and there are also tablets and inscriptions to the memory of several other persons.[3]

---

[1] See note at page 143. See also page 39. Two hagioscopes [See page 223] at the eastern end of the church will attract the visitor's attention, as will also a piscina, in its usual situation in the wall, on the south side of the altar. See page 52.

[2] The tower contains four bells, upon one of which is the inscription:—'Joseph Poope and Ellis Carter, Chvrch-vardens, Exon, 1663.' The tower is embattled, is supported by buttresses, and has a stair-turret. It is not lofty, but commands from its summit a magnificent view of the valley and the bay.

[3] See our account of Beer. The principal inscriptions refer to the following persons:—In the north aisle, 'Edmund Walrond, of Bowe [Bovey] Esq.,' buried September 19th, 1640, aged 48 years, with an epitaph 'composed and set vp by Anne Walrond, his wife,' thus:—

The church is dedicated to St. Gregory. The living is a vicarage, valued in the King's Books at £17 0s. 7½d. It has been held by the Rev. C. J. Glascott since January 30, 1837. The great tithes belong to the trustees of the late Lord Rolle, the patrons of the living. The vicarage house and schools are situated almost close to the church. The great tithes are commuted for £300 per annum, and the vicarial tithes for £260 15s. There are rather more than fourteen acres of glebe land. The Independents

> 'Here lyeth the body of my Hvsband Deare,
> Whom next to God I did both love and feare;
> Our Loves were single—we never had bvt on,
> And so I'll be, althovgh that thov art gone.
> And you that shall this sad inscription view,
> Remember it alwaies that Death's yovr dve.'

William Walrond, Esq., died at Bovey, in 1762, aged 45 years. His wife and infant son. Also, Sarah Oke, his second wife, 'by whom he had issue Sarah, Courtenay, William, and Judith Maria.' Of these the last married John Rolle, Esq., afterwards Lord Rolle. [See our account of Beer.] NORTH AISLE, 'William Henry Paulson, midshipman of H.M.S. Queen Charlotte, who, with eight seamen, all volunteers, perished in a gale of wind, off Sidmouth, whilst cruising in a galley for the prevention of smuggling,' June 13, 1817. IN THE CHANCEL:—Abraham Sydenham, of this parish, salt officer for forty years, died November 12, 1748, aged 69 years; Sarah his wife, November 15, 1748. The Rev. Robert Cutcliffe, vicar of Seaton and Beer for fifty years, died January 12, 1838, aged 77 years. Elizabeth, his widow, March 21, 1852, aged 88 years; and their two children. NAVE AND SOUTH AISLE, WALLS AND FLOOR:—John Starr, the elder [date obliterated]. Several other members of the Starr family, with the dates 1633, 1651, 1658, 1670, and 1687. [See our account of Beer.] William Head died March 25, 1833; and Henrietta his relict, June 21, 1847. Captain Timothy Head, February 19, 1806, aged 26 years. [This gentleman lost his life by a fall from one of the cliffs.] William Henry Baptist Proby, commander in the navy, eldest son of the Rev. B. J. Proby, vicar of Saint Mary's, Litchfield, died November 26, 1839.

have a Chapel at Seaton which was erected in 1822, and there is also a congregation of Wesleyans.

*   *   *   *   *   *   *

Deep in a little winding combe, among the cliffs which rear aloft their protecting heads, in beautiful undulations, and against the craggy sides of which the rude ocean beats incessantly in vain, is seated the picturesque and ancient village of Beer. It is at the distance of about a mile west from Seaton, and the walk over the cliffs from one place to the other is a treat to the lover of nature and of extensive and delightful prospects. The stranger on entering Beer will be immediately struck with its seclusion and peculiarities. The streets, the houses, the pigs—nay, the very children (and their name is Legion)—have a singularly antiquated air; and there is a half-*foreign* kind of character in the place, which may be the effect of the extensive continental intercourse, for the purpose of trade *of a peculiar kind,* for which the *natives* were, in days of yore, distinguished. The inhabitants moreover, consist of a large proportion of women and children; for it is the habit of the sturdy sons of Beer to eschew the comforts and delights of their native dell, and the 'even tenor' of a landsman's calling, for

'A life on the ocean wave,
And a home on the rolling deep.'

The chief employment of the females is that of making the celebrated Honiton lace, which is done by hand and calls for a considerable amount of dexterity

and of taste.   The Beer women are among the best
of the great number of workers employed in different
villages, and they had the honor of working the
greater part of her present Majesty's bridal dress.
The few males whom one meets in a saunter through
the streets, if not veritable sons of Neptune, at least
possess *some* of their characteristics, and strike one as
belonging to a half-sailor, half-agricultural class—
amphibious mortals, rejoicing equally in the sea and
the dry land. [1]   Beer is, in truth, a remarkable and,
in many respects, an interesting little place.   Its
principal street is long and tolerably broad, and a copious stream of water, for the introduction of which
the inhabitants are indebted to the late Lady Rolle,
flows through it—throwing itself in a respectable
cascade over a rock near the beach,—carrying away
the fishy superfluities which, as it is, appeal forcibly
to the olfactories of the sensitive,—and imparting an

[1]   The Beer men have long been celebrated as some of the boldest and
most expert sailors in the kingdom.   Schooled in their 'trawlers,' which
bid defiance to almost any storm, they become familiar, from their earliest
years, with all the arts of seamanship, and with 'the dangers of the deep.'
Among the brave and gallant fellows who compose 'Britannia's bulwarks,'
none are braver or better than they.   In former times, when the coast-
guard was inefficient and the exciseman lax, the Beer men were the very
kings of smugglers.   Jack Rattenbury, the 'Rob Roy of the West,'—
whose daring deeds have formed a volume which has left nine-tenths of
them untold—was a native of this village.   The old men tell a thousand
stories of the bravery, the daring, and the almost chivalric honor of this
impetuous spirit; and hair-breadth 'scapes,' and adventures of the
most thrilling and romantic kind, will also be related to you, reader, at
any time, if you desire it, in which a score of other 'heroes,' figure hardly
less heroically than the famous 'Jack.'

agreeable coolness to the atmosphere when the summer's sun pours its fervent beams into the hill-surrounded streets. The population of the tithing of Beer is more than double that of Seaton, being upwards of 1400. Most of the houses are built of freestone from the famous quarry which has supplied the materials for many of the public buildings in the West of England, including most of the old work in the interior of Exeter cathedral.[1]

In our account of Seaton we have translated the passage in Domesday Book which refers to the united parish. The manor of Beer, as distinct from that of Seaton, after having formed a part of the dowry of Catherine Parr, was bought by the family of Hassard,

[1] This quarry, which is of a very remarkable and very interesting character, is situated among the cliffs, at the distance of about a mile west from Beer. It is subterraneous, and extends about 180 yards into the rocky hill in which it is formed. The *roof* is supported by large blocks of the rock, left standing here and there, as the excavations have proceeded. The quarry has been worked for ages, and it ramifies into numerous avenues and passages, into which it is extremely dangerous to venture without experienced guides and abundant torch-light. A party once visited the quarry without a guide and during the absence of the workmen. Their candles became extinguished, and they had to pay for their indiscretion by remaining prisoners for a whole night. Very fortunate were they, indeed, to escape so easily, for there are deep pools of water in various parts of the quarry, and old abandoned 'workings,' in which the foot of man has not trodden for ages. The stone is nearly white, and is composed chiefly of carbonate of lime, with the addition of some argillaceous and siliceous matter, and a few scattered particles of green silicate of iron. It is soft, and easily worked when first dug, on account of the presence of water diffused through its substance; but it hardens on the evaporation of the water, which results from exposure to the atmosphere. The proprietor of the quarry is Mr. Murch, of Colyton. See De la Beche's *'Geographical Report on Devonshire, Cornwall, and West Somerset.'*

of Lyme Regis, who sold the demesnes to John
Starr, of Beer, Esq. A moiety of the manor was
afterwards sold to the father of Sir William Pole,
the historian, and Sir William himself sold it to
John Walrond, of Bovey, Esq., whose family, prior
to the year 1630, had become the owners of the
whole. [1] Judith Maria, heiress of the Walronds,

[1] The Walronds are said by Hutchins to have descended from Walran
Venator, to whom William the Conqueror gave eight manors in Dorsetshire. The family was settled at Bradfield, in the parish of Uffculm, as
early as the reign of King Henry III, [1216-1274]. A younger branch
resided at Bovey for many generations, and the marriage of Judith Maria,
the last heiress, with the late Lord Rolle, brought the property to his
lordship, by whose trustees it is held in trust, with the manor of Beer.
Bovey House is situated about a mile north-west from Beer, and about a
quarter of a mile south of the turnpike road from Lyme to Sidmouth.
It is an ancient irregular building of freestone, apparently much reduced
from its original dimensions. 'On visiting Bovey, a few years since,' says
Mr. Polwhele, writing about the year 1790, 'I was pleased with the venerable appearance of the house, and every object around it. It was then
the residence of Mrs. Walrond, relict of William Walrond, Esq. There
was something unusually striking in the antique mansion, the old rookery
behind it, the mossy pavement of the court, the raven in the porch, grey
with years; and even the domestics hoary in service. They were all
grown old together, and this coincidence was peculiarly interesting.' The
old mansion-house is now without a tenant. Many of the glorious lime-
trees which composed the avenue have yielded to the effect of time, or
else have fallen in the mania for tree-destroying which possesses this
enlightened age; and change, in many other respects, makes the description of Polwhele inapplicable to the present condition of this interesting
place. At the end of the avenue is an old stone arch, which once opened
into the entrance court. It displays the arms of Walrond, namely:—
argent, three bulls' faces, *sable*, horned, with a crescent for difference. The
date 1592, appears upon a leaden shoot, and in another place is the date
1674. The house is supplied with water from a well 160 feet deep. In
the time of Henry II, Bovey was granted by the abbot of Sherborne, to
Wide de Agevil, and it became the property of the Walronds, of Bradfield,
about the close of the reign of Henry III.

brought the manor to the late Lord Rolle, and it is now held in trust for Lady Rolle and his lordship's heirs. The family of Rolle have been munificent benefactors to Beer, and the memory of the late ·Lady Rolle is held in grateful remembrance by the inhabitants. In 1820, she gave the large sum of £7000 in the three per cents. for charitable purposes at Beer, including the founding of almshouses and schools. The almshouses are for the accommodation of twenty-five poor and infirm fishermen above the age of fifty-five years, and twenty poor women of the same age, each of whom receives one shilling per week for life, with other benefits. Both boys and girls are instructed gratuitously at the schools. They are also furnished with books and stationery, and presented, once a year, with clothing. The yearly salary of the master is £30, and that of the mistress £15. The almshouses and schools form a row of neat buildings at the northern extremity of the village. [1]

[1] The other public charities are, the interest of £20, given in 1801, by Mr. Edward Good, of Beer, and the Rev. Robert Cutcliffe, to be divided annually among the poor of Seaton and Beer, in the proportion of two-thirds at Beer and one-third at Seaton. Robert Marwood, Esq., in 1733, left twenty shillings a year to the poor of Beer, to be paid out of four fields called Muddells. This sum has not been forthcoming for many years, and the Commissioners of Public Charities in 1826 state their inability to obtain any satisfactory information about it. An old, illiterate, pauper woman, who has long been dead, and who had shared the bounty of Lady Rolle for many years, gave expression to her gratitude in many hundreds of rhyming stanzas, some of which are not without merit. We give the following as a specimen. It forms the conclusion of a series of

The church, or rather chapel of ease, is situated in
the principal street. It is a plain building, without
pretensions to beauty or to any characteristic of
legitimate ecclesiastical architecture. It was probably
built by one of the Walronds, as the arms of that
family appear on some of the stone work within
the building. It is dedicated to Saint Michael the
archangel, and has been enlarged at different times.
It contains but two tablets,—one to the memory of
Edward Good, the donor of the charity before mentioned, and the other, of an interesting character,
as follows :—' John, the fifth son of William Starr,
of Bere, gent., & Dorothy his wife, which died in
the Plagve, was here bvried. 1646.'

Few towns in the West of England were exempt
from the visitation of the plague, in the seventeenth
century, and it raged at Beer with particular virulence,
more than three-fourths of the inhabitants having
been swept away. The chapel grave-yard was soon
filled with the bodies of the victims, and the remainder were buried in a field near Bovey, called Holyhead,

stanzas on the benefits to Beer of the introduction of the stream of water,
and of the foundation of the almshouses and schools :—

' Henceforward will the name of Rolle dwell sweetly on each tongue,
And God the righteous will applaud the deeds they both have done.
God on such actions deigns to look, and doubtless does record
The same in Heaven's Eternal Book, and gives a full reward.'

[From notes on Beer by Mr. William Pulman, of Axminster, to whom
we are indebted for a mass of very valuable information on many of the
parishes in the lower part of the valley, as well as for efficient assistance
in the ' getting up' of the entire volume.]

or Hollishead.[1] At Axminster the same terrible visitation raged, in 1613, for many weeks, and carried off
great numbers of the inhabitants.[2] Tradition has
handed down a picture of the horrors of this visitation at Beer, more vivid, and perhaps not less truthful,
than contemporary records might have supplied. The
grave-yard has never since been disturbed, and, as
Sir William Pole informs us was the case in his day,
'the burials of Beare' are at Seaton.

We have only to add, in conclusion, that the cove
at the head of which this village is situated, is one of
the finest for the formation of a harbor on this romantic and too often fatal coast. Within the shelter
of a precipitous promontory is a great depth of water
extending almost to the shore. There have been
times when the government was not indifferent to the
claims of Beer. In 1792 an Act of Parliament was
passed for the construction of a harbor there, but no

---

[1] The reprehensible practice of burying the dead in the midst of the
living, was not permitted at a period in our history which we are apt to
regard as infinitely inferior, *in every respect*, to modern times. Mr.
Eccleston thus concludes an interesting account of the modes of interment which were practiced by our Anglo-saxon ancestors:—'The burial
places at first were carefully removed from the abodes of men; but
Archbishop Cuthbert, about the middle of the eighth century, obtained
permission to bury the dead within cities. The passing bell was rung,
that all within hearing might pray for the soul of the deceased; and
a payment, called the 'soul-sceat,' or soul-penny, was made to the clergy
after death. For the purpose of procuring honourable interment, bury-
ing-clubs or gilds were formed amongst the working men, the members of
which were bound under a penalty to attend the body to the grave.'

[2] Yonge's '*Diary*,' note page 1.

steps were taken to carry it into effect. Another act,
in 1820, provided for the appointment of new commissioners—all the old ones, except two, having died
in the interval. This act conferred more effectual
power than the former act, and even authorised Lord
Rolle, [1] as the Lord of the Manor, to take certain
duties from the vessels which entered the harbor.
But the result was the same as in the former case,
and hence the great national advantage of a refuge
harbor at Beer, and the incalculable local benefits
which must accompany such an advantage, are to
this moment unenjoyed.

*　　*　　*　　*　　*　　*　　*

Across the 'mighty rigge of pible stones' of which
Seaton beach is composed;—across the ferry over the
river Axe near its embouchere, at the easternmost
extremity of the beach—and the visitor finds himself
in the parish of Axmouth, and at the foot of the

---

[1] Lord Rolle died in 1842, without issue. His ancestor, George Rolle,
Esq., settled at Stevenstone, near Great Torrington, Devonshire, in the
reign of Henry VIII. His posterity became possessed of Bicton, near
Ottery, afterwards the principal family seat, by marriage with the heiress
of Dennis. [See page 377.] The family was ennobled in 1748, when
Henry Rolle, Esq., was created Baron Rolle, of Stevenstone, but dying
unmarried, the title became extinct. It was revived in 1796, in the person of John Rolle, Esq., his nephew, with whom it again became extinct.
His lordship was twice married. Lady Rolle, his relict, resides at Bicton,
and the extensive property is held in trust for her benefit and that of his
lordship's heirs. The ARMS of Rolle are:—*Or*, on a bar dauncettee,
between three delves, *azure*, charged with as many lions rampant of the
first, three bezants. CREST, an arm couped, *azure*, the hand, *or*, holding
a flint, proper. SUPPORTERS, on each side a leopard regardant, *gules*,
spotted, *or*, each crowned with a coronet flory of the second.

lofty hill called Haven Cliff.[1] The harbor at the mouth of the river is the result of the energetic and almost unaided efforts of J. H. Hallett, Esq., the lord of the manor. It is small, but quite large enough to prove, that if the government could be induced to take the work in hand, a harbor might be formed at this place which would be of the greatest importance to the commercial interests of the nation, and also be the means of preserving the valuable lives which are now so often sacrificed on a dangerous coast unprovided with a refuge harbor.[2]

We have shown, in our account of Seaton, that in ancient times the natural capabilities of the mouth of the Axe were duly turned to account, and that the commercial importance of this beautiful locality was consequently far greater than it is now. Old walls and piers, the ruins of former harbors, bear ample testimony to a fact which has been further strengthened by the discovery, in 1837, of the remains of a

[1] The view from the top of Haven Cliff, and from all the other points of this elevated range, and especially from Hochsdon or Hawkesdown Hill, which towers above the village [see page 407], is of a truly magnificent description, and produces a striking effect upon the stranger who enjoys it for the first time. Hundreds of those who pay enormous sums, and put themselves to all sorts of inconveniences, for the sake of *foreign* scenery, would find objects in this locality as well deserving of their attention as many of those for which they pay so dearly elsewhere.

[2] See a pamphlet on this subject by J. H. Hallett, Esq., and published by Hatchard, entitled '*Correspondence Relative to the Expediency of Forming a Refuge Harbor within the Portland and Start Bay,*' &c., 1837. We must apologise for an error of the press in the preceding page, which was not discovered until the sheet had been 'worked off.' The word *embouchure*, it will be seen, is incorrectly spelled.

large vessel in the bed of the river, at a considerable
distance from its mouth.   More than three hundred
years must have passed away since that vessel was
afloat, for we know that in the time of Leland 'smaul
fisschar boats' alone came in 'for socour,' and that
the ancient harbor had before his visit been choked
by an accumulation of shingle.[1]   There can be no
doubt that a great physical change has taken place at
the mouth of the Axe in comparatively modern
times; for the same authority assures us that he
found Axe Bridge, at Colyford, to be *impassable at
high tides.*[2]   That the sea, therefore, came further
into the valley, and that the Axe was capable of
receiving vessels of burden far higher up than at
present, would appear to be evident—especially when
it is known that below the surface of the marsh are
beds of sand, cockle-shells, and other marine productions of manifestly *recent* deposit (speaking geologi-
cally), and that fragments of boats, anchors, and
other similar vestiges are often found there.   And we
must add to these interesting facts, that the voice of
Tradition speaks loudly of the ancient importance
both of Axmouth and its haven.[3]

[1] See page 449. That active operations were in the course of being
carried on at the harbor in 1450 (that is, a century before Leland's visit)
is evident from the fact that in that year Bishop Lacy granted forty days'
indulgence to true penitents who should contribute to the works '*in
novo portu in littore maris apud Seton.*'

[2] See page 27.

[3] The old people say that Axmouth once could boast of fourteen hotels,
and that it covered a very large extent of ground, as is shown, they say,

Many have been the attempts, since Leland's time, to restore the harbor to its ancient condition. In the early part of the seventeenth century the Erles, of Bindon, [1] expended much time and money upon the

by the foundations of houses which are often dug up in various directions. See page 12. That Axmouth and Seaton were places of some importance at so remote a period as the time of the Romans, is almost a matter of certainty—so much so, indeed, as to have led some writers to suppose that Axmouth was the Roman station Uxelis.

[1] Bindon is a beautifully situated old residence among the cliffs, about half-a-mile from the harbor on one side and Axmouth village on the other side. It is now a farm house, but contains abundant traces of its former importance, not the least interesting of which is the elaborately sculptured piscina in the ancient domestic chapel—the work, probably, of the commencement of the sixteenth century, when the present house was perhaps erected, on the site of a more ancient structure. Among 'the men of good quality,' as Risdon calls them, who were once its owners, was one Nicholas Bach, who sold it, in the reign of Henry IV, to Roger Week, or Wyke, of North Tawton, Devonshire, in whose family it remained for several generations. Four co-heiresses brought the property, by marriage, to the families of Gifford, Barry, Erle, and Hayes. Gifford's share was purchased by the Erles, who made Bindon their residence, and who thus became owners of half the property. Hugh Barry's share was alienated to William Mallack, Esq., who sold it to Mr. Cheek, from whom it came to Mr. Bartlett, of Axminster, whose family disposed of it a few years since. Hayes's share was bought by the Rev. Edward Rowe, who was vicar of Axmouth from 1677 till 1706, and whose representatives sold it to Southcott Hallett, Esq. The Erles' moiety was sold, about the year 1773, by Thomas Erle Drax, Esq., the representative of the family, to Thomas Jenkins, of Sidmouth, Esq., of whose nephew it was purchased, in 1817, by Mr. Thomas Dare, of Colyton. It is now the property of Messrs. James and Richard Chapple and Mr. Dare. Sir Walter Erle, the grandson of Walter Erle, the first possessor of Bindon, was an active officer in Cromwell's army, and his name very frequently occurs in connection with the most stirring events in the West of England during the civil war. [See page 431.] The Erles were originally from Somersetshire. An heiress of the family married Thomas Erle Drax, of Charborough House, Dorsetshire, Esq., and the present owner of that mansion is the representative of the line. Mr. Justice Erle is a lineal descendant of the Bindon family.

praiseworthy object. 'Sir Thomas Erle,' says Risdon, 'when he had brought the same to some likelihood, was taken away by death, leaving his labors to the unruly ocean, which, together with unkind neighbours (by carrying away the stones of that work), made a great ruin of his attempt.' The labors of his son were attended with no better success, and the credit of bringing the harbor to its present state is due to Mr. Hallett.[1]

The village of Axmouth stands upon the eastern brink of the river, at the distance of nearly a mile from the harbor. Its situation is truly delightful, being at the foot of towering eminences, and in the midst of luxuriant orchards, pleasant fields, and a profusion of beautiful hedge-row and other timber. It consists of two very pleasant streets, through which flows a beautiful little stream, in all its freshness from the fountains of the hills; and the cottages are very neat and clean, with a few handsome residences interspersed.

Axmouth, as we have repeatedly stated, formed part of the Anglo-saxon royal demesne, and, as we have also stated, it was once a hundred, but has been long incorporated with the hundred of Axminster.

---

[1] In the early part of the present century, several of the farmers of Axmouth and the neighbouring parishes, attempted to dig out the ruins of the ancient harbor, and each sent men for the purpose, in numbers proportioned to the size of his farm. Considerable progress had been made, when a flood destroyed their labors, and the attempt was given over in despair.

The parish contains an area of 4534 acres, and a population of 690. It is divided into five tithings, namely:—Axmouth, Downralph, or Roosdown, Downprior, Downhumphraville, and Buckland Trill.[1] It formed part of the ancient Duchy of Lancaster, the privileges of which are duly claimed by the parishioners.[2]

[1] Downralph, or Roosdown, is an extra parochial estate of about 250 acres, upon the romantic cliffs between Axmouth and Lyme Regis,—'lying open to the south sea,' as Risdon describes it, 'and albeit wanting water.' In ancient times it belonged, with the adjoining estates of Downprior and Downhumphraville, to the family of Down, who resided at Roosdown. Many of its members were called Ralph. The property was brought by marriage to John Holcombe. The descendant of Holcombe sold it, during the reign of Henry VII, to William Mallack, Esq., whose family, after the year 1617, made Roosdown their residence. They had previously occupied Steps House, an interesting old residence at the head of Axmouth village,—now converted into laborers' cottages, and belonging to Mr. Chapple, of Bindon. In 1773, Roosdown became the property of Robert Bartlett, Esq., from whose family it was purchased by the late W. Payne, Esq. The church is an ancient little building, dedicated to St. Pancras. It is the burying-place of the Bartlett family, but has long since ceased to be used as a place of worship. From a remote period, however, it had a series of vicars, commencing with Thomas Capis, at the commencement of the fourteenth century. The living, now joined with that of Axmouth, is valued in the king's books at £2 10s. 10d. A chapel, dedicated to St. Leonard, is mentioned in the ancient records, [Stafford's Register, vol. I. fol. 238,] 'in villulâ de Dona infra parochiam de Axmouth.' It was probably at Charlton. The manor of Buckland Trill belonged anciently to the family of Trill, [see page 400,] who sold it, in the reign of Edward III, to Hugh Courtenay, Earl of Devon. It belonged afterwards to the Yonges, from whom it passed to the Bartletts. Roosdown, we should state, is subject to a modus for tithes commuted for £5 a year.

[2] See page 426. The following is a copy of the form with which the claimants of these privileges are furnished:—'*Manor and Liberty of Axmouth, Devon.* At a court leet and view of Frankpledge, held for and within the said Manor, on ————, before ———— steward of the said manor. At this court came ———— resident within this

We translate, as follows, from Domesday Book, the passage which refers to Axmouth :—The king holds *Alsemude*. It is not known how many hides are there, nor for how much they gelded. The arable is twelve carucates. In demesne is half a carucate, and four servants, and eight villains, and twelve cottagers, with six ploughs. There are sixteen acres of meadow, and eight acres of coppice wood. Pasture a mile long and four furlongs broad.

The manor and church were given, in the reign of Henry II, to the abbey of Montebourg, in Normandy.[1] Henry V seized it, among other possessions

liberty, being part or parcel of the ancient Duchy of Lancaster, therein which, by the charter of the same, is as followeth, viz :—"All and singular men and tenants, freeholders and not freeholders, as well residents as non residents, and other resiants within the manor and liberty aforesaid, are free quit and discharged of and from all manner of toll, pantage, picage, murage, stallage, panage, passage, lastage, tollage, pontage, and all other customs whatsoever, and of and from all manner of prizes and captions, carriage of horses, carts, waggons, and other carriages, and of wheat, barley, oats, rye, beans, peas, and of corn, cows and other beasts, and of all fowls and other utensils and victuals whatsoever, throughout her Majesty's realm of Great Britain and all other her dominions whatsoever." Granted in full court, &c., &c. ——————— Steward. *All persons whom these presents may concern, are to take notice of the privileges above mentioned.*'

[1] 'This property of Axmouth,' says Dr. Oliver, 'was often considered as a parcel of Lodres Priory, Dorset, which was a cell to the said abbey [of Montebourg]; but unquestionably there never was any religious community settled at Axmouth itself. In virtue of Bishop Bronescombe's ordinance, in the autumn of 1269 [see folio 42 of Bronescombe's '*Register*'] the prior of Lodres was to receive two parts of the great tithes and one part of the small tithes of the parish of Axmouth, whilst the vicar was entitled to the remainder.' The same prior also 'held the custody of St. Pancras' church, at Rousdown.'

of alien monasteries, and gave it to the Bridgetine convent of Sion, at Isleworth, Middlesex. After the Reformation it became a part of Queen Catherine Parr's jointure, and Edward VI gave it, about the year 1552, to Walter Erle, Esq., one of the grooms of his privy chamber. The Erles sold it, in 1679, to Sir Walter Yonge, of whom it was purchased, in 1691, by Richard Hallett, Esq., who bequeathed it to his nephew of the same name, great-grandfather of John Hothersall Hallett, of Haven Cliff and Stedcombe, Esq., its present possessor. [1]

The most important event in connection with Axmouth in modern times was the great landslip, which occurred on Christmas-day, 1839. The romantic cliffs on the farms of Bindon, Dowlands, and Whitlands were the scene of this extraordinary elemental

[1] The family of Hallett came from Barbadoes and settled at Stedcombe, soon after their purchase of the manor. Richard Hallett, as stated at page 378, married the heiress of Southcote, of Dulcis, and, in 1695, rebuilt the present Stedcombe House, nearly on the site of a former mansion which had been destroyed in the civil wars [See page 431.] Stedcombe occupies a delightful situation among wooded hills and towering cliffs, on the eastern bank of the Axe, about half way between Axe Bridge and Axmouth. The estate belonged, at an early period, to the Uffevilles, and, at the close of the reign of Henry III, to the Veres, with whom it remained for four generations. About the middle of the fourteenth century it became the property of the Courtenays, and on the attainder of Henry Courtenay, Marquis of Exeter, it was granted by Henry VIII to Sir Peter Carew, who sold it to Walter Yonge, Esq., and from the Yonges it was bought, with the rest of the manor of Axmouth, by Richard Hallett, Esq., in 1691. The ARMS of Hallett are:—*Or*, a chief engrailed, *sable*, on a bend engrailed, *gules*, three bezants. CREST, a demi-lion, holding in its paw a bezant.

convulsion—one of the most extensive and scientifically interesting that ever happened in this country. It was the means, at the time, of attracting tens of thousands to witness its strange effects, and the attraction is in no degree diminished although the charms of *novelty* are lost. The celebrated Dr. Buckland, who, as before stated, is a native of the neighbourhood, was present a few hours after the occurrence, and drew up a very interesting account of it, from which we make a few extracts :—

'A great subsidence has taken place through the fields ranging above Bindon undercliff, forming a deep chasm, or rather ravine, extending nearly three quarters of a mile in length, with a depth of from 100 to 150 feet, and a breadth exceeding 80 yards. Between this and the former undercliff, extends a long strip, exhibiting fragments of turnip fields, and separated from the tract to which they once belonged by the deep intervening gulph, of which the bottom is constituted by fragments of the original surface thrown together in the wildest confusion of inclined terraces, and columnar masses, intersected by deep fissures, so as to render the ground nearly impassable. The insulated strip of fields, also, which has been mentioned, is greatly rent and shattered. The whole of the tract which has been subjected to these violent disturbances, must be estimated, on the most moderate computation, as exceeding three quarters of a mile in length by 400 feet. A remarkable pyramidal crag off Culverhole Point, which once formed a distinguishing land-mark, has sunk from a height of nearly 100 to 200 feet ; and the main cliff, before more than 50 feet distant from this insulated crag, is now brought almost close. This motion of the sea-cliff has produced a further effect, which may rank among the striking phenomena of the catastrophe. The lateral pressure thus occasioned, has urged the neighbouring strata extending beneath the shingle of the shore, by their state of unnatural condensation, to burst upward in a line parallel with the coast. Thus an elevated ridge, more than a mile in length, and rising more than forty feet, covered by a confused assemblage of broken strata and immense blocks of rock, invested with sea-weed and corallines, and scattered over with shells and star-fish, and other productions of the deep, forms an extended reef in front of the present range of cliffs. This terminates, at its eastern and western extremity, in two deep basins of water. The western of these basins is encircled by the extreme arm of the new reef, in such a manner as nearly to resemble Lyme cobb, which, however, it exceeds in size. [1] Although this convulsion can only be ascribed to the less dignified agency of the land springs constantly undermining the substrata, yet, in the grandeur of the disturbances it has occasioned, it far exceeds the ravages of the earthquakes of Cala-

[1] Soon after the catastrophe the reef began gradually to sink, and it has long since disappeared.

bria, and almost the vast volcanic fissures of the Val de Bove, on the flanks of Etna. . . . . . The tract of downs ranging along the coast is here capped by a stratum of chalk. This rests on a series of beds of consolidated sand-stone, alternating with seams of that variety of flint called chert. Beneath these, are at least 100 feet of loose sand (from an obvious etymology) termed fox-mould. This bed affords the principal cause of the disturbances in question, for it readily imbibes all the atmospherical water falling on the surface, and, as it rests on retentive beds of clay (belonging to what is called the Lias formation), these waters are held up and flow out in springs along the margin of deposit wherever it is exposed to the slope of the ground, as is necessarily the case all along the face of these downs where they break down to the sea. The springs thus issuing, wash out with them a very sensible portion of the loose deposit of fox-mould through which they flow, and such an action is of course greatly aggravated by the inordinate continuance of wet weather such as has lately (1839) prevailed. Thus considerable portions of the fox-mould being gradually removed along the lines through which these springs have found their course, the superstrata will remain completely undermined; and as an excessively wet season will, by saturating the whole with moisture, increase the weight of the incumbent mass, at the same time that (as we have seen) it withdraws the support, it is easy to conceive that cracks will in process of time be formed, and that the undermined portion of the superstrata will be precipitated into the hollows prepared for them. And further, as the adjacent masses of rock—even where not thus completely undermined—rest on a slippery basis of watery sand, the motion originally impressed by the falling in of an actually undermined tract, will readily be propagated to a considerable extent in a lateral direction. These causes having acted through centuries, have produced a series of dislocations affecting all the seaward face of the range of hills lining this part of the coast, for an interval of more than a furlong from the sea beach inland. The whole of this surface presents the wildest scene of ruin imaginable — " crags, knolls, and mounds confus'dly hurled," in a succession of broken terraces, separated by deep and thickly-wooded dingles, an inland range of chalk cliffs mantled by luxuriant screens of ash and elm, wherever the declivity will allow a root to fix itself, forming the upper stage and general back-ground of the scene, and extending to the very summit of the hills.'

Axmouth church bears evidence of high antiquity, and it is therefore an object of interest to the ecclesiological student. An Anglo-Saxon or Anglo-Norman doorway, with the characteristic mouldings, appears in the north porch, which is now blocked and used as a vestry; and evidence of almost equally ancient workmanship, in the interior of the building,

incontestably proves that the original church, if not
founded by one of the Anglo-Saxon monarchs, all of
whom must have regarded Axmouth as a highly interesting part of their demesne, was, at least, of
Anglo-Norman date.[1] The building, as it at present
stands, exhibits an intermixture of Early English
and Perpendicular architecture with the more ancient
portions to which we have referred. It consists of a
chancel, nave, and aisles—(the south aisle extending
nearly to the eastern end of the chancel, and perhaps
anciently forming a chapel at that extremity), a
tower at the western end of the nave, and the porch
before mentioned, on the north side. The south or
Bindon aisle is undoubtedly of very remote antiquity. It is separated from the nave by four pointed
arches springing from massive piers,—half circular
and half square. They appear to be of Semi-Norman
construction. The chancel arch is of wide span.
Against its northern pier are placed the pulpit and
reading desk, and in the opposite pier are the remains
of the ancient rood-loft stairs. The windows have
no claim to notice—except as regards the circumstance of their manifest incongruity—the effect, of
course, of *modern* reparations. In the chancel, however, there is a blocked Early English window of two
lights with trefoil headings, and there are also the
remains of a corbel-table.[2] The tower, although not
more than fifty-six feet high, commands a delightful

[1] See page 221.   [2] See page 258.

view of the valley and of Seaton bay. It is square and embattled, with a turret, and contains three bells, upon one of which is the date 1671. The principal entrance to the church is across the ground floor of the tower, under an elegant pointed doorway, over which is a Perpendicular window. There is a curious old monument in the chancel wall, within an obtusely pointed recess. It represents, in stone, a robed priest reclining at full length, with the figure, at his feet, of either a lion or a dog, it is uncertain which. From the character of this monument it may be supposed to date about the beginning of the thirteenth century, and there are circumstances which perhaps warrant the conjecture that it may represent either the holder of the living at the time when the church was rebuilt or repaired, or else some ecclesiastical functionary, at Lodres or elsewhere, who was a liberal contributor to the work. [1] Tradition, indeed, says that the monument belongs to a person who gave

---

[1] The founder or refounder of a church, and also a benefactor to it, was, in early times, distinguished by interment in the chancel, or in some other part of the building in erecting which he might have been more particularly instrumental; and his effigy was placed within an arch in the substance of the wall. The young lion under the feet of the effigy of an ecclesiastic, had reference to the 13th verse of the 91st Psalm:—'Thou shalt tread upon the lion and adder: the young lion and the dragon shalt thou trample under feet.' Mr. Gough informs us, that after the Reformation the family supporters were often placed at the feet of monumental effigies; that before that event, a dog at the feet of the effigy of a lady represented her favorite lap-dog, and at the feet of that of a knight, his favorite hound; and that the latest instance of animals at the feet of any monument is in 1645.

to the church some land which is now called ' Dog-acre Orchard;' and in order to account for the presence of an animal, it adds that the gift was contingent upon the permission to inter a favorite dog in its master's grave.

There are several other monuments in the church; and some old inscriptions upon the floor are now almost obliterated. [1]

The living of Axmouth is a vicarage, of which J. H. Hallett, Esq. is the patron. He is also impropriator of most of the great tithes. The vicarage is valued in the King's Books at £22 19s. 2d. The vicarial tithes are commuted for £175 per annum,

---

[1] The following are the principal monuments and inscriptions:—
'Heere lye the bodyes of Dame Anne Erle, wife of Sir Walter Erle, and of Thomas Erle, their only sonne and heire; two rare patterns, the one for her pietie the other for his wisdome and abilityes. She was heire to Francis Dymmock, of Erdington, in the covnty of Warwick, Esqvire. The sonne dyed Jvne the first, 1650; the mother the 26th of Janvary, 1653.' Several members of the Mallack family, of Roosdown:—Richard Mallack, died September 8, 1724, and Elizabeth, his second wife, daughter of Sir Richard Strode, of Nvnam, July 20, 1693; ——— Mallack, January 27, 1704; John Mallack, ———, 1702. Ann, wife of Thomas Seward, the younger, September 1, 1622; Thomas Seward, November 25, 1622; Thomas Seward, his son, July 15, 1639; John Seward, December 20, 1710, aged 91 years; and several other members of the Seward family. Rev. Edward Rowe, vicar of the parish, June —, 1706; his wife and son. Hercules Pyne, Gent., 1610; Gertrude, wife of Thomas Pyne, 'Aprill' 18, 1626; William Serle, of Bradford, Somerset, April 7, 1726. Ann, daughter of Robert and Ann Dening, 'first the wife of Richard Mallack, Esq., of this parish, and late the wife of Robert Cheek, of Roestdovne,' February 18, 1744. And lastly, a handsome monument, with the family arms and an inscription, to the memory of Richard Hallett, of Stedcombe, Esq., son of John Hallett, of Barbadoes, died January 12, 1746; and other members of his family.

and the rectorial for £309. In the shape of parochial
charities, there is a rent-charge of thirty-two shillings
a year upon Dowlands farm, left, in 1726, by William
Serle, of Bradford, Somerset, for the instruction in
reading of four poor children of the parish of
Axmouth.

*　　*　　*　　*　　*　　*　　*

　　*　　*　　*　　*　　*　　*

And now, Piscator, we must say farewell;—here
in this appropriate parting-place — this quiet little
country churchyard, where everything around us is so
peculiarly in keeping. The river which we have traced
so far, through all the stages of its varied beauty,
glides gracefully and slowly into the Unfathomable.
The sun has left the fadings of his refulgence in the
glorious drapery of the western sky. The autumn
breeze sighs a mournful requiem among the branches,
as it wafts away their withered leaves. And around
us are the sad memorials of the departed—of those
who have performed the great pilgrimage of life, and
sought repose, when it was over,—

> ' Where nae mair aching tires the head,
> A-neath the turf sae grassie.'

Yea! there are a thousand things, about and around
us, suggestive of the solemn thoughts which crowd
into the mind at this parting moment—which speak
in striking language of the things that pass away,
and show the chain which unites us, link by link,
with the Future and with the Past. In truth, our

very ramble, of itself, beloved old friend, has been an *acted* moral, and we should try, at its conclusion, to reap the blessings of its application.

Is that a voice from the beetling brow of Hochsdon, which tells of the time when the old hill was the refuge of the Aboriginal, whose works outlive him by a score of centuries, while he and his race are dust? Is that a vision of the old Norman builders of this sacred fane, which even yet shows portions of the ancient handy-work, though a thousand years have nearly passed, and though the names of those old Norman builders have for ages been forgotten? Is that a warning whisper from the tombs around us that *to Part* is but a mortal's lot?

Alas! alas! Piscator, let us not pursue the painful theme when the heart is even overfull! It is enough to know that we commenced our valley-journey in all the beauty of the early spring, and in all the hey-day of an angler's anticipations. It is enough to *feel*—how deeply none can tell—that the spring has passed away, and that the journey is accomplished!

Farewell! Farewell!!

INDEX.

THE END.

CREWKERNE:
Printed by G. P. R. Pulman,
Market-place.

Lightning Source UK Ltd.
Milton Keynes UK
UKHW05f1916060318
319013UK00007B/538/P